The Funeral Casino

✣

The Funeral Casino

MEDITATION, MASSACRE, AND

EXCHANGE WITH THE DEAD

IN THAILAND

✣

ALAN KLIMA

PRINCETON UNIVERSITY PRESS

PRINCETON AND OXFORD

Library of Congress Cataloging-in-Publication Data

Klima, Alan, 1964–

The funeral casino : meditation, massacre, and exchange with the dead in Thailand / Alan Klima

p. cm.

Includes bibliographical references and index.

ISBN 0-691-07459-3 (alk. paper)

1. Thailand—Politics and government—1948–1988. 2. Thailand—Politics and government—1988– 3. Massacres—Thailand. 4. Violence in the mass media—Thailand. 5. Funeral rites and ceremonies—Thailand. 6. Death—Religious aspects—Buddhism. 7. Meditation—Buddhism. I. Title.

DS586 .K58 2002
959.304'4—dc21   2001055195

This book has been composed in Sabon

British Library Cataloging-in-Publication Data is available

Printed on acid-free paper. ∞

www.pup.princeton.edu

Printed in the United States of America

1   3   5   4   9   10   8   6   4   2
1   3   5   4   9   10   8   6   4   2

(Pbk.)

✥ Contents ✥

✜ *Illustrations* ✜

NOTE ON TRANSCRIPTION AND MONETARY CONVERSION

In this work, some of the Thai vocabulary on technical matters of Buddhist philosophy has been exchanged for the Pali equivalents from which they are derived, for the sake of comparative use by the body of scholars familiar with these terms. At other times, as when translating speech, the Thai equivalent has been retained, but should be similar enough to be recognized as equivalent to its Pali version. For transcribing Thai words, I have used a modified version of the Haas convention, with tone and other markers dropped for the purposes of typesetting. In some cases, slight alterations have also been made for the purposes of correct pronunciation. For instance, *winjaan* (spirit) appears here as *winyaan*. For personal names and words commonly transcribed in English media, the most common form of transcription is employed. Diacritical marks are included for the Pali wherever possible within the limits of typesetting. For instance, long vowels are indicated but stops on consonants are not. Thai and Pali words are italicized only at first use.

The Thai baht is converted at the rate of twenty-five to the dollar, which was the approximate exchange rate during the times represented in this text, and during many previous years of relatively fixed exchange. In 1997 the baht was "floated." At the time of writing, the exchange has stabilized for several months at approximately 45:1.

❖ Acknowledgments ❖

My teachers are Luang Bu Sangwaan, Patcharee Katasema, Gananath Obeyesekere, John D. Kelly, Vincanne Adams, and Kaushik Ghosh. Although this book is solely my own responsibility, the impact on me of each of these people—some of them theorists, some Buddhists, some both—has exemplified the fact that, given all the traces that one leaves behind, there is no other choice but to leave them with dedication and sincerity.

My aim in writing has been to explicate the parallels between various practices of visualizing death and of exchanging with the dead, but also to integrate multiple sites in ways that reflect and advocate my point of view as an author and social critic. Any other individual who would thread connections between these different sites of vision and memory in Thailand would do it differently, and Thai activists do it in their own way. This text was written, in part, by modeling its construction on Thai practices of political commemoration, and yet it is ultimately only my construction, of course, and represents quite simply an invitation to share my point of view temporarily, or not. It certainly is not an attempt to reveal an actual "Thai worldview" or, least of all, to tell Thais what they think. It is an expression of what I think, although also a continuation of the conversations I have had over the years in Thailand, after some time for reflection. Neither gestures to disperse "ethnographic authority" nor desires for the presentation of unmediated access to ethnographic subjects should distract from the fact that a critical ethnography is ultimately the argument of an author, and represents an intention to make a statement and write a historical commentary according to the vision of an author, such as it is.

I greatly appreciate everything I have learned in the discussions over the years in countless temples and villages in Thailand and in Bangkok, especially at Wat Toong Samakhi Dhamm, at Mae Moh District locations in Lampang, and in the gatherings, fortunate and unfortunate, of Bangkok. I am especially grateful to Adul Kiewboriboon and all the relatives of the dead and the injured participants in Black May who shared with me their stories, and taught me what this book had to be about. Discussions with Jarunai Dengsopha, Mali Thawinampan, Mae-Chi Liem, Mae-Chi Sa-ad, and Mae-Chi Sangiam occupy important moments in this text, and in my life.

Writing and rewriting the book after these conversations, I have accumulated considerable debt to those who have helped me tame it. I thank John Kelly for seeing to it that I went off with a proper pair of goggles, and later for countless offhand remarks that have primed a flood of new ideas for me. I thank Vincanne Adams for the conversations, all along the way of writing, that made the puzzle of how to do this not hopeless, and perhaps possible. I thank Gananath Obeyesekere especially for his removal of a blind spot in relation to Buddhism that would have been the death of me, and for stepping in always at the right moment in my thoughts and otherwise.

I thank my reviewer Michael Taussig for his adept reading of this text, and for his generosity without receiving. I thank Rosalind Morris for the daunting bar she raised and for criticisms that I reluctantly assented to, only to discover that, although I thought she was wrong, for some strange reason my book was much better after I heeded her. And I am especially grateful for the tolerance and example of Thongchai Winichakul. It took some time of rewriting to discover how correct his comments on this text were, and these discoveries have not stopped coming even as it is finished. I have tried my best to make good on them, and yet I realize sadly, in many ways, that the events I write about call for much more than I have to give. I hope there is something between the lines of this text that bears traces of the concerns that are at the heart of writing it.

I also greatly appreciate two anonymous reviewers of other work of mine whose helpful suggestions are, I think, incorporated in this text. At Princeton University Press, the editorial comments and patience of Mary Murrell, the best anthropology editor out there, made this book possible, as well as the patience of Fred Appel during trying times. And I am very grateful for trusty Mario Bick, for the support of Diana Brown, and for conversations with Yates McKee and Sanjib Baruah.

Much of the research for this book was conducted on a collaborative basis with Patcharee Katasema, a former political science student at Ramkamhaeng University.

The Funeral Casino

✢

Introduction

EIDETIC MEMORIES

In Bangkok's upscale Royal Hotel, Channel 11 is taping a talk show, a special memorial edition of "Looking from Different Perspectives," the *Maung Dang Moom* show. Three years before, here in the Royal Hotel in 1992, prodemocracy protesters had holed up until the bitter end of a month of street marches against an unelected general who had taken the office of prime minister. Here, under the beaded strings of glittering lights hanging from the atrium, they had set up their field hospital and morgue for those shot by the soldiers. Back then, the video cameras were not deployed smartly for center, right, and left angle shots as they are now. Camera crews were frantically milling about. People were shouting, and journalists from all around the world were tripping over each other, while Thais, peaking on adrenaline, would carry in faint, bloodied people whose expressions were muddled in the confusing moment of their approaching deaths. A camera was an emblem of sovereignty then. People cleared a path, as if for a king. They shouted, "Shoot, shoot, go right ahead!" as they cleared a good space around a corpse.

Then Special Forces stormed the building, and took up all the space in the world's camera lens. Yet it was far from merely unfortunate—from a media business angle as well as from a political angle—that the soldiers would then trample over and kick the protestors with big black jackboots, while the bodies lay shoulder to shoulder on the lobby's bloody marble floor. Beating them with rifle butts, the soldiers corralled them outside the hotel, and made them kneel in the sun, hands tied with their shirts behind their backs, which with a wide-angle lens looked like an endless sea of bare-backed slaves bowed before a machine gun on the horizon. Then they were herded toward trucks that looked like cattle cars and, pulled up by the roots of their hair, lifted onto the vehicles and carted away to wherever that dark, off-camera place is that military dictatorships take people.

Today is the third anniversary of the Black May massacre of 1992. The relatives of the dead have been invited here to be on TV, or at least in the studio audience. Last night, the parents, siblings, and children of the Black May dead, those who were not from Bangkok, slept on the floor in a ncarby temple. Later tonight they will sleep on the straight-backed benches of dusty, rumbling buses heading back for their provincial villages and towns. But for now, as they are at this moment part and parcel of Thai national TV in the making, they are actually let into Bangkok's Royal Hotel, where they can sit in first-class style.

Bird is bubbly, happy this morning. He got to sit up front, just as he wanted. I have set up my own video camera and sit with him and his mom for a while before the show starts, because his excitement is contagious. People with walkie-talkies and white pressed shirts are connecting cables and testing electronic things all around us. He likes TV and likes being here while it is made. But it is not his first time on TV. I saw him three years ago on satellite dish, or rather on one of the black-market video tapes of satellite transmissions that could be bought on the streets of Bangkok. The military had suppressed TV images of the violence, but the Thai video piracy industry had nevertheless quickly gotten in on the trade in these images, which was moving freely in most other parts of the world. In freewheeling entrepreneurial spirit, the street vendors and pirate video operators managed to proliferate images of the dead and dying through a local black market. At that time, only a few days after the massacre, they did not do it in the usual tourist ghettos of Bangkok where intellectual property rights are relaxed. Instead, the black market appeared right out in the open, on the actual site of the killing in the heart of the old city; and this market was transacted side by side with massive Buddhist funerary rites of gift exchange being held there for the spirits of the unquiet dead.

Bird's body was a part of this trade. It had been spirited over the surface of the globe by the BBC, and then returned and passed around in cassettes for sale by the enterprising Thai traders on the exact spot where he had been gunned down. The fuzzy pirate video showed the BBC reporter standing right here in the lobby of the Royal Hotel, in front of little Bird, who was a bloody mess on the floor. Like most people facing a camera, if he had had a choice he would have much preferred a chance to comb his hair and put on his best shirt. But he had been shot with an M-16, and the reporter was standing over him, narrating, "The military has not even spared young children. This boy couldn't be more than nine or ten." Actually Bird was thirteen at the time, but because he is retarded he has a face that looks younger, even when in pain and shock.

He was curious, he explains. He had wandered off from home because he heard loud noises not too far away. He had wanted to see what was going on. "There were lots and lots of people there. Then soldiers came with big guns, and everybody ran. It was scary, and I ran too." But he didn't get away. Now he has a plastic leg. Reporters come to talk to him and take his picture once a year. Every year there are far fewer than the previous year.

Now I sit with this boy and his actual body, the one that had wandered him into the global flow of media images, the one that had been electronically swept away in currents of international trade and transported back to the ground on which he had been shot. His had been one of the pivotal images upon which the politics of death oscillated between the military regime and prodemocracy marchers within a dialectic of local and global imagery.

"What do you think about the state of politics in Thailand?" I ask him.

For a while he is silent, holding my microphone up close to his face. He had wanted to hold the microphone. With a pained and searching expression, he grasps it for some time, and then can finally only repeat, "Thailand."

After a long wait for the *Maung Dang Moom* show to begin taping, the lobby of the Royal Hotel finally settles down, and the show begins. The TV guests soon launch into free debate; the talk-show format is both performative and emblematic of the new media freedoms earned as a result of the prodemocracy demonstrations and the massacre—a structural triumph of the bourgeois public sphere—three years before. Now the combat alights only in forms that can keep at bay from the public sphere the borderline, shadowy realm of violence, its Other.

On the first anniversary Black May taping of the TV talk show, the guests and audience actually erupted into a chair-tossing, free-for-all brawl, after the relatives of the victims were told by a promilitary guest not to "use the dead just to make a point."

The violence was cut out at broadcast time.

Because it is now the third anniversary of the massacre and they are again taping auspiciously in the Royal Hotel, a few things are said at the outset about the importance of remembering the event. But—even though the relatives of the victims have come all this way, and one of the four guests on the panel lost a son in the massacre and is there to represent the interests of the families of the dead—there happen to be other, more current and interesting issues in the air, and the discourse quickly turns toward these. The massacre is forgotten and left behind, and the leader of the relatives of the dead just sits there quietly on the stage, left out of the loop because he doesn't have anything interesting to say about new affairs. And yet. . . .

And yet as the relatives and I file out of the cool lobby on this hot day in 1995, and walk out onto the central plaza in the heart of Bangkok's old city, and they speak to me about the neglect of their dead, they are not completely dejected at the speed of forgetting that was so palpable there, in the realm of the public sphere. There is good reason for not being dispirited. The hot new news, the latest story that has displaced them one more step away from the main stage of national memory, is the story that the Democrat Party is going to dissolve parliament. The party, which came to power after the massacre, lasted just over two years in office. For the sake of democracy, back in 1992, the relatives of the dead let the "prodemocracy" parties use them to win an election and employ them as moral symbols of suffering in photo opportunities and features. The relatives voiced their support of the parties, and put aside issues of personal compensation, as well as politically sensitive issues like building a monument to their dead. All of that was for the sake of facilitating a transition of power.

After that election, the Democrat Party got what all parties want, the office of prime minister. They had nothing to gain and everything to lose by stirring up the "past." And then, when things had settled down, the relatives of the dead asked for better compensation for their loss, demanded it from the government that had come to power with the deaths of their kin. They were told by the new government, "Don't use corpses for your own gain."

When the relatives first arrived here in Bangkok two days before, the parliamentary coalition was still together. But exactly three years after the Black May incident that had put the prodemocracy politicians in power—precisely on the anniversary of the massacre—the government tumbled. It was almost as though, just as Black May commemoration rites were unfolding elsewhere in the city over the last couple of days, the neglectful new prime minister's chair slipped out from under him, despite the fact that Black May was not an issue anymore and almost no one was paying any attention to ceremonies being held for the dead.

"They call it the law of Kamma," says Pi Nok Gaow, who lost her two sons, "It is the law of Kamma. Chuan Leekpai did this to himself. Our flesh and blood died on this day so that he could be elected prime minister. Then he forgot about the dead, and neglected us, so on this day of their death, his power collapses."

THE NEOLIBERAL ECONOMY OF HISTORY

It is the project of this text to examine the appearance of an event. This event has served as a crucial plot device in a dominant narrative of Thailand's emergence from military dictatorship and its entrance into a new liberalized world order and "global modernity." In Bangkok, in May 1992, prodemocracy demonstrations ended with a massacre of unarmed citizens by the Thai military, an institution long backed by U.S. support. Around that time, the top gun in the army had displaced the government and the constitution in the seventeenth coup since 1932, then staged corrupt elections and seated himself as prime minister without standing for election himself. Prominent hunger strikers led hundreds of thousands of people in a month-long series of street protests, which proved fruitless until the army opened fire on them, hoping to disperse them. That was when gory images of violence began to circulate around the globe—and in an illegal pirate video market on the site of the massacre—destabilizing the regime on two fronts with instant photographic memories. The premier, General Suchinda Kraprayoon, was finally forced to resign.

Although the deployment of graphic death imagery was very powerful and, consequently, the political impact of the massacre very great at the time, the incident quickly faded out of memory, and "Black May," as it came to be called, had little meaning or influence in the dominant political culture that immediately succeeded it. This occurred within a longer trend in which death imagery has played a vital role in political transformations. Twice before during the struggle for democratic freedoms the Thai military had massacred unarmed citizens in Bangkok streets. The struggle over the representation of these deaths in various forms of public media has been crucial to the outcome of each these incidents, which occurred in 1973, 1976, and again in 1992. Oppositional strategies for visualizing dead bodies and commemorating violent deaths have been influential in shaping events, and in the story of this struggle the meaning of death to political culture has become increasingly subject to proliferating technologies of mass media, the economic values that animate them, and power relations shaped by a global discourse in which national image management has become central to the perceptions of investors. In Thailand, for the most part, the corpses of political victims have lent their evocative power to realizing the transformation toward a liberal free-market politics, in step with the values of global capitalism. Nevertheless—although locally the mass media profit from both the sensational value of violent death and the powerful argument for liberal freedoms that military massacres provide—the new order, as we will see, does not acknowledge the sacrifice of the demonstrators for its sake. Their death, although at times effectual and invaluable, can be rapidly divested of value. A momentous historical struggle for those Thais who dedicate themselves to it turns precisely upon these matters of accounting.

This book explores historical processes such as that between the short-term power of graphic violence and the structure of forgetting in a not-so-long *durée*. It is this power to electrify but then enervate death, this evocative power of violence and corpses in a fast-paced market of images, that I comment upon here through what may seem at first to be entirely different realms of visual and economic culture: Buddhist meditation on corpses and Buddhist funerary exchange. This book is an attempt to draw a critical position from some very different ways in which visions of death have value, truth, and power in Thailand, from the visions of death circulating over the surface of the earth, to the interplay of violence, its representation, and commemoration in the practice of radical democracy in Thailand, to the inner visualization of Thai Buddhist meditators contemplating death, corpses, and the repulsiveness of body parts, and finally to rural Thai rites of funeral exchange.

Imagine the possibility of performing an autopsy on yourself, even while you are still alive. Imagine that your scalpel and arthroscopic filament, cutting and sliding through the flesh of your corpse, left no traces, drew no blood, and that you could move through the organs without hindrance, and see and touch them intimately. Imagine that you could nestle right up next to the skeleton upon which everything hangs, and even draw so close as to lie within it—to wait quietly within, as it waits; to see and feel things from its point of view.

Such is the quiet abiding in Buddhist meditation on death, corpses, and bodily parts. In deep states of embodied concentration, relentless meditators focus their inner vision and sensation upon the parts of the body and the body as a corpse, absorbing into an interior charnel ground that festers with graphic images and insights. In Thailand it is called *asubha kammatthāna*, "contemplating the repulsiveness of the dead body," one of the most powerful practices in the Buddhist repertoire of form absorptions.

"It cracks open, divides, and separates," says the nun Mae-Chi Liem of her forays into the charnel ground within. "This body opens up for you to see. You see bodily ooze, clear ooze like in the brain; thick, filmy ooze and clear ooze. The body splits open into intestines, intestines the size of your wrist, *na*. Liver, kidneys, intestines, the stomach, you can see it all."

With this sense faculty of seeing in deep meditation, the mind's eye impinges upon the objects of its attention. It rubs itself into the gory aspects of embodied existence, brushing up against an insight into them. That is the Buddhist faith in visions of death—not only that death is certain and yet, in its own predictable way, unpredictable, but that in death, intensely examined, there resides a pressing and almost (but not quite) absolute truth about existence that can be seen and touched, intimately. *Dukkha*, suffering, is always groping at us, and those who dwell in stark lairs of its imagery discover that if you can lay your hand on it intimately you can grasp it, take its hand off you, and then let it go.

As though performing an autopsy on themselves, Thai meditators practice a form of concentration-visualization that causes absorption into graphic images of death and dismemberment. And in the practice of this art, they use gory photographs of others as an aid to realizing their own corporeality and mortality. This practice is parallel to a similar, conspicuous use of photographic memory in Thai political protest rituals and commemorations.

Political commemoration rituals, given their dual function in the presentation of both graphic corpse imagery and gifts to the dead, call up not only the particular practices of Buddhist death meditations but also the economic principles of gift exchange practiced more widely in Thai funerary rites. Such rites of exchange with the dead are a critical comment on the nature of a commerce in which so much may seem to conspire toward the obfuscation of social obligations. And yet the practice of funerary exchange is in Thailand never far from an entrepreneurial spirit, even as it embodies what Marcel Mauss dubbed, waxing romantic, the "spirit of the gift."[1] The sense that exchange objects retain a connection to the people who exchange them, rather than passing along anonymously and without obligation, is very much alive in Thai death memorials, even in the midst of an intense entrepreneurial milieu. This is important. The spirit of the gift mediates in culturally explicit ways both the relations among the living and the relations between the living and the dead, and so generates an economy that connects both people and time from within the very heart of the latest in capitalism.

This is the "funeral casino": a fusion of funeral rites with gambling. The fundamental ethnographic context to be explored here, the funeral casino is investigated figuratively throughout the text and literally in its conclusion. I find this form of freewheeling, obligated exchange performed both in the gambling wakes of northern Thailand depicted in the final chapter and in the ad-hoc black marketeering and Buddhist rites that spring up in moments of protest, danger, and mourning in the Thai struggle for freedom. Funeral wakes for the dead highlight potentials in Thai cultural practice that can establish memory in powerful and usable forms which are by no means either inimical to or washed out by the latest in capitalism.

Ultimately, this book is about the politics of telling history under obligation, an attempt to write *The Gift* into history. It is about the passage of time over the bodies of the dead, which is also a story of the apparent passing of the military-gift economy of the Cold War into the liberal free market of a new world. In Thailand, political cadavers are simultaneously catalysts, plot devices, and sublimated messages of this global story. The fusion of funerals and markets—whether accomplished in rites of mourning or in black markets of massacre imagery—offers a critique of the neoliberal economy by which a new world order can appear to sever its connection to an old order that has given it its life.

It is no coincidence that Thai political protests, tied to anniversaries of violence, are modeled upon the principles of gift exchange at Buddhist funerals, as we will see. And it is no coincidence that use of graphic death imagery has always been a standard appurtenance in their performance of social mnemonics, just as it is in the practice of Buddhist meditation on death.

In the four years of work on which this text is premised, 1989–1990, 1991–1993, and 1995, the study has encompassed Buddhist funerary exchange practices in rural northern Thailand, Buddhist meditation on death in central Thailand, and political demonstrations and commemoration rites in Bangkok. The text is an effort to bring these different arenas together into a political-philosophical association.

An instructive metaphor might be drawn from Walter Benjamin in order to imagine a way to write ethnography on such varied spheres of life, yet without relying on connective principles that are based in a logic of spatial contiguity or are purported to reflect a hermetic cultural structure. If the analytic architecture of philosophy were a palace, Walter Benjamin declared, his mission was "to fill up the walls of the palace to the point where the images appear to be the walls." He called it *Gesichtesphilosophie*, which Susan Buck-Morss explains is best rendered as "philosophical history": "to construct, not a philosophy *of* history, but a philosophy *out* of history, or (this amounts to the same thing) to reconstruct historical material as philosophy. . . . Benjamin was committed to a graphic, concrete representation of truth, in which historical images made visible the philosophical ideas. In them, history cut through the core of truth without providing a totalizing frame."[2]

What follows is, in the imagery of prose, an attempt at a similar visualization of philosophy. It is a construction of philosophical history out of the stuff of ethnography, a slight deflection of the usual trajectory of ethnography toward a sense of the architecture of ideas when one walks through them. "Philosophical ethnography" is a concept that might suggest one method, among many possibilities, for linking up mutually informative practices in a way that does not fall back on cartographic-literalist notions of culture, space, and place.[3]

Part I of this walk-through, "The Passed," is a genealogy of the political cadaver in Thailand, and investigates powerful and progressive politics in the confluence of political protests, free markets, and images of death in the recent history of the Thai prodemocracy movement.

In Chapter Two, "The New World," the stage is set by a fortuitous historical conjuncture in Bangkok, after the coup d'état led by General Suchinda Kraprayoon, as the 1991 World Bank/IMF meetings were about to be held in Bangkok—meetings originally garnered for Thailand by the previous, elected government. The chapter focuses on cleaning. It was the dawn of the "new world order," and the military sought to put forth a good public image to the world—an image of Thailand as progressive and of Bangkok as a global city. Cleanup operations performed on city space were intended to refurbish the "national image" after the damage it was believed to have sustained during the general's coup of 1991. But at the same time, the cleanup was intended to suppress unsightly street commemorations of a massacre from the Cold War past, the anniversary of which, unfortunately for the military, happened to coincide with the World Bank meetings. National identity under these conditions partakes in both a struggle over national history and the circulation and construction of identity in international arenas, an inseparable and complex relation that will be of interest throughout this text. The local history is, of course, a global history as well, but this fact is placed in a state of suspension within a discourse of new eras and a world order without history. And yet this is not the only opportunity presented by a world in which national images are adrift in the choppy seas of international imaginaries, as the unfolding series of events in this text will make clear.

Chapter Three, "Revolting History," is a reversion to the Cold War time of global community, following the lead of student demonstrators who persistently refused to detach themselves from "the passed." Violent suppression in 1973 and 1976 of prodemocracy demonstrations by the U.S.-backed military led to the public politics of the corpse in Thailand. This history, of a successful revolt in 1973 and the brutal end to its democratic aspirations in 1976, shows how powerful, potentially liberating, but also dangerous is the use of graphic death in a burgeoning public sphere, a realm that is constituted in founding violence and that therefore seeks to erase its own genealogy. This is both its unstable strength and its exploitable weakness. In the exclusion of violent ancestry and U.S. war-gifts from the memory of the public sphere, marginal and therefore potentially critical spaces of memory are generated from which contestation of these mutually bound orders of national history and global time can be launched from the sidelines, now or in the future. The recurrent time of commemoration is largely employed by direct victims of the Thai history of revolt and as a continuing inheritance by student activists, but the necromantic power of public massacre always awaits reawakening into the apprehension of a broader politics in the present, and in this "local" history the culpability of the global community can never be expunged.

Chapter Four, "Bloodless Power," resumes the narrative of the 1990s, when a protest movement against military power had the benefit both of hindsight into the death politics of the 1970s and of a far more articulated media apparatus. The chapter narrates the progress of protests against General Suchinda Kraprayoon on the streets of Bangkok. Backed by an army of mobile pushcart vendors, these demonstrators intended to force the general's resignation through nonviolent means, through the symbolism of the free market and in a contest of images in the public sphere. The protests employed mild versions of death imagery, threats of individual sacrifice through hunger strikes, and a nonviolent ideology. They made use of the presence of international journalists while under conditions of local censorship in order to place pressure on the regime, and yet it all eventually ended with the massacre of Black May. In these events it is possible to see the beginning stages of the reduction of radical democratic politics to a form amenable to accession into the narratives of the bourgeois public sphere. As a result of this process, the prodemocracy movement of 1992 has come to be known, almost invariably, as a "bourgeois revolution." This interpretation has come to enact significant and lasting effects on the performance of historical progress in Thailand; this narrative exacts a cost on radical politics in exchange for acceptable placement in neoliberal orderings of history. The demonstrators depended on the moral symbolism of modern capitalism for a construction of themselves as proper and decent citizens in step with the times, but the terms of those times made demands of their own.

Chapter Five, "Repulsiveness of the Body Politic," examines how the assimilation of radical politics into moral orders of historical "modernity" was fairly well completed through the violence of Black May. During the event, images of death were circulated in local and global media networks; they ultimately created the leverage to displace General Suchinda and significantly shift the country toward the democracy its activists had long desired. Despite state censorship, the work of death images was accomplished, on an international level through global media networks, and with even greater effect locally through an ad-hoc black market of videos bought and sold during funeral rites for the dead held on the street where Black May had transpired. Nevertheless, the incident was rather quickly forgotten by both the new government and the media, each of which had derived great benefit from the deaths. This chapter examines the serious deficiencies in media practice, as well as in its theoretical imagination, when dominant understanding is set by the terms of the public sphere's "modernity," especially where violent events are exploited to support the public sphere's own moral and historical propriety.

There are haunting similarities between theories that celebrate the new global media age and the messages on the nature of media technology that are carried by, in, and for mass media structures themselves. There is perhaps no better context in which to examine this union than one, like Black May of 1992, in which a "global mediascape," as Arjun Appadurai has termed it, appears to be a powerful source of historical agency, and is not averse to saying so.[4] What forms of exclusion enable such consensus on the place of media in global modernity? In 1995, the relatives of the Black May dead assembled for Buddhist commemoration rites and to demand compensation from the state for their losses (as they have every year since). But only three years after Black May, both the government in power and the mass media had little interest in their concerns anymore, and no longer valued the exchange relations that are consequent upon death and in which, during the event's funeral marketplace, they had themselves participated. The public sphere's persistent refusal to recognize the gift of death demands, perhaps, an equally abrupt refusal, and for that reason the text will turn to alternative critical conceptions for the principles of exchange at work in such transitional events.

Part II of the book, "Kamma," is a countercommentary on media relations of shock, remembrance, and the cultural economics of passing eras.

Chapter Six, "The Charnel Ground," interweaves theories on media representation of violence with Buddhist practices for meditating on abject images of death, corpses, and bodily parts. This chapter develops the critical meanings that can develop in the interstice between the politics of graphic sensationalism in the public sphere and reclusive Buddhist visualization of the body in death and decay. The chapter reflects on the media apparatus that can deliver the short-lived shock which has come to effect transfers of power so cleanly and efficiently. This view refuses, however, to accept facile condemnation of the essential "inhumanity" of visual media. Instead, the emphasis here is on the mutability of technologies of imaging (which are, after all, human constructions). I suggest that the most extreme form of disempowerment would consist in renouncing the possibility of making history through vision precisely at the moment of visual media's ascendance in influence. Through a detailed study of the theory and practice of visualizing death in Buddhist meditation, including the use by Thai Buddhists of sensationally gory photography, the chapter demonstrates that, like the image of the cadaver in the public sphere, this work with images of death can be chaotic and dangerous, though not hopelessly so. In a repetitive practice of taking abject imagery inwardly, Buddhist meditators create a vivid and powerful sphere of image reproduction that may seem morbid, unsympathetic in its agenda, and not directly political (if it can be said that a politics can exist autonomously of an ethics).[5] But what Buddhist meditation lacks in explicit political intent it gains in its unsettling and counterintuitive deconstruction of the human being through vision. If, as many complain, the representation of violence in modern image media is not doing what we want it to do, could it be that we ask of it something that it cannot provide, ask of it the wrong questions, need of it that it represent the fully human being where that being may not, as Buddhist meditators would claim, exist in the way we might want it to? Could it be that the most effective uses of graphic imagery need not, or must not, be grounded in the humanist call of sympathy? To answer cleanly in the affirmative is perhaps to project too literally the message of this Buddhist medium onto the public screen of image politics, and is not fully practicable in any possible or even imaginable form of society as we know it. And yet, I argue, the aims of radical democracy depend upon forestalling the closure of long-standing wounds and grievances, as well as on impeding the finalization of society in stable form.

Perhaps the political work of the abject must, similarly, find a way to wound common sense and the common senses as well, for these are media through which the peacefully violent exclusions of consensus are enforced without the use of force.

Chapter Seven, "The Funeral Casino," narrates an account of the funerary rites and gambling of northern Thais in a way that demonstrates how effective fusions of death, memory, gift exchange, and capitalism can be in Thai practices of commemoration. This chapter presents an exegesis on the practical meaning of kamma in giving and in entrepreneurial spirit, which should cast an indirect but clear light on the meaning of contemporary oppositional politics undertaken in the funereal idiom. Although the separation of gift and capital is quite possible to conceive of as well as to enforce, in economy as well as in history, this is not inevitable. Just as there is no inherent political meaning to the technological nature of image-reproducing media, so also is there no essential social formation attendant upon gambling—or in market and entrepreneurial practice, for that matter—that can serve as the bulls-eye for taking critical aim at the nature of the ills of our time. It might be noted in passing that it is unfortunate, for instance, that the term "casino capitalism" has been associated with "fetishistic" and "superstitious" monetary practices among an international underclass that supposedly has no real knowledge of the equally supposed unreal and ephemeral operations of global monetary wealth.[6] Suggesting a nonexclusive alternative to this enlightened casting of capitalism in darkness, this chapter will throw as much light as possible on socially embedded practices with money that may show how "superstitions" about value, in this case the communal generation and sharing of Buddhist "merit" (bun), can at least in some cases work effectively, though imperfectly and incompletely, from within the fabric of economic exchange as it stands. This is especially important to the radical democracy movements of Thailand, as the events of the text show that participation in market forms—of which there can be many—is as obligatory to political action as is reciprocity to the classic idea of the gift itself, offering both expansive opportunities and uncountable consequences. Drawing on funeral economies of communitarian value, this chapter puts forth an ethnographically coded philosophy of accountability, community, radical democracy, and responsibility to history. In particular it is a commentary intended to run across the grain of dominant plots for historical modernity.

This grain, what one might call "the neoliberal economy of history," concerns the economics of memory and forgetting in historical consciousness and visual culture. It is ultimately an economics of storytelling, the narrative economy by which the past is left behind and exchanged for the present, and the present is left behind and exchanged for the future, where each may go its separate way, as when one economic man comes together with another for a single moment of exchange, when they relinquish their values completely, and then depart with no strings attached.

"As a long time friend of the Thai people, we have made it clear we cannot accept the use of deadly force as a means of resolving the issues that divide the opposition and the government," said the U.S. State Department's spokesperson of the Bangkok crackdown in May of 1992. To that, President George Bush added, "Let's hope that it calms down there. We're very concerned about the instability in Thailand, very concerned about the violence that we've seen there. And we've made this position known to the Thais." This was a few days after the 1992 Los Angeles revolt. These diplomatic statements need to be put in their historical context: between two world orders. They are caught in a story about the passing away of a global military-gift economy and the arising of a liberal free market of a "new world." The words come from the country that had supplied the weapons with which the Thais were shot down in the Bangkok streets, from the country that had right up to the last minute in upcountry camps been secretly training the Thai soldiers who did the killing (while officially the United States severed relations with the military), from the country that had given and left Thailand with the martial legacy of an old world order, from the establishment that once called Thailand "America's landlocked aircraft carrier." The statements come from the country that had once superglued the Thai domino to the table with military dictatorship and massacre, and that now sent careful words condemning the violence that was so out of step with the new times.

There is here a peculiar economics plotted on the linear passing of history, which I believe is as old as the science of political economy. It can be expressed with the equation *trade replaces violence*, as Marshal Sahlins has characterized our old discourses of time, trade, and war.[7] In saying this, I am not pointing just to the ubiquitous faith in trade over violence as a symptomatic characteristic of capital culture, but also to the very cultural economy by which one appears to be exchanged for the other—the very economics of storytelling by which new eras arise and replace old ones, by which time yields an endless succession of births. Newness is the commodity form written into history: emergences, new worlds after new worlds.

In the late 1980s a Thai prime minister, speaking of Southeast Asia, the still-throbbing flashpoint of the cold war, avowed, "We will turn the battlefields into marketplaces!" This gained him worldwide respect and renown in finance circles, but at home in Thailand one West Point graduate, General Suchinda Kraprayoon, had him led away at gunpoint, thus setting in motion the series of events that make up the focus of this narrative. There was in the deposed prime minister's misfired words a peculiar sort of storytelling that packs history into the loaded phrasing of developmental time lines that imperially transform killing into clean fields of profit. *We will turn the battlefields into marketplaces.* Liberal arguments for free-market principles are seen as the nonviolent successors to a separate, discrete, violent past, to which they are radically opposed. In the neoliberal economy of history there are no strings attached. But I would suggest that our "late capitalist" economy—or, if you like, our early "new world order" economy—has accumulated a great deficit in its life-and-death budgeting, in its balancing of historical accounts and the nonviolent story that it tells about itself, nonviolently, about the triumph of peaceful trade and reason over barbarism.

Exclusion and Consensus

Only a few moments after the deaths, people were whispering in small groups about the spirits, *winyaan.* Public gatherings of over five people had been banned. In these huddled and in some cases officially illegal groups, they were not talking about what might become of them, the spirits, where they might go, or what their fate would be. It was too soon for that. There was no telling what would happen to the Black May dead, and those times had not even been given a name yet. They were talking about where they came from: "They are the spirits of those kids who were killed in October 14 [1973], come back to be killed again." In the disjointed, vacant, and yet humanly speckled streets lined with bullet holes and smoking vehicles, under a cloudy and searingly hot day—a day that was ripped from a familiar hum of normal life that is never noticed until it is suddenly gone—on such a day suspended and arrested, any relation between the times of then and now might have been the case.

"Those murdered kids were reborn and killed again," I was told repeatedly, with complete confidence.

Something undone, unquiet, not dead, not passed returns because it has nowhere else it can go. Memory manages to return among a people who so repeatedly claim they are forgetful: *khon thai rao khi lyym* ("we Thai are forgetful"). But contained in these lingering doubts about memory are both a strong cognizance of the necessity of remembering and a haunting apprehension that what was left undone exceeds the bounds of the time which forgets. Kamma, returns on death, is the subject of this text.

Perhaps one of the most dangerous aspects of the inscription of death into history is the fact that nationalist imagining obsessively does precisely that—obsessively return to the dead, especially to the anonymous dead, for the construction of its sacral continuity and encompassing logic, as Benedict Anderson has written.[8] This imagined community depends, Anderson asserts, on a simultaneous remembering of the dead and forgetting of the political conditions of their demise. Thus, one could argue, lynched African Americans can be coopted as part of a common American history, "our dead." Or—and this is more to the point of the present text—the deaths of so many Southeast Asian people in a previous world order can be brought to consciousness in a new global community only on the condition that the community can no longer remember the conditions that put them where they are, and can stare back at them or even speak on their behalf, since they are buried in time and cannot speak themselves. And this only on condition that the conditions that buried them there are no longer remembered as present, in the present.

Thai invocations of the dead do not sidestep these problematics, either. They are conducted in expressly nationalist idioms, honoring *virachon*, or martyrs, for the nation. But the refusal of commemorators to unlink an ethical responsibility to the past from a politics in the present forestalls the assimilation of violent history into a sacral and unified community that can then move happily along. Each commemoration rite voices the calls that those in the present do not want to hear, alights upon injustices that the present does not want to see, persistently demands recognition of the dead in terms that will never be accepted. This, I would argue, is the paradoxical status of calls for justice in radical democracy. Thai commemoration is a movement that perpetually forestalls consensus and refuses the terms of peace, that makes impossible demands and never rests, that creates flashes of communal unity and throws them bitterly in the face of the fiction of national unity. It is this simultaneous demand for and impossibility of recognition, this simultaneous ethical and political call, that impedes, imperfectly and precariously, the finalization of an assimilation of the dead into national imagination, and thus prevents their political divestment.

This text will adopt a similar negotiation of ethics and politics. It is, in fact, modeled on the practice of commemoration itself. Rather than merely represent Thai commemorations, however, which are being addressed mainly to the national arena, this text emulates these practices in its contemplation of its own concern, namely, the short history of the new world order. At the same time, it is a commentary on Thai rites that shares with them an attention to the breach that affords the possibility for both ethics and politics and that must remain open to be of advantage. In the special sense intended here, one could say that if radical democracy ever got what it wanted, that would be precisely not what it wanted.

In any case, that this might happen is impossible—the impossibility of justice and its necessity, as Jacques Derrida has formulated differently.[9] This is an uncomfortable conception of radical democracy. It is premised on ideas of the impossibility of justice, "the impossibility of society," and in particular on the impossibility of "civil society." The "Idea of Civil

Society" has often served as the ground of democracy's being, as it also does now, as Jean and John Comaroff have pointedly observed.[10] Questioning this idea may be as necessary to projects of freedom as the idea is itself. Is radical suspicion of the ideals of civil society tantamount to subverting freedom of thought and expression? Or are these values themselves subject to manipulation precisely because of their sanctified status? To question the idea of civil society is not a nihilistic repudiation of the political conditions that make criticism possible in the first place, but can be a call to recognize the conflictive openings that make activism possible. Radical democracy works within the fact that the exclusion upon which every consensus is based can never finally banish that which puts it in question. An agreement about what constitutes an ethical and responsible public sphere depends upon excluding disruptive and unassimilable voices, but this can never be final and sealed. And this attention to the impossibility of sealing off instability applies not only to the social body. As Thomas Keenan argues in *Fables of Responsibility*, this radical democratic apprehension must even include a deconstruction of the "responsible subject," granting no easy alibis for personal ethics to retreat from a politics. The "No One" figured in deconstructive writing still can be, must be, ethicopolitically responsible precisely because of being formed in language, itself a series of unacknowledged political and ethical processes.[11] Language, however, is not the only fable through which to inbue this far from individualized state of culpability with an ethical and political moral; this is the problematic role that Buddhist practices with kamma will play in this text. To be sure, as in the irreverent and secular practice of critical reading locked in struggle, radically democratic thought must refuse the fixation into immobilized form of either the individualized subject or the society that finally binds it. But in contrast to the sometimes severe critical energy that characterizes contemporary theory, political movements in Thailand also have their quieter and more reverent sides, which recognize, as perhaps academic theorists of radical democracy may not emphasize enough, that the openness upon which democracy depends can, and possibly must, include the actual formation of coherent social figures that can engage in collective action. That may require a kind of affirmation, an opening in a different sense, a release from antagonism that can create its own forms of opening, and openness.

The principals of connection performed in Thai rites of funerary exchange generate precisely such an opening, and therefore provide some instruction on a philosophy of radical democracy in which communitarian aspirations can exist side by side with unsettling notions of the instability of the individual and of the perpetual state of rupture that is so often called society. That this is expressed in the Buddhist and religious idiom of kamma, and in literal exchange with the spirits of the dead, is both a problem for theory and a strength for it. The use of ethnography as a source of theoretical instruction, therefore, warrants further discussion. In particular, the principles embodied in Thai funerary rites present a problem for critical theory because little space is afforded to religious assumptions in radical academic writing (though one might also note that universalist assumptions about language are accepted). Derrida himself pointedly cautions: "There has never been a scholar who really, and as scholar, deals with ghosts. A traditional scholar does not believe in ghosts—nor all that could be called the virtual space of spectrality."[12] The obsession of Western philosophy with itself is perhaps as glaringly apparent in this statement as it is anywhere else, and yet this statement is not, in its proper context, completely untrue.

At the same time, the problems for theory presented by Buddhist exchange with the dead are also its strength. Although Buddhist kamma ostensibly encompasses in its elusive logic the entirety of the world and existence, it can never serve as an all-inclusive formulation, least of all in the Western academy.[13] The presentation of Buddhism here as theory, with the same salience as what is normally accounted as theory, is impossible, like justice.

The empirical events depicted in this text show that expulsion of alterity creates both the unstable fiction of the good society and the marginal spaces from which critical purchase on it is gained. And though the movement to address processes of exclusion is expressed in an idiom of demands for inclusion, as it is here as well, if that inclusion were granted, the possibility of radical critique would be foreclosed. In fact, those who do not understand this may be the same as those who naïvely berate radical academics, and especially deconstructionists, for being "against everything and for nothing." Nothing, Buddha taught, is not such a bad thing once you get to know it. It is necessary that criticism take a form that is in some way unacceptable, that it present a gift that from the start will be, at least in part, refused. Such a breach renders the idea of consensus into clear resolution as a fiction without resolving its inherent contradiction.

But how does one proceed to see kamma in history, when so much recent history is already inscribed with its own principles of procedure, already comes with its own subtle and not-so-subtle programs running in the background, checking the grammar of historical consciousness? For the beginning chapters of the text, I write of kamma and meditation on death rather surreptitiously, through the matter and imagery of history, as Benjamin recommended. In the final two chapters, this method is exchanged for explicit theorization, which is to say for a language that departs from particular contexts and speaks across them. And yet on balance ethnographic context is enlisted here not as an object of analysis but rather as a method of analysis; it is not so much illuminated by theory as it is itself a commentary on theory. That necessarily entails difficult and irrevocable choices. Ethnography often and habitually contextualizes the exotic, pins it down in sociohistorical context while allowing, say, Roland Barthes to caper freely around the world and be brought in to comment on any situation the author finds worthy.[14] We might ask, for instance, what does it really mean to "use" theory? I am habituated enough to this practice of using theory to be neither capable nor desirous of completely abandoning it. And yet I have made the difficult choice of cutting "the ethnographic" (even, I could say, many of the Thai people I know) a little slack, too: what if Thai practices of meditation on death and ideals of funeral exchange were to be taken at a value so that they could go traveling, as a poststructuralist might?

But such traveling and traversing of traditional intellectual maps is itself problematic. In *Siam Mapped*, the historian Thongchai Winichakul delivers a principled critique not only of the discourses that have, historically, created the sense of nation in Thailand but also of the necessary complications involved when what is called *khwambenthai*, "Thainess," becomes an object of study by those designated as Thai or other, or in scholarship shared between them. He criticizes the self-ascription among some Thai national scholars who stake a claim to knowledge based on authentic insider perspective while reproducing notions of national identity that are in fact buttressed by historical processes of national construction that operate across these discursive divides. This body of scholarship and "elite discourse," argues Thongchai, ultimately contributes to the reification of the national discourse and shares a formal affinity with the booming daily military propaganda radio broadcasts in so many villages and neighborhoods around the country.[15]

This is mirrored in the inordinate attention and importance lent by foreign scholars to the role of Buddhism as a nation-ordering institution. This only amplifies the insistence of nationalist propaganda. As Rosalind Morris has put it, "Shoring up Thailand's own national culturalist self-representation . . . are the anthropological texts in which the almost uniform valorization of Thai Theravada Buddhist ideology has left questions of difference and power too often unasked."[16] As Morris implies, statements made in elite discourse about the role of Buddhism in Thai society have often been taken at face value rather than questioned as to their sources in a nationalist imaginary.

This is further demonstrated by the high degree of foreign interest in what has been called "reform Buddhism" or "radical conservatism," which Thongchai singles out for criticism.[17] Even if in some cases they explicitly reject "Western modernity," these Buddhist developments share what we can recognize as a self-consciously modernist outlook that downplays cosmology and ritual in favor of practices of cultural critique and

18

social action. The appeal to Western scholars is obvious: otherness, but not too much. The leaders and followers of this small yet influential aspect of Thai politics hold ideals of freedom and often also democracy that appear to be in step with the liberal taste of academic intelligentsia. Elaborating on Thongchai's criticism, I would argue that the progressive Buddhists hold out a difference that legitimates Euro-American values as quasi-universal, in that those values appear to originate from an "other" setting. This "other-self" might even promise a better mode of thinking or practice than that of the self-self. Ironically, the source for this Buddhist otherness is often, historically, an adoption by the purported "others" of what they themselves perceived as either Western or modern styles of thinking. Robert Sharf makes a similar case in relation to the American fascination with the Western-trained Zen philosopher D. T. Suzuki: Westerners have found in his teaching their own philosophies repackaged to them as "oriental wisdom," apparently rendering them both intuitively true and irreproachable due to their inaccessibility as Zen truth.[18]

Critiques by Richard Gombrich and Gananath Obeyesekere of the Buddhist revival in Sri Lanka and its connection to Orientalist discourses in general, and in particular to the influence of that new age precursor, the Theosophical Society, might point the way toward gaining some critical purchase on Thai reformist Buddhism.[19] What Gombrich and Obeyesekere label "Protestant Buddhism" offers, characteristically, a psychologized version of Buddhist philosophy; values the personalization of meditation and the altruism of social action; presents Buddhism as a science rather than a religion; and disfavors ritual, cosmology, "corruption," and, at least at its inception, implication in established power structures. This always-already-modern Buddhism is as established in Sri Lanka as it is in Waldenbooks. Similarly, in Thailand what is often referred to as the essence of Thainess or the foundation of Buddhism often consists of modernist accommodations and rationalizations presented as a truth that always was. The case of Thailand complicates this picture, however, in that the historical connection to colonialism (Thailand was never colonized) and the standard carriers of modernity are less straightforward than in most other cases. Many of the tenets of Thai modernist Buddhists are, arguably, considerable innovations, which calls into question assumptions about the origins of modernity in the West, a situation that in the Sri Lankan case is less obvious but probably also true.[20]

It is no coincidence that a certain bastion of liberal thinking, Charles Taylor, in his debates with multiculturalists and with proponents of "Asian Values," chose of all places around the world—and such liberal essayists can have their pick—Thailand and this particular Buddhist current, and even the prodemocracy movement that is the subject of this text, as the exemplar for how "an unforced consensus on human rights" could be possible, given human cultural diversity.[21] Western values about what constitutes acceptable actions in the realm of human rights can be held in common, argues Taylor, even if the cultural motivations are completely different. He offers, alongside the trust inspired by the benevolent Thai king, progressive Buddhist politics as the central example in a world where functionally equivalent goals of the democratic representation and respect for human rights that are held sacred in the West (in principle, we might add) are motivated by and understood through completely different cultural sources. As Taylor quotes John Rawls's *Political Liberalism* on the possibility of "overlapping consensus," "different groups, countries, religious communities, civilizations, while holding incompatible fundamental views on theology, metaphysics, human nature, etc., would come to an agreement on certain norms that ought to govern human behavior. . . . We would agree on the norms, while disagreeing on why they were the right norms."[22]

In this happy consensus, what is unmentionable is that which is excluded, irreconcilable, conflicted—in short, everything that is in fact the case in the world, and in which, arguably, politics consists. The assumption is that what Thais do with their bodies we can agree with; what they do with their minds is their own business; on those terms, there are some "Asian Values" that we can accept. What is not examined is the metaphysical existence of this other mindedness, and the readily available history, were the mind inclined toward it, which would indicate that the values in "reform Buddhism" in fact have a long and deep connection to Western discourses of human right, among a plethora of other Western and modernist discourses. More to the point, they have quite simply not been germinating in a space without world history.[23] The problem lies, of course, not in the fact that Thais are bricoleurs but in the theorist's mode of evaluating cultural difference. That Thai political thought and practice might actually inhabit the same world as that of the liberal theorist, that Thai Buddhist ideas and ideals might actually inform, contest, defeat, or be defeated by established modes of liberal political thought is not possible in a world of multiple and mutually exclusive cultural worlds—and that is precisely the point of imagining them that way. Exclusion of the disruptive is a necessary condition of consensus, after which "culture" is a favored form for readmitting alterity into liberal discourse on that discourse's own terms. Not coincidentally, the aspect of reform Buddhism that Taylor singles out as its special ethical value consists in the fact that it "attacks what it sees as the 'superstition' of those who seek potent amulets, and the blessings of monks, and the like. It wants to separate the search for enlightenment from the seeking of merit through ritual. And it is very critical of the whole metaphysical structure of belief . . . about heavens, hell, Gods and demons, which play a large part in popular belief."[24] In contrast, the alterity of a Buddhist ethicopolitics, which "popular belief" might indeed possibly present in a contest of thought, might not speak back what, and how, a liberal discourse would desire it to speak. And yet the exclusion of consensus theory does not completely prevent Taylor from perceiving in Buddhist activism that the "gamut of western philosophical emotions, the exaltation at human dignity, the emphasis on freedom as the highest value, the drama of age-old wrongs righted in valour . . . seem out of place in this alternative setting."[25] And what would one make of all this if it were not confined to its proper setting?

It is difficult to avoid the too-easy celebration of the "other self" if one engages with relatively different ideas, ideals, and practices as more than a mere gesture and, in one's work, participates in them. How does one engage in such practices and yet not in a manner that cordons them off in an unapproachable otherness that is ultimately irrelevant (save as "data")? This is the tightrope traversed in this account of protest politics and the attendant ethnography of Buddhist practice which comments on that account. This is very different from reading political movements as expressions of Buddhism or as shifts in the Buddhist structure.

Not unexpectedly, at the peak of scholarly interest in Thai reform Buddhism, just before the events of 1992, there were prophesies that this "movement" could amount to a political revolution.[26] I have to admit that my original research plan, and much of my actual effort, at first centered on investigating these "new Buddhist movements." But in fact the focus had to change, as the revolution of 1992, if there was one, came from far more pedestrian sources (from pedestrians, in fact). The consensus following the wake of the event, as depicted in the media that represented it, was an unsurprising attribution of the revolt to modernization, economic expansion, and the growth of the middle class. This interpretation of a "bourgeoisie revolt," however, is also one I take considerable empirical and political issue with. The same critical skepticism that is applied to the identity of peoples and nations needs to be applied to the overdetermined narratives of history, where the new and emerging features of global modernity are somehow not as susceptible as are national or cultural identity to criticism as discourse—that is, to criticism not for being unreal nor untrue but as practice that participates in the creation, always incomplete and unsuccessful, of the reality it purportedly only describes and knows. Although the outlines of a new and future global order must be traced, I focus instead on the complementary task of putting the imagination of our global modernity in question. This is not to declare that "there shall be no metanarratives," for this is a naïve and impossible suggestion, but to exercise critical practices on a strategically chosen subject—in this case, the short history of the new world order. In practice, Thailand was one of the most cooperative countries of all in the schemes for a borderless world economic order, and in return for that, by 1997 suffered a crushing economic blow that entailed both moral and practical submission to world economic authorities. Given this development, in fact, it is uncertain at the moment whether there is not some role that nationalism can play for countries like Thailand. I am not a little haunted by the possibility of a world in which *khon thai rao*, "we-Thai," can no longer be uttered with some form of referential meaning. It is the various uses to which such discourses are put, rather than the simple assumption of a single political meaning, that may need to be the focus of future scholarship.

In this text, neither the attempt to debunk Thainess nor the effort to identify its essence is the question in focus. Thongchai Winichakul's great contribution in *Siam Mapped* was not in discovering that Thailand never existed but in discovering how it ever became possible to believe it existed in the first place—particularly through maps, through the development of the sense of what he calls a "geo-body": a territorial-national identity dependent on the technology of mapping for its conception and distribution. On top of Benedict Anderson's idealist tendencies Thongchai overlays an attention to techniques and technologies, and so brings an emphasis on extralinguistic discourses into the analysis of imagining community.[27] What maps in particular bring to the fore—which Anderson never emphasized enough—is the fact that self-imagining is almost always in relation to other-imagining, exclusion, since the borders on maps are by their nature about precisely this dialectic. Thongchai demonstrates further that it was not possible to conceive of an "enemy within" Thailand, much less kill it, until an answer could be shown to the question, "within what?" Similarly, I would ask, what are the conditions of possibility for conceiving what lies within and without the "new" and "emerging" in our world? What phenomena count as belonging to the new global modernity and what are counted outside of it, and acted upon by it? What are the means by which it is possible to conceive of and distribute a conception of the new and global, particularly in an imaginary where the geo-body has many contenders? On a general level, I have chosen to address these questions by engaging those narrative and material media through which a passage to the present and future is granted. On a particular level, this story about storytelling is set in Thailand lest one forget that these history-making globalisms do not and cannot exist apart from the contexts in which they simultaneously declare their own existence and appear to do their own work.

In the matter of the material for writing, one must choose the enemy, and the friend, carefully. In making any choice or taking any stand, of course, there must be a certain violence wrought on the inseparable, a certain arbitrary power of the authorial hand exercised in recomposition, but also a certain respect and dignity granted where it may be, could be, just possibly, warranted and useful to see it. Here, this will amount to a manipulation of the balance not only between ethnography and theory but also between criticism and practice, in a search throughout this text for the formulation of ideas and theoretical directions that are based on values whose salience has been impressed upon me by my "informants," which are of concern and relevant to the contexts in which they live.

The possibility of this move is immediately foreclosed in the expulsion of alterity implicit in the flat figure of "hegemonic Theravāda Buddhism." This is the special danger that attends a too-eager desire to purge Thai studies of its own sins, at the expense of its subjects. It is possible, perhaps, to depict Thai Theravāda Buddhism as a monolithic structure that includes the ecclesiastical hierarchy, modernist revivalists of all stripes, and village monks (conveniently forgetting the thriving and sometimes independent practice of nuns and laywomen), all together in one male, rationalist, oppressive structure that comes on with a singular force and, coincidently, is the opposite of everything we value in America: it values order, enforces gender identities, is against imagination and dreams, and is over-intellectual and bookish. Although no specific detail I mention is untrue by itself in many contexts or among many people in Thailand, such a picture of the whole would decidedly be so, especially in its depiction of Thai Theravāda Buddhism as a whole in the first place. Although wholesale critique of Thai Buddhism, by definition, would not directly participate in the unquestioning acceptance of Thai elite discourse against which Morris cautions, a strange side effect may indeed be a reification—though not ratification—of the Thai elite discourse, mirroring exactly a certain strain in the Buddhist construction of tradition. There are Thai Buddhists who would agree eagerly with everything about the idea of a Buddhist "hegemony" except its negative moral valence, and eagerly wish for or believe it to be true. But it is not true. The antiritualist interpretations of scripture and practice are only the wishes of some, not a description of what, in fact, most Thai Buddhists actually believe or practice. The gendered identity of Buddhism as a male religion is something to be contested, not attributed to its nature. Such an approach is, at least, necessary for many of the women within the tradition, who are rarely consulted by critical scholars on these matters (while obviously Thai Buddhism is easy pickings for those who do not want to live within it).

This is a long-known and perhaps unavoidable consequence for the ethically motivated critic, especially in criticism deployed across lines of difference and privilege: in characterizing the enemy, one lends it an essential identity. Although this may serve the critical and theoretical purpose of one's own elite discourse, it may not serve as well the people for whom one is presumably concerned. For instance, identifying Buddhism as essentially patriarchical to the core does not serve Buddhist women well, since any change toward more inclusion of women in its highest established structures would amount to a change in the "essential" nature of the religion, making it, to the discourses of such essence, no longer essentially Buddhism (as has been pointed out by feminist scholars).[28] In terms of practical accomplishment, Thai Buddhist women have served their interests better by contesting the received wisdom of what counts as essential Buddhism. This does not necessarily require the creation of convenient fictions. In fact, the great heterodoxy that actually characterizes Thai Buddhism, rather than the faceless homogenizing stamp so conveniently embossed with the vague outlines of "hegemony," has long been utilized adeptly by women who have recognizable feminist goals as well as by those whose practice and achievement are defined in other terms and those who fall into both categories.[29]

Perhaps it is necessary to return to Antonio Gramsci's lesson, quickly forgotten, that hegemony can never be defeated by antihegemony.[30] To take a position of leaving Buddhism in Thailand to the pleasure of those forces that wield it so unfortunately may create a critical out for some, but for those who live within it such a surrender of responsibility is decidedly not empowering, and in any case is unlikely to happen. In Thailand, the fact is that exclusively anti-Buddhist criticism is not a viable political strategy, nor is it a significantly desired one. Although the exposure of Buddhism to radical intellectual critique is long overdue in both Western and Thai academies, it is important to recognize that this concern does not encompass all that matters, particularly to the people who are subjects of study, nor encompass all that is the case in the diverse, heterogenous, open, and leaky field which is "Thai Buddhism." Most Thais will never renounce Buddhism, regardless of how many expulsions of its alterity can be accomplished through monochromatic theories of its abuses.

The Buddhist practices that appear in this text cannot be understood solely as representative of a hegemonic structure, nor as uncritically yoked to the hegemonic discourses of a modernist Buddhism that has swept them along in an enormous historical wake seen, paradoxically, only by those few who possess the right, highly specialized training. The manner in which Buddhist practices are presented here is, therefore, in an unorthodox and problematic relation to the issues just discussed. Arguably, this text results in the "valorizaton of Thai Theravāda Buddhism" that Morris censures (though it might be noted that "valorization" can also mean "to value"). At the same time, this study of the Thai democracy movement, in the context of a globalist imaginary, is not a sociological study of the institutions of Thai Buddhism, critical or otherwise, and is neither a positive nor a negative evaluation of those institutions. It is simply not about them. Nor are reform Buddhist movements, as sources of political action, the subject of study, though that is a valid subject so long as its influence is not reified beyond the role these movements actually play in Thai activism. And, as well, this is not a study of Thai academic scholarship and theory on politics. My sources are almost exclusively oral, although that does not mean they are less edifying than academic sources. This text is an artificial employment of ethnography as theory, drawing from the instruction I have received from people, some of them illiterate, who are not normally counted as theorists and whose concerns are not normally considered accurate or usable in the public sphere that is academic writing. It would be ironic, given the premise that a consensual public sphere is founded on exclusion, if these ideas were then presented in terms we could all agree on. The moment that political thought can agree on what constitutes political thought is the moment politics is effaced.

Whether this approach can function as intellectual capital is not a conclusion I am making but a question I am exploring here, a question of unsettling the exclusions of validated political practice, language, and thought—a concern that some would argue has long been important to the aspirations of cultural anthropology. The following text is merely the only way, given my limited abilities, I could figure out how to express the insights I know are there in "my material."

When I returned from the field I was asked, "Did you get good material?" The answer, in fact, is yes, "but not just the way we want it."[31]

In comparison with many people I know, I almost feel I have no right even to speak of this material, or of death, save for the fact that I have been taught well that what matters is not how much of death you have seen but how you handle it, and what you are willing to do with that accursed portion. My preoccupation here is the question of what to do with these matters, rather than a focus on the violence itself. The anthropology of political violence has voiced its share of cries over "the horror," staked its share of claims to authority over "the things I have seen," its words wielded conspicuously, almost violently. It should not be difficult to understand and acquit this anger at the world, especially if one has no desire to transcend the political worlds addressed by ethnography. It should be possible even to empathize with the fact that the invocation of these accursed matters always carries the potential for rebounding on the one who invokes them. What follows is an attempt in some way to do something with this lamentable share—in this case, not the greatest in scale, by world standards. What follows could be thought of as an attempt to translate a sensibility of Buddhist meditation on death imagery and village funeral rites into something quite different from them (and so not to be confused with them): ethnography and history, words, images, and storytelling.

25

"I don't know who to tell our story to," Pi Gai, mother of a son crippled in the Black May crackdown, said to me. "Who can I tell it to?" She did not really see my ear as the answer. Nor did I. What could I do for her, after all? But then again, there must be something.

These stories of those with whom I have had direct connection, the saddest stories I know, will not necessarily be so when at the end of the day they are dissolved into the great connections between minds that dwarf that here in this text, between you and me. And as each day passes and the history in these tales gets farther and farther away, my connection to its spirit becomes only more tenuous. It is more difficult to give anything at all back to it, even memory, let alone honor. One only ventures, however treacherous it is, to write about death—their death, our death—in the face of dangerous possibilities of evoking its sensational aura, or inciting fear, or fascination, or in abusing the very sentiments between people by manipulating them by faking them, by maudlin or pointless repetition of them, by indulgence in them, or by linking those sentiments to some ideological or philosophical program in order to hide the collapse into which all that must always lead, or through analysis or cleverness, or histrionic twitching, or narrative incompetence. To do so would be to destroy the meaning of the lives and deaths behind these tales, to commit a form of murder that drains the life not only from the living and the dead but from death itself.

But even my torturous list does not exhaust all the possibilities for that which kills, which recapitulates what already seems to be a severed consciousness of meaning in death and a severed connection between the living and the dead. I am not sure, anymore, if I have what it takes to care enough about these stories or spirits, any more than I can exhaust all the forms of little murder that conspire against our caring.

And yet the repetitive tasks of memory performed in Thai funerary rites keep orienting attention toward the salience of such preoccupation, just as the repetitive mental motions of Thai Buddhist meditation keep returning to a similar practice of reminder, within the very process of passing away itself. Whether there are dangers in mindfulness of death cannot be in question. Nor can there be doubt that there is often proffered some purported standpoint that remains outside implication in these matters—due to a more sophisticated critical armature wielded from a transcendent position or due to an historical "lateness" in intellectual progress beyond the concerns of people who recognize a need to present the passed and to exchange with the dead. But these are not accurate and useful positions for, at least, some small proportion of the people in the world today. In a time of the global ascendance and proliferation of a particular and unfortunate form of accounting, perhaps other forms of accounting should also count for something.

Forgiving the Debt

Even later than the events recounted in this text, but only a bit, the hulking skeletons of unfinished high-rises in a perpetual state of suspension hang over a city dried of its liquidity. Perhaps they will never be finished. The crash of currency has arrested them, causing these girder ghosts to come back from the future to scatter all the Thais and immigrant workers who depended on them for their lives.

All in all, it has been said, the collapse of economies in Asia may be a good thing in the long run. Asian ways have been cut down through an inevitable power and plot to the biography of the world market, and the free world will eventually visit in their stead. At least to a certain portion of the world's financiers, what was deserved was received, and for them the question of an Asian way of progress has been settled once and for all with the return of the real. That is, at least, one way of keeping accounts of what must be traded in for an upgrade.

But where is, when was, the deal settled? This book looks elsewhere. It is a short history of the new world order, set in Thailand before the crash and during the hopeful period heralded as one of world transition. It is a study of the Thai democracy movement of 1992 and its entailments both in the legacy left to it by the county's partnership with the United States in the Cold War and in the altered array of possibilities and restrictions when the field of power changed. This is difficult terrain to traverse—the changeful. It is not easy to write about political action in what has come to be called "global modernity" without capitulating to the demands that the idea of global modernity makes on a picture of the world, especially that of a "new" world. The same remains true for Thai democracy, of course—a movement that has taken great advantage from the integration of international finance, the expansion of world media communications and, at least for a time, the burgeoning of wealth beyond the capability of existing hierarchical structures to absorb it, all of which have created fissures in state power and have made numerous political contests potentially effective. But the trade for agency in this situation must of course come at a cost, and the terms of the deal with these forces do not always make themselves clear at the time of exchange. Perhaps, in the underfinanced concrete waste of the time being, it has become clear. And it is the strange and awkward purpose of this book to explain that it is not people like the relatives of the dead of 1992 who do not understand how this exchange in history does its work.

In the Southeast Asia of the new world order, people still die and are maimed by the previously undetonated bombs and mines of the Cold War. In southern latitudes, the Cold War was never cold, and it still is not. But the historical imagination of this presence-of-the-past-in-the-present need not be limited to the easily graspable concept of buried explosives. Far more is in order, and this book, such as it is, is an attempt to reach askew—to other, unobvious and unorthodox accounting practices for the processes whereby new world eras are born. Somewhere the lines have crossed, demanding an audit.

That an alternative historical accountancy might be relevant to assessing what is at stake in the world today can be no better indicated than by the present penchant for discourse on forgiving third world debt. The idea that the world's debtors might be "forgiven" by the same countries that previously had colonized or imperially governed and exploited them certainly could not have come at a more auspicious time.[32] The methods of calculation are all ready and in place, so that this forgiveness need not be articulated in a language of historical justice but can be reasonably calculated in the econometric equations of greatest good in the present time. The case can certainly be made—I am not denying it—for the economic perspicacity of forgiving the debt: to free oppressed economies and bring prosperous returns, in different degrees, for everyone, and far out of proportion to the loss of the unrecovered credit. But even before this thought can be grammatical there must be a production of forgetting to condition the possibility that such forgiveness might occur in the first place. Where is this place, this first place that forgives the third place?

PART I

✤

The Passed

The New World

BANGKOK AND THE WORLD ORDER

WITHOUT HISTORY

> Each epoch not only dreams the next, but also, in dreaming,
> strives toward the moment of waking. It bears its end in itself
> and unfolds it—as Hegel already saw—with ruse. In the convul-
> sions of the commodity economy we begin to recognize the
> monuments of the bourgeoisie
> as ruins even before they have crumbled.
>
> WALTER BENJAMIN[1]

THAI INTERNATIONAL

October 14, 1991, was a curious day in Thai history, when two histories collided as if by some divine plan or irony. On the one hand, it was the opening day of the World Bank and International Monetary Fund meetings, the triennial foray of the Washington-based agencies out into third-world conference centers, which that year was hosted in Bangkok. It was to be the first such World Bank and IMF meeting since the collapse of the Soviet Union. Arguably, it was to be the first World Bank meeting of the new world order. On the other hand, in a bizarre twist of kamma, the date to discuss the fate of nations in Bangkok landed exactly on the anniversary of an event from what seemed, then, an entirely different era. In that other, faraway time, there was a notorious massacre of unarmed Thais by a U.S.-backed military regime. In Thailand, the successful student-led revolt of 1973 was so charged with memory that to this day it is simply referred to as "October 14" to recall its history. No need to refer to the linear scale of time: the same day perpetually returns, once a year.

So in October 1991, the linear history of economic progress had, uncannily, fallen into the lap of an eternally returning sense of past massacres unaccounted for, of commemoration and anniversary. And within this wrinkle in time, two separated histories of the gift seemed almost to seek each other out for an exchange—military aid and development aid, martial and Marshall plans—two gifts, two histories, two powers, two world orders, collapsing the past, present, and future. The correspondences defy description. But, as will be apparent in the following pages, the efforts of some people to keep those correspondences separate can well be described.

It cannot be emphasized enough that Thailand is intimately acquainted with the obsolete world order, a military gift economy in which it has participated for some time. Long before hosting the World Bank, Thailand was host country to the war of Indochina. In fact, it was the key domino superglued to the table with military dictatorship and the massacre of restless civilians. "America's landlocked aircraft carrier," as the Yanks used to like to call it. Fittingly, since the world had already arrived at the future, it was only fair that the victory of linear progress be celebrated in Thailand—which was after all *the* success story of World Bank/ IMF plans for development and structural adjustment, with double-digit GNP growth, with a transnational flow of tourist bodies and foreign exchange replacing the lost Vietnam War economy, and, by the late eighties, with three years as number one on the economic growth charts.

And yet, with the anniversary of the October 14 killings, the old order seemed poised to return in the circumambiance of a different, cyclical scale of time, for what made this collision of the bloody past of October 14 dictatorship and the bright future of October 14 development even more uncanny was that in 1991 the Thai government had itself been set in place only months previously by a military dictatorship and coup over an elected prime minister.

Such things are not considered attractive, either at home or abroad, and now abroad was coming home, so to speak. Past massacre, present coercion, the eye of the world and of the nation—too many matters mingling in space and time. The government installed by the military ordered sweeping measures to clean all this up before the 1991 World Bank/IMF meetings began. The city was to be clean and orderly. The "national image" was on the line, they asserted, and any unsightly memories and present flaws were to be subjected, mentally and materially, to the logic of the national image.

But by the time the World Bank was coming to town, although eighteen years spanned the divide between two October 14s, somehow development in Thailand had failed to cough up progress in the expectable manner—there was a successful democratic revolution in the past and a successful dictatorship in the present. Now, with the engineers of world finance poised to sink their counting fingers into this gritty grinding of history's engine, which had popped out of gear, it was felt that Thailand had somehow to be presented as spankingly smart—and no kicking the tires. And it is here that our story begins. Constituting and constructing, constructing and constituting, like busy culture bees, the latest administrators of the state were tidying up their habitus in full consciousness of the new world order, as though the new world was hovering over them judgmentally—as, in fact, we are doing as we eavesdrop on their production of October 14 for the world, licking our chops at the whiff of something we might anticipate as nothing other than transnationaliscious.

LAND OF SMILES

General Suchinda had given several warnings over channel 5 and channel 7 ("color channel seven, T–Veeee, fo-o-or . . . you!"), the army-owned television stations, as well as 3 and 9, the state-owned channels, to the effect that no troublemakers would be tolerated during the World Bank meetings. There was to be no embarrassing the country in front of the world, and that meant especially no embarrassing the military strongmen who had "grasped power" (*yud amnaad*), a phrase they preferred to the more militaristic sounding "coup d'état" or "overthrow of the government" (*radthaprahaan*). Steadily, from October 1 on, General Suchinda boomed warnings over TV and dictated to newspapers that swift action would be taken against anyone who stirred up trouble. He promised that the army would back up police in a crackdown on criminal rackets that prey upon tourists and on any trouble arising over commemorating October 14, or having to do with the persecution of the environmental activist monk Phra Phrajak (who, along with his coterie of monks and villagers, had recently been driven from the forest by army troops who shot up the monks'—*kuti* ascetic huts—to bits and pieces with recoilless assault rifles).

"The success of the meeting," General Suchinda declared, "will be crucial to the country's economy for the next three to five years!"[2] And he explained,

> The military is always watching out for security, both inside and outside the country, because preserving internal security has on many occasions required that the military enter in and supervise. . . . The military must always be ready. . . . And in the area of terrorism, we have information that foreign terrorists have entered the country to disrupt the World Bank meetings . . . the military is following this information closely . . . and with respect to various popular protest movements, I want to say that they shouldn't engage in any activities in this period because that will disrupt the World Bank meetings, and these meetings are going to have a effect on our economy for the next three to five years. If these people with money and power see that Thailand is quiet and peaceful they are going to tell their clients that this country is a good place for investment.
>
> I want to ask each and everyone to help make our country clean. May the people be cheerful and smiling. The tourist industry which has become so

sorrowful since the Gulf War will get better, and various investors that are involved with the World Bank will get recommendations to come to Thailand.

I don't want to see any kind of demonstration or gathering. I ask for restraint and patience until this period of World Bank meetings has passed. Divisiveness and divisive thinking can wait just two or three weeks, it won't wither away.

Any gathering concerning October 14 by the students this year—I ask that you quietly refrain for just one year. I don't see what would be so bad about that. This is a request I make in my capacity as supreme commander of the Armed Forces, vice-chair of the National Peace-Keeping Council, and commander of the Capitol Guard. Because I have so many positions I call on all my positions.

I have information that there will be a movement to sow chaos within the country.

But I can tell you now, when I play I don't play by the rules, but when I play with the head-horsemen those head-horsemen better watch out, because I don't take legal protocol as my principle. And wherever those head-horsemen are, we always know. If we must get violent then we must get violent, for the sake of the calm of the country and the nation.[3]

"So I take it that if any incident arises, the military response will be severe, is that right?" a reporter asked.

"Definitely. Because you already know that I smile and smile like this, but I am stern all the while," swore General Suchinda.[4]

And so the commemorators of the October 14 dead and sympathizers with beleaguered Buddhist monks were lumped alongwith con men, thieves, murderers, and terrorists into that criminal element that can extend its clutches into the pockets of every decent citizen. General Suchinda promised he would put a stop to all that, that he would come through for the nation and protect the country's image from anyone and anything that would spoil it, especially a return of the historical dead. And indeed, as anyone could see in the clean-up operations let loose on the city, the government did seem serious about the national image and were doing their utmost to further the national interest by presenting the nation in a clean, clear light.

THAILAND, NEW AND IMPROVED

The strategy was, as they say, *phag chii, rooi naa:* "coriander sprinkled on top"—that finishing touch which, while so little in itself, makes all the difference in the world for the presentation of cuisine on a plate.[5] In the run-up to the World Bank meetings, hundreds of soldiers, policemen, and prison laborers were let loose on the streets to deck them with finishing touches. The army dredged the canals to handle rains better, while prisoners scrubbed and washed down both the streets and the sidewalks, planted new bushes and plants, and clipped the old ones on the road island gardens. Road railings and traffic signs were repainted. The police rounded up whomever they could think of among small-time crooks and illegal aliens. The city buses were repainted, and the worst of the black smoke belchers were temporarily sidelined, as were fat policemen.[6] Were portly policemen signifiers of official corruption? Perhaps they signified inefficiency, a corporeality spilling forth from the national image of a lean mean developing machine. In a series of draconian transfers, portly policemen by the dozens were moved out of town for the week.

Twenty first-class hotels were reserved for delegates, and a brigade of several hundred health officials were sent out sniffing through all their kitchens so as to scour away any dangerous impurities.[7] One by one, the auspices of gem dealers were visited by officers of the law who declared a temporary halt to the massive fraud regularly foisted on tourists.[8]

University scientists calculated the best traffic routes between hotels and the convention center.[9] These routes were to be jealously guarded by the police—no Thais allowed on these streets—which permitted the delegates to buzz to and fro while subjecting the local citizenry to some of the worst traffic snarls in their lifetime (but just wait a few years, with five hundred new cars on Bangkok streets every day). A fleet of helicopters to whisk delegates from rooftop to rooftop was put on standby in case of floods.[10]

The busiest days of the meetings, Monday and Tuesday, October 15 and 16, were declared a national holiday to encourage residents to leave the city and return to their places of provincial origin for a four-day weekend, and to keep people out of rush-hour traffic. For those who did not leave, the state arranged for good movies to be broadcast on TV every night so people would stay home to watch them. The masses that populate the huge government bureaucracy's offices and the classrooms of Bangkok schools, colleges, and universities were all relieved of their duty to move their bodies, as were workers in banks, state enterprises, and the state tobacco monopoly.

And then a bizarre aura began to hang over those particular, reserved streets that were chosen for depopulation. A ghostly and unnatural quiet settled into the high-class shopping districts. Miraculously, one could sit on the city buses, and pick and choose wherever one wished to go, and then just putt on over there, so long as it was within the World Bank version of Bangkok. This portion of the city had not been that lovely in fifty years.

THE FEELINGS BANK

Chintana Bunnag, the notorious madame to the rich and famous, announced her state of preparedness on TV, albeit indirectly, as she was
warned by the police not to engage in her kind of contribution to the
cause of national development too brazenly, or risk being shut down. And
so it was, by intimidating Madame Chintana into announcing her new
"Feelings Bank" in thinly veiled niceties, that state orchestrators of the
World Bank meetings began to fine-tune their image, as best as they could,
to the ideal pitch and harmony between purity and the nasty, nasty. Her
"Feelings Bank," set up especially for the world finance meetings, was to
offer "loans" of "service girls." Following the Feelings Bank philosophy
of government, the state hurriedly set about altering the image of its notorious tourist sex den, Patpong Alley. Officers of the law combed the area
days before, issuing threats and warnings, picking up transvestites (except
the "nice ones"), capturing illegal aliens and assorted sordid criminal elements that prey on tourists, and laying down the temporary code for the
Patpong experience: no fucking shows, no visible child prostitution, no
foul language when beckoning customers to enter the bars, no physical
intimidation or cheating the customers with engorged drink bills or surprise retroactive cover charges, and all dancing boys and girls must at all
times don their respective pants and panties.[11]

This image fetish, the pornographic-and-puritanic complex on the sexy
fringe of capital culture's rationalized system of fair exchange, became a
crude patchwork construction designed to last only as long as necessary.

For their part, the world's financiers arrived in Bangkok ready to party
up a storm at a favorable exchange rate, and not a few reported to the
Far Eastern Economic Review that they were rather disgruntled and dis-
appointed that it was so difficult to find anything but the watered-down
version of the Patpong experience.[12] That goes to show that it is not always with functional precision that excursions into the phantasmagoric
realm of the image sphere are embarked upon.

THE TEMPLE OF WEALTH

The Queen Sirikit Convention Center (see figure 1) was completed at a
cost of 2.5 billion baht (US $100 million).[13] Although built especially to
hold the whole world in its hands as it were, on this auspicious occasion,
it was justified as an all-purpose building that would help make Bangkok
one of the business world's favorite rest areas on the highway to the global
village and corporate conference heaven of the future. The last time I saw

Figure 1. The "Temple of Wealth": The Queen Sirikit Convention Center

it, it was being used for fiscally disastrous pop rock concerts bouncing sound along acoustically dysfunctional contours, and as replacement office space for the state's Public Relations building, which had been torched during the public revolt against Suchinda's dictatorship seven months after the World Bank meetings. Be that as it may, obviously it was, at World Bank time, the centerpiece of the Thai state's representation of itself. If, as everyone was supposed to be led to believe, all future prosperity hinged on the framing of that representation squarely along the lines of image fetishism, then no price was too dear.

The convention center was the nucleus of a singular history, the history of the future, a history of objects contained in the material contours of visual worlds. With the expansive red-tiled roof of a Buddhist temple, with the steel-rib and glass walls of a postmodern corporate skyscraper, with a palatial setting amid a sprawling fir-tree-lined garden pond and fountain-head, the convention center was erected behind a new, forty-foot-tall mystical sculpture. This was a flaming golden halo fanning up into the sky, a strangely unarticulated form, neither exactly the flames often depicted rising off the crown of a Buddha image, nor exactly the gleaming of a shiny gold coin, but a lumpy shape that calls attention to itself as a unification of values—of the modern in its abstractness, of the traditional in its evocation of the Buddha, of material possession in the goldness of gold, and of spiritual transcendence in the ephemeral rays of enlightenment.

At 2:06 in the afternoon of October 14, 1991, the sun hit the mystical sculpture at just the right angle, sending a beam of divine light across the four-lane, divided street, straight through a door-sized opening on the other side of a gaily painted fifteen-foot wall of corrugated steel sheeting. There it passed into Khlong Pai Singtoh slum and landed right on twelve-year-old Gope Januwong's forehead, causing him to squint as a trio of Swedish journalists pointed their snub-nosed camera at him through the corrugated sheeting to reveal the slummy innards behind the facade. The image was bounced off of satellites and into Swedish TV sets, which made it look as though Gope's little squinting face was strained with the pains of hunger.

CLASS CLEANSING

The number of blights on the cityscape that held the potential to disrupt the whitewashing of history were many, and yet Thailand was in many ways the darling of the world finance-scape, the pride and joy of macro-economic management strategy. Most top Thai economists brought into state institutions to manage the economy were subscribers to the IMF's style of conservative fiscal policy.[14] All sides were pleased with the results. Since the oligarch Field Marshal Sarit Thanarat took power with U.S. backing in the late 1950s, world financial circles have had a great say in the workings of the Thai economy. And since the end of the economic boom of the Vietnam War, Thailand had managed, after some stumbling, to renew its growth into the Reagan eighties without appreciably violating World Bank/IMF policies of structural adjustment.

Despite all that, while the elite classes became larger and a middle class even larger, many Thais were left out of the boom—as is no surprise. With development came urban pollution and overcrowded cities, most of in all Bangkok, which was swollen with traffic jams, sour black canals, noise, dust, row after row of drab egg-carton-box buildings; everyone was gassed by thick noxious fumes spewing forth from the motionless vehicles on the searing pavement. This is a material history of development that adheres in the thingness of things and is embodied in the chronic ailments, cancers, and respiratory failures that carve strained lines around the eyes of beholding. It is to this material history that the scouring practice was directed. For the sake of a spatial representation of promise in the phantasmagoric moment of the World Bank/IMF's end of history, a thin house of mirrors was set in place to simulate a materiality to the ideal types of development conveyed so purely in the formulaic equations of GNP percentages. The phantasmagoria began with the Temple of Wealth at the center, radiated out on spokes of reserved, scrubbed streets lined with slender policemen and cleared of rabble and maddening crowds, led to a rim of first-class, superclean hotels under strict disciplinary vigilance. Attempting a sleight of hand using air conditioning and velvety high-tech environments as distractions, the bases of sensory perception were supposed to be edged from tactility toward the singular sense of sight, the most manipulable of all.

Months before the opening of the World Bank meetings, the state began to remove, as the National Housing Authority put it, "an eyesore in the heart of Bangkok." As it happened, the Temple of Wealth had been constructed at the core of what was, in fact, a large squatter settlement area. The contradiction of two large slums rubbing up against the vision of a new world future, a naturally occurring spacial-historical irony, was a prime target of the cleansing operations. Unfortunately, as so often happens in the uncertain realm of the image fetish, scratching at the rash may only inflame it more. The Thai press raised a ruckus over the government's planned forcible eviction of over two thousand slum residents, and the international press seized upon the irony, provoking a continuous stream of image-managing discourses and practices surrounding the slum/ conference center architectonic of development. Representatives of the World Bank quickly announced that they had no part in this plan and that it was all initiated by the Thais, and that they did not request it. Then they took the high road by suggesting publicly that the Thai authorities go easy on the people, citing the worldwide phenomenon of slums and the fact that they are familiar sights to all the delegates.[15]

Apparently the negative publicity was considered an acceptable loss by the government agencies planning to go ahead with the relocation. The authorities claimed that they were enforcing this move not for the aesthetic benefit of the World Bank delegates but because they had planned it since 1986 and now was the "right time." From this we might gather that now the national image could be invoked in defense of the surgery. But in apparent contradiction to claims that it had nothing to do with the World Bank meetings, the slums were at the same time professed to be a terrorist threat to the delegates that had to be cleared out.[16]

Neither appeals to the national image nor the association of slum residents with terrorism was sufficient, however, to hoodwink the Thai press, which has long been familiar with the underhanded tactics used to clear out slums to make huge profits on sky-rise development. The slums are usually set on fire under the cover of night, and the survivors, homeless and vulnerable, are then easily carted away to shelters, sometimes apartments (a move that then appears as charitable action rather than coercion). However, setting things on fire is not a viable option when the

Figure 2. Painted ghetto covers

national image is on the line. In the end, some apartments were set up, and only the smaller of the two slums was forcibly removed. The army arrived at Duang Pitak slum and carted the residents away on GMC trucks (the same trucks that seven months later would cart away corpses from the Democracy Monument). Meanwhile the government negotiated a bizarre compromise with civic groups of the larger slum: they could stay but only on condition that the length of their slum that faces the convention center be covered with a fifteen-foot wall of corrugated metal sheeting (see figure 2). Their children were provided with paints and brushes to color the wall brightly with images of their own choosing. They painted bright fantasy scenes of green trees, blue skies, orange suns, happy-faced children and spacious homes amid unspoiled nature.

The new wall presented various different aesthetics of power depending, literally, from which angle you viewed the resulting dialectical image. Viewing at an oblique angle from air-conditioned buses that whisked the delegates past the embarrassing mess, you saw only the gaily painted façade of a child's dream for a good world, before making a ninety-degree turn into the adult's phantasmagoria, the Temple of Wealth.

An alternate view, of the innards behind the façade, was the one so valued by international journalist camera crews who aimed their guns straight through doorways that opened up to reveal the dark, chaotic space of the slum. That is the straight-on view, where you penetrate to the id of capital culture.

But the strangest angle was the parallel view, from which you could take in the contradiction between the two worlds, the futuristic world of capital culture facing down the urban barnyard of the squatters, and right smack in the middle the mass media ogling for images with pointed surveillance machines, penetrating an exposed subject.

Then there is the viewpoint looking out, from within, through doorway slits in the gray backside of the corrugated sheeting, looking out into rectangular shapes of color, partial views of the Temple of Wealth's red roof and the golden mystic halo before it, and into the blue sky above the convention center, under which matters of the largest scale, of world scale, were being decided. The children of Khlong Pai Singtoh slum with whom I talked were proud of their painted creation. For the record, the adult residents were just glad that they did not get carted away, and in sighs of relief only spoke of how their colorful corrugated aluminum wall was helping the national image and how it showed that they were willing to do their part in the interest of national development.

Yet surely they too will one day face the scouring operations of class cleansing, the fear of which is common among slum residents who, in the majority, prefer their squatter settlements to the scarcely available government-run housing. In 1991 in Bangkok there were an estimated 1.3 million residents in 1,500 slum areas, out of a total of over 6 million people living in the city.[17] This was 20 percent of the population—hardly statistically marginal. One can imagine the mounting desire of city planners and their entrepreneurial backers to be rid of this blight, and it is in this context that the government's feeling that "now is the right time" can easily be read. The World Bank meetings provided a convenient pretext for class cleansing, as it provided a pretext for so many other sweeping power operations.

The slum residents face great pain should they be carted to the outskirts of the city. Most make their living from cheaply paid service jobs and, more commonly, self-employment in taxi driving or street vending, be it of food or the smallest trifles like candy and cigarettes. Bangkok traffic jams practically seal off the inner city from the outskirts for those with limited means who require long hours to produce their income, such as taxi drivers and vendors. Class cleansing, in its attempt to produce what is like a superstructural correspondence in spacial aesthetics to the marginalization of class—that is, to spatially marginalize people who are already economically marginal and so reproduce that economic divide— stirs up for already troubled people fears about remaining marginally alive, or not remaining so at all.

The clampdown on their livelihoods, meager as they already were, was not just a dark storm looming on the horizon, for the World Bank phantasmagoria demanded instantly spacious, clean streets and orderly shopping, not the aesthetic chaos of street hawking. A decisive blow was struck in the long-running struggle between municipal authorities and the masses of Thai street vendors who serve the working class its food at affordable prices, though not without taking up space in an informal and chaotic-looking manner. For the World Bank meetings, all the best spots in the city were to be cleared of street vendors for the duration of the meetings, to show off those sidewalks scrubbed clean by prison laborers, to keep primitive marketeering out of the new world vision. So like government service workers, slum residents were also given a holiday of sorts: a vacation from their income.

And when the class-cleansing operations commenced in and around the Temple of Wealth, army trucks wound up with such a bounty of unwanted bodies that no pretense could be made of housing them all. One slum area was carted off to the outskirts and lined up like checkers on a vacant lot, each family given a 3 × 5-meter plot and each 3 × 5 plot a family (renewable annually), and 6,000 baht (US $240) to build a shelter.[18] Many families were even left out of this square deal, and were forced to live under an expressway—expressways keep off the rain—and suffer through respiratory problems from the dust and smoke. To them the government bequeathed only ten days of electricity and water.[19]

THE DISCIPLINE COMMODITY

Long-term economic goals apparently depended greatly on hospitality and facilitation, on combining the seemingly limitless sensual pleasures of seduction with the most ephemeral electronic information and financial technologies. But the goal of the business community, to make Thailand the banking and business center of Southeast Asia, was threatened by the image of danger flashing up in this picture of cleanliness the military-installed government was so desperately trying to paint. Because Thailand had been listed by U.S. intelligence as high risk in international security matters, the World Bank meetings were as much a disastrously risky venture as they were a priceless opportunity to get new, improved images circulating. The government pumped 70 million baht (US $2.8 million) into overt security and an unspecified amount into covert surveillance. They mobilized between seven and ten thousand security personnel to ensure the safety of no more than twelve to fifteen thousand delegates—at least one security officer for every two delegates.[20] And most significantly, they put this security apparatus on continual display, so that it could be circulated in photographic and video images. Every day of the week before the meetings, and for every day of the meetings, a portion of the security force was on photogenic "training maneuvers," which were elegant displays of uniformed bodies performing simultaneous movements in rows and columns, cadenced marching, simultaneous manipulation of segmented body parts, and so on, much as Michel Foucault has described in *Discipline and Punish*.[21]

Security officers were no doubt having a particular form of disciplinary power impressed upon them, as some interpreters of Foucault might have it, through their embodied participation in these practices. But discipline here is more than a bodily practice. Discipline is a commodity; in fact, it is even more than that when it is a commodity circulated in the realm of image discourse. Here disciplinary spectacles were quickly converted into media spectacles with a variety of significations to a variety of audiences. The security apparatus, made so accessible for international journalists and so excessive as to attract the media hunger for the bizarre, sent a positive signal to the world. On the other hand, it was not just a positive message but also a real technical capability to prevent negative messages: should any terrorist incident occur while such a deluge of international media networks was focused on Bangkok, the damage to the national image would be unthinkable. The material presence of a security apparatus thus helped ensure a material absence of things that could endanger the imagery of cleanliness. The signifying image of a secure and orderly city under surveillance, embodied in a disciplinary metonym, proved as positively desirable as its breakdown would be horrific.

The performances went on unabated through the meetings. The signification of disciplinary images was not, however, exclusively engaged at the level of the national image circulating over the surface of the globe. For it is important to remember that the daily torrent of security images streaming in on local TV screens and front pages in the days running up to the World Bank meetings were simultaneous with the discourse about political dissidence that could destroy the national image, and with the daily threats from the junta to crack down on any protesters. There were visions of power circulating to back up, and acting as a backdrop to, the threats. Military- and government-controlled television kept it coming. And given the Thai dailies' flair for drama motivated by the competitive drive to sell, those photographic images appeared on front covers next to large, eye-grabbing headlines that reiterated the military's threats, thus accomplishing the association by another twist in the image-value of discipline (and history) as a commodity.

The double entendre of signification in which the military was engaged is a tricky business, however, and depended most of all on keeping the two realms of reference, local and global, entirely separate. In such a tactic, one hopes to threaten the populace with the rational instruments of

violence while signifying to the outside world that one has an environment clear of all such violent dangers. A long history of human rights
violations and the embarrassing fact of military dictatorship are dusty
irritants in the world's vision, and can always be called to mind by such
a forceful presence and magnet of militant associations. The aesthetic
logic of power in the new world order was intended, of course, to cleanse
not only the aftereffects, vast disparities, and tragedies of structural adjustment and development throughout the Cold War era but also the political structures resulting from decades of U.S. military support. Thus, in a
camouflage move, in order not to "make the delegates nervous," the army
soldiers, who formed the bulk of the security apparatus, were dressed up
in police uniforms. These army troops, decked out as "police" to the
world while Thais would know perfectly well who they were, could be
seen carted around in GMC trucks all over the city, with greatest frequency passing, in a reflection of the double entendre, through the high-
tech shopping districts where delegates would be enjoying themselves
and, ominously, through the area around the Democracy Monument,
which had been for many years the staging area of mass politics. Were it
not for the absence of tanks in the streets, one might think there was
another coup going on.

And that would be a particularly prickly conclusion to draw from the
visual display, for investment and tourism had been steadily wilting since
February, coincidentally—now that we are talking image—around the
time when General Suchinda launched his coup against the constitutional
government. How's this for an image: Prime Minister Chatichai Choonhavan, steward of 11 percent GNP growth years and U.N. hero of capitalism—so often referred to, by his own catchy phrase, as the one who "turns
battlefields into marketplaces"—led at gunpoint by the military from Bangkok airport and from the premiership.

After the coup, the United States issued a mild rebuke, called off indefinitely the annual Golden Cobra joint military exercises, and suspended
$100 million in military aid (a paltry sum, scoffed at by the junta, when
compared to the Vietnam War years). Yet the Bush administration still
allowed the Thai military to purchase U.S. arms. The Bush administration
also continued, despite its public assertions to the contrary, the covert
deployent of U.S. Green Berets to train Thai Special Forces (who, several
months hence, would in the service of General Suchinda kill unarmed
Thais in the Bangkok streets). And the United States was willing to recognize the military-installed government when Suchinda, in a smart move
aimed at garnering "international credibility," appointed an internationally respected business leader and former diplomat Anand Banyarachond
to be the junta's frontman and caretaker prime minister. Thus did the
United States renew negotiations on their favorite subject, intellectual

property rights, with a pleasantly technocratic businessman. The Japanese commented on the coup in only the vaguest terms.

But the recently dispelled illusion that coups in Thailand were a thing of the past, widely believed within and without the country, and the apparent shattering of a progressive development of the GNP-democracy tandem, were enough to shake down the economy while it still rumbled in the after-tremors of the Reagan boom years.

A general like Suchinda who rules by a coup over constitutional government naturally did not want to see protests in the streets. But more was happening here than rule by force of arms. This was rule by force of image—within a discursively ethereal sphere of imagery interlaced with twists and turns—and we are embarking on a journey into this misty realm at one of its most compelling and inviting points of entry: the new world order.

It had become obvious to all who tuned in that Thailand was part of a global community: a country whose GNP was tied to massive tourism, commodity exports, and foreign investment, and which was thoroughly penetrated by foreign commodities and advertising, electronic media networks, even cable and satellite dish access for the urban middle class, and video often across classes—always up on the latest fashions, celebrity scandals, and political or natural catastrophes around the globe. In short, Thailand was ripe for articles in *Public Culture*. Something had emerged as a significant cosmological entity, the national image (*phaab phod kaung chaad* or *phaap phod kaung pratate*), which circulated in an unspecified medium among other such images and which issued forth from that worldwide public realm with the spoils of productive wealth. Furthermore, the reality of images as forces of production was brought home by the shock conditioning delivered to the country's economy attendant on image-making and image-breaking events—Suchinda's coup over constitutional government in February 1991 being a recent example. Just before that, George Bush and Saddam Hussein declared the Gulf War, and so also the end of the Reagan boom era. By the time of October 14, 1991, the new world order had already had its crowning moment: Saddam Hussein and his renegade state were put down, their black-and-white case of antisocial behavior in the global community was closed. With such ready access to the world news pool, Thais had every opportunity to ride the missile's camera eye on government or military broadcast TV (it being somewhat of an exception even among the poor not to have any access to TV). This whole Iraq affair was more than just TV images of a new world enforcement: a worldwide stock market plunge in the wake of Iraq's invasion hit heavily in Thailand. A worldwide economic recession followed, and the international tourism fallout fell out in Thailand as well. It had become an obvious point of fact that Thailand had a

45

stake in having the United States win this police war, just as it became obvious that Thailand would suffer casualties from it as well, when the coagulant threat of "Muslim terrorists" would clot the flow of bodies on tourist and business networks. And not only did the foreign exchange reserves suffer but the Thai national image suffered twice over when the U.S. State Department delivered a crushing blow with a widely publicized travel advisory against any movement through Bangkok's international airport, as many known terrorists had slipped through Thai customs without impediment.

The rapid economic growth that everyone knew was being siphoned off an international flow of capital was brusquely cut off with the advent of an equally international phenomenon. That is how the crowning moment of the new world order was delivered into palpable reality, by a combination of world historical events and TV images with almost immediate shock associations of economic loss and pain.

It was common knowledge that the economic slowdown that was threatening everyone's lifestyle at the turn of the decade was due to world-scale, global-type phenomena. And it was well known that the "national image," the amulet that sucks wealth to itself by seductive powers of appearance, and which circulates in this global realm, was being tarnished by various publicity problems—among them AIDS, prostitution, and military dictatorship. But although the national image suffered globally in the sense of being tarnished, image discourse itself—and especially the belief in the reality and efficacy of public images—gained ascendance locally in the sense that the reality effects of the national image (as tarnished) were proven to be real by the unpleasant sensations in the economy.

In this particular form of economic logic, images are no longer the bygone ideological smokescreens for material forces of production, but the very stuff of economy: images are products to be exchanged and consumed in a realm of their own, and image management is a means of production. Images themselves are no longer mere accessories for promotional purposes only, as with simple advertising that refers to a material product and delivers it up to its material consumption, as it were. Not only are images the products trucked, bartered, and sold but images also produce their own autonomous realism and economic ground such that their manipulation is as productive of value as the manipulation of a hoe in the earth, or more so.

So what, then, *is* a "national image?" In Thailand, *phaab phod kaung chaad* (national image) has been heavily promoted as an absolutely vital principle in the production of wealth. A good national image will materialize investment, tourism, prosperity, and economic power in the new world order. But handling it is not easy. You cannot point to a national image, much less hold one in the palm of your hand. It may be promoted or demoted through visual images and all kinds of talk, but it isn't—itself—any one of these material things. Of course, one might polish a national image, but not by wiping it directly, as it were—it is only possible to disseminate missives that are believed and hoped will affect it, such as advertising campaigns, publicity stunts, and so on. On the other hand, a national image can become tarnished or spoiled by such notorious things as military brutality or rampant sexual diseases, when caught in printed text, photo, or video. But then again, campaigns can be launched to repair the damage, to counter it, or to dilute it with positive refurbishing images. Dispatching these images to the beyond, one can then even statistically gauge the effects (it is so real) as those reality effects come back to show themselves in the economy and foreign exchange reserves. But what a national image is in itself, out there, is ineffable, empty you might say, or beyond the pale.

And so, though there may be talk of the ascendancy of the visual image in an ultramodern historical beyond, it is of perhaps even greater interest that not only do visual images seem to absorb into themselves powerful persuasive forces, which as theorists show are charged with all manner of futuristic media, but there is a realm of images, "public images," that cannot really be seen at all, that circulate almost godlike beyond even the material signifiers of image and word that are dispatched toward it like offerings, gifts, always in exchange with an ineffable next world, a presence that presents real effects in return.

Strangely, it is as though this economy is deeply involved in exchange with a spirit world, or with a realm of the dead. It is not unlike the way some people dispatch gifts to dead ancestors in a spiritual beyond. But after all, of course, here the dead appear to have nothing to do with it at all. In fact it seems that death is anxiously swept under the rug in this sort of economics.

October 1991 Bangkok was to be filled with *birth*, with newness and anticipation for the birth of a new world. And now was the chance to set the national image right, as well as the chance for the discourse of international images to ascend almost to sovereignty by drawing upon the mystical history of a new world phantasmagoria. Bangkok was set to host the most auspicious of days: the first of the triennial World Bank excursions since the collapse of the Soviet Union and its domination of Eastern Europe; the end, so it appeared, of the Cold War ideologies that had been disrupting and coagulating the free flow of capital in a world market. October 14 was in a sense, then, the first day of a new world. It was the dawn of new possibilities, of a world where image matters. And Thailand was poised in such a good position to get its image out and circulating.

No, General Suchinda wasn't going to let anything spoil that. And so by the logic of image exchange, his fate became locked into the fate of the image discourse. His brother-in-law General Issarapong Noonpakdi, as interior minister controlling the police and bureaucracy, echoed Suchinda's threats against political activism, and warned that all historical commemorations would be vigorously suppressed if they turned into "pretexts for other political issues." In other words, he made it clear that a separation of past and present was to be strictly enforced. All the power and influence in the world to enforce the order of history is not quite enough, however, in this strange confluence in the forces of the phantasmagoria, for a violent suppression is not a good image to be creating when the world's eye falls on you.

The reasonable recourse was to tap into the phantasmagoria itself, to bend the power of image discourse to your own purposes. It was by this fateful intuition that the military vigorously campaigned for the *reality* of the national image (a campaign, we will see, with long-range consequences), ardently trying to establish that the national image was real, and really on the line—going to extremes to clean up a national image in which they may have had more faith the more they saw their fate reflected in it. Thus it was, amid an army of soap bubbles erupting in a massive scrubbing of the material signifiers of the city, that they appealed to the nation's citizenry for moral support in defending the national image from troublemakers.

It was all quite logical: since military dictatorships are bad for the country's image, and since we are now having a military dictatorship, any protest against it calls attention to that fact, which further damages our image. So the best way to manage the damage that a military dictatorship causes is to allow it to go on in a strictly orderly fashion.

Imposition of military power must be enhanced by a superimposition, erasing the effects of actions by erasing the actions; only by eliminating all reference to the ugly business of military dictatorship could the country recover from what the military dictatorship had done. The more the national image is promoted, the more justification for repression. But in an undertow, the more the national image is promoted, the more the unsayable reality of the military's previous damage to the image is affirmed. The phantasmagoria begins to lock in on all possibilities, but for the time being the military believes itself to be prudently navigating the currents of the flip-flopping logic of image discourse—by which the "troublemakers" come to be the destroyers of the national image, and it is the military dictatorship that must save the country from . . . well, the military dictatorship! If you see what I mean. And if you can follow all that, then the phantasmagoria may already be working on you, just as I am already seized.

DUELING IMAGES

Then it was party time. As always at these triennial excursions out of Washington, the conference evenings were bubbling with hobnobbing, crisscrossing, party-hopping international exchanges. On occasions like these hotel parties, hosted by various governments, various international banks, prominent personalities, and so on, an internationally respected business leader like Prime Minister Anand, along with his technocratic friends, can come in handy for putting the best foot forward. As they were hosts to the World Bank, the Thai government's parties were naturally visited by everyone who was anyone in international finance. This was a perfect time to make a pitch in a competitive world of national images, a post–Cold War world in which the economic sympathy votes were centering on the Soviet Union and Eastern Europe, true to the World Bank's origins in the U.S. Marshall Plan to rebuild Japan and Germany.

And it is in this context that the cleverly crafted seams of the image fetish started to come apart, for the military was navigating the most turbulent crosscurrents of authoritarian rule and national promotion, while the front-man prime minister was a businessman through and through. He apparently had a different understanding of the efficacy of images.

Much to the embarrassment of the inner circle of Thai elites and to the chagrin of the military junta, Prime Minister Anand set out on his own independent foray into the manipulative morass of the phantasmagoria. Along with his sidekick health minister, Anand kept pointing out to surprised delegates—who are rather more accustomed to whitewashing—some of the mildewy stains the military was so desperate to rub out. They spoke frankly of the problems of rampant AIDS, the decaying environment, and the widening gap between urban rich and rural poor, all the while passing out specially wrapped condoms as "World Bank Survival Kits" in Health Minister Meechai's style of laissez-faire pragmatic lyricism. Apparently questions were raised among the Thai elite as to whether this was the proper way to handle the Thai image, and whether Anand, educated in Oxford, and Meechai, half Scottish, were less Thai than *farang* (Western).[22]

It was a clever strategic ploy to attract sympathy and interest in the Thai economy after it had fared so well, and in light of the collapsed communist bloc that was the focus of so much attention. What was most interesting is the AIDS sympathy-commodity, since both Anand and Meechai, although in some senses the true heroes of AIDS consciousness-raising *within* Thailand, had always been consistently allied with the philosophy of not letting the issue of AIDS out of the country to tarnish the national image. They had supported the policy of suppressing international publicity or films depicting the AIDS problem, as well as all foreign research not solely concerned with "epidemiology." Although I have never heard either of them link AIDS as an image problem to scaring away sex-tourism, on several occasions other prominent politicians, in parliament and while on national television, have argued against AIDS publicity as making Thai women unattractive and sending businessmen elsewhere. In the new image wars of Southeast Asia (the "battlefields turned into markets," I assume), one can see the regular barrage of publicity about Thai AIDS printed in Malaysian and Singaporean newspapers. These countries are Thailand's best competitors as a next world business center.

But if Singapore has in some way realized the Thai military's wet dream of authoritarian development, orderly streets, spanking white gloves, and efficient banking—obviously all this had been working for Singapore, and certain elements were trying to form, through an argument of images, a consensus that it could work for Thailand, too—the shaky Thai military-business complex might still win out by delivering the other, sensual side to capital culture, the visions of excess on the horizon that complement and round out the austere discipline of technologies and mirrors of power and production. "The World Bank Survival Kits," with their cartoon cover of a "superman-rubber" flying through the air, were a free-market latex-technology death repellent, a promise of endless sensual gratification in atmospheric, limitless, safe sex, the genital root of the body and all that is solid melting into air as the flying phallus and fantasy of super-power is circulated in palm-size packets from financier to financier, and don't do anything I wouldn't do, wink, wink.

When the party was over, much to everyone's surprise as far as the World Bank meetings usually go, only one banker (Turkish) lay dead in his hotel bathroom, dead of a drug overdose. Despite the government's attempt to sweep away development's ugly and dangerous side, however, 937 delegates of development were treated for respiratory disorders, gagging as they did on Bangkok's high-lead, brain cell-dissolving fumes.[23]

All in all, it was a smashing success: buttery smooth international finance meetings without a smidgen of terrorism, lots of mingling and networking in squeaky clean first-class hotels, and a raucous good time in Patpong Alley. As many delegates put it, the meetings were neither as strictly authoritarian as the previous meeting in the Korean army's Seoul, nor as lavishly indulgent as that in the Marcos' Manila.[24] It seemed that the Thais had struck just the right balance in the seeing eye of the clean new world, between visions of excess and technologies of power, between disciplined consumption and consumptive discipline, between manipulation of the image discourse and subjection to the discourse of images.

The Market Is Elsewhere

On the local front there were gains, as well. For those fortunate enough not to have been carted away on military trucks, for those whose livelihood was not cut off by various government decrees, for those who were too busy to be bothered by all this hoopla, and for those who have little feeling for the other, negative side to the history of October 14, the World Bank simulational city actually was, perhaps, a dream come true. Newly decongested streets, cleansed of the flurry of bodies and colors and smells that in many places usually boil up around every square inch of available market space, at least hinted at the image of sleek functionality that is the modern dream city, where the market is elsewhere, with no visceral assault on the senses, and certainly with neither connection to a bloody history nor any exchange with death, nor any corpselike corporeal presence—where business is transacted in an imagined nether atmosphere of electronic information transfers or in the climate-controlled passageways of the mall environment. The rabble of street vendors is displaced, and this brute, aesthetic power over the free market, under the guise of liberalism, transforms capital culture by a technology of spatial control and sensory sublimation into a great price markup, visual and physical access to the market guarded by heavily owned walls surrounding it on all sides, thus setting all prices and all the conditions of possibility for trade.

This dream city floating in a deathless realm is not merely a fantasy, for just as plagues and leprosy mobilize new disciplinary technologies that prove to have enduring presences and unintended uses,[25] so too one does not rework the aesthetic city, mobilize thousands of security personnel, remarginalize thousands of the poor, disperse the unclean free market, banish history, and exile the signs and recollection of death and decay without revealing new possibilities for power and establishing new desires and future visions. Among those fortunate ones who did not bear the brunt of the assault on the city, who did not suffer the weight of these ten to fifteen thousand representatives of finance, one could hear about the town a nostalgia for the future—oh, if only it would one day be like this! And although, as we will see in the next chapter, everything in the new world did not go as swimmingly as the military junta would have liked—*in fact, the students eventually erupted on the street with funereal protests, in utter confidence that they were protected by the very power of image discourse and an onlooking world, a situation that was supposed to stifle them*—nevertheless the generals must have been pleased at the efficient manner in which they were able to occupy the city as a practical exercise in martial maneuvers, not to mention wield at least a shade of the omnipotency to banish death from their virtual economy with one crisp, clean sweep of an airbrush over aesthetic space.

THE RETURN OF THE REPRESSED

A few days after the world financiers had cleared out of the city, everyone did not just come back, willy-nilly, spilling onto the streets and public spaces again. They were afraid to be out in the open. First, it was talk that ran wild, of an "AIDS stalker," a grungy, long-haired young man, sticking infected hypodermic needles into innocent passers-by. "Here, share some of this," they said he said, before sticking it to you. The TV news interviewed a police chief who confirmed the ghastly crimes, and then TV took to the street with a hand-held camera as they told the story. The jiggly camera would walk through the busy sidewalks, up the street crossing bridges, and through the passageways of department stores, eyeing a woman's exposed thigh here, an arm there, or focusing a bulls-eye shot on someone standing unawares. The camera eye would thread and meander like that through public space, while the voice-over would tell infectious tales of young women getting pricked and to beware, the AIDS stalker's favorite haunt was shopping malls.

Actually it turned out several days later that, contrary to what certain police captains connected to the junta had claimed, there was no one who had in fact seen any incident, that no actual victims were found, that it was safe for people to shop and be in the streets again, and that the phantom of death was never real.

Revolting History

THE NECROMANTIC POWER OF PUBLIC MASSACRES

> Revolt—its face distorted by amorous ecstasy—
> tears from God his naïve mask, and thus oppression collapses
> in the crash of time. Catastrophe is that by which
> a nocturnal horizon is set ablaze, that for which lacerated
> existence goes into a trance—it is the Revolution—it is time
> released from all bonds; it is pure change; it is a skeleton
> that emerges from its cadaver as from a cocoon and that
> sadistically lives the unreal existence of death.
>
> GEORGES BATAILLE[1]

THE HISTORY OF THE WORLD

World Bank delegates prowled the electric illuminations of Patpong Alley. Meandering through its arcades of sumptuary excess, they perused the sidewalk maze of outdoor stalls that sell counterfeit first-world merchandise, and sampled the indoor sights of simulated sex in the go-go bars. Patpong Alley was, on the eve of the 1991 World Bank meetings (as it was every night, always returning), a space of violation: of sexual propriety, of underclass bodies, of children, and of intellectual property rights. This last violation, one at the very heart of what was at stake for the first world in this new world order, was therein erupting into a kinky perversion of the fetish values of high-capitalist markets—Gucci, Rolex, Levis, Stallone—all signs of value, all signatures, fashions, brands, here only skin deep. I watched, curious, the representatives of international governing organizations on that night as they milled about the stalls of Patpong, holding up for all their colleagues to see the counterfeit watches and handbags they had bought with silly grins on their faces. Devilish, their underhanded dealing in commodity fetishism. I followed them into the bars and peeped in on their peeping. But I didn't follow them any further than that. Unfortunately, I also missed out on a party where, as one journalist reported, delegates in one of Patpong's premier discos "were decked out in costumes as devils with bags of hell-money."[2]

October 1991 was a time to celebrate, after all. The future had emerged victorious. It was a time to rake in the spoils on that developmental gift economy that had been circulating over the surface of the earth for the latter part of the century. Thai governments, headed largely by generals for the duration of the military gift economy, had received quite a bit in that exchange.

What follows is a story about returns. The Thai military took its gifts, and for a time allowed the U.S. Air Force to take off on death-dealing raids from Thailand into neighboring countries. The stories to follow are about what happened to Thailand in that global gift economy, the one that immediately preceded our new world, and from which that new order was born.

But these are not simply Thai stories. These are not just Thai history. This is not simply because this story about imperialism has been replicated in countless other places, all over the world, and so represents a particular instantiation of a worldwide and general event (which is certainly also the case). That what follows is truly world history can be apprehended better, actually, by scrutiny of its particularities, of the very intimate matters of personal matter that are manipulated, created, and destroyed here, and the truth, however unstable and bottomless, that is opened up here by the figure of death. There is an immense debt hanging over the new world and its public realm of images, a violent history replicated but hidden in the cleanliness of the moment.

Bloody Octobers

Confident in the phantasmagoric power of the World Bank meetings, with The World roosting near and its news-eye surveilling the city, the students march, despite the military's orders not to do so. It is the afternoon of October 14, 1991. A modest procession of about two hundred demonstrators march from Thammasaat University to the small sculpted memento to the military's victims that was allowed to be built near the Democracy Monument, behind the cluttered market of national lottery vendors just off of Ratchadamnern Avenue (the "King's Promenade" that passes the Democracy Monument and connects the residential palace to the Royal Temple-Grand Palace complex that is the ceremonial center of Bangkok). As always, here as in many other Asian countries, political protest is performed in the idiom of funeral.[3]

Offerings of candles, incense, fruit, and flowers are made at the base of the statue to the spirits of the dead. Alongside gifts to the dead are placed funeral wreaths and colorful signs commemorating the victims and carrying messages of protest. The marchers place framed black-and-white photographs of their fallen loved ones, the same kind of portraits that are always presented with the coffin at funeral wakes and often hung on a wall after the cremation beneath a Buddha image in the most honorable corner of the home. Most of the photographed victims are in school uniforms.

Student leaders speak on a podium and do in thought and speech, if not yet in deed, exactly what the military fears: implode the past and present, connect the spirits of the dead and the past days of terror to the death and terror of these days. As reporters and military intelligence point their recorders at this historical commemoration, student leaders detail the present-time terrorization of the monk-hero Phra Phrajak and his village followers, who are trying to preserve the National Reserve forests against encroachment by loggers and resort builders and resist the forced relocation of the rural poor, only to be beaten up and arrested, the monk's huts ripped apart with the fire of assault rifles. They rally around the criminal cases pending against dissidents, including one of the founding parents of Thai critical discourse, Sulak Sivaraksa, who spoke out after the February coup. They recall the disappearance of Thanong Pho-an, popular leader of the labor union Federation of Thai Workers, of whom General Suchinda, while admitting nothing, said he should never have been talking to foreign reporters about the suppression of Thai labor.[4]

Offerings to the dead left behind, the demonstrators march back to Thammasaat University, under police "escort," with relatives of the October 14 dead in the front rows carrying the memorial pictures of their brothers and sisters and sons and daughters as they were in their student days, their last days. Behind those who hold the images of the dead in their arms flows a stream of college students, many of whom will soon meet the same fate. In a few months, in May 1992, many of them will be carried so, photographic impressions in the arms of loved ones.

But they will also be carried differently, as truths and values embedded in images that circulate in satellite orbit over the surface of the globe.

NECROMANTIC POWER

For some time, the Thai resistance had been occupying the only public space left to them: funereal space. In 1991, the Thai resistance, with the student movement at its nucleus, had neither the means nor desire for violent confrontation. Lacking capital and a mass-communication apparatus, sidelined in the public sphere by the people's absorption in media diversions and the spectacle of consumer goods, it has for some time come to occupy the peripheral public space of mourning and funeral ceremony. The student movement keeps a pact made with the past corpses of the military's power operations, a pact used as the baseline of meaning with which it tries to keep in constant contact.[5] Centered in the universities, this historical mediumship with the military's victims is imparted in art, music, drama, sit-ins, and in yearly commemorative rituals, the combination of which forms a steady dirge of funereal memoria.

But in a clean new world of public images, how can this funereal space shift in social location, filling the clean space of modern image markets? Or are they ever truly separate to begin with? This is to ask what possibility is left for liberating work with images in a realm of public culture that has the power to plow the evocation of killing into clean fields of profits. Although the military tried to set its hooks into the express train of futurism—the new and emerging birth—the student movement draws its force from the space and memory of death. Such funeral protest culture has become common for suppressed and hunted people around the world. It is a culture people seem almost instinctively to know their way around. But perhaps, as the following story may show, it is not so easy to know what to do with violent death, how to represent it, or, by summoning the death to public space, harness its evocative power to one's purpose. Perhaps both funeral protest in particular and the representation of death in general border on something like the practice of magic: difficult to master, highly unstable, and usually overshadowed by more mechanical means of producing power.

What makes a public culture based on the proliferation of mechanical reproduction so powerful? In this regard, the mythic narrative of progress would have its legendary agents resurfacing the world and shifting like earth-trembling tectonic plates: technologies of mass communication, financial orders of global capitalism, democratic-enlightenment ideologies and values. Here on planet earth it is always a new world.

The events I attend to here certainly take place in such a world, but is it these new historical implements that make the critical difference? One may, in explaining public culture, write the history of national development in Thailand and show how it brought material gadgets and ideological tenets, wealth, a middle class, and globalizing technologies, as though these things in themselves are the sufficient and reasonable conditions for the power of public culture. But this clean history obscures the death that animates this arena and that gives it its life. The history of the kind of public culture and sphere of power that can contest or even overthrow the instrument wielders of state terrorism does not exist in a sovereign sense, that is, in a sense that can rule, until it somehow incorporates into itself the killing, until the power of the corpse coronates it. And this brings us to consider the odd postulate that the "peaceful" persuasive power of public images, circulated in what may seem like an ethereal, high-capitalist market, disguises a visceral violence fundamental to its constitution.

The World Bank phantasmagoria of 1991 Bangkok tried not to admit into its arcades the truth about its genealogy in war gifts. But, as it turned out, because not every Thai has severed that connection, because the Thai resistance is never far from its memory of the past victims of state terrorism, the national image was not able to liberate itself completely and become a true national fetish, blinding all. The clean public space was trespassed upon by an exiled past. Through these funeral rituals, Thai students remained connected to something that drags on new eras.

What follows here is this other side to the story, a side that shows that no one can fully possess the powers of public images—an insight that is both hopeful, in the sense that the military cannot control the powers of the national image it unleashes, and fearful, in that the power of images created for contest in public culture is not fully possessed by *any* maker, that meanings of signs in an historical field are not fully determined by the one who means them, and especially that drawing on the historical power of the dead—perhaps the only hope—is the most dangerous imagery of all.

October 14, 1973: The Gift Economy of the Old World Order

The U.S. State Department had secured for U.S. manufacturers a virtual monopoly on the Thai market for weaponry. The U.S. military had created in Thailand a massive system of military airfields and ports, radar surveillance stations, communications and signal sites, military training camps, and intelligence networks that supported the U.S. military's fight against communism in Southeast Asia. And by 1973 the United States had invested over 2 billion (preinflation) dollars into the Thai military.[6] Since a 1950 treaty, the United States had been sending military advisors to Thailand to shift the Thai military thinking over to U.S. methods and theories of combat and training, especially in the curriculum and structure of Chulajomkhlao Military Academy.[7]

Thailand had followed U.S. foreign policy goals faithfully and, in return, a virtually uninterrupted period of military dictatorship did not abate, from the 1948 coup of the former fascist General Phibun Songkram over the socialist-leaning Pridi Banyamong, to the 1957 coup of General Sarit Thanarat over Phibun, to the death of the great oligarch Sarit and the passing of his power to his underlings, the incorrigible trio General Thanom (prime minister), General Prapat (military commander in chief), and Army Colonel Narong (son of Thanom). All of these military men amassed great wealth both from overseeing the wheelings and dealings that go with military aid and weapons purchases, all that goes with facilitating development loans and foreign investment, and from influencing the arrangement of business relations within the country. Only two strings

CHAPTER THREE

were attached—compliance with U.S. military interests, and compliance with conditions for economic aid. The tyrants were only too happy to oblige, and provided over twenty continuous years of development under military dictatorship, a most reliable island of certainty amid the ring of fire in surrounding Cambodia, Laos, and Vietnam.

Development loans, aid grants, military aid, machine guns, rifles, tanks, artillery, helicopters, "advisors," spies, counterinsurgency expertise, psychological warfare tactics, American anthropologists for intelligence gathering and advice—these gifts the military rulers were more than happy to receive. It enhanced their own gift networks. They passed what they could down the line to their exchange partners. Thai dictators had always depended for their power upon patronage relations whereby the *phuu yai*, "bigman," is the one who can provide the most for his underlings, and the longer he can do it the longer he can rule. Every Thai connected through this gift economy to the juntas was, in turn, connected to the U.S. gift.

But by 1973 the patronage relations were showing signs of petering out. The U.S. military was beating a retreat from Southeast Asia. And although Thailand's hatches seemed securely battened down by an authoritarian regime, U.S. foreign policy was failing everywhere else, with U.S.-backed regimes in Laos and Cambodia on the verge of going the way of Vietnam.

The chance for dissidents to break the cycle of exchange came in early October 1973, when the police arrested a group of activists in an emerging middle-class shopping district for distributing pamphlets calling for a constitution to be drafted by December 10, the anniversary of the first constitution in 1932.

In the clampdown against constitutional activists in early October 1973, the police eventually seized a total of thirteen people, among them Thirayuth Boonmee, the former general secretary of the National Student Center of Thailand (NSCT), who had led the student movement to national prominence after a long period of escalating protests over issues ranging from the trade imbalance with Japan to dictatorial expulsions of university students.[8] The NSCT, which had become the only viable opposition force at the time, was unlikely to sit idly by at these arrests.

"The Thirteen," charged with treason, began a hunger strike in their detention center, which helped fuel the protests with a threat of death and suicide against the social order. In response, students and teachers filled Thammasaat University's football fields, coming from technical colleges, high schools, teacher's colleges, and all major universities. Across the street, on the large field of Sanam Luang, the sprawling weekend market was being set up as usual, and the students spoke from megaphones to the vendors and onlookers assembling there. By the time the market started business Saturday morning, the students, climbing atop buildings to wave flags and speak through microphones to the market, had recruited thousands of shoppers and vendors with their calls for a constitutional government with an elected prime minister and the king as head of state.[9]

A long process of historical agency was culminating, a new form of political power coalescing. The culture of protest in public spaces had been gaining momentum in two decades of slowly but surely growing confidence in the ability to call attention to issues of public policy and U.S. cultural imperialism, all led by student activists. Now, finally, in 1973 the public sphere was coming into its own, carried on utterances that vibrated across the marketplace: it was, finally, "mass politics," with its battle of images, its displays of bodies, its occupation of public space and of visual spheres in which power is contested, and its link to the market.

Questions of power had for a longer time been decided in secreted corridors, among a small and powerful elite. They were invisible questions—which faction was to prevail over which other—while a largely excluded populace waited in the sidelines. Often political parties were permitted to form, but these parties rarely had any ideological leanings and were simply vehicles for factional interests. Since the 1950s, when the U.S. gift started playing a heavy hand, strict dictatorship had been the rule, guided by a system of "despotic paternalism" in which patronage alliances forced out virtually all contest for power from nonelites.[10]

Although vested with the summary power to kill all enemies, Thai dictators needed to use it only sparingly, and for that matter, mostly on other elites, in a behind-the-scenes space of death and threats.[11] At the same time, however, military regimes again began conspicuous public executions, which had not been seen since the early 1800s, in order to advertise the sense of a strong hand in control of the state. As Benedict Anderson writes of this time, "arsonists," for instance, were lined up on the wall of the Royal Buddhist Temple Wat Mahataat and shot before the public and journalists; at the same time, and in secret, sometimes whole villages were tortured and killed off for suspected communist sympathies.[12]

But now no small part of the power of public spectacle was shifting toward public access politics. As Frank Reynolds relates in his account of the rise of Thai "civic religion" during the October rebellion, it was the students who were able to speak powerfully in the public image arena of spectacle. All the while that the students were encamped at Thammasaat University, and were being photographed by a largely sympathetic press, they had erected a stage next to the bo tree in the courtyard (this is the species of tree under which Buddha made and realized his vow of enlightenment), and had a large Buddha figure placed prominently next to the stage, an image that proved to be highly photogenic. Every morning of the protest, student leaders and demonstrators organized a large almsgiving to monks, which was also liberally photographed. Over the stage hung two large pictures of the king and queen. Between political speeches the crowd would often break to sing national songs, especially the king's anthem. And, of course, the whole pretext of the demonstration was the arrest of activists calling for a return to constitutional rule.[13] By these tactics, and with the aid of a newsprint apparatus willing to circulate the images, the students were able to counter the image assaults that the government attempted to cast on the demonstration as communist and terrorist by conveying the power of what Reynolds called the key symbols of the "civic religion."

When the deadline that the student demonstrators had set for the release of the prisoners passed at 12 P.M. of October 13, 1973, the crowd of demonstrators had swelled to over 400,000.[14] Students spilled out of Thammasaat University and led the crowd the short distance to the Democracy Monument. There were numerous portraits of the king and queen held aloft the whole way, lots of waving national flags, as well as plenty of yellow Buddhist flags.[15] It was the largest crowd ever assembled for a political protest in Thai history.

The march of 400,000 people was cleverly organized to face off as well as possible whatever violent force the three military rulers, Thanom, Prapat, and Narong, were planning to unleash upon them. Students from the vocational-technical colleges, some armed with clubs, were in the front row, as they were perceived to be brawny and fit, suitable for frontline confrontation.[16] They were followed by a row of young girls carrying pictures of the king and queen, dressed in the school uniforms of a prominent girls' school to which the children of army generals were often sent.[17] In line with a gendered division of protest labor that would continue into the 1990s, boys were behind and flanking the girls with thick sackcloth to be used against possible dogs and barbed wire. Other special groups were formed, each with its own colored armbands, to handle duties of first aid, technical work, intelligence gathering, and donations collecting.[18] The last of these functions was taking on a striking resemblance to Buddhist *dāna* (almsgiving), with the wealthy and reluctant giving money to the ones who would forge ahead in their stead, just as nuns and monks do in the project of Dhamma.

After the march commenced, the king, who had himself been accumulating great moral capital to his public image by remaining aloof from "profane" political matters, summoned first Thanom and Prapat for an audience, and then student leaders.[19] He had recently been restored to a position of prominence in national ideology by Field Marshal Sarit Thanarat, the premier just before the Thanom-Prapat-Narong regime. Back in 1932, the monarchy had been deposed by a military coup led by generals and bureaucrats of diverse political persuasions but unified in an idealism for a new and modern Thailand. Eventually, however, the king was brought back into the picture as a powerful symbolic figure to work alongside the centralized military authority. Though governments and generals have since come and gone, the king has remained. The monarchy has managed to gain in power, in part because of the king's astute maneuvering all these years, in part because of public sentiment and a massive image promotion campaign, and in part because of a law of lèse-majesté, which has been interpreted as meaning a ban on any and all forms of public criticism of the monarch—a law that has been used, often without the assent of the king, relentlessly to jail and exile people who make trouble for whatever government happens to be in power.

By October 1973, the symbiotic relation between the military and the king had been fully cultivated, and yet rifts were developing. One of the king's main sources of moral authority comes from the people's belief in his moral character. In an ideological sense the king is supposed to stand as the head of state, and by October of 1973 that meant being at the apex of a state that was going sour fast. The king stepped in, calling for an end to the demonstration, claiming that he had brokered a settlement with the government and that all student demands would be met: the military promised an unconditional release of the prisoners and a new constitution by the same time next year.[20]

More than half the crowd of 400,000 did not disperse, however, after the student leadership declared the protest a success. They were not content with mere promises from the military regime, whose word had been broken so many times before.[21] As is clear in the character of this massive display of bodies, the incident was about far more than the release of thirteen prisoners. The regime had to go.

In this situation, where a giant protest had pushed the military regime to the wall—and with night falling—it was prudent to divert the protests, for the first time in the history of such public demonstrations, away from the municipal center and toward the royal residential palace. It was felt that the most disgraceful place to hurt people would be near the king's residence, and if there was a violent clash people could run into the palace grounds to find safety. There at the palace they could appeal for more royal confirmations and intervention.[22]

In the darkness of the morning of "October 14," a representative of the king was sent out to meet with the demonstrators and express the monarch's desire that they disband, as all their demands would be met. The students sang the king's song and the national anthem, and prepared to return home.[23]

The police, who had hemmed the demonstrators in the courtyard beside Chitrlada Palace, demanded, however, that all demonstrators exit from a well-controlled point. The urge to command these bodies and have them file along official channels proved fatally destructive. The police refused demands for the unwieldy crowd to be let out of two exits. Thousands of corralled people swelled against the police lines that were forcing them through a single, narrow gauntlet. The police responded to the disorderly crowd by clubbing some of the students. Many students fought back bare-handed, and several were badly beaten. Then some Molotov cocktails were thrown by people in the crowd, and the police fired rifles and pistols (shots that could be heard as far away as at the Democracy Monument), and most demonstrators ran away in a panic.[24]

Word of the police brutality spread all over the town. A rumor, never substantiated, that three young girls had been beaten to death, spread throughout the crowds. Angry students, mostly male, ran from the scene to spread the news to people still gathered at the Democracy Monument, tipping over cars and smashing windows along the way.[25]

In the meantime, Thanom, Prapat, and Narong were putting into action their plans for a violent recoup of the situation. By now the city was humming with news of the events, and word had it that for anyone who wanted to be involved, the area around Sanam Luang commons was the place to be. Police clashed, first in hand-to-hand combat, with students playing a cat-and-mouse game of defiantly running into police lines and then running away. Sometimes solitary students would face off police armed only with a stick, which drove home the point that the demonstrators were now refusing to disband, refusing to show fear, refusing all intimidation.

There was no beat of retreat when two tanks were brought in to assist police, along with five hundred footsoldiers armed with assault weapons. The assumption among the crowd was that their moral authority was irresistible and the regime could not turn such heavy weapons on an un-armed crowd of youngsters. But the regime did just that, firing automatic weapons and tank-mounted machine guns on the crowd. As the bullets ripped into the stunned demonstrators, the army seized the airwaves, declaring that the protestors were rioting communist agents, armed with machine guns and killing Thai soldiers in the streets.[26] But the move back-fired, only enraging the urban viewers more and further disgracing the regime, as most Bangkok residents had ample information about the situation through the hyperefficient rumor mill (as opposed to rural TV viewers, many of whom were surprised to find that in the aftermath there wasn't going to be a communist government in Bangkok).[27] At this point, clearly the regime was incompetent in its control of images. It turned up the volume of violence instead.

THE POWER OF THE CORPSE

Gunning down demonstrators, spectators, and even a few police, the soldiers kept up a barrage on the crowds, driving them into Thammasaat University. After tanks fired machine guns into the grounds of Thammasaat University, the hounded students dove into the Chao Praya River, which runs behind the university, and were picked up by sympathetic ferrymen.[28]

Rumors were circulating that thousands of unarmed civilians were gunned down. The rumors were believable, given the fact that army helicopters were touring the city skies in pairs, for all to see and in clear view of everyone, firing their heavy machine guns on condensed and helpless crowds below.[29]

By the afternoon of October 14, 1973, several hundred students had gunshot wounds, and more than one hundred were dead.[30] But students fought back again through the medium of public visions, thus enacting a critical turning point in Thai history. They paraded through the streets with what corpses they could retrieve, carrying them on their shoulders, displaying to the public the outrageous truth of the military regime's moral order. The crowds witnessing the display quickly multiplied the images in a flood of word-of-mouth reports. The utterances embodied in the cadavers held aloft, circulated physically and verbally, began to draw in even greater numbers to the new public body.

As this steady stream of the populace emerged the military regime was desperately trying to control the image of the corpse, to erase it or transform it. On the radio and TV, government spokespeople enjoined the public not to believe the wild rumors cascading through the city. They informed the public that what the students were holding aloft was their friends who were faking being dead, that in fact the students had been infiltrated by communists who were putting them up to this charade, that the corpse-act was another of those communist ploys that turn all truth and righteousness in the world upside down.[31] But the broadcasts managed only to spread news of the corpses all the wider.

The truth, and the power, at this moment adhered stolidly in the corporeal moral order that left its official seal stamped into bodies of the young lives beaten down, now rising again to a new life they did not choose, where their most private spaces are turned, inside out, into public power. This led to the last and greatest gathering amassment of the masses, under the sign of death, an overflow of people in the streets, alleyways, and byways around the Democracy Monument—the body politic numbering more than half a million.[32]

Some groups ransacked and burned nearby government offices, crashed and burned city buses as barricades in the streets, and torched symbolically significant offices: the Public Relations building (the launching pad for the propaganda about fake corpses), the State Lottery auspices (widely believed to be manipulated by Thanom and Prapat), and Colonel Narong's "anticorruption" center, which he used as a personal tool to criminalize contenders for power.[33] Large groups of teenagers toured the streets in commandeered municipal buses, expressing their outrage by smashing

63

traffic lights, ripping down traffic signs, and burning the streetside booths of the traffic police, in the process destroying most of the state's emblems of reason and power to control everyday public order on the streets of Bangkok.[34]

By early evening the government gave in, or at least they pretended to give in, and the king went on national TV and radio announcing the resignation of Field Marshal Thanom (the prime minister in the Thanom-Prapat-Narong regime), and the appointment of an interim prime minister.[35]

The area in and around the Democracy Monument erupted in celebration. Most of the crowd dispersed in an air of jubilation. Many students and their leaders remained, however, speaking angrily of the murders of their friends and family, and of the fact that the perpetrators remained in the country. Although they had ceded the premiership, Thanom, Prapat, and Narong would still remain in control of the armed forces. Some were demanding the complete ouster of the trio of tyrants. Others demanded their execution.[36]

Making the situation worse, and despite the announcements by the king, the metropolitan police at their headquarters across from the Democracy Monument, which was manned by trusted commandants of the regime, were still taking potshots at the demonstrators, killing and wounding several students. It was not long before a group of incensed demonstrators, dubbing themselves the "Yellow Tigers Suicide Squad," vowed to take out the cops by any means necessary.[37] Lightly armed, they tried to storm the police headquarters, heaving bricks and Molotov cocktails through the windows, with little thought to their own lives. Many died fighting the small number of well-armed police defending the building, while several doctors and nurses were shot trying to attend to the wounded. The siege lasted through the night and into the afternoon of the next day, when the "suicide squad" emptied the water tanks of a commandeered fire engine, refilled them with gasoline, and then sprayed the gasoline into the building, forcing all the police to evacuate the building before it was torched.[38]

As it turned out, rival factions in the military proved unwilling to back the regime up when the situation began to deteriorate. After a rival general to the junta, Krit Srivara, had refused to dispatch more troops to do the trio's killing, Field Marshal Prapat and Colonel Narong had been desperately scheming to call in army divisions from the countryside, including the severely trained Special Forces division based in rural Lopburi (soldiers trained by U.S. Green Berets who will kill anyone and anything on command). When word got out of Field Marshal Prapat's plan for a new and larger massacre, General Krit threatened to cordon off Bangkok with his troops, finally leaving the trio of tyrants no recourse but to pack up and leave the country, apparently at the king's insistence but no doubt also at General Krit's.[39] For his part, the sniping police commander holed up at headquarters was several times turned down in his request for support by military generals. As one eyewitness claimed, he finally cursed and spit into the phone when General Krit refused to send help.[40] And then the gasoline smell started wafting in.

By nightfall, more announcements were flooding the national airwaves: Thanom, Prapat, and Narong were gone, having left the country on secret flights in the late afternoon.[41] Prapat and Narong were reported to have shown up at the airport with thirty overstuffed suitcases weighing 1,500 pounds. At the airport, Colonel Narong was seen running zig-zag, zig-zag across the runway, to avoid sniper fire, and on reaching the boarding stairs, he turned quickly to announce "I will return!" and then ran inside the aircraft.[42]

The release from martial law had finally come. City buses gave free rides to help disperse the crowds, and students and other protesters helped fire companies put out the flames. Not a single policeman was to be seen on Bangkok streets for several days, and Boy Scouts directed the traffic.[43]

There were, of course, many factors that contributed to the fall of the regime, as is the case with any historical episode. The behind-the-scenes maneuvering of military and elite factions was certainly as critical as anything else in effecting change, especially in the crucial moments of the aftermath, and as such seems to show us that October 14 was essentially another instance of Thai politics as usual. But what was very different about this behind-the-scenes maneuvering was the pronounced degree to which it was also a public image act. The army's survival of the epic moments of aftermath could only be accomplished with a simultaneous public image campaign. General Krit, who subsequently took control over the armed forces and organized and funded a political party to do his bidding, saw to it that in the aftermath the story was told and retold of how he faced down the trio of tyrants. His famous words to them were played over and over in the national imagination of the episode: "They are our children. They want democracy. We cannot shoot them." After the massacre, the army was quite rightly very concerned about its public image, and for a few years seemed content to contest for the public's sympathy by peaceful means.

Above all else—above the heroic stature the student movement had attained, above the heroic stature the king had added to his image by brokering the power transfer to constitutional and parliamentary rule, above the self-promotion of the self-styled "new professionals" of the army brass—what October 14 impressed upon the collective memory was a heinous deed, the brutal killing in the streets of unarmed boys and girls in their school uniforms. This had never happened in recent memory.

There had always been limited executions, semisecret killings, and discreet assasinations. There had been some close calls between small groups of demonstrators and police during the years that had led up to October 14, 1973. But in fact it was only now, in a new and prosperous modern Thailand, that common citizens were killed in the streets in such a brutal manner, with machine guns, tanks, and helicopter gunships. There is no question that October 14 marked (and I say marked because I do not want to imply that one episode can alone create such a massive historical development) and catalyzed a new era of mass politics, an era in which image really matters.

But just as it was the dawn of a new public culture, it was at the same time, *inseparably*, the dawn of the new public cadaver.

Politics of the public sphere in its full-fledged form was from this time, its first sovereign moment, a politics of the corpse. The student demonstrators had successfully charted the stormy seas of image management, or as Reynolds has put it, taken over the moral force of "primary symbols of civic religion": nation, religion, king, and constitution. But October 14 was more than a struggle for possession of a preconstituted symbol system. It was the generation of an evolving moral force field, a field of death. The consequences of these deeds cannot be erased, only made to lie dormant for a time, and then only seemingly so. With the dawn of the new mass politics and the new public sphere—and the new public cadaver— a force was unleashed that it is hard not to wax mystical about. For as will be clear in what followed, there is something about these public cadavers that is extremely dangerous, unpredictable, uncontrollable, and that makes difficult any normalization into social scientific discourse. If it is possible from time to time to get a smooth system of public images up and running so that it can simulate something like a clean new world, that should only further impress one with the danger of the corpse when it is happily cast from awareness by public image productions. It proves dangerous to forget where the public sphere came from in which public images are constructed, deployed, manipulated—dangerous to forget that *that sphere itself* has entered into a deal that is difficult to settle.

The student movement clearly occupied the positive moral space of the "civic religion," but it was the shock and horror of the massacre that brought the regime down so quickly and unexpectedly. One moment they were totalitarian despots who arrested thirteen activists for distributing a handful of fliers calling for a constitution in the near future, the next moment they were fleeing the country. In the void left by their absent despotic figures new public profiles rapidly arose: a constitutional convention, political parties, elections, parliamentary rule, civilian prime ministers, and a heady three-year period of the most open political freedoms the country had ever known. The power of horror was the catalyst for all this whirlwind change.

But about that whirl in the wind: what I mean to suggest by associating the public sphere with the genealogy of the public corpse is a moral economy of signs that is to a degree cut loose, as evidenced by the contest for the meanings and means of signification that animate much of public demonstrations. There can be a great degree of plasticity to the structure of power formed in a public image, which is what makes this power so dangerous, however heroic it may appear; for the genealogical ancestry of public culture is a violent one. As we shall see, the moral onus and the horror of the public cadaver—its unpredictable power and its danger—is a free-floating danger once it is unleashed, irretrievably, into the public realm, providing the often unrecognized force of animation to the phantasmagoric dreams of capital culture.

October 14, 1991: The World After

While the World Bank meets in the brand new convention center, at Thammasaat University students are busily painting long cloth signs. Some students whom I haven't met before tell me, with paintbrush in hand, that no, there won't be any big protest tonight, only a little memorial ceremony in the afternoon. I could be the CIA. Their trepidation is perhaps justified as, after all, General Suchinda's threats against a major demonstration were explicitly violent, though surely he has his spies in the student movement anyway. And yet, the government's double entendres in the terror and reason of public images are peculiarly difficult to navigate with equanimity and direction: the more the regime throws its discipline-commodity, threat-advertisements behind the national image, the more powerless it makes itself to wield those implements of death that lurk behind the new world. If the whole future of the nation rests on the smooth production of the meetings before the world audience, on the military saving the national image from the damage that its recent coup has done, how can they kill anyone just then?

It is the night of October 14, 1991/1973. As evening expires, the real thing erupts into the streets: the largest display of a mass body in eighteen years. The student leaders notify the authorities to show good form, and proceed out of Thammasaat, marching toward the Democracy Monument. They are now twenty thousand strong. Thousands watch by the side of the road. Surrounding the mass of people is one continuous cloth sign as their boundary and circumference, declaring the space within a "democratic zone, free of dictatorship." But the students are not merely cloaked by a thin cloth adorned in painted figures, they are secure in the heart of the World Bank phantasmagoria whose reason demands that they not be harmed, at least not while the world eye is focused here. The power of the national image begins to outrun those who promoted its reality with the most zeal—and it would not be for just a day that the national image would linger on in the new world imaginary.

Surrounded by the students are small groups of farmers. One group is fighting World Bank–financed dams that will flood their lands; another, larger group, is objecting to displacement by draconian land reform measures instituted by the military in the name of environmental protection, but which will actually move rural people out of forests soon to be cut down. The dead have been remembered in the morning; at night the victories are celebrated in advance. The energy is fantastic; the students are beaming with happiness. They chant "Out with NPKC, bring back democracy" which in Thai has a symmetrical, sharp, pounding rhythm between the two phrases. They sing out phrases from banned popular music of the rock band Carabao.

The corpse is evoked—a coffin for NPKC figurehead General Sunthorn. It is laid at the monument, which they call the "tomb of dictators." At this point, when the coffin prop is brought out, the steady flash of journalist cameras erupts into a rapid fire volley. It is protest drama, death drama, corpse drama. It sells well, but more than that it also seems to speak well, powerfully.

And yet . . .

And yet at the steps of the Democracy Monument on this day of collapsing histories, the Thai student leadership announces that the coffin, set down at the tomb of dictators, is not to be set on fire, so as not to provoke violence, as if there were some special danger associated with flames. They circumscribe a certain limit to the signal flare of their theater, as though their death images ought not be too powerful.

For a few hours the crowd surrounds the Democracy Monument, and careful policemen redirect traffic, obviously under orders not to let any untoward incident arise while the World Bank is roosting in Bangkok. Obviously they are there to keep the local history on hold, to keep things right side up, to keep the cadaverous roots of the new world from turning upward.

After political speeches and songs are rung out on loudspeakers, catapulting over the mock coffin, the leaders call for a satisfactory close. They made their point. They filled the broad avenue around the monument with a solid mass of people. They created a spectacle for the onlookers, one that would certainly keep them coming back for more.

As the crowd disperses, the leaders urge everyone, for the sake of the movement, to return home peacefully. They show every sign of cooperation with the authorities, both sides operating as smooth as butter. The students are careful to avoid any incident showing them to be rabble rousing, riotous, or, especially, ruinous of the national image. The police avoid all confrontation, not wanting any violent episode to call up the terror side of the equation. The students are defiant, the military keep hands off, and the police walk on eggshells. In this first, moot court of historical battle, neither side makes a false move.

At the steps of the monument there are a few hangers-on. There remain about sixty, mostly male, students from Ramkamhaeng University, the open university whose students have the reputation of being a bit more radical, rowdy, and free-spirited than their counterparts at Bangkok's prestigious Thammasaat or elitist Chulalongkorn. And Ramkamhaeng is home to the Satchathamm (truth-justice/Dhamma) student party, a more radical group than the Student Federation of Thailand. The students are a little tipsy, and are singing songs. A couple of boys in the corner set a single sheet of paper on fire, and a police sargeant runs in and stamps on it angrily with his black-heeled boots, "No fires! You can't burn things here!"

One of the drunk boys yells at him, "The military regime is corrupt. The people need things that they don't have!"

The police sargent snaps back, "I have enough to eat. My family is happy. The money is enough."

A few glowing embers fade back into darkness. This little transgressive episode of fire is over quickly. For most, October 14, 1991/1973, has passed smoothly enough, and it seems that few have seen the forbidden flare.

OCTOBER 6, 1976: REINCARNATING THE OLD WORLD ORDER

Following the revolt of 1973, the junta was finally gone, and then there was the stench. Details of corruption and excess spilled out into public discourse in an incontinent stream of conspiracy. It was just like the aftermath of the death of the Thanom-Prapat-Narong junta's mentor, Field Marshal Sarit Thanarat, when there was for each of the first hundred days after his demise a new story about a new mistress and a new mansion in a new part of the country.[44] Likewise, the sordid details of the Thanom-Prapat-Narong regime's twisted, cynical networks of extractive gift relations of official power abuse were dissected and exposed with fascination and anger.

The outrage over October 14, 1973, was massive, and for the first time in ages, the country's leadership was completely shamed and disgraced. In the climate of free speech that was released by a public culture generated from the horror of the corpse, the public media seized upon the moral onus and lay it firmly at the former junta's feet. Immediately following the massacre it became widely agreed, through the media, that it was all to be attributed to the "trio of tyrants." Two highly charged images reigned at the time: Field Marshal Prapat (the military chief in the regime), as he was attempting to call in the Special Forces from Lopburi, had allegedly signed orders permitting up to 2 percent of the demonstrators to be killed, while army communications monitors reported that Colonel Narong, son of Prime Minister Field Marshal Thanom, was personally on board one of the helicopters that could be seen swooping down suddenly and raking the people with gunfire. It was, and still is, widely believed that Colonel Narong personally had his hand on the trigger of a machine gun.

In the immediate wake of the disaster, the king, having already involved himself in the public sphere of politics during the incident, stepped in to lend his newly sparkling legitimacy to the transition to constitutional rule, and used the moral capital he had stored up from years of the new style of removed, untainted, almost holy kingship he had been promoting since the dictator Sarit Thanarat enlisted his aid in legitimating power in the 1950s. But he did not let up on the image making either, as he and his family members could be seen reproduced on TV and in papers visiting the wounded victims, capping off an historical episode in which both the national and international press saw the king as the decisive personage who made the transition to democracy possible. He emerged as the hero of the story, more adored than ever in both local and foreign media. It was like a second coronation.

The new parliament and constitution were put in place in 1974, and until October 1976, Thailand had its most democratic period of politics ever. Farmers from around the country organized the Peasant's Federation of Thailand. Unions gained a right to organize and strike, and did. The press was uncensored. Students stepped up their pressure on the government. Political parties went forth and multiplied. Popular culture—music, literature, poetry—flourished with the new social conscience and new freedom efflorescing since the massacre, and even Marxist political tracts were sold on the open market, including works by authors too close for comfort, like Mao and Ho Chi Minh. But in the short space of only three years, the moral and emotional topography would radically change. The United States was pulling out of Southeast Asia generally, but wanted to keep its air bases in Thailand. Students successfully capitalized on the moment and directed a popular, nationalist protest at the new elected government, demanding the complete withdrawal of U.S. air bases. It went on to become the first such effort in Asia to oust U.S. military installments—perhaps a sign of more to come. The United States was not about to stand by idly and let its gifts be refused, nor was the Thai military going to let anyone stand between them and their patron.

The United States began to reduce drastically its aid to the country after the student uprising, and the "artificial" economy pumped up by war dollars started to go into a dive just as the new democratic parliament was taking over. The military, although bitterly divided into factions, was unanimous in its desire to roll back the clock, both in terms of reasserting its control and in garnering more dollars from the United States. The "anti-U.S." students were particularly loathsome in that respect. Meanwhile, within the armed forces, the uncertain future was simply a question of which faction was going to win out over the others and seize power again.

A new moral alignment was coalescing around right and left. If the students had at the height of October 14 occupied the high road by being the pioneers of a new image-driven mass politics, by 1975 there were new forces at work on this very same frontier, forces desperately connected to the U.S. gift, focused narrowly and incessantly on the students as a focal symbol of evil. A propaganda war began. With the implicit knowledge that death and corpses were the most powerful of the forceful images unleashed in this new public space, it is not surprising that the cadaver was the telos toward which the events of this period moved with the unswerving purpose of a predator chasing its prey.

THE RIGHT

A paramilitary group of ultra right-wing activists, dubbed the Red Gaurs after a mythical wild ox, was created as an all-purpose anticommunist, antidissident organization that engaged in covert operations and counterinsurgency propaganda. It was organized through the leadership and funding of the Internal Security Operations Command (ISOC)—which was itself the creation of the CIA.[45] The ISOC recruited, trained, and armed the Red Gaurs, whose ranks were made up mostly of unemployed youth and vocational students, ex-mercenaries for the United States from the war on Laos, and discharged soldiers. Red Gaurs were on call as counterdemonstrators and incendiaries for any situation on the streets, in return for which they received generous pay that they would never have been able to garner on the labor market, as well as free alcohol and brothel visits, and a fanatic ideology that gave them a sense of righteousness.[46] In the name of the *lag thai* (Thai pillars) national ideology—nation, religion, king—which became the battle cry of the new mass right, Red Gaurs assaulted labor protests, protests concerning the drafting of a new constitution in 1974, and protests of American military bases in 1974–1975; they also assaulted Thammasaat University in August 1975, causing many casualties, even among journalists who tried to document the violence.[47] When government instability led to calling new elections in April 1976, Red Gaurs proved the most instrumental of all right-wing groups in intimidating politicians and their constituents, and disrupting campaigns by lobbing grenades and sniping.[48]

Also connected to the ISOC was the organization Nawaphon, which was an ideological compliment to the Red Gaurs. Nawaphon was made up mostly of urban and rural elites, an association of merchants, businesspeople, conservative Buddhist monks, and high-society types gathered together under the pretense of building a new communitarian society.[49] Conducting much of their discourse in a Buddhist idiom, and alleged to have the support of the king and queen, Nawaphon recruited a great number of adherents, some of them secret members, from influential elite circles.[50] On Nawaphon's executive council were figures like the right-wing monk Kithivuddho, who gave headline-making speeches about the Buddhist merit and good kamma to be earned by killing communists, and Thais who had been brought over from CIA training in the United States to teach psychological warfare to the ISOC.[51]

A third right-wing group was the ostensibly politically neutral Village Scouts, whose patron is the king. Funded by wealthy businesspeople, the Village Scouts were intended as a rural community organization to organize cultural activities such as village bazaars, beauty contests, and parades, in which the populace was to be indoctrinated into national values like nation, religion, and king, to counteract the influence of the Communist Party of Thailand in rural areas.[52] Their practices included mystical mass initiation rites and invocations of Buddhist teachings, which had religious-revivalist effects on many of the youth subjected to them, as Katherine Bowie explores in her ethnography of the movement, *Rituals of National Loyalty.*[53] Toward the end of the post-1973 democratic period, the Village Scouts increasingly came to be employed in orchestrated political strategies in the urban center of Bangkok. During the April 1976 election campaign, while they were heavily involved in the campaigns of right-wing politicians in the provinces, at the same time they were increasingly appropriated into the intimidation tactics of Bangkok street politics.[54]

Although the student movement had pressured the government to agree to demands that the United States withdraw its air bases, they could not possibly have forced the United States to withdraw its covert agents. An insidious web of counterinsurgency advisors and informants, possibly numbering in the thousands, was left in all places and levels of government, military, and police.[55]

Added to all that was stacked against the students, there was a generalized propaganda campaign delivered through army TV and radio and conservative newspapers, which effectively claimed the national symbols of nation, religion, and king as belonging to the right wing. All others were represented as a direct threat to the pillars of the nation. Commie-mongering was the standard fare of the day, and a great discursive effort was applied, backed up by U.S.-trained experts in psychological warfare, to establish the reality of a right-left political split. By late 1975, after first the Cambodian king and then the Lao king fell, the latter to communists, and with the Vietnam War ending in defeat for the United States, the domino theory provided a great deal of manipulable angst. The Thai king began making speeches calling all Thais to gather their strength to fight the enemy, internal and external. He foretold of a great struggle ahead, as he increasingly lent his imagery to photographic sessions with top-ranked military officers and with the troops fighting the small, Chinese-backed communist insurrection in the provinces.[56]

Around this time a terrorist campaign was launched against the left, which within a year claimed the lives of at least thirty peasant leaders and eighty urban activists, student and labor.[57] Among prominent incidents were the assassination of the secretary general of the Socialist Party, respected academic Dr. Boonsanong, who was gunned down in a drive-by, and the killing of a leader of the NSCT, shot to death while asleep in an up-country Buddhist temple when he was on a field trip with some friends.[58] Red Gaurs killed four students and wounded eighty others with a hand grenade tossed into an NSCT protest against the U.S. military in March 1976.[59] By this time, prominent student leaders, such as the leaders of the 1973 revolt, Seksan and Thirayuth, had already left the country, to return underground with the rural insurrection later.[60]

Not only were student leaders driven off by the violence and ominous political instability within and around Thailand, there was a great capital outflow as well, with foreign-controlled capital extraction almost doubling its rate from 1974 to 1975. Thai-controlled capital also went packing as Thailand suddenly became the third-largest investor in Hong Kong behind the United States and Japan. While the United States was drastically cutting its aid to the Thai government, Japanese investment in the private sector almost halved.[61]

In a flip-flopping logic of appearances, the right wing continued to stir up violence so that it could blame the students and the new democracy for the instability in the country. The right-wing propaganda machine ferociously persisted in singling out students and labor as the destabilizing elements that were scaring away foreign investment and causing the economic depression as well as destroying the national development goals drummed into the populace since the 1950s. Dr. Puey Ungpakorn, rector of Thammasaat University at the time, reported on what would become a new wave of common sense communicated through highly organized channels well tuned to the new power of the public sphere: "After the October 1973 incident . . . it was said that if Thailand could be rid of 10,000 to 20,000 students and other people, the country would be orderly and peaceful. . . . There were other public statements that the slaughter of 30,000 . . . would be a 'cost-free investment.'"[62]

The United States was withdrawing its gifts from Southeast Asia, and the Vietnam War era was trickling down to a close. If the students were not stopped, it was established, they would soon drive the country into economic collapse, bloody civil war, and communism.

FOCAL IMAGERY OF RIGHT-LEFT PRODUCTION

By 1976, right-left political polarity was becoming a reality. The right wing had occupied the space of national symbols and the lag thai ideology—nation, religion, king—while relegating to the left all others, including all politicians against military dictatorship (most of whom were as "leftist" as a moderate U.S. Republican). It was not long before the military leadership was able to disrupt the public sphere sufficiently to force a new election, to try and oust the first postmassacre government, which had given in to student demands for the withdrawal of U.S. air bases.[63] The campaign trail of the resulting April 1976 election was the bloodiest in Thai history. Many candidates and campaign leaders, identified as "leftist" and so also communist, were assassinated. Their campaign offices were burned. Hand grenades and pipe bombs were tossed into election rallies. An orchestrated and incessant propaganda campaign identified the liberal parties as destroyers of Buddhism and the monarchy. It was capped off by a series of catchy, militant pop tunes encouraging people to destroy the enemy, the "scum of the earth" and "disease of the land."[64]

Pramarn Adireksan, a key patron of Nawaphon (the mystical counterinsurgency group described above), as interior minister with the Chart Thai Party, used his control over the media to launch an effective redbaiting campaign. It was a constant daily barrage of virulent speeches accompanied an incessant, chanting mantra over Armed Forces Radio— "Right Kill Left! Right Kill Left! Right Kill Left!"[65]

A 29 percent turnout and a sound though not total victory for the right brought in a new center-right coalition government, with the Democrat Party as the core. But the right-wing terrorism did not abate. "Leftist" elements were perceived to be involved even in the relatively conservative Democrat Party, while several military factions were vying with each other to gain enough influence over the armed forces to put together a coup. Something much more powerful than red-baiting was needed to win out.

In 1976, former Prime Minister Thanom, who had fled the country in disgrace only three years prior, returned to the teetering country in a production intended to polarize the situation. The former tyrant Thanom stepped off the plane from Taiwan and was greeted by a storm of media attention. His head was shaved. He wore the yellow robes of the Buddhist order. He claimed his aged father was dying, and as all good sons must do, he was returning to Thailand to be ordained as a bhikkhu (monk) in the Buddhist Sangha (order), in order to dedicate the merit so made to his father.

He had already been ordained as a novice in Taiwan so that he could be photographed in the robes when he arrived. Air-brushed with Buddhism, Field Marshal Thanom was hurried off to be ordained as a Buddhist monk at Wat Borworniwet, the flagship temple of the royally created and patronized Thammayut sect.

Soon after, the king and queen visited the temple in liberally photographed sessions, with the ostensible purpose of conferring their support on the temple which was, according to the establishment's claims, supposedly besieged by leftists waiting for the chance to raze it. Then the crown prince returned to the country after a long stay in Australia at a military academy. One of the first things he did was visit the temple and produce more royal photographic images to circulate. Thainess, Buddhism, and monarchy were discursively fashioned into a tight configuration of propriety that admitted no one who begged to differ, while students were identified as corrupted by un-Thai elements of communism and infiltrated by Vietnamese, as Thongchai Winichakul has pointed out. And every day in the papers, there was the new Buddhist monk, Thanom, the ruler from the October 14 massacre, walking on alms rounds with shaven head, yellow robes, and bowl, with soldiers on his left and an escort of police on his right.

EVEN THE DEAD ARE NOT SAFE FROM THE ENEMY IF HE WINS

Thanom the monk, redeeming himself by living the holy life, was trying to shuck his historical role as father of the Thai public cadaver. Thus was the spirit of the October 14 dead let loose.

An eagerly expected outcry followed his return. Now it could be made plain to see who was on which side—indeed, it could be made to seem that there were in fact two sides, as a mounting crisis built on the controversy. While Prime Minister Seni Pramoj waffled, his Democrat Party split bitterly into "left" and "right" factions, a tenacious debate arose in parliament, and the house finally passed a resolution for Thanom's expulsion. Trying to handle the chaos, Seni temporarily resigned, declared his government null and void, and put together a new cabinet that was due to be presented to the king for approval on October 6—a cabinet that made a few too many concessions to liberal politicians for the taste of many forces aligning behind Thanom's monkhood for a final stand. What followed became the darkest memory ever in Thai national history.[66]

Soon after Thanom arrived in his monk's robes, student and labor organizations set to work on a protest, knowing, as most did at the time, that a coup was now imminent and the window of opportunity in the public realm might soon be closing. Desperate to rescue their assailed democracy, they turned to staging evocative images of cruelty to convey arguments in the visual sphere, which was the last place left to them. They managed to produce some effective counterimages with their recently acquired artistic-dramatic flair for agit-art. One act, with an actor dressed up as a monk and parading with soldiers carrying heavy weaponry, got a lot of circulation in newspaper photographs. But the right wing had its own images in reply. Two young men from a labor group, who were handing out anti-Thanom leaflets in a Bangkok suburb, were seized by police. The police strangled them, then hung them by the neck on a wall for all to see. At first they left a police insignia at the scene, but later removed it before photographers and journalists arrived. Then they quickly buried the bodies, claiming no relatives had come forward.[67]

Although the material cadavers had disappeared, photographic image-cadavers were replicating rapidly. For the next few days the two dangling corpses, lifeless heads bent at the neck, were prominent images that circulated along with the Buddhist monk Thanom's media circus in the national news. The bizarre juxtaposition was the onset of an impending eruption in the image realm.

At first police denied any involvement, while students demanded that the culprits be arrested and tried for murder, threatening a mass demonstration if action was not taken. But Prime Minister Seni would do nothing, even after the police later admitted that they had in fact killed the two youths.

In protest of the murders, a group of relatives of people killed on October 14 went on hunger strike in front of the prime minister's office, supported by "heroes of October 14," wounded survivors of the October 14 killings, and NSCT student demonstrators. Police arrived soon after, looking to start a fight, and the protest was moved to what was thought to be the relative safety of Thammasaat University grounds, where it remained until the bitter end.[68]

Outside the university, on the vast fields of Sanam Luang, an orchestration of right-wing might was forming on the empty space of the weekend market. Red Gaurs showed up in force, as well as Nawaphon members, Village Scouts, and hundreds of the right-leaning public, where they were all incited by virulent right-wing politicians and organizers and whipped-up with the violent songs and chants they all knew so well.

Inside the university grounds, at least two thousand students and workers gathered to listen to speakers and music and watch political dramas. On October 4 they staged another, more fateful image of cruelty for their following and for the press. The students put their hands again to the politics of death imagery that had worked so well for them on October 14, only three years before. The image went like this: one student was dressed like Phra Thanom in monk's robes, while another student, reenacting the earlier killings of the labor activists, was slung in a harness and "hung by the neck" over Phra Thanom's head, while a "soldier" with a Nazi armband presided over the scene, which was rimmed by a few other students lying about like dead bodies. At "Monk Thanom's" feet was a sign-caption reading, "STUDENTS DON'T WORRY, I ONLY ASK FOR A FEW MORE CORPSES."

It was an eerie image. Its aura crept over the university field for most of the day. It was a powerful death image launched into the turbulent space of the political battlefield. But to skillfully evoke the power of the corpse is not to control it; to sign and to mean is not to control the circulation of your signs or the meaning that they carry.

The right-wing newspaper *Dao Siam* ran the image of the dangling corpse in front-page photographs, interpreting it with headlines that announced that what the students had done was hang the crown prince in effigy. The new meaning stuck, and of course the students could not take back their image now that they had already set it loose into the image realm. All day and night of October 5, Armed Forces Radio railed against the students as antimonarchist communists. Announcers chanting the "Right Kill Left!" mantra extolled the public and the police to charge into Thammasaat University and exact vengeance. In a coordinated image-assault, Armored Division Radio repeatedly rang out their call for violence against the students who had staged the "mock hanging of the crown prince," encouraging listeners to buy *Dao Siam* to see the truth for themselves. Seeing had already been established as believing.[69]

By early morning of October 6, 1976, hundreds of angry people from the general public heeded the call, bringing along hundreds of photographs of the mock hanging, which they held aloft as visual truth and imaged proof, joining up with the right-wing organizations outside the gate of Thammasaat.[70] A new and different union of political action groups and the public was fusing on the market commons of Sanam Luang, joining under the photographic sign of the corpse that they held above their heads.

At the same time, police encircled the campus compound and declared their intention to break up the protest and arrest those responsible for the crime against the monarchy.[71] The crowds outside began setting small fires near the gate and then throwing burning objects at the students. Around 5 A.M., Red Gaurs lobbed Molotov cocktails and a hand grenade over the gate, seriously injuring many students, and then started climbing over the gate, until one Red Gaur cadre was shot in the chest; he died later. Police suddenly fired an M-79 rocket launcher at the student gathering, killing one and injuring sixteen others, after which many of the two to four thousand people inside ran into school buildings for shelter. After sporadic fire of M-16 and AK-33 assault rifles through the university gate, a few student snipers, holed up in class buildings, fired back.[72]

At that point, most of the people inside did not know that the police were attacking them, but thought the Red Gaurs were exchanging fire with student guards. When they realized the truth, most wanted to get out, but the police had sealed off all the exits. At first, a few wounded demonstrators were brought out by boat in the river behind the university, but the police, patrolling the river, quickly cut off further evacuation, and fired at the protestors on the bank. At the same time, Red Gaurs and police intermittently fired on the other three sides of the compound.[73]

Meanwhile, NSCT leaders were trying to negotiate an audience with the prime minister, to get the police called off and to explain the truth about the hanging corpse skit. The prime minister's secretary promised them an audience on condition that "the student who looks like the prince" come along too. Desperate, they eventually agreed and were snuck out past the mobs in an ambulance and brought to the prime minister's house, where instead of meeting the prime minister, they were arrested.[74]

Around 7 A.M. the students sent someone out with a bullhorn to announce a surrender. He was gunned down immediately with an M-16. A half hour later, the metropolitan police chief arrived, saying he was "ready to die." The prime minister had signed "fire at will" orders, based on orchestrated rumors that the students had heavy weaponry "of Vietnamese origin" secreted on campus. As the students saw the eerie black uniforms of border patrol police—police trained to ambush the jungle caravans of opium warlords—filing in to back up the metropolitan police, they begged that women be allowed to evacuate the area. They were refused.[75]

At 7:30 the police began their assault on the university. Red Gaurs and Village Scouts used a hijacked city bus to crash through the university gates, while police and others climbed over the fence. The police, apparently believing rumors about Vietnamese weapons, proceeded cautiously, while allowing the right-wing mobs to stream out and expose themselves to light pistol fire. Townspeople, climbing on rooftops to get a better view, could see that the students had no heavy weaponry, and shouted and gesticulated wildly to the police, egging them on.[76]

Some students tried to escape via the Chao Praya River behind the university. Many drowned or were shot by patrol boats.[77] Most of the rest were exposed to the crowds and police who stormed into the university compound, shooting rocket launchers and grenades into the classroom windows, gutting the buildings and then in a frenzy scouring the grounds to get their hands on the terrorized students hiding within. Eventually the police and crowds got to everyone trying to hide. The students were made to crawl on their stomachs out to the football field in the central quad of the university. There both girls and boys were made to strip to the waist and lie still while police rained down rifle-butts or boot heels on their heads and backs. The right-wing mobs sat in the football bleachers cheering wildly, waving national flags, and singing their ghoulish killing songs while the boys and girls were brutalized on the field.[78]

Other students tried to flee over the fence or come out of the front with their hands up, only to be captured and tortured. Red Gaurs and Village Scouts dragged students out of the university where they were being made to lie prostrate, including two girls who were raped, and then beat them to death, strung them on trees, and mutilated their bodies. One girl was stripped naked, hung on a tree, and shot repeatedly while the police watched. Another group of four students was doused with kerosene and their bodies burned, one while still alive. Four students tried to get out the front gates with their hands over their heads but were immediately met by Red Gaurs who beat them and shot them. One of them, a girl, was mutilated by a plainclothes policeman who shoved a stick up the dead girl's vagina.[79]

Most of the police stood by and watched. Bodies were dragged out, mutilated, and burned by the right-wing groups who were even so brazen as to tear captured students out of the hands of the police to beat and lynch them.[80] With clubs and metal bars, the right-wing crowds rounded up students and beat or kicked them to death. They mutilated their corpses with blows from classroom chairs or metal shards torn from the university gates.[81] Hanging corpses on the trees that line Sanam Luang commons across from Thammasaat University, people took turns beating the dead bodies with sticks, gouging out their eyes, slashing their throats.

Hundreds of students were killed in the massacre.[82] Three thousand demonstrators were taken prisoner, loaded on buses, and carted away, driven past the line of corpses of their friends dangling on trees outside the university. If one of these buses stopped at a red light too close to the killing field, crowds would board it and beat and loot the prisoners. If any prisoners tried to escape, they were gunned down on the spot.[83]

At one o'clock it rained. The streets around Thammasaat University were literally soaked red. Meanwhile the cheerful crowds had been gradually filing out of the area and moving toward their own demonstration at the "Equestrian Statue" of King Rama V across from the royal palace, led there by Village Scouts. There they remained until six o'clock, when the crown prince (the real crown prince) appeared amid wild cheers and addressed the crowd, asking them to disperse and announcing that a "National Administrative Reform Council" had executed a coup, and the military was once again in power.[84]

NECROMANTIC POWER

In the 1700s, the Burmese razed the kingdom of Ayudhaya, just north of what is now Bangkok. But the phoenix of Thai kingship reemerged under the charismatic, millennial King Taksin. The present dynastic history has it that Taksin was crazed with megalomania, among other things calling himself a Sōtapanna, a Buddhist stream-enterer, a nascent enlightened being who was putting off full enlightenment for the sake of the kingdom. The founder of the present Chakri Dynasty, nine kings ago, ascended to power after Taksin had been killed, and moved the power center across the river from Taksin's Thonburi to what is now Bangkok. There the rulers constructed the Grand Palace, ceremonial center of the city and its kingly power. After the 1932 coup over the monarchy, Pridi Banymong, the socially conscious ideological whip of the 1932 "Promoters' Group," had Thammasaat University built almost next door. The large field that fronted both edifices became an open free marketplace, the grass commons of Sanam Luang. Later, of course, the market area became the staging field for the public sphere of oppositional politics and, inseparably, for massacre.

Across the field of Sanam Luang is another construction from the days of the regicide: the *lag muang*, the city pillar, built as the magical pole around which a sorcerous power to protect the city would circulate. It is a stupalike construction, with a wide base narrowing in level geometrical increments to a pointed apex. It is ignored and forgotten by many people, but it is a favorite site of spirit mediums, those who commune with the dead, and it is a special fount of power to practioners of magical arts. I have been told rumors that before they laid the foundation for the city pillar in stone, they dug trenches in the ground, brought young, pregnant slaves to the site, and there slashed their throats with swords and cast the corpses with their dying fetuses into the earth. It was believed, or so I am told, that the collective force of their murdered spirits would empower the pillar.

Regardless of actual truth to this bit of exotica about necromancy and the lag muang pillar, there is nevertheless a truth of sorts embodied in the story of this white, geometrical stone edifice of power, erected over a pit of corpses. The lag muang's cleanliness and rational order, its symmetry and proportion, not only signify this particular, magically centered power but can also speak to the duplicitous layering of the clean public sphere over its own revolting history. Is not the 1991 Bangkok phantasmagoria—created in one sense for the World Bank and in another to keep the populace in line—is it not a monument rather similar to the city pillar, a construction of smooth angles that rests, in a sense, on a pit of death? The victory of the new world order and its efflorescent visual market has just this malodorous history about it. Although the neoliberal market can claim to operate by nonviolent principles of free trade, although prime ministers can become heroes in world finance circles by "turning battlefields into marketplaces," nevertheless the metamorphosis was here accomplished by means that only in their surface dimensions appear to be the nonviolent ordering power of the global market. Southeast Asia was in some respects the premier arena in the battle over the old world order. At least in a mythic sense, this was so for the United States, which was itself traumatized by its gift-patronage relations to the region, especially Vietnam, but which scored perhaps its only victory in Thailand on October 6, 1976, on the fields of Sanam Luang, the common market—a market transformed into a battlefield. Underneath the victorious new world lies the historically buried cadavers of those who had to be murdered in order that a clean and orderly monument of public imagery could be constructed. The erection of this orderly image realm is nothing less than necromancy, death magic, power culled from the corpse.

The art by which powers are culled from corpses is a powerful magic, but also a dangerous, unstable magic, as it aims its taproots directly into the spiritual matter of decay and death. During October 14, 1973, Field Marshal Thanom, Field Marshal Prapat, and Colonel Narong, the fathers of the Thai public cadaver, tried to raze the populace with lightning bolts of state terrorism, but instead unleashed the power of the corpse, which sent them reeling out of the country almost immediately. In a public sphere where image matters, a public sphere crystallized by the magic of murder, the collective force of the spirits of the dead roam. And this makes it a doubly dangerous conceit to infer that simply invoking the dead, simply tapping into the historical claim with which they haunt the present, will bring a redemptive, positive, predictable, or controllable result. In October 1976, the students tried again to draw on the power of the corpse. They created, staged, and circulated its imagery. But they were no match for the CIA, its child the Internal Security Operations Command,

81

or their tactics of psychological warfare and their orchestration of mass murderers. Nor were they a match for the power of mechanical reproduction, which almost stands up like the city pillar and demands to be recognized as a pole around which power circulates. First the police strung two young men up on trees, evoking the corpse. When the students tried to harness the imagery of the corpses with which they were to be terrorized, the magic backfired, and the necromantic power of the public cadaver ricocheted back upon them. The cruel artistry in the students' eerie agit-art performance was at the same time its danger.

Michael Taussig has suggested that the kind of evocation Benjamin, for instance, had imagined for his enigmatic "dialectical image" was like a magical power; "we can see that such images are created by the author but are also already formed, or half-formed, so to speak, latent in the world of the popular imagination, awaiting the fine touch of the dialectical imagician's wand—not unlike Victor Turner's description of the central African herbalist whose adze, in chopping bark off the chosen tree, arouses the slumbering power of material already there awaiting the copula of the magician's touch."[85]

The "dialectical imagician" can with a magic wand tap into the slumbering power of the dead, and Taussig also compares this release to that of the "chaos and danger" of "liberating signs" in Antonin Artaud's Theater of Cruelty.[86] In response to that one might emphasize that such magical power is not an instrumental power—unlike the simple application of a magic wand, perhaps. Nor is it exactly like the well-proportioned and ordered magical geometry of the lag muang city pillar. The chaos and danger of liberating signs is more like what festers—at least in stories—underneath Bangkok's pillar of power: decay and instability. Once an image is created in the unstable field of public culture, it is no longer under the control of its maker, least of all an image of death—how quickly the decay set in, how quickly the image of the dangling corpse, which the students unsurped and reproduced, fell into the brew that the CIA and mystic counterinsurgency necromancers were simmering. The power of the public cadaver only increased in the rapidity with which it was tossed back and forth. Rather impersonally, its power accumulated in the intensity with which it was *used*, and in the ferocity with which the death spells and counterspells were woven: first raising the memory of the October 14, 1973, dead, bringing their executioner back into the country in the bhikkhu's robes; then stringing two young men up on a wall; then taking that image and reenacting it in political drama, only to have its meaning recaptured and spewed forth in yet another form, into a photographic death's-head emblem under which murder and a fluorescence of dangling corpses were produced, the devastating onus of the public cadaver eventually falling on the students. And add to this the exchange relation that mechanical reproduction has not only with the production of copies but also with the production of more originals—or, in other words, its mass production of real violence through its reproduction of violent images. This is perhaps one of the greatest disasters and plights of necromantic power in our time. The mutilated corpses of the students bloomed like flowers on the trees that line Sanam Luang's market field. And what followed was the most vicious reign of reasoned state terrorism that Thais have ever known.

Today, Thai student leadership is among the most circumspect, and astute, of all progressive forces in the country. Thai students know the danger of the graphic very well, directly—a danger that others may not know so well. Having touched the sign of the corpse, the students now have an eidetic memory, dated October 6, of real and mechanically reproduced corpses, each imitating and reproducing the other, finally in serial repetition lining the streets with rows of dangling remains.

Public images are fraught with free-floating significations, with indeterminate meanings, with a lack of bedrock to their signifying functions. Here, the sign of death epitomizes the qualities of all signs. In other words, the public sphere is a corpse—a site of impermanency and uncertainty. Its images decay. Its signs decompose. Its meanings have no self-essence, whether disguised in the reasonable cleanliness of the public sphere or not. In such a field the historical effects of intentional acts realize persuasive discourses and produce reality effects that soon outrun the intentionality of the actor. The remainder, that excess, that genealogical residue washing up in the wake of the act as it slips away, is history and ruin: decomposing agencies and decaying intentions running their course toward dissolution.

The pictures of death from October 14 and Bloody October went underground after the democracy movement of the seventies had failed, into a student publication banned, I am told, for many years after. *Samut Phap Duan Tula*, "October Album," is a collection of mostly pirated photos from international and some local correspondents in which the multiple languages of the captions, with screaming exclamation points, are left untranslated and the pictures are for the most part left to speak for themselves (see figure 3).[87] Sometimes it is better not to have a caption. And to my knowledge no news agency has stepped forward to claim its property right to the cadavers. So they still sit there, waiting.

Whether in photographic or other forms there is a return of the corpse always waiting to happen, because underneath the clean image realm lies a trench of charnel ground. What our critical attention must do, when turned toward the battlefield of public images, is prepare us to recognize

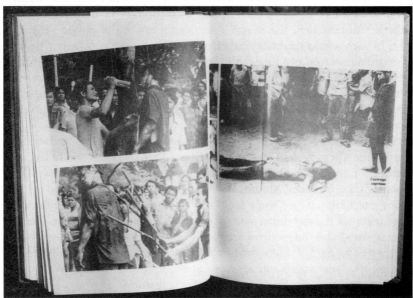

Figure 3. *October Album* (Student Federation of Thailand)

death magic as magic indeed, to share in the insight that every moment is a moment of mortal danger, which must include both the times in which history is patently revolting, and the times in which danger is suspended and order preserved in a public image.

BOUGHT TIME

In a letter from one former student from those times to students two decades past his own brush with the day known as "Bloody October" or "October 6," and four years past the massacre in May 1992, the historian Thongchai Winichakul writes:

> Thai people might think that Thai society is just like a village from the past, only larger, in which everyone knows each other well . . . respecting and loving community, and they believe that conflict is something abnormal and wrong. . . . In this belief, and in a history that sticks only to the unity of the people of the nation, the revolts of October 14, 1973, and May 1992, and the massacre of October 6, 1976, are things that are opposed to nature and to the history of the Thai people. And therefore the act of remembering hits this belief with a violence. . . .

> Thai society thinks that remembering October 6, 1976, is like pouring salt on an open wound that hasn't dried, and hopes to buy time for the wound to dry and the scab to drop off, to avoid any search and struggle for establishing justice and a means to address the conflict in Thai society. . . .

> Hundreds of lives went on that day, and society didn't value, in any way, their sacrifice.

> It's as if it never happened, or as if its only value was to teach people how to forget.

> Sometimes I feel that many of my friends are dead without eyes closed, and still wander around to witness the killing one more time in May 1992.

> If they are victorious, people who sacrifice themselves get honored as *virachon* ["martyrs" for the nation]. We send their spirits to heaven and can herald their honor. Defeat has the sacrificed pass away in silence, vacant and unthinkable. In the mornings of October 6, every year that has passed, there are so few people who know that there is [Buddhist] merit-making beside the student center of Thammasaat University every year. Even when the organizers invite monks and arrange everything, still there is hardly anyone. No wreaths for saying goodbye, with no words written in honor, for the place where they passed away. It's a good thing the remembrance for October 14 [1973] every year helps to uphold them along with it, somewhat inadequately. . . .

Our friends who sacrificed themselves on that day did not do it out of some official duty. They were not forced to face the bullets, nor were they hired to be the victims for inhumane torture. And it was no accident. They were fighting for ideals and they passed away with ideals, a brave dream to see that the lives of everyone would be happy ones. That was their spirit.

They offered their lives, one time, for the whole world and for the lives of all those who remain.[88]

This letter is addressed to students who were planning a twenty-year commemoration of the 1976 massacre. Against the consensus of Thai national unity and the state-as-village, which was precisely the ideology that was used at the time to identify Thai students as an enemy within, the unthinkable stands in violent relation to that which generated it. And it might be noted in passing that while the dead of the more or less successful revolts of 1973 and 1992 are locked in reincarnating wheels of exchange—that is, "The kids who were killed in Black May are the same ones come back from October 14, 1973"—no doubt because they can in some ways be rendered into a story of Thai democracy, the vanquished dead of Bloody October watch restlessly from the outside.

This outside, which none of the events of massacre manage to escape completely, and this gift of death, especially the unanswered spirit of the gift to the whole world, are the subjects of mediation for this narrative ethnography. This gift hangs not only over the Thai nation, and the avoidance of open wounds could fairly stand for the situation of the world today. In any case, the gift was for everyone. How does one realize this?

But there is no one who can fully reciprocate, least of all someone from the same country that built up the Thai military for these exercises in stability in the first place. What right is there here to even attempt it? An answer would only serve to buy time.

Anthropology, skirting the world, must leave such questions open, and wounding. There is no out: no way to avoid responsibility, no way to succeed in fulfilling it. This is the incomplete and unfinished business that can never be expelled, either from the clean new realm of the public or from the public sphere that is academic writing.

"BLOODY OCTOBER," 1976

Strangely, after the chaotic violence in what was to be called "Bloody October" was over, the police assembled themselves into a smart, symmetrical, and orderly marching formation and trotted off in two neat, straight lines while the right-wing crowds sent them off with cheers—which shows just how quickly the spectacles of both reason and terror can flip-flop back and forth from one to the other (which is the "magic of the State," as Michael Taussig explains).[89] A few days later, the new prime minister addressed the nation on television. Backed by large portraits of the king and queen, Thanin Kraivichian, former justice of the Supreme Court, delivered his moralistic spiel in the same manner as he had as an occasional guest on the TV show "Democracy Talks," where he had been flogging his right-wing view; it was the only forum in which most people would have had any acquaintance with their new prime minister. Thanin was a secret member of the executive council of Nawaphon, described above as the mystical anticommunist group with ties to the CIA, responsible for disseminating hate, whose most prominent member was the infamous monk Kitthivuddho.[90] As Charles Keyes has argued, the perpetrators of Bloody October were inspired not only by the invocation of nation-religion-king and the symbol of a royal temple under imagined siege by students, but also by the increasingly influential movement of right-wing Buddhism, at the time most prominently figured by Kitthivuddho.[91] Thanin was also connected with the royal family, and was a close advisor to the queen. The new military junta, formed from the remnants of Krit Srivara's clique, had their own ideas about leading the country, but Thanin was the surprise choice, possibly at the insistence of the monarchy. In his television address, Thanin propounded his fantasy of a clean and orderly Thailand, promising to clean up government corruption, uphold the monarchy and Buddhism, and keep the chaos of politics safely at bay until the Thai people, whom he spoke to as children in need of the paternal guiding slaps of the state, were ready.[92] It would take about twelve years for Thais to grow up and be ready for democracy, he said, and in the meantime he would see to it that Thailand had the right constitution and force of law to keep order and peace in the country.

Gatherings of over four people were outlawed. All talk of politics was banned in universities and public schools, including any mention of the word "democracy." Thousands of people were arrested for thought crimes. Libraries and bookstores were raided and great Nazi-style public book-burnings were held in public squares. Several newspapers were shut down, and the others were forced to cooperate with close supervision by the regime. Under a new law, anyone could be arrested and held without charges for six months. Being a "danger to society" was declared a crime, and in four months following October 6, up to eight thousand people were imprisoned for being regarded as such.[93] There were sporadic killings and a steady stream of disappearances.

General Kriengsak Chomanan, a leading figure in the junta with close ties to the U.S. gift, explained emphatically that there was no cause for worry: "We will not persecute anyone who is not guilty!"[94]

Immediately upon assuming the reigns of the state, Thanin instituted a draconian program to clean up the public space in Bangkok. A few days after the massacre, the city governor, under Thanin's orders, promulgated the "Cleanliness Act." Beggars were to be rounded up by the city administration and brought to special places set up by the Public Welfare Department. Street-cluttering vendors would be given an allotted, limited number of spots to conduct their business, and those who disobeyed would have their license revoked. Effective immediately, the entire populace was to conduct themselves in a clean and orderly fashion:

Littering outside shophouses will face a fine of 100 baht.

Bathing and washing on side-street water taps or in public places which attracts attention will face a fine of 200 baht.

Illegal putting up of posters in public places will face a fine of 500 baht.

Drawing or scribbling on roads or alls of public places will face a fine of 200 baht.

Hanging out clothes to dry, in a place which attracts attention is subject to a fine of 200 baht.

Kite flying or playing football on public streets is subject to a 200 baht fine.

Picking flowers is subject to a 200 baht fine.

Destroying public trees will be fined according to the damage caused to the trees.

Urinating, defecating, or loitering in a public place is subject to a 100 baht fine.[95]

Loitering, and that must include any suspicious gathering, is like defecation—how easily public weal and the dream-displaced traces of recent memory mix in the power aesthetics of cleanliness. No "scribbling" on walls, no putting up posters, no airing dirty linen: in this, the genealogical ancestor of the 1991 World Bank phantasmagoria, the "unclean" market of street vendors is to be contained, elsewhere; beggars are eyesores to be scoured out by class cleansing, while public space is to be cleansed of dissenting messages and memories.

The clean new world of public image space was from the start forged in violence—but from now on the prohibition on damaging public trees, apparently, would preclude the hanging of heavy objects from their branches.

Bloodless Power

THE MORAL ECONOMY OF THE THAI CROWD

A dark night, a Bangkok street, speckled
with headlights, plugged with cars wedged and jammed into
columns. But there is one car that outshines the rest.
Inside, a man at the wheel with a worried, furrowed brow.
And next to him, almost pressed up against and bulging out of
the TV screen, is his wife, pregnant and sighing because she is
about to deliver any minute. Gridlock snaps its metallic,
smoking jaws around this nativity scene, casting it with danger.
But the husband pulls out his Worldphone cellular telephone,
dials 911, and the word "emergency" lights up in
liquid crystal display. Instantly, a helicopter with a
red cross on its belly swoops overhead. The couple are lifted by
tether, and brought into the cabin: safe, air-conditioned, with
a view of Bangkok, the endless dotted tangle of headlights
below. The next moment they are smiling under the sanitary
lamps of a hospital room, cuddling a baby in milky white sheets.

Alone, and without even a hand to support it, the
heroic cell phone appears again, standing
upright next to the Worldphone logo.
TELEVISION COMMERCIAL

BIRTH

One of the first things that the government installed by the National Peace
Keeping Council did, after the February 1991 coup, was lower the steep
import tariff on cars. It was a bone thrown to the Bangkok monied class,
who were eager to get their own personal vehicles out on the streets and
who at first almost seemed to tolerate a military takeover rather than
remain under the corruption of political parties who had purchased state
power at an average rate of 200–300 baht per villager's vote.

On February 23, 1991, the army seized all mass-media installations.
The prime minister at the time, former general Chatichai Choonhavan,

was taken away at gunpoint. Eventually, the new junta appointed a squeaky-clean and well-respected businessman to the interim premiership, and promised a new constitution with free democratic elections within a year. And last but far from least, General Suchinda Kraprayoon, the coup-maker, made public oaths stating that he had "grasped power" only temporarily and only in order to clean up politics. He promised he had no designs on the premiership, that he was doing all this for the sake of the nation only, and that he would never stoop so low as to get involved in politics. It was all a quick rerailing to get back on track to the efficient future of a competitive nation in a new world order.

He vowed that he would never seek or accept the position of prime minister in the future. "I do not play politics," he promised, and this was echoed on air and in headlines everywhere.

After the swearing of that oath, an exchange of tobacco. Besides lowering the import tariff on cars, one of the other things that the military-installed government did was lift the ban on foreign cigarette companies. Marlboros passed above the counter instead of under it. The military-installed government let there be commodities, and it was good.

Astute businessmen and -women presented General Suchinda and the National Peace Keeping Council with gifts of wreaths and flowers of congratulation for their successful coup.

"I don't play politics," declared General Suchinda's glossy color face on the magazine covers, the words written over his forehead.

The "National Assembly," which NPKC had hand picked, began drafting the new constitution. In the military's new version of constitutional rule, the prime minister did not have to be an elected member of parliament. It meant that the next prime minister—theoretically speaking, of course—could be a general who didn't have to stand in an election.

Politicians began flocking to the new party established by the junta, Sammakhi Thamm ("unity-justice"), as it soon seemed clear that it would be the winner. It was not preelection polls that foretold this. Whatever certainty existed in Thai politics, at least at that juncture, was due to the entrenched gift-patronage system by which much of the voting is orchestrated (later, issue driven politics would eventually become a contender).

Each province has its local kingpins, who if not candidates themselves can often determine the winners in their region. Most prominent politicians are so because they secure the support of the other politicians who are indebted to them. They secure that loyalty by giving money to these lower-tier politicians' campaigns, to their pocketbooks, and for further distribution of obligation. These less prominent candidates and office holders keep up, in turn, their own local system of vassals. The patronage system is saturated at the local level, where canvassers, *hua khanaen*, are responsible for turning out the vote in each village, the gift money eventually trickling down to the voter. Most hua khanaen are like subcontractors. They are given a lump sum of money, for which they are expected to return an agreed-upon number of votes. It is then up to them to decide what portion of that fee they will keep for themselves and what portion they will give to voters in return for their vote. At the end of each election, the national murder rate soars. Many hua khanaen wind up miscalculating.

The winners in this system are those who come together out of common self-interest in getting control of central government, and they disband and rearrange themselves according to what seems at each moment to be the most propitious configuration. Once in power, leaders receive kick-backs from all sorts of interested parties, which become the return on their investment in vote buying. The patronage relationships formed by and through gifts, then, are at the same time also fields in which to sow returns on capital investment.

But in order to get started in the game one must first enter into those gift relationships. Thus, when the military-formed Sammakhi Thamm started to fill its coffers (it is believed through embezzling state funds and especially secret military budgets), it had no trouble recruiting members from the coterie of political kingpins. In fact, they garnered their strongest support from the very same politicians the junta had ousted with the February coup, and whose corruption was cited as the primary justification for the coup.

After a delay long past the day that had been promised by the military, past the World Bank meetings in October of that same year, and past the start of the next year, elections were finally conducted in March of 1992, and the promilitary parties won as expected. The leader of the military's Sammakhi Thamm party however, immediately resigned, ostensibly because the United States considered him a drug lord—which the military junta already knew was the case. Immediately, General Suchinda was proposed as the "only" person who could step up in this crisis and take over the country, this time as an unelected prime minister.

By executing what was called a "bloodless coup" in the public sphere, the clique of generals had secured control over the armed forces for themselves, control over the mass media, and control over the constitution. And now they had the prime minister's chair. "The only things we do not control," announced General Suchinda, "are the moon and the stars."

Many of the politicians who had been branded as unclean were appointed right back into their cabinet positions, and they all supported General Suchinda for prime minister.

There was still, of course, the matter of General Suchinda's public promise not to seek the premiership. Still claiming he had never acted for personal gain, he announced that he had to go back on his word. He must, he proclaimed, "sacrifice my honor for the sake of the nation."[1]

On national TV, General Suchinda announced his resignation from the military. He cried profusely while the cameras rolled. Later, he was sworn in as prime minister.

After that, his wife announced to reporters that she had had a prophetic dream in the night. She was floating and flying through the air, and passed over a massive mountain range—a dream that she interpreted for everyone as an omen of the future, meaning their reign would sail on into the next decade. A new era and new order of government was born.

With control over the armed forces, the TV stations, and the appointed Senate, and with the junta's own version of constitutional government with General Suchinda sitting in the prime minister's chair, it could hardly be argued that the prophetic vision of a floating Mrs. Suchinda was wrong.

However, I should mention that in Thai dream interpretation theory, the symbols ordinarily have inverse meanings. For instance, shit in dreams means wealth is coming your way. When someone dies in a dream that means you will see them well.

DEATH

On the day that General Suchinda was sworn in, Chalad Worachat vowed not to eat until the unelected prime minister resigned and returned democracy to the people. Without any more of a plan than this, he sat himself down on the sidewalk outside of Parliament House, where he had once held a seat for one term as a member of the Democratic Party. Some friends and sympathetic observers put up a tarp over his head so that the April sun—it was the hot season—would not beat harshly down on him. They put up some signs and slogans, and waiting with him thus began a modest vigil of conscience, outside the walls of the institution for which they had high hopes and aspirations but which for the time being had cleverly and effectively been usurped by the military.

I thought at the time that Chalad must be crazy (and after getting to know him later, my sense is that he is a bit eccentric). Almost everyone I knew shared this feeling. There was no point to dying like this. How could it possibly work?

General Suchinda obviously also found this hunger strike futile. After all that the general had gone through to become prime minister, he could hardly be expected to resign just because one man refused to eat. "Big Su," as he was called, let loose a great sneer of public derision, taking great pains to broadcast his flippant and cold rebuffs. He put Chalad down as "abnormal" and a suicidal maniac (though the army-controlled TV news reports that carried the attacks did not make any mention of what, exactly, Chalad Worachat was on a hunger strike for). Suchinda said that if Chalad wanted to kill himself he could go ahead and do it. "I'm not a dictator who is going to take away anyone's freedom of individual choice."[2]

A week after he started the fast, Chalad was sent a gift. A teak coffin was delivered by pickup truck to his protest site outside Parliament House. Curious supporters opened the coffin to see what might be inside, but it was empty. The contents within the gift were obviously to be the bodily remains of the receiver himself. The coffin arrived draped in a white sheet with a message printed on it saying, "This coffin is to support Chalad Worachat and I would be glad to sponsor your funeral rites for one night." At the bottom was printed the name of a member of parliament for the military's Sammakhi Thamm Party, the core of the Suchinda government.[3] It must have cost a pretty penny, and Chalad was happy to add the coffin to what was rapidly becoming a shrinelike funereal display area under the plastic tarp that had been set up over his head. Just like at a funeral, there was an altar of Buddha images, a photographic portrait of Chalad, for remembrance, and black wreaths and flowers arranged in a display around a not-yet corpse and his waiting coffin. Just like at a funeral, and now a quietly growing number of mourners came to pay their respects.

After Chalad wove the coffin into his protest display, the police took the coffin away, claiming that a coffin was not suitable for display in front of Parliament House.[4] But the supporters still trickled in, and having come to like the idea of having a coffin around, and thankful for the suggestion from the military's party, they acquired another coffin, in funereal white with gold-colored inleaf, to display beside the dwindling figure of Chalad.

DECAY

Several newspapers had a regular daily front-page feature on Chalad's fast to the death. *Matichon*, popular with educated young urbanites, was most faithful in this respect, printing a front page color photo every day of Chalad on hunger strike with a big countdown-to-death caption: Day 1, Day 2, Day 3 . . . along with an extensive textual update on his condition. Every day in the newspapers, there to be seen was Chalad's body steadily wilting away, while Suchinda refused to take seriously any of the criticisms that were beginning to poke at his image with increasing bellicosity, it seemed, as Chalad's condition deteriorated. The hunger striker began to look pained, weak. In subsequent days he seemed to be on the border of shock. To keep him going, volunteer nurses hooked him up with glucose and saline intravenously. Then he started appearing in the daily photographs lying with plastic tubes inserted into his limbs and veins, with plastic medical apparatuses piercing his body, and coiled, tubular symbols of suffering emanating out of it. There were always people in the background with grave, distressed faces.

With this continuous apparition of suffering visualized, this focus point of imminent death established, prodemocracy organizations stepped up their efforts to protest the unelected prime minister. The four opposition political parties, with cooperation from the Student Federation of Thailand and the Movement for Popular Democracy (an alliance of academics), held their first rally on April 25, which for Chalad was Day 17. An electrified crowd in the tens of thousands assembled at the monument of King Rama V riding a horse, on the plaza in front of Parliament House. The rally leaders, mostly politicians, railed against General Suchinda's illegitimate rise to power. The prodemocracy organizations proclaimed their intent to fight for freedom, and began extolling to the crowds the virtues, and powers, of nonviolent protest, *ahimsa*, in attaining their goal. The goal was General Suchinda's immediate resignation.

Skeptical, I asked an old hand in Thai street politics if he really thought that anything would come of this protest, and he assured me that it would for sure, that this is how it always starts, with small rallies one after the other that get bigger and bigger. This was how October 14, 1973, started, he promised. Probably because Thailand, unlike most other countries, superficially resembles my native United States in the great degree to which consumer fascinations appear to predominate over political consciousness, I did not believe that October 14 could possibly return. At the time, many Thais—including the junta, apparently—shared the opinion that people would rather just shop. But many others, especially those with some experience in these matters, were well aware of how inspired and idealistic the so-called "pragmatic" and "sheeplike" people of the country can be.

The rally ended with all standing to sing the national anthem and an anthem to the monarchy. The rally organizers called for a new and greater rally on the grounds of Sanam Luang, the grass commons, and former marketplace and battlefield, for May 4.

As the countdown-to-death numbers kept accumulating, Chalad's body would appear in greater and greater states of visual suffering. When it reached "23," his body could be seen curled half-fetally, as he was being rolled onto a stretcher with a shiny aluminum frame. He was encircled by a womb of nurturing supporters, bent over and around him and gently lowering his unconscious body onto the wheeled device. He looked both as helpless as a newborn baby and as old and beloved as an elder about to die. The feature news stories were all about how Chalad had gone into shock, and had to be whisked away to the hospital. On Day 24 Chalad was in the hospital, on the brink of death.

UNIVERSAL BEAUTY

What with the corruption, the coup, the unrest, and the protesters at Parliament House, what with the tourism industry's steady plunge since the very beginnings of all this, the stock market's nosedive since Chalad stopped eating, the capitalist elite's public warnings about wary foreign investors, reinforced by that of the hoteliers who experienced a sharp slowdown in bookings—as though all that were not enough, the local organizers and promoters for nothing less than the 1992 Miss Universe beauty pageant were adrift amid the whirlpool upon which the national image had been set afloat. This was surely bad timing. During the previous elected administration, Thailand had scored for itself both the World Bank meetings and Miss Universe. But then there was the coup d'état, and then this hunger strike, and now demonstrations. The beauty pageant was supposed to be, once again, an important showcase of the national image, for the world. The promoters were divided as to what should be done. In the mass-circulation dailies, the chairman of the committee for hosting the pageant was on the front page actually advocating cancellation or at least postponement of the affair, in order to protect the national image, which promised to suffer a disaster at the hands of a herd of international press present in the country for the big to-do. The world's eye could be focused on Thailand at precisely the same time that a street protest might be amassing and violent measures taken in response (after all, this sort of response had happened before). How would they ever live that down? The estimates were that a worldwide TV audience of several hundred million people, in sixty countries, would watch the show.[5]

But most of the others involved in managing the affair came out with the opposite view, which eventually won out. The show must go on, went their response in the public controversy. Imagine the embarrassment to the national image, not to mention the international lawsuits, if Thailand could not muster enough peace and quiet to host an innocent beauty pageant. To a country that has loved beauty pageants right from the first time the cultural form had been diffused into its kingdom, there was some measure of bated breath over the production of Miss Universe. As it turned out, the promoters took their chances on going ahead. They restricted individual interviews with the contestants so that they would neither be asked nor answer political questions. Or, as it was put in the publicly offered reasoning, the national representatives would be kept in the dark about the political developments so as not to compound "the pressure that they are already under as contestants."[6]

Chalad's body had been folding under the fast, but in the hospital it stabilized. The doctors announced that Chalad's heart and brain were in serious danger, and his stomach lining had developed threatening lesions. He had come to, after being put on a respirator and given a glucose and saline solution intravenously. The doctors, citing their ethical duty as overriding political concerns, could not condone his return to the hunger strike.[7] But Chalad had mumbled a vow to return.

The "Day 24" photos on the front page of some newspapers had the grim image of a corpselike Chalad in ICU, out flat on a sterile aluminum bed, his open mouth with a transparent plastic accordionlike hose thrust into it, his limbs pierced by intravenous tubes, and the whole visual scene ensconced in a life-preserving, death-evoking web of medical technology.[8]

Meanwhile Chalad's young daughter, a university student, went on hunger strike in his stead, and her words of devotion to her father were disseminated in newsprint. As a gathering was called for on Sanam Luang for May 4, to demand that Suchinda resign and Chalad live on, the face of the young woman, a picture-perfect image of a good devoted Thai daughter, shared front pages with the sight of her poor father lying on the edge of death and with snapshots of Miss Ecuador, who in preliminaries had won Miss Photogenic, and Miss Paraguay, who had won Miss Best Costume with her peacocklike dress.

CONSPICUOUS RENUNCIATION

The second protest rally on May 4 was held on the vast field of Sanam Luang. It was, as expected, bigger than any other since Suchinda's coup. While crowds filed in at dusk, speakers from the Student Federation of Thailand, activist groups, and some politicians kept up a steady harangue over the speaker system they had set up. When enough people were assembled, they read out a soulful letter from Chalad Worachat's daughter, which told how much it hurt to see her father dying. Then each of the four opposition parties spoke. The party leaders and members, dressed in funereal black to mourn the death of democracy, went on stage to deliver speeches against Suchinda. Chamlong Sri-Muang—a famous ascetic and founder and leader of the Palang Dharma Party, "Force of Dharma"—had asked the others that he be the last one to speak. He had something extremely important to announce, though he would not tell anyone what it was.

It was at that point that Chalad Worachat gained a powerful ally. Chamlong's story is a convoluted history in itself. Child of a civil servant, Chamlong Sri-Muang entered the military academy through achieving high marks on the standardized entrance examination. He eventually became a key officer in the "Young Turks" of Class Seven, a young officer clique of ambitious and idealistic reformers, and the bitter rivals of Suchinda's Class Five. Back in Bloody October of 1976, the "Young Turks" were involved in antistudent organizing and were firmly behind the tyrannical order of things that followed the massacre, though soon after they were pushed aside by Suchinda's Class Five. Class Five and Class Seven were, ever after, bitter rivals.

After the worst of the post-October tyranny had passed, Chamlong served in the government of General Prem in the 1980s, but he became increasingly disaffected by military and bureaucratic politics, and took to studying Buddha-Dhamma instead, first through studying the work of the great reformer Buddhadasa Bhikkhu, and later by involvement in a small, odd, but growing reform movement burgeoning around the charismatic monk Phra Photirak and his Santi Asoke ("Peaceful Abode") organization.

The eighties were strange days. "Democracy Thai style" was the ideological order of the day, which meant that the Thai version of democracy, according to the generals in power, meant centralized control over bureaucracy and public media. Nevertheless, as the massacre of Bloody October 1976 drifted into the distance, a nonexecutive public culture was creeping, bit by bit, back into bloom. The untiring efforts of veteran politicians and activists were eroding, ever so slightly, ever so slowly, the established order of things that had kept the military in powerful influence and deeply involved both in government and lucrative state enterprises. At the same time, these were the boom years of national development, market expansion, foreign investment, and tourism. Although the government kept strict control over TV, using it as a propaganda instrument of their policy (as it had always been used), the newspaper industry was breaking away. The papers were floating on the intense fiscal liquidity of the boom economy: the print news corporations were making big profits for their investors, while the journalists themselves apparently began to feel confident again. They started to call for the lift of unchecked censorship, which the military had imposed since Bloody October. It was a point of both principle and profit, for the more TV was controlled, the more fiscal interest there was in having an alternative to offer, and a free press is a spicier press. In 1988, under the administration of the soon-to-be-deposed Prime Minister Chatichai, they succeeded in having a repeal of the censorship laws that had been put in place during the turbulence of the seventies.

As it turned out, the first test exercise of their newfound freedom centered precisely on news surrounding the monk Phra Photirak and the Santi Asoke movement in which Major-General Chamlong Sri-Muang had become involved. The Santi Asoke reform movement had grown by preaching against the traditional Buddhist order, and its members had garnered a good deal of attention through their conspicuous differences with monks of other temples, including the fact that they ate no meat and practiced no traditional "superstitions." This led to considerable conflict with the established Buddhist hierarchy. Although Thai Buddhism is a diverse field of practices and organizations, of religious and even political ideologies, the entirety is encompassed in a state-mandated bureaucracy that tightly integrates the periphery with the center, the common monk with the ecclesiastical hierarchy, at the apex of which stands the supreme patriarch and Sangha Supreme Council. The 1980s saw a proliferation of subnational Buddhist temple organizations grow in autonomy, and the Santi Asoke movement soon came to embody everything that was threatening and dangerous about these heterogenous movements as they sought, through increasingly pervasive and articulated national media and transportation channels, broad reach and autonomous alternative national followings. But the conflict between the Sangha Supreme Council and Santi Asoke only reached a public crisis point when, not coincidentally, Chamlong and Santi Asoke started a new political party in Bangkok, which ran on a platform of contesting elections without buying votes. Eventually, Phra Photirak was likened to the vegetarian turncoat from the Buddha's time, Devadhatta. When Santi Asoke and Chamlong Sri-Muang began to work together on forming the new party, the ecclesiastical authority decided to move against Phra Photirak. They enlisted aid from the Chatichai Choonhavan government, which, given the threat of this new and popular anticorruption party, was only too happy to oblige. Phra Photirak was arrested and defrocked for "impersonating a cleric."

The arrest and conflict was far and away the number one news story in the new journalism of the late eighties. The government pressed the newspapers to stop sympathizing with the radical monk. The story disappeared from TV broadcast bands, but newspapers did not appreciably give in, and the new free press established itself over the Santi Asoke controversy. It was the first test case of the public sphere, and it was a success.

The second test was the Suchinda coup of February 1991, a test in which the journalists immediately failed. Afraid of a crackdown, for the most part the papers fell instantly in line with the Suchinda junta. At the time that the NPKC junta took over, all the gains so slowly made since Bloody October seemed dashed away in a single moment.

But in fact, the third and by far the most decisive test case was yet to come: the hunger strike and protest against the unelected prime minister, General Suchinda. The night of May 4, 1992, was the point at which the struggle for free democratic expression in Thailand took a decisive turn, precisely at the moment when the Santi Asoke ascetic, Chamlong Sri-Muang, took the stage.

Major-General Chamlong endorsed the Buddhist eight precepts, became vegetarian, celibate, ate one meal a day, and wore the denim farmer's garb like other Santi Asoke lay ascetics. And just like Phra Photirak and the Santi Asoke movement, he made a great public spectacle of his extra asceticism. He rode this conspicuous renunciation into the hearts of the Bangkok populace. He was a Buddhist ascetic politician for the people, who were fed up with corruption, dirty money, and cynical politicking. "Maha Chamlong," they called him (a religious title meaning "great," like "Mahatma"). He formed a new political party, using Santi Asoke followers as its workforce. When, in the slow trudge toward democracy, elections for Bangkok governor were held for the first time in history, Chamlong entered the race, campaigning with his people on the streets. Bangkok was said to be in the throes of "Chamlong fever." He was called "Mr. Clean," and he walked into the governor's seat easily the first time; the second time (after threatening he would resign from politics if he lost), he won by a huge landslide, garnering 700,000 votes. After Suchinda abrogated the constitution and set up new elections, Maha Chamlong resigned the governorship to contest at the national level. The Bangkok populace routed all other parties and Chamlong and his Palang Dharma candidates took 31 of 33 Bangkok seats, seen widely as the city's summary rebuke of the NPKC junta.

But his meteoric rise to celebrity had been spotted for a time by a past that came back to haunt him. People had identified him as involved in the premassacre rabble rousing outside of Thammasaat University in Bloody October. He denied being involved in organizing the right-wing crowds, and claimed only to have been a misinformed witness in the crowd. After several intense and highly publicized meetings with student leaders, they let him off the hook, for what they would later report were pragmatic political considerations. Mr. Clean was severed—at least in public reckoning, or at least in some measure—from the spirits of those who had died violent deaths, and by the night of May 4 was about to soar toward his greatest height of prominence.

Till Death Do Us Part

I joined the large crowds that were beginning to assemble around Chalad Worachat's fast. Now that the hunger striker had taken a turn for the worse, and seemed close to death, Chamlong was going to seize the moment. On the night of the May 4 protest, and as he had asked, he took the stage as the last speaker, to make the mysterious announcement he would not divulge to anyone. Dressed in funereal black, he read out a letter, which he said was his "final letter." He bid the people farewell. He was going to fast until Suchinda resigned, or he himself was dead. And it wasn't going to be a fast like Chalad Worachat's. No, this was going to be an "ultra-strict fast" (*yang kreng-krat*), an ascetic fast to match his ultra-strict observance of Buddhist precepts and practices: none of those intravenous injections, no medical checkups, no taking him to the hospital. He informed the crowd that medical authorities had it that such a strict, water-only fast would permit him to live for no more than seven days. That's right, he would be dead in seven days—unless enough people turned out to demand that Suchinda resign (those in the audience who could muster some hope, in the midst of the shock, pointed out the landslide 700,000 votes he got in the last gubernatorial election). He called for continued protest. For him, it would be a protest to the finish, till death do us part. He was going on to Parliament House now, where he would remain, in silence, to the end. He would do no more speaking now, to preserve his strength. These were to be his last words.[9] It was almost as though he was already removed from their midst.

Everyone around me in that crowd was stunned. They loved Chamlong. A few people were crying, and many others were groaning in disbelief as he read his farewell letter. I had, at least, become accustomed to and fond of seeing him on the cutting edge of national politics, and like most others there was sad to see him have to die. He had seemed to be the last hope, and now he was gambling it all away. Few people really believed it was possible that Suchinda would resign. Why would he? The demonstration came to an official close and petered out with Chamlong's last words, and everyone turned to each other in rapt conversation. Many student leaders, experienced in demonstration politics, were taken sharply aback by the decision. "Now is not the right time," they were saying. "It is summer recess. If he would wait until the term starts, we could turn out one million students, no problem." But the prodemocracy movement, from this moment on, was no longer in the students' hands.

Chamlong's political party, his party's allies, and apparently even his wife Sirilak, a fellow ascetic celibate, were also all taken by surprise. Some privately called it a dictatorial move. This hunger strike had pitched the conflict into a whole new key. He had wagered a political gamble with death, on behalf of the whole country, but entirely on his own. The next morning, the stock exchange of Thailand plummeted, and small-time investors lost their shirts even before Chamlong's stomach started to rumble. The next morning, Chalad Worachat discharged himself from the hospital, resumed his hunger strike, and joined Chamlong outside parliament to await the end. He dropped to his knees, pressed his palms together, and gave Maha Chamlong a great big *wai* (kowtow) of public respect and veneration, perhaps also with a personal sigh of relief.

THE MOVEABLE FEAST

The protest was jump-started to an entirely different velocity. By the morning of May 6, tens of thousands of people streamed outside Parliament House to pay their respects to the strict Buddhist ascetic and dying hero. Thirty others joined in the hunger strike, but most could not endure

Figure 4. "Maha" Chamlong in the initial stages of hunger

for many days. One Democrat member of parliament went on hunger strike but gave up after he went into shock.

Chamlong, back in his denim farmer's garb, was sitting cross-legged against the stone wall of the park zoo, which borders on Parliament House (see figure 4). A coterie of thirty to forty people sat around to guard him, while thousands of people passed by to get a look at him. He had a necklace of prayer beads in his lap, and with eyes closed he slowly passed the beads through his fingers one by one. Sometimes he would look up, and assess with cold eyes the amount of the turnout. He was gambling his life against a payoff of supporters. He looked neither pleased nor displeased, but very grave. Sometimes he would jot instructions down on a notepad. His characteristic winning smile was gone as he wrestled with the first few days of fasting, which are the most trying. As Chalad Worachat has explained to me, once you punch through the initial hunger, weakness, and revolt of the body, it gets easier and one almost sails through it. At Maha Chamlong's feet was a sign asking that he be "granted permission not to speak." Up on the wall, fanned around his figure, were more signs:

"I'll fast till Suchinda resigns or I die."

"Although I might collapse . . . you must have the strength to watch me collapse. Don't let anyone give me glucose or send me to the hospital."

"We can pay to preserve our organs, and sacrifice body parts to save our lives. So we'll sacrifice our lives to uphold the right principles."

"Don't cry for me now. If you must cry, cry before you come here."[10]

May is a hot time to be fasting. Office workers accustomed to air conditioning were filing through on their lunch hour. It was humid and upwards of 42°C (108°F) on the thermometer, and hotter on the city pavement and in a dense crowd of bodies. They were sweating in shiny shoes, dress slacks, pleated skirts, collar-buttoned pressed shirts and neckties—and black funereal headbands with white lettering, "Suchinda get out!" Protest workers were hard at work to make it possible for such people to endure. Santi Asoke adherents were also there in force, cooking and handing out vegetarian food from their own foodstores, laying out mats, and draping over large swathes of the crowd black plastic tarps on bamboo poles to filter out some of the hot sun. They were an all-purpose, celibate workforce that quietly provided minor comforts for the less practiced and newly ascetic masses that were weathering long vigils, sitting on the hot cement. But Santi Asoke ascetics would have failed in their work were it not for an army of streetside vendors who rolled their wheeled carts onto the scene, selling noodles, refreshments, fried meat and vegetables, and desserts.

The protest site became a marketplace (see figure 5). Along with the army of pushcart vendors, spur-of-the-moment entrepreneurs emerged, carrying their wares through the crowd by hand. Many had invested in selling newspapers, a hot item read voraciously and then folded into a hat to keep off the sun (there were volunteers on hand to teach paper hat folding). Other entrepreneurs toted buckets of Coke and Pepsi bottles or cold compresses soaked in ice water. The paper towelettes were three baht, the cloth ones were five baht. Mixed with the sound of the protest stage was an orchestra of hawking calls to get your this, get your that, get your cigarettes and your breathmints and your cold cloths to keep you fresh and cool.

The demonstration was a market, and the protest stage was the mass media. Students, politicians, public celebrities, and articulate members of the public gave speeches, alternating with performances by musicians, including the rock star Aed Carabao, who played his banned tunes about democracy and "Big Su," a satire of the general's endeavor. Forty-something-year-old semiprofessional musicians played in breaks between speakers, and more often than not drew on the songs of their own political youth, protest songs from the seventies.[11] Tears came to the eyes as the crowd quietly sang along, nodding to the memory. Other times the crowd sang out loud, and vengefully, when they were led in singing against the Suchinda regime the same killing songs once meant to target them by the

Figure 5. Moveable feast

propaganda engineers of Bloody October: "Scum of the earth, scum of the earth, people like this are scum of the earth!"

Nga Caravan was on the protest stage once again; he had been the biggest "Art for Life" singer of the seventies and a leading inspiration of the protests against military rule in those days. After Bloody October, he had escaped to the jungle with the students, until amnesty was granted. In those days his lyrics were about underprivileged people, but his songs for the nineties were educational ballads about democratic rights.[12]

Aed Carabao, who was too young to have been involved in the seventies protests but was greatly inspired by Nga Caravan, had taken the originally Marxist-inspired Art for Life movement to contemporary heights of commercial success. He shone with the bright light of stardom, while still carrying something of a flickering torch of political conscience onto the stage along with him. His last album, containing songs critical of Suchinda and the NPKC, was banned from the radio. If you wanted to hear it played in public you had to come to this live performance.

Then someone who was the last personage you would imagine to be banned from the airwaves miraculously materialized, in the flesh, on the protest stage: Arisaman, teenybopper heart throb from whose precious lips were rung those songs of love and loss that continue to echo in your mind long after you have left the department store floor. To the immense

103

delight of everyone, he set protest lyrics to the melodies they all knew so well, harnessing his biggest hits, *Jai Mai Daan Phor, Thad Thai, Mai Jam*, and so on. He was never on stage for very long but he was always coming back for more, like a commercial break. The tunes were catchy, with snappy little melodies that I can still hear wobbling around in my mind. The words were simple, like "Suchinda, Suchinda, get out, get out." And once he got involved in the prodemocracy demonstration, he stuck to it also like a jingle in your ear. RS Promotion, his record label, was far from pleased with this development.[13] But people loved it, and those that went home late at night, which was a majority of the crowd, told all their friends and relatives about how Aed Carabao and Arisaman were there and sang songs and how they would be there tomorrow, too.

The military had all music by performers who appeared at the rallies banned from radio and TV. This too was exciting news. The sweet trolling croon of Arisaman's current megahit, about someone his heart just could not resist, suddenly vanished from the airwaves with an abrupt silence that loudly called attention to itself.

The crowd size was reaching toward a hundred thousand in the peak hours of lunchtime and evening. Casually dressed military observers with camcorders reported all that was going on back to central command. Air Marshal Kaset Rojanin, supreme commander of the armed forces, senior junta member, and a thinly disguised force behind the military's Sammakhi Thamm Party, began to threaten violent measures to disperse the crowd. In the afternoon he had a "state of warning" announced over the TV, and flew a propeller airplane over the protest site with a big microphone to boom the threat over their heads, to which the crowd responded in a raucous "ho! ho!" booing. Then it dropped leaflets, which were written versions of the warnings, but the wind blew them all away and they landed in the zoo and on the lawn of the king's palace, which drew enormous guffaws from the people.

Student Federation of Thailand leaders, however, began announcing instructions about how to prevent a stampede in case they were attacked, and how to protect themselves from tear gassing by wearing a plastic bag on the scalp, using cloths over the nose, mouth, and eyes, and taking only shallow breaths. This talk quieted people down a little. In the hush, the hawking vendors with buckets of cold towelettes could be heard more clearly now, as they milled through the crowd, "Cold towelette, great for a gas mask, get your gas mask here five baht!"

That night Chamlong decided that the narrow space they had occupied outside Parliament House made it difficult for so many people to escape should they be attacked, so he decided to pick up stakes and head for Sanam Luang, an expansive commons with 360 degrees of escape routes.

By now people were giddy with excitement and righteousness after listening to days of protest speeches. As they flooded the streets on the way to Sanam Luang, they sang songs or chanted insults of General Suchinda. Casually dressed military men brought their video recordings of it all back to army command.

Somehow, by passing through night streets that were eased of the rush-hour congestion, the protestors actually managed to gain in numbers. People walked off of city buses to join in. Cars honked their horns and flashed their lights in sympathy, and the two-kilometer-long trail of bodies made a defiant counterstatement to the TV blackout of the whole protest, a blackout that began from Chalad's fast, to Chamlong's fast, to this throng. For a time, they gathered the largest crowd against military rule since the massacre of October 14.

But once they wound into Sanam Luang, and it started to get late, many did not dare to stick with it for the whole night. After all, that day the generals had openly threatened violence for the first time.

Those who stayed on had to keep the vigil on their own, and somehow make it through just one more critical, long night and into daybreak, when the big crowds would be back again. The dark air was thick with rumors of an army crackdown planned for the middle of the night. They kept someone on stage all night. Many students stayed up. I couldn't. After all that time on the hot pavement, Sanam Luang's dried-out grass was like a soft and inviting feather mattress. The distant bright flashes of buses, taxis, and three-wheeled tuk-tuks were circling the field like vultures. The ground was still hot, but a cool breeze wafted gently close to it. People were afraid, a little. We were right on the killing fields of Bloody October. And in the middle of the night the group was at its thinnest and most exhausted point ever. If they are going to kill, it was thought, they would do it now. There were only the diehard protestors left now, mostly young students. The middle-class and urban professionals thinned out late at night, leaving the same sort of crowd whose corpses, once not long ago, were slashed open, burned, and hung from these very trees and mutilated like piñatas.

The rumors of a crackdown seemed to coalesce somewhere, out there, into a dark, seething and intangible circumambience just beyond the range of vision. Art for Life musicians were on stage late through the night, and in the starless darkness played grim songs from the seventies— acoustic, funereal laments of heroism and suffering. The singers raised the memory of the dead, and dedicated the music and the moment to those who were once slain here at the hands of a hideous power. Nightmare lullabies were sinking me deep into the void between sleep and wakeful fear, sinking in circling lights, encircling night, in the secret dark where murder can be committed and no one will ever see it except in tales.

Suddenly, I would startle up out of sleep and whirl my head around to see nothing but the usual vulture lights circling the field, one of which had probably honked a horn for no particular reason.

❖

The predawn light diffused from behind the uncertain distance and thinned the night. But the hope of a new morning is like a magician's distraction, a ruse of the truth that it has always been right before dawn that they have chosen the first strike. Yet this time, at least, dawn passed. Soon enough the almost welcome sun was making the tops of our heads unbearably hot again.

That day was way too hot for a big crowd in an open field, but a steady influx of thousands still came by to pay brief respects. Maha Chamlong was weakening now, and the tent canopy under which he lay seemed like a shrine. Devotees sat around him as he lay out flat on a table, wearing only a blue denim sarong. Still enigmatically silent, he was a bit closer now to death. Huge blocks of ice were placed on the ground around him in the hope that they would cool the air. Journalists and protesters filed by reverently.

But by evening the crowd was back to full strength, and more. Now, with over a hundred thousand demonstrators, the political leaders were ready to move through the streets again. Student leaders disagreed, feeling it was too dangerous. But the politicians won out, and the crowds flooded out onto Ratchadamnern Avenue. It is believed, based on an order placed for a hundred thousand candles at the time, that Chamlong's intended destination was the king's palace, where the people would hold vigil and beg for intercession as on October 14.

As they overran the Democracy Monument on the way, there was a thrill of mobile confidence in the air. But just a few hundred meters after they passed Democracy Monument, the police, in riot gear, with barbed wire and with fire engines as water canons, formed a cordon preventing them from getting through. A backup of bodies was swelling against the cordon at the cutoff point, the Paan Fa Bridge, exactly the same site on which so many had died in the student-led revolt of 1973. There was uncertainty about what to do next. Some of the Student Federation leadership were largely still back at Sanam Luang. They had not agreed with Chamlong's decision to move out. It seemed safer on the field. The students wanted a long and protracted battle for democracy, which might last through several years of Suchinda's rule. But Chamlong saw this moment as the window of opportunity into which to launch their strike.

A weak and delirious Chalad Worachat, standing atop the cab of a pickup truck, arrived at the Paan Fa Bridge. He was waving floppy hands for the people to move forward, weakly yelping "Charge, charge." But some Student Federation and Palang Dharma leaders got him to settle down before a clash started. A white and quiet van arrived, the van that carried the sacred cargo of Maha Chamlong. Then politely worded threats were issued to the police over loudspeakers, announcing that they were facing two hundred thousand people and that they had better get out of the way (it was, at least, one hundred thousand). But the police did not move. The protest organizers let the pop singer Arisaman get on the loudspeaker, but just as quickly Palang Dharma leaders had to drag him down again, when he started yelling, "Stupid police idiots get out of the way, I have a bachelor's degree!" Eventually protest leaders had a summit with the chief police officer, and the officer informed them of what the military high command might have in store for them if they tried to force their way through.

After this point, Chamlong went back on his vow of silence. By the time the protest had picked up stakes from Parliament House, moved to Sanam Luang, and then moved again from there onto Ratchadamnern Avenue, he felt compelled, he later explained, to begin issuing instructions over loudspeakers to help control the demonstrators. He had the demonstration step back from the cordon of police blocking the way. They called the cordon the "Berlin Wall." That first night at the Berlin Wall, Palang Dharma members were on stage beginning to put forward the idea that Chamlong might also give up on his hunger strike, asking the people if they wanted Chamlong to call off the strike or wanted him to go on to die, telling them they had to cheer loudly for him to get the message through the walls of his little white van. Finally, in the morning, Chamlong himself was on stage and asked an early morning crowd of a few thousand for a vote, which as expected was unanimous against his dying. And that is how he would justify it—as decided by the people. He explained later, to hounding reporters, that the situation had totally changed, and that "there is no hunger striker anywhere in the world who could continue his fast while being forced to walk, run, and climb up on top of a van at the same time."[14]

Thinking that the worst was over, the Suchinda government gleefully announced the good news on TV and radio. They aired some messages commending Chamlong for backing down on his promise to fast to death, thus "preserving peace and unity in the nation," yet also broadcast messages ridiculing him for his spineless duplicity.

And after it was all over, months later, Chamlong further justified going back on the vow to exchange his life for democracy by citing the brief handwritten note that was sent to him from the revered monk Buddhadasa Bhikkhu in the southern province of Surathani. Chamlong may have used the note as a rationale after the fact, but I also suspect, knowing the care and attention one gives to the words of a teacher, that the terse words from the great monk may have snapped his will like a twig, days before he announced the decision:

> Mr. Chamlong,
> If you still have good mindful-awareness left, I ask you that you please do not do anything on the order of exchanging gold for dust. And you know perfectly well what is gold and what is dust.
>
> Buddhadasa Bhikkhu[15]

The organizers decided to settle down indefinitely to a face-off right there at the Democracy Monument, behind the police wall. They set up stage on the monument, and blocked off the roads around it in all four directions. With each night at the Democracy Monument, the crowds swelled. The stage had spotlights, music, famous politicians, and national figures. People sat on mats and newspapers in the relatively cool night air, and there was room for anyone to spend the night if need be. It was the place to be in Bangkok. Ratchadamnern Avenue had become a stadium. And you could not see it for yourself unless you went there in person, because TV was censored.

The attendance for the live political performance was breathtaking, and the audience itself its greatest attraction. The protest promoters improvised an auditory self-representation of the crowd. Dividing the crowd in thirds, they had each section pound their plastic water bottles (purchased from the protest market) on the pavement. The fantastic roar, which you could hear so clearly when your area was quiet, was only a third of the truth.[16] That cascading sound you just heard, those footsteps greater than a thousand giants, the people were informed, was *palang prachachon*, people power. People first sighed wide-eyed in amazement at the oceanic sound, and then cheered wildly for the greater self within which they had been living but whose proportions they had never quite realized.

Those were good days. I regret that I can only describe them in rose-colored language. It seems that in times like this the best side of people comes out. Within the temporary community of the protest, people were incredibly nice to each other. They wanted justice, morality, and truth to prevail. They were willing to sacrifice and endure together so that greed and avarice would be defeated. They sat peaceably for hours and hours listening to talk of right and wrong, justice and injustice, and received hour after hour of education into social values and the noble methods to achieve a better society through nonviolent struggle. It was very much like listening to a sermon in a temple. The stage was like an altar, and the audience was like the laity, the way they sat politely on the ground, enduring the same painful aching, cramps, and sleeping limbs that one endures through a long sermon. Only this was bigger, much bigger, than any temple—any temple so far.

Protest leaders announced on stage that the street vendors had started price gouging, such as charging ten baht instead of eight baht for a bottle of Pepsi. The violation of moral economy quickly and obediently ceased after that censure. Prices dropped.

The audience was given the examples of Chamlong and Chalad, who were willing to suffer and endure, and ultimately sacrifice their lives. In a huge banner over the stage, in Thai for the audience and in English for the large core of journalists already in the country for the Miss Universe beauty pageant, were the words *ahimsa* and "nonviolence." Any picture that included the center stage would have to circulate the word "nonviolence," send it into outer space and refract it in a kaleidoscope over the surface of earth. . . .

IN THE EYE OF THE BEHOLDER

In matters of more universal import, Miss Thailand didn't get as far as the first cut, and all that Thailand had to show for its entry in Miss Universe was runner-up for Miss Best Costume. As it turned out, the beauty pageant experienced no scandalous disruption of its global proceedings by local violence. The Miss Universe local promoters, the beleaguered Suchinda government, and the elite business community could relax, at least for a moment. It was another public image coup d'état, a gamble that paid off. The Miss Universe pageant had actually served as a protective umbrella. The military did not kill anyone while it was on. And although the international media were certainly following the political uncertainties, at least the national image had this counteracting image production, which could partially offset and repair some of the damage. Dick Clark hosted. Miss Universe cried. And although she and other contestants were later peppered with reporters' questions about the Thai political situation, all the national representatives declined comment, on the grounds of their ignorance of politics (except Miss Philippines, who said street protests were more volatile in her country and nothing disastrous ever came of it). A Suchinda cabinet minister declared the pageant a great success for the country, and that it had refurbished the national image. Given the coeval political unrest, he expounded, the country was "lucky to have had them occur at the same time." Furthermore, he could now affirm that the government could go full steam ahead with the "clear Thai image" worldwide publicity campaign, which was to repair further the national image, a campaign planned a year earlier during the military-installed Anand administration.[17]

Locally things were not going so well. Prime Minister Suchinda's body-guards beat up reporters in front of their cameras, for pressing in on him too vigorously. A TV personality and executive editor of the English-language paper *The Nation* had his car vandalized. And the Thai TV audience was complaining. It had become accustomed to the increasing openness in the media, especially in the run-up to the election, in which politicians were subjected to frank and disturbing questions about their pasts by a talk-show host and by each other. But now that Suchinda had taken the reins, heavy blackouts on speech were again in effect. The opposition protests were the top stories in the newspapers, but were not to be seen on TV. Army chief (and General Suchinda's brother-in-law) General Issarapong Noonpakdi had several newspapers banned from army installations because they had printed references to him as "shorty."

MOB RULE

The greatest struggle over public images was mob struggle. The biggest battle for the protesters was to resist the image that the Suchinda regime had the government-controlled TV paint: a picture of the protesters as rabble-rousing, national image-tarnishing, riffraff malcontents trying to overthrow Buddhism and the monarchy and install a Soviet system. Picking up on what was at first merely the Thai newspapers' typical play with language, the government began wielding the fashionable word entering the Thai vocabulary, *maub*, from the English "mob." The legitimate prime minister was not going to bow to "mob rule."[18] The constitutional ground to contest his leadership was within parliamentary procedure and not outside of it (despite the way he had himself come to power), and certainly democracy was not to be conducted in the streets, where people were being paid and deceived into joining a "mob" against him.

The construction of the identity of this crowd was a major site of the contest. For one thing, as is usual in such battles, a debate was waged over the actual numbers in attendance at the live events (as it was waged over the actual numbers of corpses later). The Interior Ministry was on the airwaves denouncing the newspapers' inflation of the attendance statistics, while quietly planning measures that would enable the government to censor or otherwise intimidate journalists without seeming repressive to the public. Suchinda would appear on TV defiantly every other night, claiming that the demonstration represented a fringe minority of the Thai populace of sixty million, repeating that he wasn't going to bow to "mob rule."[19] Yet he promised that no harm would come to the demonstrators at the hands of the military or his government, "Soldiers and police are also sons of the Thai people and will never use their weapons against them."[20]

Periodically throughout the day and evening, the TV channels would interrupt regular programming and air compulsory announcements denouncing the protest, which were always preceded by a few minutes of a Muzak renditon of "I just called to say I love you." People were warned away from the dangerous area. Sometimes the announcement would warn of strict measures if the "mob" became a "violent threat."

Another forum the junta used to wage combat in the public sphere was the popular *J.S. 100* traffic call-in radio show. Normally, this show was all about the Bangkok streets. Motorists, using cellular phones, would hook up to the radio and give traffic tips to the rest of the city. It was one of the most popular Bangkok forums of collective talk, and the only live talk-back show that was permitted to air anywhere in the nation. Only a few weeks before, the whole city was in the grips of an episode in which a woman gave birth in a taxicab and on the air, while a doctor who was himself stuck in traffic led the cabbie through delivery by cell phone—an incident later to be immortalized in a popular cell phone commercial.

Now, after first defaming the mob as stranglers of Bangkok traffic and the national economy, the call-in show was suddenly transformed into a political talk show, to discuss what was happening. Infuriating the crowd on Ratchadamnern Avenue, all of the (prescreened) call-in guests were suspiciously hostile to the democracy movement, while the moderator was obviously leading the discussion as a propaganda piece.

There was at the protest site a very clear feeling, and fear, that there were two realities going on simultaneously—the one here on the streets, and the one out there. Power lay in the ability to manipulate the relationship between the two.

Against this image of mob rule, the newspaper industry reconstructed the Thai crowd in the clothes of a morally positive economic symbolism. Newspapers called the crowd the "yuppie mob." They dressed it up in economic signifiers of moral value: affluence, education, in step with progress and national development, in touch with the future. The newspapers' protesters were clean-shaven and wore neckties, held briefcases and cellular phones. They were called, more frequently than anything else, *maub myyr tyyr*, the "mobile phone mob." They were "middle class." Many drove automobiles to the protest sites rather than rely on public transportation, it was written. They ate yogurt, a foreign food, expensive and difficult for traditionally trained Thai palettes to acquire a taste for. Then they were called the "yogurt mob."

They also were constructed against the contrast of an otherness in time and class: the "hippie rabble" of the seventies (even though many of them

111

were the same individuals). According to this reckoning, the seventies protesters were long-haired students in T-shirts, jeans, and sandals. Now in the nineties, on-the-spot survey questionnaires were being passed out in the yuppie yogurt cellular telephone mob's midst, asking them to check their income bracket and list what commodities they owned.

Meanwhile, the vast majority of protesters, in my personal witnessing, were passed over by the newspapers. They were those I would characterize as the "as-yet-undemoralized urban poor." They are not apparently newsworthy people. The as-yet-undemoralized urban poor are ordinary people barely getting by on the strength of their values, which they are ready and able to apply to the moral universe around them. The equivalent in countries that were colonized is, perhaps, the class of politicized poor. This class of poor urban Thais has taken on the ideals imparted to them from both state-organized channels and a more traditional inheritance, a moral inheritance that has often been twisted around for use against them. Through aristocratic ideologies, state propaganda, primary school education, popular Buddhism, and through their family ties, they have incorporated ideals that they can take quite literally at times, and that have provided them with some measure of stability in their personal lives, despite all economic odds—which they can clearly see are stacked neatly against them. But then, as people are wont to do, they begin to apply these ideals to the literal reality before their eyes, as E. P. Thompson has said of the moral economy of the English crowd in the eighteenth century.[21] In this case, the object was Suchinda's rise to power: the corruption, the hypocrisy, the misrepresentations piled one atop the other, the backdoor entrances.

Suchinda said, to justify going back on the promise not to seek office, "I sacrifice my honor for the sake of the nation." Chamlong came back with his own slogan, "I sacrifice myself for the honor of the nation."

The moral imaginary of the "mobile phone mob," by contrast, was bound up in an economic morality constructed in the embrace of capitalism, modernity, futurism, progress, and development, and in the closely related significations of wealth itself. The ones who read the newspapers were precisely the class of people represented as making up the mob, the yuppie cell phone-wielding yogurt-eating briefcase-bearing middle class. History in the information age appeals precisely to a class of consumers who wish to see themselves expressed in it, and who will consequently purchase images of themselves as its main protagonist.

And yet, the cell phone was not just an auspicious symbol associated with capital culture's moral nature but also a practical and tactical material advantage. Cell phones were efficient organizational tools, which the "yogurt mob" possessed and security forces did not. Renegade radio operators, using Zorolike pseudonyms, clogged the radio bands with falsetto gibberish and curses, and security forces could not use their communications system. They were forced to go to streetside pay phones or ask to use phones in the lobbies of hotels in order to communicate with central command. The "yuppie mob," being far beyond the ancient technology of radios (now rendered defunct), had none of these problems. Bypassing censorship, protestors could be seen everywhere calling in information to the home, office, business, and their provincial hometowns, reporting events on a minute-to-minute basis. One cellular telephone company boasted about how greatly they were cashing in: the normal rate of 160,000 calls in a week had leapt up to 268,000 during the protest.[22] Meanwhile office workers everywhere spread information throughout Bangkok and into the provinces with instant fax transmissions that cost them nothing and could not be monitored by the authorities. The techno-public sphere was booming with the business of conversation and free-market information—something the print media, of course, were quite self-interested in harping upon—while the authorities were dependent on pay phones and the kindness of strangers.

INTERMISSION

At the blockade set up on Ratchadamnern Avenue, dubbed the "Berlin Wall," the crowds got larger and larger with every day that passed, reaching hundreds of thousands in the night. The government, failing to pin the traffic jams on the protesters, proceeded to try and get them for anti-monarchical sentiments. The Buddhist holiday of Visakha Puja was coming up, and traditionally that meant that the crown princess would travel by motorcade through Ratchadamnern Avenue and on to religious rites in the heart of the old city. The "mob" was in the way, and government propaganda began to focus on this affront to the monarchy. But protesters seized the moment to demonstrate their loyalty by clearing the streets just so that she might pass, in a highly orchestrated and orderly demonstration complete with thousands of little national flags for everyone to wave as she passed. But it was decided she would take a detour. Instead, international journalists occupied the open spaces of the royal promenade, cleared of all Thais (see figure 6).

As crowds continued to grow, the government parties started to waver. Late one night, they offered what seemed to be capitulation. An intense discussion among protest leaders followed. People in the crowd were tired and on edge. The next day was Monday, which would make them vulnerable to even more harangue about disrupting traffic. The holy day of Visakha Puja was coming up, and they might get blamed for heresy. And Miss Universe was over, and that meant less international media atten-

Figure 6. International correspondents occupy monumental streets
cleared for sovereignty

tion, and less safety. So they announced a tentative victory, and informed everyone to reassemble on Sanam Luang the next Sunday night, after all the Buddhist events would be finished, to go back at it if the government reneged on their word.

The very next day government party leaders were denying that they had ever agreed to anything. One, in a slip of the tongue, admitted that they might have said some things just to get the protesters to disperse.[23] The protest leaders consequently went all out to promote the next and final wave of protests, beginning with a rally on Sunday, May 17.

Chalad Worachat had disagreed with the decision to disband the first gathering and broke off to set up camp in front of Government House. He was followed by a few remaining hunger strikers and a hundred or so sympathizers. There he vowed to go on alone. He set a deadline for May 24, giving just enough time to pass a constitutional amendment that could prohibit unelected people from leading the country. If Suchinda was not out by then he was going to stop drinking water, which for someone in his condition would mean certain death in a couple of days.[24] No one doubted at this point that he meant what he said. He would stop drinking water after the deadline of Sunday, May 24, two weeks away.

Chalad sat for photos atop his coffin to emphasize the promise.

114

THE MOVEABLE FEAST II

Meanwhile, the prodemocracy groups in provincial towns began to organize large crowds in Khon Kaen, Chiang Mai, Songkhla, and other towns, which was the first time this kind of political activism was coordinated between Bangkok and the provinces. Although they were small protests by comparison, they carried the suggestion that a crackdown in Bangkok would not put an end to everything, that the movement was mobile, diffuse, and had multiple points of entry, escape, and above all, witnessing. The provincial protest sites were hooked up by fax and cellular phone to the Bangkok organizers, and by satellite to the world TV news pool, and so one could have a vicarious experience of the Bangkok protest by attending a provincial gathering.

The protest in Bangkok reconvened on May 17, with the largest crowd ever seen since the seventies. The military first tried to drive them off with rain. Air force planes tried cloud seeding, or so it was believed, on the night of the Sunday gathering. Unnaturally minuscule raindrops fell in a bizarrely sparse pattern, with a ten-meter space between each drop. The shower lasted about fifteen minutes, and was a great source of amusement to the already very entertained audience on the field. That night was the peak of the amassment, announced on stage as five hundred thousand or a million people, but more like two to three hundred thousand. Contrary to what the military apparently believed or hoped, it was a firm conviction of the outrageous moral breach committed by the regime that drew the crowds to the protest spectacle. This moral breach seemed to be an endless fount for producing quality entertainment material: speeches, songs, comedy monologues.

The military tried to counter all this with its own media event, a "Concert for Drought Victims," to benefit suffering rural farmers—a free concert with free drinks held at two Bangkok stadiums. It was an attempt to capture audience share, and it was also an attempt to work a discourse of real economic need against the intangible, superfluous ideals of "democracy." But even with bribe money and the busing in of elderly farmers, they could not fill more than a small fraction of the seating for their gala of pop stars. They could only lose in their ratings war. Meanwhile, the vast field of Sanam Luang was teeming with people waving flags, demanding Suchinda's resignation to the cadences of protest leaders who led them with speeches of rousing cheers, biting irony and, most of all, farce. There was a jam-packed program of Art for Life music, quickly composed protest ditties, and even a traditional-like Thai opera performed in celestial regalia that delivered in its whiny, high-pitched songs a satire of the regime's foolish scheme to take power.

It had been no problem to draw in a battalion of pushcart vendors to support the crowds. The more that the bodies of hunger strikers withered away, the more appetites there were to satisfy in the throngs paying their respects to the protest movement. So even the street-vending rabble, whom Chamlong as governor had striven to sweep off the streets in the clean aesthetics of the market, as elsewhere, were willing and eager to open shop and deliver meals on wheels wherever in the city his crowd was moving. Some vendors reported astronomical profits, returning to the slums with ten thousand baht for a few days' work.[25] Sanam Luang's nightly noodle market was supernaturally multiplied and doing a brisk volume. Through the milling bodies, stalling against each other in the flow of their masses, wafted grilled dried squid smoke, the smells of woks frying pork, and visions of coconut ice cream steaming in the night heat. Big glass jars displayed jellied desserts in all the colors of traffic lights and floating in creme and chopped ice, flanked by Coke, Pepsi, Sprite, Fanta, and Vita-milk soy drink. The various refreshment stands included the market's regulars and vendors from all around the city and even distant provinces. There were protest T-shirts for sale everywhere. Many people donned black funereal headbands, and almost everyone had slogan flags and balloons. Small paper national flags and protest banners were passed out for free.

It had been almost a week since the steadily accumulating protest crowd had broken off. That was a lot of time for word to spread. While the nationally broadcast benefit concert for drought victims went on as orchestrated, and while at the same time the military took the cloud-seeding planes away from where they were most needed in order to drop rain on the urban field that was cultivating nothing of the vegetable variety, the protest culture absorbed into itself more delighted members than ever.

WORLD CONQUEROR AND WORLD RENOUNCER

It was then that I witnessed the turning point in Chamlong Sri-Muang's life, the apex of Maha Chamlong's attempted ascension toward both world conqueror and world renouncer. Sanam Luang was filled with so many people that they had to erect two protest stages on the field in order to speak to everyone, despite the high-powered amplifiers. I was on the fringes of the field, in the street, and Maha Chamlong was marching by on his way to the stage, surrounded by a devoted retinue holding hands in a circle around him. Cameras were flashing, videotape rolling, and everyone's head turned as he passed, as though they were obeying a law of nature. I could swear he was almost shining. Uniformed in his ascetic denim clothes, he basked in devotion and bounded forward with the determination of a warrior general, knowing full well that the historical power to do something momentous was in his hands, that now was the moment, and that he was about to do it.

Who would have realized that it would be for that moment alone? Who would have thought so, seeing him march at the height of his powers, to make the first and fateful announcement, of plans to move out, to mobilize onto Ratchadamnern Avenue?

This time there would be no embarrassing split decisions. Realizing what a long shot victory in this struggle would be, the students' leadership had committed themselves to a united front. If the Federation for Democracy was to lead them down Ratchadamnern, they were to follow. Individually, though, some students balked at the idea and stayed behind. And up to a quarter of the hundreds of thousands of people at Sanam Luang went home at that point, partly because it was getting late and partly because they feared what might be waiting for them at the end of that road.

On the other hand, many people rushed off down the street. To get a good seat near the next stage, you had to get there early. As soon as Chamlong announced the mobilization, people ran down the street, with a cascade of motorbikes flashing through their midst and into the lead. Just as a week before, at the Paan Fa Bridge they were met by a cordon of police in full riot gear and backed by fire engines as water canons. This time the hoses were on full blast as the people began to clog up the end of the street.

What happened next continues to this day to be a contentious issue. A coterie of aggressive youths were already at the scene when the crowd arrived. Who planted them there has raised a question of a mysterious "third hand." Given the history of such events, an interested party might have tried to instigate violence in such a way as to bring a return of October 14, in order to displace the government, or the military itself might have sought a return of October 6, in order to crack down violently and consolidate power. My sources upcountry told me of political operatives from one of the prodemocracy political parties—not Chamlong's—soliciting rioters to stir things up in Bangkok, while the military's plan for "security" at the protest was called "Operation Annihilate the Enemy." Most likely there was more than one "third hand" at work, as the history of the prodemocracy movement clearly indicates to all involved that it is death which brings change—which the student leadership, in their reluctance to march down Ratchadamnern, as the ones who have always done the most dying, were more aware of than anyone.

Although water hoses fired off, the crowd at first easily broke through police lines. Some boys got aboard the fire engines, took over the hoses and began spraying water straight up into the air to the jubilant cheers of the others. But the police quickly beat the crowd back with batons, which left the boys stranded atop the fire engines. They were pulled down and savagely beaten by hordes of police. Photojournalists captured the scene in powerful images for the next morning's edition: boys on their knees with hands behind their heads, cowering in submission while police kick them and poise for full-swing hacks on the head with their batons.

I was with a protest worker who was reporting all this on her cellular phone back to the protest leadership, which was only beginning to proceed from Sanam Luang. We were positioned on the castlelike walls of a temple at Paan Fa Bridge. We climbed up there after the police charged the unarmed demonstrators. The people ran back in a short-lived panic, then cautiously advanced again. In the space of an hour, however, the seesawing flow settled down again, and it looked as if it was going to be another test of staying power at the Paan Fa Bridge.

Despite the clashes with the police, despite the bloodied faces and limping, wild-eyed people being carried back from somewhere off in the distance at various times throughout the night, things had seemed to settle down again, just as they had the previous week on this spot. All were sitting peaceably, shoulder to shoulder in the street. Chamlong and Aed Carabao and Arisaman and the Ramkamhaeng student turned comedian, Luk-Yee, were there as before, keeping things calm, keeping them light and peaceful.

For me there was an image in that calm that arose vividly. We were all sitting there, our attention divided between what was on the protest stage and what lay beyond the barbed wire, distracted by the inkling and wonder of what was being held in store for everyone behind the razor line. Sometimes volunteers with low-volume bull horns would come around and tell everyone to remain calm, remain seated, to stick firmly to ahimsa. But more convincing was a middle-aged woman that went by. She was a portly woman, with softly clenched fists and elbows out, dressed neatly but plainly in well-cared-for, inexpensive clothes. Her head and chin were up and she was strutting with out-thrust breasts in the direction of the police line, declaring loudly, "They can't kill us. They can't touch us. They can't do anything to us." She was just an ordinary aunt, or maybe a young grandma. She was absolutely confident, and I and anyone else there who understood her feeling could only be further inflated with her contagious certainty.

It was so clear from where we were sitting, and I mean both physically in the street and in an historical sense of progress, that the force of right was on this side of the fence, that we were sitting in the center of modern morality, pursuing through peaceful means an end to the illegitimate regime, which itself was founded on violence or the threat of it. Everyone felt that in the 1990s the military could no longer afford to harm them, as the people had absorbed all that was proper about modern civil society into their midst. In this day and age—and this was truly the crux of it—if civic-minded citizens peacefully express themselves after almost two decades of whirlwind progress since October 14 and Bloody October, two decades in which there was no such highly visible atrocity committed, then there really was nothing the army could do with all the weapons they were amassing somewhere out there behind the barbed wire. "They can't do anything to us" was among the crowd a widespread and firmly held conviction right to the end of that night.

The Angel of History

The bitter aftertaste, the bitter afterimage of that portly aunt or grandma strutting down Ratchadamnern Avenue, puffed up with people power, with the certitude both of being fixed here and now in the center of moral righteousness and of being whisked forward into the future by the spiritual forces of history—that her vision of historical ascesis would explode, just as my own vision of her has gone tragically sour—it is this bitter taste that lingers long after. And who knows, maybe she was eventually shot in the face, or in the back of the head while fleeing.

But from where we were sitting, there was only an occasional and slightly injured bloody person carried by. Every time the army tried to scare people by firing their weapons in the air, people would thunder out unblinkingly in an outraged chorus of "ho! ho!" booing. At first there was just an occasional single round fired, or maybe two, but even just one soldier or policeman who lay his finger on just one trigger was morally intolerable to the crowd, who would castigate him severely with their own sounds. Later, off in the distance, there would be sudden flashes of light and a big booming explosion here and there. Off to the right, to the left, to the front. Each time the crowd would boo and hiss vehemently, with the amplification of hundreds and thousands of larynxes aligned behind one idea of truth and justice. Chamlong was on stage denouncing the explosions as the work of elements trying to instigate violence, trying to create a pretext. On the loudspeaker he told everyone not to fall for it, to remain true to the principles of nonviolence. But people in the inside circle of the protest organization later told me that, though he was aware that people had been injured and many might be killed, he would harbor no discussion of pulling the protest back to Sanam Luang.

Most people stayed on all night, even when the singular gunshots that were meant to scare them began to be orchestrated into mass volleys of automatic rifle fire. The army was shooting three- to five-minute rounds of continuous machine-gun fire over the crowd's heads. During the bursts the crowd would lie out on the ground together, while it lasted, then rise up back into sitting position and yell out boos and hisses again. Back and forth it went on all night, lying flat, sitting up, booing, and gunfire again. In the darkness of the streets this furious argument of sound waves seemed to suck all time and thought into itself, as though the exchange of these missives was all that existed in the world, all that had ever happened, and all that ever would happen. There was only this moment, filled only with evil words aspirated by the combustion of gunpowder, and the condemnation shot out in return.

Most people believed the bullets were aimed over their heads, or were blanks. Something like this may have, at first, been largely the case. Nevertheless, there was no denying the fact that once in a while someone would be carried by with gunshot blood. I retreated onto the plaza that fronts an old temple adjacent to the Paan Fa bridge. There I got a good look at gunshot wounds, because at first that was the place they would try to bring the injured, before the abbot got a call from the authorities and quickly complied with their request to turn away the wounded. There on the temple's plaza, I waited out the night with others who believed the temple grounds would be a safer spot than on the adjacent street, even though the temple plaza was unwalled and open. The later it got into the night, the more difficult it was for people to remain calm. Lying out flat to avoid bullets began to seem a more and more uncertain gamble. Sometimes sharpshooters would fire at the protest stage, but it seemed they were careful not to hit anyone up there. Sometimes Aed Carabao played. Chamlong was on stage most of the time. And when it started to get really scary, Luk-Yee, a student leader, would keep up his endless comedy act to cheer everyone up. Aed Carabao later wrote a song in honor of the amateur comedian, because it was really true, as the song went, that without Luk-Yee they never would have made it through the night.

And it seemed that everyone was going to make it. Dawn, the critical time, was approaching. Their collective historical memory intact, many people were nervously searching the lightening sky for the signs and sounds of helicopter gunships. But the chopper blades never appeared. Instead, monks came out in the dawn light, rolled up their bright orange robes and flapped them over their shoulders, on their way to alms round. It seemed from where we were lying on the open temple plaza that a signal had appeared—the monks on their way to alms round—the signal for a dawn that had finally come and passed.

Journalists and other observers, who had taken positions on top of what remaining buildings army sharpshooters had not commandeered, had a different bird's-eye perspective on the dawn, recorded on tape. Their video shots took in the early light and a march of cordon after cordon of soldiers armed with heavy assault rifles, headed for the police line. The police backed off to make room for them to go through.

It was now fully morning, but not bright. The army battalion was marching forward, while the crowd had come up off the asphalt, where they had been lying prostrate, and were now standing in unison, thankfully singing the national anthem.

Then the crowd sang the anthem to the king.

With that, the soldiers stopped their advance, held their firearms at their side, and stood at attention. For the duration of the anthem to the king, both sides stood at attention. When the people finished singing, they erupted into applause and cheers. For the soldiers' part, as soon as the song was over, they charged. The ones in the back roared out M-16 gunfire into the air. The soldiers in front, with guns at their hips, spattered the people with bullets.

With many of the others in the temple plaza, I hit the dirt, and got up to run, hunchbacked, whenever there was a break in the shooting. By following the auditory cues, running and ducking with the machine gun bursts, we managed to move toward an alley leading out of the main street. People running through the alley would stop at people's doorsteps and beg to be let in, but no one was having any of it. Everyone turned and kept running, not knowing what lay at the end of the road, given the explosions and gunfire they had heard coming from all directions in the night. But eventually the alley ended in the open space of a canal, and there was no military blockade. There on the edge of the canal people reassembled, and began discussing with local residents, who had heard the shooting all night, what might be going on. The local residents were of the mind that it must have all been fake bullets, as no one could believe that in this day and age the army would try to pull off another massacre. Witnesses, however, began telling bits and pieces of what they had seen, a few bloody bodies, or a few dead bodies.

Young students were already milling about telling how they had seen hundreds and hundreds of people killed in the last few minutes. With single-minded purpose they sought out everyone and anyone who would listen, and systematically filled them with tales of atrocity on the grandest scale.

Repulsiveness of the Body Politic

AN ECONOMICS OF THE BLACK MAY MASSACRE

> you will see my present body
> burst into fragments
> and remake itself
> under ten thousand notorious aspects
> a new body
> where you will
> never forget me.
>
> ANTONIN ARTAUD[1]

THE ECHO CHAMBER OF GLOBAL CAPITALISM

Estimates for the year's GNP growth were scaled back from 8.1 percent to 7.3 percent by Merrill Lynch's Asia-Pacific desk, while Bangkok Bank forecast 7.0 percent, down from 8.9 percent, and other local forecasters put it down even further, below 7 percent.[2]

The stock exchange of Thailand sank 8 percent, and went into a day-by-day tailspin to reach a yearlong low. Liquidity evaporated as stock analysts forecast a pullout of foreign investment. Siam City Bank credit card department predicted it would be a long time before forgetting set in: "Maybe in three to five years, people will forget the inhumane scenes they had witnessed. . . . After the coup on Feb. 23, we recouped the situation by holding the World Bank/IMF annual meeting. But our image now is difficult to redeem."[3]

While the body count of "Black May," as it came to be called, climbed higher and higher—even the government's count—so too did the interest rate climb on loans for foreign investment in the country. Standard and Poor announced a review of Thailand's credit rating, threatening to move it from "A–1" and put it on "Credit Watch with negative implications."[4]

Mastercard changed the venue of its upcoming Asia-Pacific meeting from Bangkok to Singapore, and Thai bankers reported personal spending, investment, and tourism were plummeting so severely during this violence, and were likely to remain dormant because of the tattered national image, that the whole personal and corporate credit industry would be thrown into crisis.[5]

Travel warnings were issued in major Western countries of tourist origination, while Western travel agents announced that they were monitoring the situation and reviewing their own decisions about marketing packages to the country. Bangkok hoteliers were granting dismal interviews to anyone who would listen about the devastation that the violence was wreaking on their industry. Hoteliers in upcountry and beachside areas shared the gloom-and-doom predictions, though in the short run they were raking it in as foreigners went on mass exodus from the city, while tourists already out of Bangkok were extending their stay so as not to have to return to the city.[6]

The Thai Hotels Association and the Tourism Authority of Thailand quickly announced meetings to decide on a cooperative venture to revive the national image.[7] Meanwhile, the Board of Trade announced that it was planning an international meeting with representatives from all of the thirteen foreign Chambers of Commerce established in the country by its major trade partners.[8]

Local financial analysts began to cry out that a quick solution to the crisis was the only way to pull the national image back from the brink of disaster. Hong Kong bankers, the major backers of large-scale government projects like highways and power plants, issued warnings that all loans were at risk, while European and U.S. bankers were quoted as saying that all further lending was on hold.[9]

Foreign governments were sending in statements of condemnation, despite the fact that when all was told the military had received a rather mixed bag of reviews. Most prominently, the United States, age-old supporter of the Thai military elite, called off its annual Cobra Gold joint military exercises that were just starting up. To that President Bush added a statement of concern over the situation, and his disapproval of violent means of ending the conflict. But the Thai military would be allowed to continue its extensive arms purchases, as it had since the February coup in 1991—an event to which the U.S. government also claimed to be opposed.[10] Ever since the February coup, the Bush administration had officially canceled military aid (although, secretly, U.S. Green Berets were still training Thai Special Forces right up to the last minute, when their pupils were ordered out of their rural training camps and into Bangkok to do the lion's share of the massacre). After the Green Berets' students demonstrated their training, the Japanese government sent their best wishes for a quick solution, and denied reports that they were contemplating cutting off Thailand's largest source of economic aid. European nations, however, as well as Canada and Australia, tended to be harsher on the military government and more supportive of the democracy movement. Though the European governments made little public mention of economic issues, their investors were running from the baht to the dollar. By contrast, some Asian governments expressed regrets and concerns over the investment climate publicly, while privately their entrepreneurs tended to make no significant moves to pull out.[11]

Thailand was up for review of two major loan projects from the World Bank for June, and human rights organizations in the United States began demanding that the Bush administration oppose the loans.[12] The international trade union ICFTU, with 108 million members worldwide, called for trade sanctions against Thailand. Asia Watch reported that they could not keep up with all the human rights violations.[13]

The discourse of the world's financial elite pushed for a quick solution, and some of it even explicitly suggested that the quickest possible means of said solution would be for General Suchinda to step down.

The interest rate on foreign loans rose another half a percentage point.[14]

After whatever it was that happened on Ratchadamnern Avenue, Thai International Airlines announced it was getting a flood of cancellations. Bookings were plummeting at rates between 50 and 80 percent per day.[15] Hitting the corporation hardest was one striking BBC image, of a British couple and their son being escorted out of the Royal Hotel after it was stormed by Thai Special Forces. First there were brutal scenes of soldiers kicking, stomping over, and beating with their rifle butts defenseless Thais who were quivering prostrate on the hotel's bloody marble floors (they had holed up there to care for the dead and wounded). The BBC followed that up with the knockout punch of poor British tourists whose door had been kicked open by the same jack-booted soldiers who were now leading them out of the lobby. The woman and man told of being too terrified to let any terrified Thais, who had come begging and knocking at their door, come into their hotel suite to hide, while their adolescent son was completely confused and couldn't blurt out any answer at all to the international correspondent.

At this moment, at the end of a siege on the Royal Hotel, the army had finalized the advance of its troops into the shadowy heartland of the new world phantasmagoria. Here, the confluence of multitudinous local and global forces that have been circling this history converge in a dense pith of sieges within sieges. With the fluorescence of international media images arising from the crackdown on Thai protesters, the forces of integrated structures of global finance and mass mediation erupt in the compound of this local power struggle in ways that signal the complexly imbricated nature of local and global formations. As the troops surround and then storm the makeshift morgue in the heart of a major tourist destination, they are surrounded and enveloped, in turn, by the echo chamber of global capitalism. They are herded into the coreless core of a world that David Harvey has characterized as one of "space-time compression" in the advance of telecommunications, where local and global geographies fold in on each other in the instant transport of a global space-time machine.[16] They march into the radical disembodiment that Anthony Giddens delineates, whereby space and time are each disembedded from the other in the exchanges of finance and communication that render transactions over space without regard to time.[17] The event occurs within the experience of an increasingly pervasive consciousness of the world as a whole, and yet paradoxically occurs alongside the simultaneous global disjuncture and fragmentation in the noncontiguous flows of capital, resources, and people in "disorganized capitalism" and the dispersal of ever more complex identities in "global mediascapes" and novel forms of the public sphere that defy geopolitical borders and "confound theories dependent on the continued salience of the nation-state."[18] In this, at least as Appadurai registers the spirit of the times, "the states are under siege."[19]

But of course these nearly mystical reflections on the nature of a new world are, themselves, an overdetermined constituent of the world they narrate and evoke. What the following story about the global collateral damage of a local massacre may indicate is how tightly integrated are, in fact, the structures of these seemingly disembodied agents swirling over the surface of the earth. It may demonstrate, at least, one among many possible arrays in which ideologies of the public sphere, technologies of global communication, virtualization of financial transaction, and principles for the narration of modernity can, at times, arrange themselves into an ordered configuration that is not so disorganized as it may seem at the first shock of the new. Indeed, disjuncture itself—especially that disjuncture accentuated between past and present eras—is a principle upon which their order is founded. In this, theories of mass mediatization in global modernity can often echo the plot devices of dominant forms of historical narration.

To be sure, there is more than a little unhinging of the nation-state as a result of the global proliferation of suprastate communications networks, which prompted Arjun Appadurai to claim that "electronic mass mediatization and transnational mobilization have broken the monopoly of autonomous nation-states over the project of modernization."[20] And yet that power to override power is itself the express declaration of agency that the very same media structures often claim for themselves in their own moral and modern positioning in history. Their claim is bolstered by the possession of the material means to produce and distribute such proclamations. Jean and John Comaroff have questioned such recent eruptions of faith in civil society consequent upon, and also obscuring, the violence to society enacted by recent transformations of global capitalism. The "Idea of Civil Society," argue the Comaroffs, "conflates an analytic concept with an ideological trope."[21] And the same observation might be applied to the idea of "diasporic public spheres" and "global mediascapes," as well.[22] Although these technological suprastructures may provide the material means for new forms of imagined community, they are also symbols of modernity in their own right: imagined media. The twist is not simply that imagined media are as much imaginations about the historical movement of modernity as they are the means for imagining community, which is the case, but also that these imagined technologies have the power, materially, to speak for themselves. Thus they bear more than a trace of the centralization of capital upon which they depend for their existence: the contents of their ideological tropes and the plot devices for rendering their place in the narrative of modernity are carried by and in the media themselves. Like the "Idea of Civil Society," which the Comaroffs point out "has served as a remarkably potent battle cry across the world"[23] and in which faith in imagined media of global modernity itself partakes, there are echoes in analytic concepts for theorizing new media forms that may mirror too closely discourses embedded in the phenomena they purport merely to describe. For that reason, perhaps no better context could interrupt this plot than the one at hand, which appears to be nothing less than the global mediascape flexing its might—so as long as one does not look too closely at the particular switching mechanism by which the media at large extracts from the ground of history the message it tells about itself.

THE COLLATERAL DAMAGE

Since, as we have seen, so much about power relations within the Thai state depended on strict divisions between local and global significations, the presence of international journalists who saturated the scene of protest and massacre in 1992, and were connected to the massive technological, capital, and moral structure of global media and finance, required that all the more strict censorship over information and images within the country be maintained, even if the global mediascape required a different sort of brinkmanship.

It was Thursday, May 21, and the army had been killing for three days and nights. That much was clear from a few Thai newspapers that were brazenly defying threats and decrees to silence the information. Announcers on Thai TV continued to mouth only the army's prepared reports, declaring that Chamlong Sri-Muang had been taken prisoner and that the "rioters" were captured by Special Forces and interned on military compounds. Everything would be back to normal soon. But with the blackout on accurate TV news, which is the people's primary connection to the stage of the nation, rumors lit up the night like wildfire, some of which put the death toll up to as much as ten thousand killed, while it was also widely feared that the junta had taken the king and queen prisoner. There was speculation that the army generals were divided and a "shining knight," as they called it, might pull off a coup. There were stories that Chamlong had been tortured and killed.

But finally Chamlong was presented on state TV, still in his denim farmer's garb, under arrest, announcing that he was alive and well treated, and asking the people to remain calm. He managed his trademark winning smile.

After whatever it was that happened for those three days and nights, students led those who had not been captured or killed across the city to the campus of Ramkhamhaeng University. There they vowed to hole up to the bitter end. Despite the crackdown it was as far from certain what would happen there, as it was far from certain, in the public sphere, what had already happened. The students would hold out to the end, whether that be Suchinda's resignation or an even more brutal and systematic massacre.

In the evening of Thursday, May 21, the junta appeared on TV, in apparent unison, all officers present, where they proceeded to deny all rumors that the armed forces were divided, that they had killed thousands of people, or that they were holding the monarch hostage.

Then there was an announcement that sometime soon the king was going to appear on TV, and that there was going to be a resolution of the crisis. After weeks of desperate calls for his intervention in the run-up to Black May, finally he was going to step in. The critical moment was at hand: would there be total mass murder in the name of the Suchinda government, or another coup, which would without doubt be the bloodiest one ever, or would Suchinda finally give in, put an end to it all, and resign? Everything was hanging on this appearance.

After long delays, with people both in Bangkok and upcountry waiting apprehensively by their TVs, the king finally and dramatically appeared on screen, sitting stiffly on a luxurious couch in a waiting room of the royal palace. First Suchinda then Chamlong entered, and falling to their knees, they bowed down, touching their head to the floor at His Majesty's feet. Chamlong apologized for the improper farmer's garb he had on, saying that since he had been held, he was given no chance to change (though that wasn't good enough for a lot of the viewers, who later had bitter words for him because he would dress in so slovenly a way for an audience with His Majesty). The king then proceeded to order a halt to the conflict. He said that the country did not belong to you two, that you two should settle your personal differences in another manner, that neither of you two could possibly win, and, rather, that it was a loss for everyone else in the country. He also mentioned, looking down on Suchinda, that the country already had a good constitution before his February coup, and that now there should be amendments made to fix the constitution as befits the best interests of the people.

Soon after, a pretaped video of Suchinda announcing his resignation was aired over all channels.

The king had looked glorious up there, while it was an embarrassing moment for Suchinda and Chamlong. They looked exactly like two bad boys being scolded by their father.

Both home and abroad, this scene of the king, with Suchinda and Chamlong at his feet, was the front-cover photo and the lead footage in newspapers and newscasts—by far the single most widely circulated image of the incident.

Prices on the stock exchange rose 9 percent, the most for a single day's trading that year.[24] If it was speed of resolution that the local and international financial elite wanted, that is what they appeared to get.

The Tourism Authority of Thailand sent out its first image-bolstering message to the world, dispatched to tour agencies everywhere:

> His Majesty the King has intervened to solve the political crisis in Thailand. His Majesty appeared on television with the leaders of the two conflicting parties. The situation is back to normal. Knowing the nature of the Thai people, and their respect and veneration for His Majesty, we believe that all parties and the protestors will be submissive to his command. We believe that everybody should work for a peaceful solution to solve this political difficulty. Your clients will be able to travel as before without any problem. Only a few countries in the world can solve such a crisis in a very short time.[25]

The Foreign Ministry, which had been controlled by a party supporting Suchinda, was sending out dispatches to governments the world over, encouraging them to send tourists to Thailand now that everything was "normal" again. In their dispatch they heralded the martyrdom of those who died (though without mentioning that they had died because of government actions). "Thailand is achieving full democracy resulting from the sacrifices of the people . . . we had some clashes but now the concerned person has already resigned and everything is returning back to normal."[26]

Although Thai citizens were the targets of the army's fire, there was, as in all military actions, unintended and unavoidable damage to bystanders. The national image had been critically wounded. To the business elite, the image of the king was the only salve miraculous enough to mend the collateral damage inflicted on the economy. Anand Banyarachond, the respected businessman and former prime minister installed by the NPKC after the February coup, announced to the country that he was on a mission to the rest of the world, where he was going to explain to foreigners the power of the Thai king. He explained to the Thai reporters, who passed his message on down the line, that if the West could be made to understand the power of the monarchy, their fears would be allayed, the horrible images of chaos counteracted, their faith in the Thai economy restored.[27]

His was an influential voice cast in at the start of the maelstrom of uncertainty within the country: the particular uncertainty within the country, that is, over what the exact effects outside the country on their image would be, the uncertainty over what images of domestic uncertainty were going to do to the perceptions of uncertain perceivers abroad. This kind of epistemological chaos over the state of the national image creates only one kind of certainty: that the national image is real, that image matters.

At the very least, immediately after the killings it was abundantly clear, from what everyone was saying, that the national image was now on the front line, and the shock of this reached new heights of shocking with the chaotic scramble over what to do about it. The more uncertain one is about one's image, the more one's very real image itself suffers, because the worst image you can project is that you have no control over your own image. Because the world is ready to buy into it (or at least so it appears on the home front), a desperate importance is lent the sovereign's image in the local balance of power. That is the necessity for image prophecy: there must be an epistemological clampdown, a sovereign hermeneutics to show that in fact the national image can be manipulated. There must be decisive measures taken, even if they only appear to be decisive and effective. In fact, it is not completely necessary actually to control the national image so much as it is to appear to control it, because that in itself is a good image to project in a realm of public images where the appearance of being effective is itself a real effect. In the argument of images and international economics, at least in a time of radical uncertainty, reality and appearance are not mutually exclusive. Or rather, we might say at least that appearance is nine-tenths of reality, which is quite large enough a margin to base an investment decision on.

With the sovereign hermeneutic of the king established, further measures were then taken, though with less unanimity. The foreign minister announced that he was spearheading a coordinated effort to revive the national image, an initiative that would pool the efforts of state organizations such as the Tourism Authority of Thailand, the Board of Trade, and the Commerce Ministry, in conjunction with the private sector, including the tourist, banking, and hotel associations.[28] But the private sector wanted no part in that. Locally, the business community began a campaign in the public sphere that was unprecedented in terms of its political overtones. Although big business always maintained relations of convenience with military and party cliques in the behind-the-scenes machinations of power, CEOs and prominent entrepreneurs were now speaking out publicly and banding together to take a political stand. Between the military, the government, and the opposition, a mess had really been made of things, and the business elite were being as vocal as they could about the ruined national image and what they could do to save it. The Federation of Thai Industries, the Board of Trade, and the Thai Bankers Association would eventually issue a joint political statement demanding that parliament be dissolved and new elections held, to put a decisive end to the uncertainty with a fresh start for the image of Thai democracy.[29] They asserted that a "neutral person" should be named interim prime minister to oversee the transition. Renegade, middle-level managers in Thai International Airways began an anonymous fax campaign calling for the ouster of Air Marshal Kaset Rojanin from the chair of the board of directors, as his overseeing of the massacre was ruinous to the company's image.[30]

Thailand hardly makes a regular appearance in the imaginary of the countries that fly in most of its tourists. Being a relatively peaceful country, it has little sensational appeal, the only images breaking the surface, of late, being the February coup, AIDS, and sex tourism with its sensational appeal and unappeal. But none of these news items carries a sensate value on the level of lead news. By stark contrast, from the time the protests began to get big, and throughout the killing, Thailand had gradually ascended to top headline news in those foreign newspapers that concern themselves with international coverage, and in the United States it was a top-of-the-broadcast feature on the evening news, as well as receiving continual coverage on the international networks of BBC and CNN.[31] So it was that the biggest doses of visual imagery ever to be foisted on a world audience largely unacquainted with the country were painted in the dodgy video colors of violence.

A hundred times more shocking than the country's profile in worldwide media, however, was the local perception of that very same proliferation; many people were convinced that the whole world was just as riveted to the spectacle as they were. The shock in the aftermath was greatest not with the impressionable foreign audience—for whom, after all, such images come in serial regularity and blur into one another—but locally, within the very discourse through which the economic equations of public images are sold to the Thai public. It was the sovereign moment for this discourse. Up to that point, the World Bank meetings and Miss Universe had heated up this discourse of the national image to its highest degree historically. But Black May was its greatest, and crowning, moment.

Eventually the wobbling state's Tourism Authority of Thailand would have to announce over local TV and radio its own multipronged international scheme to revive the country's image internationally. In the "Back to Normal Inspection" program, they were to foot the bill for both local media representatives and foreign tourism agencies to come to Bangkok and see for themselves that everything was just fine now, beginning with Asians, who were, presumably, less sensitive, and then Westerners to follow after. The "Clear Thai Image" program was to work the other way, sending reps from Thai tour agencies out to the agencies in foreign countries to assure them personally that everything was A-OK. The "Come, See, and Tell" program was to be a more broadly reaching program of discounted fares and guided tours for any and all travel agents so that they could spread by word of mouth the news of Thailand's new political stability.[32]

But this top-down image-mending strategy, which as always carries the multiple entendre of mending the government's image locally because it appears to mend the country's image globally, instantly became controversial in the newly uncooperative private sector. The five largest tourism associations joined in outcry at the prospect of a hokey campaign that could spell disaster if launched at the wrong time—like right now, when everything was in fact so uncertain, with no new government, no assurance against yet another military coup, or against a resurgence of street demonstrations, or a devolvement into assassinations, bombings, whatever. To prevent the move, the tourism associations contemplated signing on with the powerful alliance already forming between the Board of Trade, Federation of Thai Industries, and Thai Bankers Association.[33]

Realizing things were not going their way, and that the top generals were facing transfers, the junta assembled two hundred officers to read out a joint statement that proclaimed their intent to defend the honor of the military institution if they were harassed, and that they were willing to stand behind their leaders if necessary. To that the foreign minister responded that they had better keep their morale boosting to themselves and not let any of that threatening talk leak out into global circulation (which it did). The world was monitoring the situation carefully, he explained. The European Community was going to meet on reviewing their policy with respect to Thailand. Several international lending agencies had rated the country in the high-risk category, which was rocketing interest rates for investment loans, while diplomats from Western nations were demanding that the situation be settled peaceably and by democratic principles.[34]

The United States, Britain, and France had all issued warnings against visits to Thailand. To that the foreign Ministry responded that there were plenty of peaceful spots, like the islands, for tourists to go.[35] But some published forecasts had the country losing up to one-third its projected five billion dollars worth of tourist trade for the year, and the industry was the country's biggest earner of foreign currency.[36] And that was not even counting other sources of incoming foreign exchange. Two weeks after the incident, one billion dollars had already been pulled out, mostly from the severely battered Stock Exchange of Thailand, sometimes at the rate of remittance of foreign investment from the SET of 200 to 300 million dollars per day.[37]

But foreign governments and agencies were not nearly as gloomy as the local forecasters. The U.S. Chamber of Commerce announced its concerns while expressing confidence in the long-term strength of the economy, forecasting a GNP growth rate of 6.5 to 7 percent despite the ugliness. Japanese investors, representing $1.79 billion of the previous year's $5 billion in foreign investment, were even more confident, and did not even make substantial withdrawals from the SET.[38]

In the meantime, advertising agencies (almost all backed by foreign capital) began jockeying with each other to secure the government contract for a newly proposed megacampaign dubbed "The World: Our Guest."[39] As for that, the tourist industry tried again to get it across that this would all only look like more stiff-necked propaganda, and just make things worse.

The United States would eventually modify its travel warning to be a travel caution, and the Foreign Ministry would go ahead and stamp its final approval on the coordinated image crusade.[40]

THE LOCAL IMAGE

The bombardment of national economic and political borders persisted, carried by the instantaneous transmission of international news imagery around the world and in the network of financial discourse and exchange. The transfer points between international images and finance inhere in the global media network of economic forecasting and rating, but carry more than mere messages as they transmit their reality into the economy through the superconductors of a highly liberalized financial policy developed through years of cooperation with international governing organizations like the IMF and World Bank. The liberalized policy was boosted by the neoliberal ideological turn of the decade and by neoliberal policy initiatives set in place since the February coup of 1991: the nearly frictionless regulations for the insertion or extraction of short-term capital, the uninhibited extension of foreign-denominated debt in the private sector, the integration of Thai equities into international investment protocols, and the continued dependence on the largest foreign reserve earner for the country, tourism.

The price for inclusion of the Thai economy within this global market, as for so many other states in the same position, was, among other things, supposed to have been enforcement of regimes of intellectual property right, that brake on an immaterial globalized space which, through an intellectual pointer, centralizes and localizes the material means of production upon which continuous relations of asymmetry are furthered within the "free" market. Along with pharmaceuticals and software, media imagery, as Annette Hamilton has explored in her studies of Thai media, has been at the forefront of this structuring of the global in Thailand.[41] But although talks with U.S. trade commissions broke down over drugs and computer code, the Thai state, as Hamilton argues, had an overdetermined interest in enforcing audio and video copyright, and had featured most prominently in its demonstrations of cooperativeness a crackdown on a massive video piracy and rental industry. Given the tight censorship laws and enforcements for radio and television in Thailand since the seventies, especially with regard to politically unwanted messages, the proliferation of video throughout the eighties had led to a huge and almost acephalous network of image exchange in which state censorship had little role to play. A video store, chock full of pirated tapes of all conceivable contents, could be found almost anywhere one went in the kingdom. The crackdown on video rental practices in the late eighties, by contrast, had led to a centralization of distribution among certain licensed channels and the demise, at least for a time, of the proliferated mom-and-pop stores scattered throughout the land. To that I would add, only furthering Hamilton's argument about local state censorship as the driving force for what she called the "Sacrificial Pirate" in intellectual property law, the crackdown was not nearly so severe on the pirate catering to foreign tourists. As far as I have observed, by the early nineties there was no detectable inhibition on open sales of pirated content in tourist ghettos, and urban Thais, at least those with capital enough for purchase as opposed to rental, frequented these markets regularly. Meanwhile, frequent features of media spectacle within the country itself were great confiscated-cassette-burning events that sent photogenic thick black plumes of smoke into thin air and, presumably, into the offices of the U.S. Department of Trade. These smoke signals, we might say, were double entendres that signified one thing to the global audience and, following Hamilton, quite another locally.

To ensure this double entendre, during Black May state- and military-controlled TV kept as close a grip as it could on information. The promilitary government parties were still in place. The highest ranking generals refused to rule out another coup, while top junta figures warned against anyone trying to "corner" them. Under these conditions of silencing within the country, it was still far from clear which way things were going to go. It was far from certain whether the full significance of whatever it was that happened would ever make it into the public sphere, given state control over electronic media, and far from certain what effect there would be if it did.

Once troops are slowly but surely withdrawn from the streets, the turn of events is no longer something that can be decided simply by force of arms. Nor, with the cessation of massive street demonstrations and with no control over official public channels, is there a collective means of recourse with which to exert bodily pressure on the situation. The next few moments, hours, days, weeks, would be decisive. Where the moral onus for the death should fall, who would gain and who would lose— this battle had now to be fought over the construction and interpretation of the event, the classic battle in such situations. It is a battle waged over the formation of memory, even a few moments after the event. Especially then. Now was the time when establishing what had happened would have its greatest impact, when there was the most interest in knowing the truth, and the most consciousness of the fact that it was an event worth remembering. But the material means of production for such historical memories—at least when ascribed, as is so often the case, to mass media structures as though they are its given right—were not in the hands of the demonstrators, regardless of what may have been occurring in the world at large.

Although General Suchinda may have resigned under the barrage of the media and finance networks, the military had not been routed from power within Thailand—far from it. Perhaps they would ride it out, last through this global storm, and seize power again. Many within Thailand might know, privately, that something terrible had happened, but that is not the same thing as having the knowledge on public display before everyone. The military controlled the electronic media, and it is there in the surface dimensions of established structures of public culture that one might think that the power to construct the event resided.

THE CHARNEL GROUND

The morning after the king appeared on TV, soldiers still held Ratcha-damnern Avenue, though they were not shooting at anyone. Those citizens who dared to sneak into the area through an alley were able to wander through the scene of the crime for the first time without getting killed.

The whole street is a smoking gun.

Blackened with soot, seven metropolitan buses are burnt-out hulks, scattered here and there, crumpled and overturned like skeletons and husks. One bus is punctured by bullet holes, many of which are in the windshield in obvious contradiction to the army's claim that they only shot out the tires. Another bus has bullet holes in no place other than the windshield. Exploded pickup trucks and passenger cars are strewn about on different sides of the street. Broken glass is all over the pavement and sidewalks. Newspapers and bloody articles of clothing have been discarded everywhere.[42]

Firemen hose down the smoking carcass of the Public Relations Building. Municipal workers are out sweeping up garbage and the thousands of rounds of spent cartridges littering the avenue. Others wash off anti-Suchinda graffiti in Thai and English, *Hia Su*, Fuck You Su, and so on.[43] Water trucks are dousing the bloodstained sidewalks.

But the whole crime scene is far from clean. Astonished crowds have trickled in, and have portions of the street cordoned off with their bodies, creating sacred spaces not to be defiled by cleansers and rinsing. Only the flies can get through the circle of people surrounding pieces of skin, blood, and bones left behind like roadkill. One group has a piece of brain sitting atop a block of ice, with a makeshift incense burner made from a plastic water bottle placed beside it. There is a small sign that reads, "This is the brain of our patriotic friend who loved the country and democracy. His name and surname are not known. He was shot at 3:15 this morning."[44]

Other pieces of brain are still unattended, rotting in the sun along with shreds of bloody cloth, as well as a few entire articles of clothing soaked in blood, strewn about. Here and there, bits of skin and pools of blood and water that have not drained properly accent the air. And then there are the sandals—thousands of them, rubber ones and leather ones, cheap and expensive ones—all over the place. Some people are scavenging, hunchbacked, over the avenue, gathering up bone fragments into little baskets.[45] In the background, a droning, chanting sound wafts over the scene, emanating from a small group of angry protesters out with big national flags and a handheld megaphone.

Having returned to the scene of the protests (I had run away upcountry), I find that most people mill about in less dangerous groups of five or six, as no one knows what will happen next in the politics of the world out there, beyond this scene. The military could launch another assault at any moment. Yet all attention in these small groups is centered on what has happened, not on what might happen. Giving eyewitness accounts, exchanging queries and stories, many speak of the GMC trucks that came in to cart off corpses almost as soon as they had fallen. Newspaper and TV reporters hover over these people. Many people complain bitterly about being shot at while trying to retrieve the bodies. But other protesters proudly tell of how they had snatched up a few bodies before the army could stop them. Some of these corpses, no doubt, were the ones carried atop big national flags held like tightly strung hammocks and paraded through major intersections in the city. To deal with the symbols of death escaping from their grasp, the high command had plainclothed sharp-shooters, riding in teams on motorcycles, drive up and try to gun down anyone holding up a corpse, though this risked producing more of the same, so they called it off and returned to the motorcycle assassins' original mission, to chase down and kill joyriding motorcycle youths, who were smashing traffic lights and throwing Molotov cocktails at police booths.[46]

Horror stories are circulating through the milling crowds. No one really knows how many were killed and injured. The government is saying only forty-six died, but all of those were injured people who died later in the hospital, when it was more difficult to cover up their bodies. Witnesses say hundreds were gunned down, their corpses placed in fertilizer bags and carted off in GMC army trucks. These witnesses tell how they were made to lie face down in the street, and shot at if they looked up, and how they did it anyway (doctors and nurses later make angry public announcements about the people who were shot in the back of the head, at point blank and near point-blank range).[47] In fact, there is no telling what happened to the dead bodies. Residents of the northern quarters of the city claim they saw the bagged corpses brought into a nearby temple, where they were cremated one after the other in smelly, smoky, all-night sessions. Meanwhile, sources inside the army and navy claim other bodies were thrown out of helicopters over the jungles across the Burmese border, while others were weighted down and tossed into the sea outside the naval base in Sathahip. Other spectacular stories allege that the corpses were dropped into the crocodile pond at a major tourist attraction, or that the army buried the dead bodies in trenches they dug right inside their own compounds in Bangkok.

Activists drive by in pickup trucks with megaphones, distributing pho-tocopied leaflets with the "latest information." People crowd in hungrily and strain against each other, reaching out for the leaflets. Some batches of leaflets, streaming in anew each hour, announce the death toll to be five thousand, ten thousand, twelve thousand.

Most people are quickly drawn by the flow of others sucked irresistibly toward the Royal Hotel. A clot of people are lodged outside the hotel, the site from which the goriest images of corpses were broadcast. The lobby doors are locked, but the people peer through the windows, trying to get a look at the space of death. There is confusion and mystery passing from lip to lip. Some say it was the field hospital for the wounded, others say it is the morgue for the military, and the corpses of the missing are being hidden inside. Troops pass by in GMC trucks. Instantly the soldiers are assailed with verbal abuse hurled from the bystanders. The soldiers fire their weapons in the air and disperse the crowd, but soon enough the people are back, pressing in once again to snatch a look at the lobby of the Royal Hotel.[48] There is a bullet hole in the glass so big you can stick your thumb in it. The outer wall, made of solid stone, has bullet dents two inches deep. But inside, you can no longer see the bloodstains on the gray marble lobby floor which were once vivid scarlet on the satellite transmissions to the world beyond.

Eventually the hotel management gives in to the crowd, and lets the people stream in to get a look for themselves. They find no corpses inside. Management pleads with them to leave so that they can get back to business. It had taken them two days to wipe up all the blood. A few days ago the hotel was full almost to its three-hundred-room capacity; now there are thirty guests.[49]

All around the scene are hundreds of little black circular stickers that have been stuck up on phone booths, the sides of buildings, lightposts, some of which say "5,000 Dead," and most of which say "Liar-Free Zone."[50]

A single tree on the curb of Ratchadamnern Avenue is riddled with telltale bullet holes, and a meter-long section of bark has been completely ripped off by gunfire. Faint bloodstains have soaked into the wood, and there is dried blood on the sidewalk beside it. People there say that is where soldiers tied up a young man and executed him with machine guns. They tie up a sweet-smelling, jasmine-flower garland around the trunk, above the grisly, impressed evidence. They call it the "Tree of Democracy." Later, for effect, they douse it with a bucket of cow's blood.

The next day, after all the soldiers are finally moved out, crowds stream into the area. People gather in groups to discuss the events, and to see for themselves the barbed wire barricades, charred vehicles, the occasional trace remnant of a human body here and there, or the shredded blood-stained clothes and numerous scattered shoes, to get a look at the bullet holes and dents in trees and shopglass, traffic signs and stone walls, the piercing holes and thudding indents that leave little to the imagination as far as what the army's assault rifles can do to a fragile human body. People hold handkerchiefs to their noses or, failing that, pull up their shirt collars to cover their noses as they inspect bloody articles of clothing or traces of bodily remains.

Spontaneous shrines pop up everywhere, especially at the Democracy Monument and around bloodstained trees and articles of clothing, around brains, bone, or fragments of flesh found drying in the intense heat. Jasmine garlands are strung in great numbers from the bloodstained Tree of Democracy. People crowd around, reaching out to feel the bullet holes with their fingertips as if they were touching a living saint. Small paper flags are stuck into the bark, in the end, hundreds of them, many more than even the bullet holes, which cannot be touched or seen now because the tree is a bursting red, white, and blue beehive covered in the national colors. Crowds come to the tree and bring offerings of fruit, food, and water for the spirits of the dead.

They kneel on the asphalt with lighted candles and incense, holding up their offerings first at heart level, then at head level, and inwardly make a concentrated mental determination and wish that the spirit is well, at peace, and released from its torments, finding an easy rebirth in a heavenly realm of existence.

From another tree, which has also become a shrine with incense, candles, and lotus blossoms offered at its roots, is hung a bloodied shirt and a sign reading "Two dead here."[51]

A procession of students and prodemocracy organizers, carrying black banners and black wreaths and dressed in funereal black clothes, moves down the street, passing the Democracy Monument, passing through the new marketplace that lines both sides of the street, and on to the Royal Hotel. About five hundred doctors, nurses, and staff of nearby Siriraj Hospital join in, followed by about two thousand from the crowd of ten thousand who were gathered into hundreds of discussion groups mixing in the avenue's heat, dust, and noisy sidewalk vendors. The doctors and nurses complain bitterly that children were not spared, and that the victims were mostly shot from behind.[52] There is not a single police uniform in sight now, even though the traffic is severely backed up. Municipal workers have to get in the road and the cars themselves. Every once in a while a traffic helicopter passes over the scene, and the crowd erupts into boos and hissing, because it is the helicopter that checks out traffic for the *JS 100* radio show, the only uncensored form of talk-back public discourse permitted on the airwaves, which was nevertheless used as an anti-demonstration propaganda instrument during the protests.[53]

The funeral procession lays wreaths at both the Democracy Monument and the Royal Hotel, inaugurating them as sacred sites. Soon the Democracy Monument becomes a great big tomb. A huge black sash is wrapped around the center structure. Black wreaths and cloths are draped from the four giant eagle's wings. Thousands of incense sticks are placed on the steps, sending fragrant smoke up to heaven, where before burning buses had belched up black clouds into the sky. Thousands of people pass in and out, lighting candles for the dead, laying down black or white funeral wreaths, and gifts of thousands of lotus blossoms. The Democracy Monument, thickly coated in funeral wreaths, and breathing up clouds of incense, pulsates with burning offerings left by the tens of thousands who have knelt there, focused on the well-being of the dead, tens of thousands of determined wishes let loose here so that the unquiet spirits of those who died violent and unnatural deaths might escape torment and gain rebirth in heavenly existence.

In a Thai Buddhist conception, the moment of death is crucial for the destination of the spirit afterward. A mind dying in anger, fear, or confusion will arise again in a form suitable to that state, in hellish anguish or, more likely than not, as a "hungry ghost" (*preta*) who hovers over the scene of life and death like a broken record, playing and replaying with obsessive hunger the state of mind at the moment of death. All of the conditions of living before that moment come into play, of course, for after all the mind that encounters a violent death has characteristics it has inherited from previous, conditioned states of mind. But the extreme added conditions of anger, fear, and confusion at death may overwhelm what has come before. The enigmatic concept of *kamma* (*karma* in Sanskrit) accounts for these processes of cause and effect. But intervention in this process is possible, through building up beneficial mind-states during individual acts such as kindness, generosity, charity, direct cultivation of the mind, and—by far the most widely practiced form of religious observance in Thailand—"merit making" and "merit sharing" (*tam bun, phrae bun*). Merit sharing is intersubjective kamma: dedication to others, especially to relatives and the dead, of the effects of meritorious deeds including but not limited to alms giving to monks, nuns, and temples, observance of Buddhist austerities, and meditation. In a Thai Buddhist conception, the only way to intervene in the shock of violent death on the spirit of its victims is to share merit for them and assuage their torment.

But the funeral exchange at the site of violent death in Black May was at the same time a political performance for recognition of the violence. The special province of merit making in Thai Buddhist culture—by the very nature of its intersubjectivity—is its ability to absorb into its ritual form disparate entities and intentions, whether that be a disparity between the living and the dead, or that between any other social formation and the individual intentions of the merit sharer. Political programs of both progressive and reactionary politics are routinely expressed in merit-making idioms, ranging across everything from the meritorious killing of "communists" and students, as Buddhist counterinsurgency groups encouraged in the seventies, to large collective donation rites sponsored by large Bangkok banks to perform their legitimacy in the countryside,[54] to this Thai oppositional funeral exchange on the steps of the Democracy Monument.

Merit makers on Ratchadamnern Avenue vary in the degree to which they think of their performance in these rites as strictly religious; almost no one to whom I talk believes that she or he is not also demonstrating sympathy with the protests and lending merit to the cause itself. A few say they are only expressing solidarity through a form in which they have no literal belief. As the wafts of incense rise into the sky, and gifts of food, flowers, and candles pile up on the steps of the monument, surrounded by the grave aura of charred vehicles, slight traces of bodily remains, and the shell-shocked storefronts speckled with bullet holes and broken windows, the rites become a giant, centralized, and condensed expression of the numerous and scattered rites regularly held all across Thailand's roads by close kin for the accident victims of its rapid and uninhibited progress. The traffic in this accident is in moral sentiments, telescoped into the center of national history. The expression of solidarity and connection between the living and the dead here are only metaphorically that between kin, "brothers and sisters of the people" (*pi naung prachachon*). The rites for this side effect of progress may not finish so precipitously as those roadside funerals that allow families, arguably, to pick up and move on at the same speeds. And this funeral may never be completed.

A formal merit-making ceremony for the spirits of the dead is announced for the next morning. Tens of thousands of people are drawn in, most of them dressed in black-and-white funeral attire. They stream in to the accompaniment of a tape recording of monks chanting, blasted out of loudspeakers, wafting over the gigantic funereal marketplace. Large continuous billboards line the sidewalks, displaying thousands of photographic prints, taken by everyone from foreign and Thai journalists to student amateurs and common folk with Instamatics. Meanwhile, all over Bangkok, and in the provinces and especially the provincial towns, a small portion of the population takes to wearing the colors of mourning in a nationwide movement that centers around the dead. At Ratchadamnern, doctors and nurses dressed in their white uniforms and wearing black armbands move through the incessantly chattering crowd, complaining to everyone about how the soldiers blocked them from getting to the wounded with ambulances, blocked them from getting through to the dead and injured, how they were assaulted and shot at when trying to tend to those they could reach. A big black banner hung from one of the monument's eagle wings reads, "Why block ambulances and assault doctors and nurses helping the wounded?"[55]

Scores of Buddhist monks file in. In a long line, they receive alms gifts from the people before sitting on the Democracy Monument, filling its sooty gray steps with their orange and ochre robes. They chant, dedicating the merit made to the spirits of the dead. As in almost any other rite of funeral exchange, the people then ritually transfer the goodwill made by the act of giving, and give it over to the unquiet dead. A list of the names of the missing is burned as a stand-in for cremation.[56]

THE FUNERAL BLACK MARKET

There are other supplements, however, for the presence of dead bodies on this charnel ground. There are other substitutes for cremation here, embodied in a giant market of massacre splayed out over the funereal space.

140

Newspaper stands all along Ratchadamnern are doing a brisk business. The English-language papers, as well as *Matichon* and *Pujadtgaan*, which had been the most forthright all this time, quickly sell out, even though they are cranking out papers at maximum capacity. The mass-circulation *Thai Rath* is the only news corporation that has the means to keep up with demand, and is turning out several editions each day. Both English dailies turn out a special edition that carries nothing but massacre news. It is not only the regular newsstands that make out so well, however, for there are enough customers in the thronging crowds for small venture capitalists to get in on individual street vending, which is normally the province of the destitute. People go to the offices of the major newspapers and buy bundles wholesale. All along the avenue, hundreds of mats are laid out with various newspapers on offer.

Many other forms of public media join in on the market. More prepared than any other, the always gory crime magazines print out hastily put-together editions, sporting all the blood-and-guts photos they can muster, and reach the highest sales levels in their history. These magazines—the two most popular are called *Crime* and *911*—regularly publish the most graphic death scenes they can find. They have always existed in a symbiotic relation with Sino-Thai benevolent associations that seek out unclaimed corpses from murders and accidents, usually the poor or unidentified, and perform Buddhist funeral rites for them. This elaborate system (a story in itself), produces profits for the gore magazines, fame and large donations for the benevolent associations, and merit for donors and for the dead. This everyday religious commerce in corpses, death images, and funeral rites, while representing an established media apparatus ready and able to absorb Ratchadamnern's circulation of graphic imagery and funeral consciousness in market form, is also in some ways a prototype for the avenue's funeral market itself.

All kinds of magazines, however, get in on the funeral market. Special one-time edition "Black May" magazines spring up for sale everywhere, with gory pictures and text. Vendors lay out sheets on the sidewalk to display the ten to twenty varieties of death images they have up for sale. Soon after, it seems that almost every genre of magazine has transformed itself, in whole or in part, into the crime-gore format, so that even the TV digest and soap opera weeklies, which keep one up on all the latest celebrity gossip with glittering snapshots of stars on and off the filming scene and glossy color bra advertisements, now have bloody centerfold sections of glossy color corpses, and scenes of atrocities committed by police and soldiers.

At some quickly set-up curbside stands, one can purchase original photos of corpses with their brains spilling out of cracked skulls, or wrapped up in and drenching the national flag with blood. The most commonly available pictures come from a single roll of negatives smuggled out of the gory scene of the Royal Hotel before Special Forces stormed it. The poor-quality prints are mass produced so hastily and in such great numbers that the colors come out blotchy and smudged with bright, vulgar color, as though the photographic prints of bloody bodies were themselves mashed with a truncheon. There are a few print enlargements of better quality, and these larger corpse images are being held aloft for display among the crowds, some by activists spreading news with megaphones, some by vendors advertising their wares.

As many as one-quarter of the thousands of people streaming into Ratchadamnern in the first few days after the killings come in armed with their personal cameras, and take pictures of everything from the elaborate shrine constructed out of the Democracy Monument to the spontaneous shrines constructed around body parts left in the street, to the evidence of bullet holes and bullet dents left in the trees and walls of the buildings lining the avenue. To aid them, activists go around with chalk to make big circles around every hole in wood or stone they can find. Many of the visitors leave the avenue with not only their own photos but also photos they have purchased on the street, whether they were prints or some form of gore magazine. A few sidewalk vendors have on sale a collection of sandals, shoes, and other belongings reputed to be those left behind by the dead.[57]

At this turning point, though it was the physical destruction of bodies on this space that has attracted first the funeral and then its attached market, relics no longer dominate the scene so much as representations do. The pieces of brain and bone are gone now, and videos quickly become the bestsellers.

Unlike October 14 and Bloody October, this massacre is caught on video. On October 14 the demonstrators had managed to retrieve some of the corpses, but this time they have retrieved their images, which in a strange way may almost be better.

The first day after the soldiers have left, a few cautious vendors set up stalls selling video footage of the murders—warily, not sure if they are doing something improper. But, after all, upcountry protest sites have already been selling videotapes of BBC and CNN satellite transmissions, virtually from the moment the first shots were fired. The first daring entrepreneurs on Ratchadamnern Avenue make a killing, selling tapes at prices up to one thousand baht per cartridge. Soon others buy tapes, retape them, and set up their own stalls. Many of the vendors have TVs hooked up to running cars and vans so that they can display their wares in support of their hawking cries to the crowds that their videos are the good stuff, the uncensored stuff, the foreign stuff, jampacked with dead bodies. Those vendors who don't have the capital for hooking up a TV have

Figure 7. Previewing massacre at the video market

the smudged and hastily reproduced photographic prints from the Royal Hotel on display instead, some taped to the video cases or just propped up against them to indicate that there is death, blood, and corpses in these black boxes. They give money-back guarantees that the advertised blood, gore, and corpses are indeed to be seen on the tapes.[58] By the third day, Bangkok's massive underground infrastructure for pirating videos has engaged itself in the funeral market, and there are hundreds of video vendors in hot competition, lined up and down both sides of the half-kilometer stretch of street from the Democracy Monument to the Royal Hotel. Lottery vendors sit neglected, as what was once the favorite hot spot for gambling with the state has now been transformed from official state casino to an illicit casino for selling pirate videos. Potential customers, along with those who come only to see and have no intentions or money for buying, crowd around the numerous TV sets, oohing and ahhing, yelling out and wincing in tandem as they watch. Others mill about from set to set, skipping over the boring parts and finding a set where they can catch a good part (see figure 7).

As the market expands, prices fall to between two and four hundred baht per video. Bangkok's elaborate means of production for pirating video, which has been earning the country top priority for trade sanctions from the United States because it is hijacking Hollywood, are now churning out their own material, local images captured by international business but taken back again, for an audience that cannot get enough.

143

As Annette Hamilton has argued, in distinction to prevailing views about the relation between world economic regimes and the nation-state form, the enforcement of international copyright laws in Thailand have in the case of media served to reinforce, not diminish, the power of the state over its populace in its desire to insulate them from undesired messages in audio and video emanating from the world at large.[59] The strength of this conjuncture of interests between global and local power could be indicated no better than by the fact that its opposition is embodied in an alternative production regime that flourishes in black market practice. But I would suggest that the the property-right regime is far from a completely successful hegemonic alliance. This is attested by the fact that video crackdown in the eighties only drove the means of production further underground. There it proliferated through increasingly more informal networks, and its structures only became more antistatist in form—and by Black May 1992, in content as well.

The pirates of the new world order become the most powerful resistance to national media control. Under the sign of death and the space of funeral exchange with the dead, the black economy thrives on a power that can no longer be controlled by the Thai military, the state, or by Disney. The means of production and black marketing have already been set in place, ready for implementation should the occasion ever present itself.

The mass-produced tapes quickly spread from Ratchadamnern to all the major marketplaces where pirated videos are sold, like the sex-industry district of Patpong Alley. Even ultramodern and luxurious shopping malls have massacre videos running continuously, on display in the multiple screens of the video stores where, as everywhere else, they vastly outsell the usual market leaders Sylvester Stallone and Jean-Claude Van Damme, who are just faking it, anyway.

On the street, the tapes that had the hardest exchange value were the ones reputed to have the most graphic and violent scenes. Australian film crews were reputed to have the goriest images, followed by the close seconds of the BBC's Royal Hotel footage and the Japanese NHK team, which held its ground along the army firing lines. In form not unlike the prestige afforded foreign whiskey in Thailand, the more the video contents are made up of gory and foreign footage, the higher the price.[60]

The content and value of the tapes widely vary. Some tapes are hour-long edited compilations. Others are two- to six-tape sets that feature uncut taping of the protest, compilations of foreign news broadcasts, or tapes made by Thai TV camera operators and smuggled out to prodemocracy groups during the events. Some versions are narrated and others are raw.

Almost as soon as the video market heats up, the military infiltrates it by starting to market its own tapes in dozens of roadside stands, though their ingredients are not labeled as having come from the military. These videos contain scenes of protesters running around in the streets, screaming, throwing rocks and bottles, and long shots of buildings and cars burning, all sorts of flaming images and fiery destruction of property—this all cut in with shots of soldiers getting in trucks, soldiers getting off trucks, soldiers marching this way and that in an orderly fashion, soldiers manning roadblocks, soldiers leading people this way and that, soldiers giving aid and comfort, wiping a brow, administering water to a thirsty protester, and so on. These videos are offered at a cut rate of 200 baht (and I even saw some at 170 baht). Although they do accomplish, to some degree, the promotional goal of getting out into circulation favorable public images through the unknowing purchases by the more uninformed consumers, the military videos also quickly help to bring the general market prices down, thus also bringing the price of the truly damning and gruesome images more within reach of the average consumer.

At Central Department Store's largest shopping mall, customers and employees alike are treated to multiscreen video replays of the violence on a huge bank of video screens, which normally displays advertisements for gigantic commodities, beautiful twenty-foot tall models, and loud music videos that blare tunes throughout almost half of the shopping mall's floorspace. But back at the technologically less-well-endowed entrepreneurial funeral, vendors of bootleg pirated videos use unassisted vocal cords and hawk out competing calls of "Ratchadamnern!" "Paan Fah Bridge!" "Royal Hotel!" (major sites of killing), or cite the foreign news services: "BBC here!" Some use Xeroxes of the most sensational newspaper photos and headlines they can find and tape them to their video cartridges in order to package their merchandise, while a few use only the top of their lungs.[61]

The goods continue to be hatched in the hideouts of the bootleg video pirates who want to lay low and out of sight of the U.S. trade reps who keep pressuring the Thais for more crackdowns. The "Robin Hoods," as they say in Thailand usually of those who illegally migrate for work and foreign currency, are now not only taking entertainment from the rich overseas and giving it to the poor over here, but taking back their own intellectual property rights, taking back the dead bodies snatched from Bangkok streets, dispersed over the surface of the globe, then shuffled into the living rooms of the first world, and bringing them back from there to their point of origin.

COMMODITY PATHS OF NECROMANTIC POWER

While the killings were still going on, occassionally national TV would feature shots similar to the military videos, of burning cars and rock-throwing protestors, followed by state buildings aflame, public property being destroyed by roving bands of motorcycle gangs, with traffic lights and police booths all smashed up. The images of mayhem would be juxta-posed with gentlemanly scenes of police and soldiers acting in an orderly fashion, helping out distressed protestors, and so on. With that image established through the media form that is by far the most widely attended to by the populace at large, the junta had announcers read out text about how this chaos before one's eyes was destroying the national image and how that was going to deplete foreign investment and wreck the national economy, which by implication implicates everyone else alike in the hard-ships to come.

The establishment of a national image on the line had long been smelting in the forge of international business, and the military had, up to now, been bending the discourse, to some degree successfully, to their own ends. All the while—during the February coup, the World Bank meet-ings, the Miss Universe pageant—the logic of public images was picking up more and more momentum as more and more claims were being made that images are a real field of productive value, requiring a strong hand to care and nurture. Such arguments could be made even more convinc-ingly now, as they were combined with a frenzied business elite's discourse on image damage measured and gauged in interest rates, foreign reserves, capital in- and out-flows. But hovering over everything, and hanging in the balance, would the national image prove any more dependable, har-nessable, any more under control, than the image of the corpse proved to be for the dramatic students of the seventies?

Immediately after the smoke and embers fizzled out, the interior minis-ter in the Suchinda government, former police general and Class Five ally Anand Kalinta, tried to shore up the government's image with a local press conference, but the enraged reporters only yelled out hostile ques-tions about the murders, to which he responded with what became the week's hottest headline, "Line up the corpses to prove it!"[62]

Military censorship of TV was fairly tight, but newspapers were a dif-ferent story. Some were merely suggestive at first, but others were explicit the whole while. Interior Minister Anand Kalinta ordered the shutdown of those newspapers, but they refused to comply. Still, most people in the country did not the read newspapers so much as watch TV. And it was true that in the end they could only locate around fifty of the corpses (almost all of which had died in the hospital).

But the visual imagery of the event was quite different abroad. Prime-time news in Australia would feature a full five minutes of soldiers holding their weapons at body level and then firing them into crowds of unarmed Thais. ABC and NBC had violently embarrassing scenes on the nightly news in America soon after they took place. BBC and ITN of England had its crews on the scene, as did the Japanese news services of NHK, TV Asahi, and Tokyo Broadcast systems. And news crews from Canada,

Germany, Australia, Sweden, France, Korea, and even Luxembourg were all also running through the Bangkok streets.[63]

Thai TV workers, in fear of severe retribution, did as they were told and aired only official announcements and approved central-pool footage, put together at the army-owned Channel Five and distributed to the other stations from there. But although they reluctantly slopped the standard fare out locally, they allowed foreign camera crews to use their facilities in order to route footage to a satellite transmitter, and broadcast an uncensored version to the rest of the world.[64] A frequently recited anecdote went: when Thais abroad saw the gruesome scenes on their TVs in the United States and Britain they phoned home to Thailand to see what was going on, only to find their friends and relatives asking *them* for information.

Satellite transmissions in Thailand are all routed through a central, state-controlled transmitter. There were a few incidents where worried Thai TV station managers put up some interference with the foreign journalists' satellite links. Sometimes, Thais manning the broadcast facilities would garble transmissions when the pictures got violent, or sometimes one station would refuse service and they would have to go to another, or that one would suddenly turn coat and they would have to go back to the first. But whenever it got to be too much trouble the foreign news services would pool their footage or simply send tapes out on the next flight to Hong Kong and link up there.[65] Whatever the case from moment to moment, the reporters did manage to get the images electronically encoded and shot out into space. So in France, where the crown princess was visiting the high society appropriate to her station, there were almost instant replays of soldiers shooting directly into crowds, while the bloody results of that shooting, strewn about on the morgue, field hospital, and lobby of the Royal Hotel, would show up in England. But this was not the only direction in which the death images were moving.

Some Thais are linked up to CNN on cable, and BBC on Asian Star TV. So it was only a matter of a few moments delay before the same images were viewed and consumed locally. People in Bangkok above all, but also some upcountry townspeople, have access to satellite and cable, especially in apartment buildings, and this audience was easily amplified by video taping, copying, and redistribution of the footage to those who don't have that access. The junta did its best to stop the flow of the images returning from the world back to their native country. They set up some electronic interference of CNN on cable, but there is nothing to be done about satellite transmissions.[66]

Moreover, the foreign news services shared their footage with local crews on the spot, and these quickly shuffled it off to those swarming pirate video operators who plague Thailand's economic relations with the United States. Even the local news services, though they could not actually broadcast anything, could not be prevented from at least taping things for the record. So through the practice of black-market economics, there was actually a surplus of death images, regardless of the fact that so few bodies could be found.

There, in the very same street where the people were killed and their bodies—most of them—stolen away and permanently made to disappear, the dead now reappeared not only as gruesome evidence of atrocities committed locally *but also as images that have passed through the hands of foreigners*, as concrete and corporeal evidence of the state of the national image in the eyes of the world.

The death images returned from the sky beyond and sought out their point of origin. And from that point of reception at the Ratchadamnern funeral ground and black market of massacre, the images once again fanned out, radiating to the various other video markets of Bangkok, and on to provincial cities and towns. So it was that the original images of those corpses that slipped out of the grasp of the army on Ratchadamnern Avenue, those images that also got past on-the-spot confiscation of negatives and tapes by police and security forces, would move on to Thai TV facilities, and from there be broadcast on to a central satellite link transmitter in the ground station at Sri Racha, and from there into outer space and bounced all the way over to the first-world headquarters of the news agencies, where they were edited and then sent back into outer space, through satellite transmission, to the country of their origin, where they were tape-recorded in Bangkok and other cities on video, copied, and redistributed in little black boxes carried by plane, train, bus, and automobile, first to the towns, and later by democracy activists to the rural countryside in traveling shows. The world system expanding and contracting, contracting and expanding, like a galactic polity.

But even this was not the only pattern in which the news flowed (though being visual, and viewed by an audience largely accustomed to taking their truth through the eyes, it was perhaps the most influential). Mobile phones, first criticized in public discourse for being a nuisance in public spaces like movie theaters, now became heroes of the revolution. Phone carriers reported another massive surge during the second wave of protests and the ensuing violence, as more on-the-spot reporting radiated out of the space of death.[67] And as injured bodies trickled out of that center, the hospital workers who received them would then also get on the phones and report the gruesome consequence all over the city and countryside.[68] Fax machines, which normally carry naughty and forbidden messages with the latest gossip about the royal family, were now pressed into the service of a massive bypass of censorship, moving reports of atrocities and other subversive messages from office to office in Bangkok

148

and between Bangkok and provincial towns. On-line bulletin boards were flooded with real and false information, anti-Suchinda messages, and flaming hate mail. Then wildfire chain faxes leapt from office to office carrying astronomical body counts and accounts of devilish corpse-hiding tactics.[69] Photocopied pictures of violence and leaflets of firsthand accounts were passed though the streets and marketplaces. In a continuation of a strain of misogynist discourse that accompanied some of the affronts to the generals, one popular photocopy featured Suchinda's head placed atop the bikinied body of a Miss Universe contender.

Rumors multiplied. A few of the more enterprising individuals, armed with cellular phones, fax machines, and on-line computers, turned themselves into information clearinghouses, working in groups to collect information, sift through it for the most likely reflections of reality, and then send it back out again through the same channels.[70] In some cases, a single report or rumor could have a path that passed through every form of media several times, reprocessed at each step along the way. Everything from talk on the street to phone calls, to electronic information transfer, to broadcasts in outer space, was interconnected in multiple ways. The communication links could rapidly fire out information from the street into outer space, or it could double back on itself in circling loops, transformed and sifted by a massive, informal consensus.

To an attention captured in such a manner, the censorship of TV news seemed only to backfire. The only centralized medium that could possibly have established a single, authoritative version of the truth was bypassed. And in its stead a wildfire of public exchange raged—truth, rumor, gossip, and gripping tales all jumbled in a complex of exchange—gifts, commodities, and communal discourse reflecting and transmitting the sheer excess opened up by the gashes in the body politic and the necromantic power that had been unleashed.

Although the pink afterwash disappeared down the curbside drains, it was quite fruitless, in fact, for municipal workers to hose down the street. With the dead bodies gone, only more and more vividly did they exist, and the more sensational did their disappearance become: burned in fertilizer bags, in a temple, in secret, thrown out of helicopters and into the jungle, tossed in crocodile ponds, in the ocean, in secret trenches.

The lack of cadavers for physical handling only multiplied their discursive presence. In the week following the killings, the hottest stories in print journalism, and by far the hottest items of gossip, were centered on the whereabouts of the missing corpses. Several hot lines were set up to locate the missing, and government reports started to add up to between one and two thousand, though individual lists varied. As time passed, government counts of the missing would dwindle slowly but surely, but at the time it was the most charged of issues. Army spokespersons were on TV daily to refute the latest reports, trying as best as they could to keep up with the accumulating rumors that piled one atop the other, amassing in the informal and underground realms of communication, surfacing by the force of their excess, like corpses stacked up in a secret grave that cannot be dug deep enough to prevent them from spilling out into the open air.

The military made reluctant TV camerapeople from the army stations film footage of great trenches that the soldiers dug out of the grass on military compounds in the city, which "proved" that there were no such corpses hidden away on their grounds. To back that up, they got what newspaper reporters they could muster to photograph the orchestrated hole in the dirt. All that might have proved something to those eager to believe, but in another sense it was just foisting another image on the public that signified nothing but empty space, just another instance in which what should be solid and grounded looked vacant and mysterious. The necromantic power generated by the empty trench had already moved elsewhere, to the charnel ground of the Democracy Monument, there rising with incense and chanting and passing on to the spirit worlds.

And so, even without much coverage by the usually all-important Thai TV stations, the onus for the crimes was shifted decisively on the military. Funeral rites gathered to themselves all other forms and media of exchange, including the illicit and forbidden. On the very site of the charnel ground, under the aegis of the protest funeral in which the spirits of the dead were given the honor and remembrance due them, a funereal and black market absorbed into the image of death the nature of several economic systems: international image trade, small-time marketeering, illegal trade in artifacts and political messages, trade in historical memories, and gift-exchange with the dead according to Buddhist funerary principles of remembrance. The black funeral market turned the political tides in a direction that had seemed unimaginable at the time when Suchinda was sworn in and Chalad Worachat volunteered to be the first one to die.

He didn't die. Against any reasonable expectations, Suchinda was miraculously forced to resign. The military, despite their grip on the mass media, was unable to control the public image sphere and the national image discourse to which they had themselves first tied their fate. In the end, they received the brunt of an outrage effectively delivered in sensational imagery of death and violence. Since that time, the idea of military intervention in Thai politics has gone into a deep coma. Most of the junta generals were transferred from power. Given the widespread condemnation that the circulation of massacre images achieved, they did not dare resist.

Parliament was soon after disbanded, and new elections held. The opposition parties went on to win those elections by a narrow margin.

Sovereign Power

And yet that incense which floated from the charnel ground and the steps of the Democracy Monument burned for only a short time, and the chanting sounds passed away, as vibrating molecules in the air dissipated their clusters of pulsation into the vast expanse of the atmosphere. The sheer excess of that moment, an excess that could not be pressed down or rubbed out from above, or pinpointed with truth and accuracy in any of the multiple, complex, and mutually intermutating forms of eruption in which it had passed—that surplus energy unleashed by the power of the corpse passes, in turn, from these material rites into an elsewhere, and the fuming residue left over is mutated yet again, into a sublimated power visibly and tangibly real, public, cultural, publicly cultural.

There were two signs that took palpable form in a strange alchemy, transubstantiating from the malodorous remains, two sovereign powers that emerged. The first was the public sphere itself, which discursively refashioned itself out of the stuff and spiritual matter of the charnel ground. The sheer excess opened up by the violation of killing and the unquiet souls of those who died violent deaths became in the weeks of aftermath a story—told by and in the media—about the importance of media freedom and the power of the public sphere. In their retelling of the story, the television and print media had the throngs of people out there in the streets—the ones who refused to back down, who joined in as more death and danger was unleashed, who afterward filled the funereal market of the charnel ground—they put these people there for the sole reason of wanting the *news*, to know what had happened. It was because of the censorship and misinformation that the crowds had swelled. In their version of history, the more the junta suppressed information and the more it foisted its own pale lies on the educated, middle-class, techno-literate public, the more the hunger for information grew, and this information-starved public was therefore flushed from its individual private entertainment nests and out onto public space, searching desperately for the highly priced and valued commodity which by the law of scarcity, animating great demand under limited supply, had burst an invisible hand right through new ceilings of value.

In this balancing of historical accounts, the market on the charnel ground of Ratchadamnern Avenue, which evolved out of a funereal and spiritual exchange with the dead, is actually a pure expression of free-market capitalism, reemerging where it was unnaturally suppressed. The law of supply and demand and the marching forward of its historical and inevitable expression is raised to the level of truth-effect: the information-starved masses fill the streets demanding the goods that are due them. Media technology is the hero of the story. The charnel ground is buffed up with the phantasmagoric sheen of an advertisement for a new world. This new world is both the heroic agent of history and the primary martyr and victim, as well. But it rises again, inflating itself with the life force of surging demand for information, free information—information is scintillating everywhere, and everyone is middle-class, wielding sacred weapons of truth, justice, and the moral order of historical things: satellites, VCRs, cellular telephones, fax machines, computers, yogurt.

Alongside with the moral coronation of the public sphere, the sovereign power of the monarchy also flashed. For it was at the cusp of climax, when the king stepped in for a televised audience, that the demonstration was made not only of his local power but also, and inseparably, of lightbeams radiating outward, signifying the power of the king as a public image in the eyes of the world.

The power of the king, in fact, is directly linked not only to traditional categories—the Ashokan empire, Dhamma kingship, and so on—but emanates from his exchange value in a worldwide network of images.[71] For those who follow business at home and abroad, the monarchical power is linked directly to the fluctuations of stock-market prices, to the adjustments of fractional percentage points in the disbursement of foreign loans, to the evaluations and devaluations of the Thai capitalist elite's credit rating everywhere from Wall Street to Hong Kong. In the wake of violence, the stewards of the foreign exchange promote the image of the king repairing the damage to the national image. The idea that the image of the king will have power in the eyes of the world can enhance his power locally among those desperate for a solution. If his power is enhanced locally by this idea, then the king will therefore actually have more power locally, which, in turn, also proves to the world that they are not wrong in their estimate of his power, and that does have the desired effect of assuring investors. That, in turn, proves the reality of the power locally yet again, and so on and so on. The loop does not really have a beginning or ending point, but rather turns upon itself and signifies itself, which is perhaps the meaning of sovereign power. It makes itself. Like the sun, it reflects nothing.

This is a power exceeding the bureaucratic and rational power of the state, for neither force—neither the media nor the monarch—actually wields the dangerous and deadly material means necessary to wreak violence on the people nor, we can presume, would either the corporate media or the personage of King Bhumipol ever wish to do so. This is not the power of Leviathan—to cow the awed and frightened populace into submission—for that kind of power lurks elsewhere. The power of Leviathan is wielded by proxy, as it were. It is sublimated into an innocent power by the apparent fact that both the monarch and the media are what stand between the people and such a terrible force. Without the monarch, the military could run roughshod over the populace—something local people and global investors take notice of. And, similarly, the public media hold back murderous violence, a violence that were it not for the media would be given free reign.

A surrogate Leviathan arises from the charnel ground, with the sovereign power to tell its own story, to make itself. A new era in the communications industry stepped into the picture and shone therein, while stepping over the bodies of the Black May dead. Competition for the most sensational stories but also for the burgeoning profits to be made was launched into a new stratosphere of intensity after Black May. Along with another brilliant moment for the monarch, it was this coronation of the information industry that became the most lasting and most profitable effect of the violence and death, the most lasting legacy of Black May. In the media's story that it told about itself, the sheer excess opened up by the killing was transmuted into scarcity, the spiritual economy based in violent death flip-flopped into a political economy of information. A surplus of meaning in the general economy of the charnel ground was transmuted into a narrow and rationalized economy of hunger, need, and scarcity, reified as information.

The work of history in the information age shears off that repulsive excess of mortal animation, the death that gives it life, shutting out from its narrow vision of economy that exchange with the dead, that deal which is, in fact, dealt, whether the eyes to see it still exist or not.

Between the high-capitalist exchange of international media, and the local, spontaneous marketplace of image exchange, it was only a matter of weeks before all responsible commanders were transferred, the government and parliament disbanded, new elections held, and the prodemocracy opposition parties finally took control. And the Thai mass media were finally released from censorship.

End of story. Trade triumphs over violence.

And, you could say, the new world replaces the old. The military gift-economy of the Cold War is exchanged for the neoliberal market of a new world order.

The battlefields are indeed turned into marketplaces.

The New Leviathan

The proliferation of paths for the exchange of Black May valuables was not merely a naked, empirical fact. It is no coincidence that all the details about information transfers and electronic images, as discourse, were in themselves a constant object of focus and fascination for the print and electronic media for a long time afterward. It was as though, just as in this text, it is not only the content of the images and information that is of sensational appeal here but also the very fact and manner of their circulation and proliferation that shine forth and capture the attention.

In the battle for possession of the Thai state, alternative public spheres reconfigured the channels of power and influence in the Thai prodemocracy protests of 1992. Attention to these paths and linkages of local and global media is crucial to understanding these events. But attention is not enough. Recounting the paths by which images are exchanged and public spheres formed and dispersed does not necessarily address the powerful forms of imagination, and especially historical imagination, that are shot through globalist narratives about the significance of mass media. This is especially true where practices with media are in fact embedded in social formations, such as Buddhist funeral rites in this case, which defy the organization of selective attention in global neomodernist principles of inclusion.

The plot device of technology in the narrative of the public sphere and its moral valence cannot be separated from the broader structural movement of the ascension of the public sphere as a dominant economic and cultural institution. To look askance at this development is not necessarily to critique the idea of free speech and expression but rather to be aware of the cornering of those same values by an apparatus founded on highly centralized capital, the wheels for which are always greased by a corresponding centralization of moral capital for imagining new claims on territory. One has to wonder whether the fragmentation of media spheres within states, attendant upon the globalization of mass media, may be just a step toward increasing conglomeration on other levels, through the centralization of a global means of production, and in the multiple replication within local contexts of a modular version of imagined media. Black May shows how counteractive media practices with highly localized valences can be absorbed into a more universal discourse of the public sphere, made conceivable and moral on its own terms and in its own, quasi-sovereign, right. The exchange of the military-gift economy of the Cold War for the neoliberal order—a fair enough one when considering only the short-term project of the demonstrations—has a closing cost that may be nothing less than the institution of a new Leviathan.

This analysis, however, emphasizes the value of counteractive media practices that are themselves only conceivable after the technological implements for their delivery have proliferated, as, for instance, the neomodernist theory of Appadurai also underscores.[72] The radical potential of Thai counteractive media practice in Black May was undeniably amplified by an illegal production chain made possible through local proliferation of recent technologies on the one hand, and through a global mediascape already in place on the other. The "darker" mirror of these means of production were forms of "civil society" in charnel-ground funerals that are unassimilable to public-sphere discourse—"black" business models that are outlawed by international treaty and subject to suppression in exchange for the Thai economy's legitimacy as a trading partner in the new world economy. The counteractive media of Black May opposes this new order not only as an alternative material means of production but also with alternative structures of social relations that are irregular to that order. These even include, in this case, cosmological orientations and exchange principles that run counter to the dominant discourses that are abstracted in the "Idea of Civil Society" attending to the public sphere generally.

Anyone closely following the protest cannot deny that material control over the representation of the incident was crucial to the event. There would have been no hope for the protesters without at least some international presence and without some degree of free expression for their messages. In fact, the entire course of the movement and massacre, as the account of the month of demonstrations indicates, was largely navigated with image positioning, this being absolutely crucial to the outcome at every stage, from the construction of the crowd as a mob or mobile phone mob, to the depiction of the military order of barbarism, to the apportionment of legacy as organized largely in the idiom of the public sphere's ascendancy as opposed to other values such as exchange with the dead.

In her article "Surviving Pleasure at the Periphery," Rosalind Morris argues that fascination with the violent imagery that was circulated up-country during Black May was due to a form of "survivor's pleasure." On the basis of Roland Barthes's essay *Camera Lucida*, Morris argues that these images which were so deliberately circulated during and after the Black May events are to be understood as providing an experience of satisfaction for people who realize that their own life continues, consequent upon realizing that others are dead. Thais were provided with a self-satisfaction in death images made uniquely available through modernity and its media. My research among everyday consumers of mass-circulated crime gore magazines certainly confirms the partial validity of Morris's reading, that indeed a pleasure—which I would specify as the pleasure of intensity and shock more than that of survival (which would require at least an interview or two to establish)—is a significant factor among repeat customers of these magazines, who often describe their patronage as "an addiction" (*did*).[73] Additionally, as we have seen, the material means of production and the marketing models for graphic magazines were also directly engaged in the promotion of the market in the massacre of Black May. But reduction of the conscious and deliberate methods by which Thais circulated graphic imagery to a thin vision of the meaning of the market as producer of desires and pleasures, which are therefore to be taken as the prurient indulgence of modern excess, expels the alterity inherent in Thai practices with death imagery. It is possible to have an interest in death that is not simply one of self-interested pleasure in life but is also about death itself; a market can embody multiple practices simultaneously, including pleasure, profit, and desire but also displeasure, political insight, religious meaning, and collective conscience and consciousness—all this can create an instability in the heart of mass media theory and its object, an object that depends far too often on flattened historical consciousness in its performance of itself as the ground of the really modern.

In fact, a great deal of what has come to be common sense about the representation of graphic violence in modern mass media could benefit from fundamental reconsideration. The history of Black May admittedly suggests that the media employed within the representation of the event lent their powers to a quick transformation that bypassed the intentions of those who were either dying or honoring the dead. But were I to read back from that fact in order to discern a political meaning inherent in the nature of technological form, I would only lend more salience to the narrative principles of modernity discourse that are crucial to performing that transformation. The process is one of extracting some of the values and practices in place at the time and taking them to be major elements in the outcome because they are easily assimilated into modernity discourse. This process is closely tied to the broader development of an emerging, legitimated public sphere replicated locally many times in modular form but supported by an increasingly monolithic mass media structure of centralized global capital.

The most significant force of historical agency is largely attributed to the implements of "modernity" in both the media's own representation of itself in the events and in two articles depicting Black May in the journal *Public Culture*.[74] This attribution speaks to that resonance in the echo chamber of global capitalism in which the analytic tools of anthropology bear striking resemblances in form to discourses closely tied to the mass media's own project. In fact, the technological agency of electronic media cannot stand for the whole of the event—but even more important, cannot even stand for the whole implementation of the media within the event. The exchange of Black May media images in the funeral market was, in fact, bound up in a charnel ground of funeral rites and exchange with the dead, even as it was quickly bound again into the service of performing an accounting for "modernity." This social and cultural embeddedness must be sloughed off if a hypostatic version of the free market is to prevail. In the continuous funeral rites staged on Ratchadamnern Avenue—precisely on the scene of the killings—we can witness, in a matter of days, this transformation occur: from the confluence of Buddhist gift-exchange for the dead with an entrepreneurial casino of death images to an extraction of historical meaning and agency out of these embedded rites for the sake of a thin description of "modernity." This is done for the sake of a story about media as agent and a certain commonsense version of the free market cut loose from the social bonds through which it was, in fact, constituted. But this distillating mechanism does not only pertain, as we will see in the chapters to follow, to this "turning point." Here, analysis of a "pivotal event" has included more than situating it in a causal narrative between what comes before and after, but also inspection of the turning point itself for the pivotal principles turning within the point. I would suggest that the pivot within the pivotal event of Black May was precisely this transformation of Buddhist funeral black markets into the hypostatic free market and the Idea of Civil Society. This particular pivoting principle has had a longer legacy and effect than has the event of massacre itself. The "free" market and mediated "modernity" extract themselves from the charnel ground that gives them their life, so that they might, as imagined entities, symbolically perform their existence and virtue, and like sovereign power and the sun be nothing but a reflection of themselves. In the process, the modern market and the modern media aspire to become realized versions of the ideal image of themselves, performing a crucial work on history in the turning of the event but also furthering a project that is of far grander ambition.

THE VALUE OF THE DEAD

The integration of the Thai economy with the new vision of the world market was fairly well completed by the time I returned to Thailand in 1995. Only three years after Black May, the alignment of neoliberal financial policy with the privatization of industries and relaxation of state interventions into the economy had picked up great momentum. The "bourgeois revolution," as the ultimate victors had performed it, was successful, and without a subsequent reign of terror. And yet curiously, three years after Black May, the military's constitution was still in place. The Democrat Party, which eventually won the premiership, was unwilling to take steps toward a new constitution after it began enjoying the powers that the military's version afforded. A demonstration for a People's Constitution had been staged in Bangkok the previous year, two years after Black May, and was led by another Chalad Worachat hunger strike, but it failed due to the public's lack of interest.[75] Chalad called off his hunger strike, seeing no point in dying if no one was going to pay attention. The next year, for the third anniversary of Black May in 1995, he just sat outside parliament alone. There, he complained to me:

> I have been sad and disturbed all this time, all three years. If not, I wouldn't have come here today. I am sad thinking about those who died that May, and how we did not get anything from it all. I don't use people's lives to campaign for fame. I don't use people's lives to seek my self-interest. I honor them. I

will finish their task, so long as I have a life to do it with. I want democracy to be real. One day, if there is real democracy, the heroes will get what they deserve. I think of them always with a pure heart, and not to make an image for myself. At the very least, I will do something to exchange with the martyrs. . . . If I see the flow of the people is right, I might put my life on the line one more time. But this time is not right for that.

Surely politics is all about timing. But if so, then timing, and so politics, is also all about the nature of time itself. Student activists and relatives of the dead, whether from October 14, Bloody October, or Black May, believe that there is great political potential to the time of recurrent return, of commemoration and anniversary. This is a countertime that cuts against the grain of a system that would have itself move rapidly from era to era, that would stress this aspect of time against others that might drag on its heels. True, things seem better in 1995 than in 1992. Democracy and a free press, though not fully realized, seem to be more robust than they were when the military seized power at the turn of the decade. There is certainly no way to fight tyranny without these things, above all the free press. But there is, perhaps, more to the story, even more that it is necessary to be vigilant about. For those intimately involved in or affected by Black May, at least, the accounts are far from closed.

In May 1995, I returned to the site of the charnel ground on Ratchadamnern Avenue, a year after the failed People's Constitution protest, three years after that original, absorbing moment in Black May when all sense of time, all thought of the past and future, fell away and all that there was, was here and now, at the center of history. Massacre commemorations were being staged by student activists, and attended by an organized group of relatives of the Black May dead. Together they would perform a ritual exchange with Buddhist monks, on behalf of the spirits of the dead, on a site by the side of the avenue where they also hope, one day, to erect a monument to the Black May sacrifice. They assembled with some sympathetic monks for the merit-making ceremony in which alms gifts are presented to the Buddhist order, and a merit-sharing ceremony performed for giving the value generated, by these gifts, over to the spirits of the dead.

But there were, this time, no tens of thousands of people out on the streets to exchange with the dead. The commemorations were not even covered by the television media that had derived from the event their newfound freedoms. A few print journalists showed up, but their brief stories would appear far from the front pages. A few politicians showed up, but the government that had been put in place by the sacrifice of Black May wanted to put the incident in the past, where it could no longer stir up trouble.

A government led by the Democrat Party's leader, Chuan Leekpai, was formed out of the ashes of Black May. The campaign for the election held three months after the 1992 massacre was the first period since the commie-mongering days of 1970s massacres that the political landscape was again sharply polarized on an issue. The division of political interests into multiple party factions that had little ideological basis had again begun to take on a clearer binary coding, although this time, rather than being a premurder division of left and right wing, created by and for the right wing, it was a postmurder apportioning of positive and negative moral value, with the parties behind the demonstrations raking in the moral profits. They narrowly edged past the former government parties in an election that, as always, was largely determined by vote buying and patronage networks but that also definitively proved that public media, opinion, and discussion could have a decisive influence. The newspapers and television had divided politics into the *Phag Maan* "Devil parties," those who had supported Suchinda's outsider premiership, and the *Phag Theeb* "Angel parties," those who had supported and helped organize the May protests. The relatives allowed themselves to be part of the political movement to shore up democracy after the massacre. They cooperated with the Democrat Party's government, invited party leaders to their commemorations, and allowed their symbolic value, as martyrs to the cause, be associated with what were then called the Angel parties. The relatives posed for pictures, gave endorsements, and promised not to act too militantly.

The media represented the Black May protest crowd as middle-class—in other words, they represented the media's primary consumer base as being in the driver's seat of history, the representatives of an inevitable historical order of things. But most of those killed were urban and rural poor, in many cases breadwinners of their families or sons expected to support their parents. After the massacre, it was decided that the state should compensate the families of victims: 200,000 baht for death (about US $8,000), and half that for a disabling injury. The new government was also to oversee an investigation into the whereabouts of the missing corpses. They didn't find them. Those who did not have a corpse to show would have to wait three years and be cleared in an investigation before they could collect their money.

As soon as the relatives learned the terms and rate of exchange for their dead, they set up an advocacy group. Many of the families were not going to survive. The government began to ignore their plight right away. The families had to band together if they had any chance. With the help of a lawyers' association they pursued a criminal case against the perpetrators of the massacre, but since Suchinda's government had issued an amnesty decree for everyone right before they resigned, and since the military would not remain quiet if they were not allowed to go free, the case was thrown out of court. So the families are pursuing a civil lawsuit, and rely mostly on charitable contributions for their monetary support. In three years, they have not gotten very far in the courts, and most of them do not hold out any great hope. They've seen how things work.

And now, three years later, the relatives of the dead join together for several days of commemoration ceremonies. They have no choice but to band together and continue reiterating their demands, which ultimately can be reduced to the simple request that they count, that they and their dead be readmitted into the economics of this system. And to their demands for compensation the government responds—to their faces and also in highly publicized statements—that these people should not "use the dead to make a living" and should not "use the dead to strike bargains."

"From the prime minister who came from our flesh and blood," commented a father whose daughter was killed.

"And *now* look at the papers," another father adds, slapping a front page with the back of his fingers, "since the start of this ceremony there has been no news about the families of the dead. Just ordinary murders here and there. They should announce the progress of our case. They should ask who is going to take responsibility for our situation. They should announce who is helping us and who isn't. There's only headlines about sensational crimes and accidents, but nothing about our heroes' deaths."

"It's totally silent. We Thai are forgetful. We forget too easily."

Under some cool trees on the commons of Thammasaat University, right on the killing fields of Bloody October, I sit with the relatives of the dead before the start of their Buddhist ceremony of remembrance. They keep coming back to those two things—the forgetting, and then how everything gets twisted around. It has become a commonplace since the 1970s massacres that "We Thai are forgetful" (*khon thai rao kii lyym*). Everyone was saying that even a few days after the 1992 May massacre, during the height of the national pathos, that very soon everyone would forget all this. But I suggest that in a way this ubiquitous perception of forgetting also indicates an extraordinarily strong consciousness of the importance of remembering.

The group of massacre victims and families call themselves the *virachon* relatives. Virachon, literally translated, is "courageous person," and in practice means a combination of martyr and hero. Generally it means any heroes who sacrifice themselves for a collective cause, but in common discourse I have heard the word used most often (though this is indicative of the kind of company I keep) with respect to people gunned down by the military while fighting for democracy. In this usage, the term embodies the theory that it was specifically these deaths that engendered social changes in the balance of power toward popular participation and political freedoms. With complete accuracy one can sum up the purpose of the virachon family group: they seek both a rightful recognition of the political value of their kin's sacrifice and the material means to survive without their presence. And the former ought to beget the latter, according to their inherent sense of a law of exchange.

Mindful Economy

As the merit-making ceremony is about to begin on Ratchadamnern Avenue, a mother who lost one son dotes on her remaining one, twelve years old and pudgy on sweets. She pats him gently in the direction of the politicians: even though he is a shy and quiet boy he doesn't balk at sitting on the teak bench with Vice Prime Minister Chamlong Sri-Muang. Many press photographs are taken, and Chamlong makes some small talk, kind talk, about what a handsome, intelligent, strong young man this boy is. The boy neither smiles nor frowns, neither warms nor turns away.

Later, as the monks begin to arrive under the tent's canopy, Chamlong mills among the people who came to attend this ceremony. He must stand close to every one of them because the buses, trucks, cars, and motorcycles that roar just a few meters away make it hard to hear anything. Their smoke wafts under the hot canopy. Like foul incense, it seeps in from behind the monks, who sit in a row upon a raised platform. Chamlong takes his seat on the teak bench with Uthai Pimchaichon, commerce minister and leader of one of the smaller government parties, also with no power to change its policy. The virachon relatives sit in collapsible chairs. Everyone presses their hands together at heart level, and they begin to exchange chants in Pali and Thai with the monks. The laity pay respect to Buddha, and ask for the five moral precepts. The monks pay respect to Buddha, and recite the five precepts to them. The lay people repeat after the monks, in Pali, "I will refrain from killing, I will refrain from stealing, from lying, sexual cheating, drinking."

Then alms gifts are presented. One person goes down the line handing over gifts to the Sangha of monks: robes, tinned foods, soaps, toothpastes. Another hands out envelopes with money for each.

Everyone recites a chant for making merit, willing that the act of giving benefit the Buddhist Dhamma and produce results of well-being, health, long life, good fortune, and nibbānna (nirvana). The monks then continue the exchange with a chant of blessing, focusing on projecting their chants over the sound of engines gunning on Ratchadamnern Avenue and projecting their good will out into the laity. Almost everyone—the senior monks, the junior monks, the senior political leaders, the student leaders, the virachon family, the spectators, even some of the reporters, and myself—focuses on transferring the good will and the merit to the Black May dead. While the monks chant blessings over the scene, and in fact over the precise space where many of the people were killed, the guests of honor who sit on the teak bench perform the "pouring water" custom for dedicating merit. Water is poured from tiny pitchers into small bowls, spilled from one container over into another. Everyone else presses their palms together at heart level and recollects the dead.

It is in this moment that the spirit of the gift is transferred to the other side, to the ones to which the debt is owed, according to a law of symbolic exchange.

Of the guests of honor, only Chamlong refrains from the pouring water custom, as is taught in the puritan Santi Asoke sect that he participates in. The controversial leader of the sect says that this water-pouring ceremony of merit transference smacks of primitive and magical superstitions.

No one faults Chamlong for that, however. At least he showed up. And after all, he wouldn't be "Maha Chamlong" if it were any different. He carries himself reticently, appearing small and almost shy before the official monks. Within this scarcely attended ceremony, submerged under a high, beating sun and almost inundated by a gigantic city's traffic jams, there are few or none who gravely doubt Chamlong's sincerity, unlike many of those out there in the bustle. None that I know of in the virachon family blames Chamlong for the deaths of their loved ones, despite the fact that they could just as easily blame him for some of the more confrontational and controversial decisions he made, if not also for the deeper past of student massacre in the seventies. But they understand the difference between a political ally and a foe, and see through the manipulations by more directly culpable parties who have gained by laying the blame for the deaths on the one who led the protest, by tying everything up in a loop that points nowhere.

Quietly, the monks return to their temple, everyone retires, and the ritual paraphernalia are packed away. Some lingering family members point out to anyone who will listen that there is still a score to settle. "It rains, and before anything gets dry they already forget," complained a woman whose son died from complications of a gunshot wound to his lung. Another, younger woman was pregnant with her only child when her husband was killed in Black May. She was there in 1992, with a contingent of virachon family, when they met with the Chuan government soon after it formed itself out of the May dust. She was there when they said, right to their faces, "Don't use the dead to complain. Don't use corpses to make money."

"They said that and my heart fell out."

"If I was there I would have cursed them out," chimed in a rich lady whose son was murdered. "At that time, I was too shook up. I was so sad. I was in a bad situation so I couldn't get up to go. But if I was there I would have really given it to 'em." Since she is so wealthy, she argues, where is that assumed avarice with which the government wants to camouflage her pain? She is one of the most avid supporters of the virachon family's civil lawsuit against General Suchinda Kraprayoon and his partners. "Even if it is for just one baht, I will still sue. I'll grab any chance I can get—whatever right is still left to me I will take it. Either that or give me back my child, right?"

One mother of a disabled son came to the commemoration ceremony selling little cloth change purses her son sews, one-handed, at home. "They said if they became the government they would help those who sacrificed so that they could rise up," the mother says calmly, resigned, "but once they got to be the government they weren't interested anymore. At first Chuan Leekpai came around . . . to our ceremony. He mixed with us, you know, like 'the prime minister speaks with the citizens' kind of thing. He asked how we're doing, about our suffering, and so on. But when he got out the door, he probably forgot the whole thing. He would forget; he doesn't care. And then later they'll say we are using corpses to make money!

"They make promises and then break them . . . I have to look at my son who can't do anything. It is real pain. I feel alright to come here and remember the dead, the heroes, those who disappeared, but it still hurts. Because nothing is the same anymore. Nothing will ever be the same. They say we are after money, that we're greedy, hungry. But really, we are worse than that—there is nothing that can give us satisfaction anymore, ever. This is just how we live. We can just watch and listen from the outside."

Although in the wider public culture there is deep resistance to a return of that Black May ugliness, the families will always return. They will come out for the annual commemorations every May. There they have value; their dead have value. But otherwise everything is upside down. And that, precisely, is what characterizes the economics of this movement in time. In this economic system, members of the living family are almost like dead spirits. To haunt is to be a ghost in the next world, over there somewhere, unseen and almost undetected. To be a ghost is to be marginal, to have no role to play in the economy of the living. A haunting spirit is dissatisfied, restless. Preta, "hungry ghosts," are what Buddhists call them in Thailand.

Today the virachon family are just like these marginalized dead, whereas in that past—the past that was not so long ago, after all—their dead, the true dead, were paradoxically like living bodies possessed by spirits in a reverse mediumship by which they were seized by political interest and then discarded, the reverse possession by which the corporeally living rode the bodies of the dead and bound them to their will for a time.

One mother, Pi Nok Gaow, has a special complaint: not only did she lose two sons to the army's gunfire, and not only did she lose the corpses of her two sons to whatever means the army used to make them disappear, but now the state has decided that she should only be compensated for one of the two dead children. They claim that the rate of compensation is 200 thousand baht per family of dead victims. It is not 200 thousand per victim, they told her, it's 200 per family. So now that the three-year waiting period is over and she is entitled to the money, they will only give her 200 thousand for both boys. Of course, the virachon family are outraged when she tells everyone about this. It is perfectly natural and obvious: she lost two boys, so she should get 400 thousand, 200 for each boy.

"They were never interested in politics," she says with utter seriousness in answer to one of my questions, "they were interested in making a living." The last part about making a living she says with serious emphasis, to communicate the fact that only people like her people, and not like mine, can understand how much more meaningful the latter can be than the former.

What happened for the two young laborers was that the path of their commute to work passed directly through an area where the army was engaged in sporadic shootings. In a gun's sight, workers wearing working clothes are indistinguishable from rabble rousers rabble-rousing. The two young men had been staying at a temple where they could ask for food from the monks, and so have money left over to send home. And sometimes they would bring sacks of rice back to the temple from their home village's paddies. They used to show up at home every New Year's and every Songkran Water Festival (Thai New Year). Then one day in May they didn't show up for work, and they never did show up again anywhere at all.

"If I could have had even one bone to chant over and pour water! They are dead, and I don't even know where to look for the bones, so how could I do any of that, right? Gone, completely gone. Both the person and the corpse, both gone. This weighs on me, greatly. I can't clear it out of my heart. I can't cut it out. They are my children whom I love. The greatest love is loving one's children. My love of myself can't equal my love for my children. Think of it that way, the life of a mother.

"The other boys, the young ones, have already promised that one day they will take care of me. 'Mommy, don't go away somewhere to work,' they say, 'just stay home.' Where we come from, we take care of our own. We owe each other at least that much."

And the state owes her 400 thousand baht, 200 for each child.

The three-year waiting period for missing corpses is over, but out of seventy families in the relatives' group, only eighteen have been compensated for their dead.

As Samyote, paralyzed by a gunshot to the back, says, "What politics has given me is this chair."

PART II

✤

Kamma

The Charnel Ground

VISIONS OF DEATH IN BUDDHIST ASCESIS AND

THE REDEMPTION OF MECHANICAL REPRODUCTION

> History, in everything it displays that was from the
> beginning untimely, sorrowful, unsuccessful, expresses itself
> in a face—no, in a skull. . . . It articulates as a riddle, the
> nature not only of human existence pure and simple, but of
> the biological historicity of an individual in this, the figure
> of its greatest natural decay.
> WALTER BENJAMIN[1]

AN ALTERNATIVE SENSE OF GORE

Why did the market of massacre on Ratchadamnern Avenue—the corpse photos, videos, relics, and even the spiritual economy of exchange and offerings to the spirits of the dead—have such a short shelf life? The shock effects ran deep. The traffic in death images was brisk. And the political tides turned in a way that seemed miraculous, given the impossible situation in which the antimilitary forces found themselves at the time of General Suchinda's first swearing in. It seems that it is only with the death of people that the power to change things is armed. They must die. There must be death—if they are to win, or so it seems in short sight. But what of them, then, and their deaths after that?

The shock effects delivered through the medium of imagery made, in the critical moments of aftermath, a victory for the forces aligned against the murders. The imaged corpses of victims were the hottest item for a few days in May 1992, especially with the real cadavers banished to a mysterious elsewhere. And as could be heard in the guarantees of vendors called out over the market floor in this trade of death images, the aesthetic of the corpse that achieved the highest exchange value was precisely the antiaesthetic, the most graphic and repulsive depiction. It is gruesome images, which serve death straight up, that carry the evocative charge—a sacrificial charge that was then transmuted from an excess of graphicness into a leaner, cleaner story about the liberation of free-market information flows, crowning the shining public sphere and a mass media glistening with sovereignty and profit.

There are, of course, other dangers that beset the necromantic power of graphic imagery. The neoliberal economy of history of Black May shows how this power can be tamed and sublimated into the ordering of new-era constructions and a particular teleology to the moral authority of historical movement. The exclusion upon which exchange between eras depends cannot erase, however, the traces of its peaceful violence. The living ghosts of unquiet relatives produced by that exclusion—if not, at least in the minds of many, the spirits of the dead themselves—still haunt the scene of modernity, returning in yearly punctuations as well as in continual acts of insistence. The clean order founded upon violent death is inherently erratic and in a state of contradiction. This fact is easier to see in events that are less assimilable than Black May, or completely unassimilable, to the narratives of modern democratic progress and process—as Thongchai Winichakul has argued with respect to Bloody October of 1976.[2] As Thongchai has written, although the revolts of 1973 and 1992 are taken, at least by some, as steps forward in the Thai national history of modern progress, Bloody October of 1976 was far too violent and ugly to be assimilated, and has always been marginalized in historical consciousness. The attributions of "communism" and "un-Thainess" still hang over the memory of the victims, ensuring that they remain cast out, excluded from fully human accounting as virachon, or those who have sacrificed themselves for the nation.[3] As a result, regular yearly commemorations of Bloody October are, in my observation, always far less well-attended than those for October 14 (1973) or Black May.[4] But as Thongchai himself suggests, it is perhaps the extreme atrociousness itself that renders Bloody October unthinkable and that may never permit its rightful entrance into the history of Thai democracy.

It is uncertain whether this is entirely unfortunate or not, at least so long as the terms of exchange with the dead would be the same ones "negotiated" unilaterally by the forces that emerged victorious after Black May. The transmutation of the graphic power of revolting history in such exchanges leaves a huge blind spot in the purview of the dominant order. Its fount therefore remains uniquely available to those who have the sense, and sense of duty, to draw upon it. That is where all the other dangers of necromantic power arise, having always been there. Not only can the power of graphic death be tamed through historical misdirection and sleight of hand but also, as we have seen, the unstable and dangerous power afforded by directly touching the most hideous and gruesome imagery—as the turn of events within the event of Bloody October itself demonstrates—can escape all control whatsoever and even ricochet back upon those who would make use of it. There is, as I have suggested, something in the political use of the cadaver that epitomizes the quality of all intentional meanings. As Katherine Verdery has also stated, the symbolic effectiveness of dead bodies lies in "their ambiguity, multivocality, or polysemy. Remains are concrete, yet protean; they do not have a single meaning but are open to many different readings." In a separate note, she recognizes that "most symbols share these properties" but that "corpses are particularly effective in politics because they embody the properties particularly well." Moreover, this power is compounded by the fact that "[t]he link of dead bodies to the sacred and cosmic—to the feelings of awe aroused by contact with death—seems clearly part of their symbolic efficacy." All this calls up the question of the affective efficacy of symbols, which Verdery argues is long-standing in anthropology and "troubles other social sciences as well."[5] And troubled they ought to be.

Many well-planned violent programs are legitimated with affective appeals to the symbolism of death. Before the war on Bosnia, there was a disinterment of mass graves of Serbians from World War II—a huge, orchestrated media event within Yugoslavia—that eventually led to even more mass graves for Bosnian Muslims. Sensationalist photography of aborted fetuses has led to fatal bombings of clinics in the United States, among other violent speech acts. The examples are endless. And yet, at the same time, a cognate peaceful danger lurks here as well: through no coincidence in historical timing with the concerns of the present text, Verdery was writing of the politics of reburial of dead bodies, particularly of famous figures from the past, in the performance of transition to new-order postsocialism in Eastern Europe, and saw quite clearly that "[d]ead bodies, in short, can be a site of political profit."[6]

The affective efficacy of death symbolism is by definition perhaps the least of things amenable to routinization into social scientific discourse. This is no less a problem for those who would, in practice rather than in theory, address, traverse, and negotiate these dangers. With the clean transmutation to political legitimacy on the one hand, and the chaotic propensity to escape control on the other, the graphic presentation of death is besieged on all sides. This is all the more powerfully problematic when visions of massacre are stilled in photographic memories—stilled, but not finally so—no less dangerous or powerful than the bodies themselves. For this reason, I would depart from conventional forms of explanation and direct attention to a work with graphic images of death that has not been conducted by social scientists but instead by a committed coterie of Buddhist meditators who employ graphic visualizations of death and corpses within their own agenda. In a way, of course, their investigations do not completely take leave of Thai imaginaries, especially where they concern the violently marginalized and unquiet dead. And I suspect, given conversations on the subject with Thai student activists, that this overlap of Buddhist meditation on death with broader cultural idioms could potentially make its philosophical insights especially usable to those so inclined, since political ritual in Thailand is conducted, in part, within a Thai Buddhist idiom from which most commemorative movements in Thailand draw upon, in part. But at the same time, the strictly Buddhist meditative approach to visions of death lies at an oblique angle to the political implementation of death. Although it is far from usable as an autonomous, totalizing frame that could provide an explanation of all the possibilities and potentials inherent in the affects of death imagery, this wealth of practice does have the value of seriously attempting contemplation of these forces in depth and breadth. Buddhist meditation on death represents a distinctive practice in negotiating the dangers of corpse imagery and in traversing the ground of the marginal and unquiet dead. It is not so idiosyncratic, however, that it has nothing that it can say to us on this matter.

THE TEMPLE

A corpse with skin sliced open, revealing the innards; another on a table with rinds of charred meat dangling from the bones; one cadaver lying flat on its stomach with bloated gray flesh, swelling, as if about to burst . . .

Framed photographs of corpses line the altar of the small meditation hall, at the foot of a smooth, gold-colored Buddha statue—serene, ideal. To either side of the statue dangle a pair of full human skeletons, suspended from the ceiling, their dried-out bones connected by thin wire. Candles cast soft light, and incense floats randomly. Flowers, some fresh and vibrant, some old and dry, are placed at the foot of the Buddha image, among the framed images of corpses in various stages of rot. More skeletons are pinned up against pillars along the hall floor. Rotating ceiling fans circulate air over the heads of white-clad Buddhist nuns, who sit still among the human bones.

The golden Buddha statue, with its idealized grace, is a form of representation that may have been diffused since the contact of early Buddhists with ancient Greece and its sculptural humanism.[7] The photos of decomposing corpses are also diffusions—of Buddhist "contemplation of the revolting" into the realm of mechanical reproduction.

Asubha kammatthāna is a Buddhist practice of meditating on death, corpses, and the repulsiveness of body parts. In many ways, the thought of such a practice may seem to resonate counterintuitively with the values of ancient idealisms, not to mention present-day valuations of beauty, romance, and "the power of positive thinking." And even though the practice of contemplating the revolting may partake in humanist ideals—

as the altar's juxtaposition of photos and an idealized figure seems to say—at the same time, it flashes out with a sensational focus on the negative side of things.

In a sense, this meditation hall, steeped in images of death and corpses, participates in a very different economy from that of the media images circulating over the surface of the globe. Here, people practice an economy of images that goes under the surface of their skin. Under the skin, too, there are objects of desire and attraction, and powers of horror every bit as dangerous and liberating as those faces of death that circulate in a political economy of material images. The spiritual economy of Buddhist ascesis values death as an end in itself; it confronts death straight on, and exchanges its repulsive visage for release. And yet because of the chaos and danger of liberating signs, the attraction and repulsion of sensational depictions of graphic death, these forces of liberation and disaster are just as problematic in this other, very strange arena of image production and consumption, a realm that for most people is radically different from any other they know.   .

The practices pursued at Toong Sammakhi Dhamm, a Buddhist temple in rural Suphanburi province of central Thailand, thrive upon a form of meditation on death modeled after the ascetic adventure of the abbot and founder, Luang Bu Sangwaan Khemiko, an elderly monk and resident teacher. Asubha kammatthāna employs a mode of seeing that takes place in high states of concentration, called *jhāna*: meditative absorption with the image. Jhāna affords a special sort of seeing, born of intense training, that has intense effects on the mind. But however alien this mode of seeing may seem to be, meditative visualization in Buddhist ascesis shares with the necromantic power of public image politics a genealogical origin in the field of death. The subterranean killing field under Bangkok's lag muang city pillar is hardly the most notorious among spaces of death— in tall talk, in gossip, or in truth; nor are the sites of political massacres that return again and again. Hauntingly pervasive, tales of death—especially the violent, strange, and ghostly—have for a very long time been envisioned and interred in a domain of decay displaced to the outskirts of cities, towns, and villages. For much longer than there are historical memories, a piling compost of corpses, spirits, and wildness has fermented there, a space of death skulking with bodies and stories, in which the most frightening rot between the living and the dead is expurgated: a charnel ground.

When Luang Bu Sangwaan was ordained as a bhikkhu (monk) and went off to practice meditation at the age of thirty-five, in the early 1950s, he went straight into the heart of death's domain, to dwell alone in the *paa-chaa*, the charnel forest. In those days, and to this day in many places other than towns and cities, only the cadavers of monks were ever cremated on temple grounds, which is within the domain of the living. Regular cremation of corpses was usually held in a designated area of adjacent forest, or sometimes in a remote section. And for those people who died violent, accidental, or mysterious deaths, especially if there were no relatives to claim their bodies, corpses were quickly burned, buried, or cast out in the charnel forest, and special rites were performed to keep them from coming back out of it. Such a charnel ground more or less encompasses the ghostly traces Robert Hertz has drawn for the collective representation of death: "All those who die a violent death or by accident, women dying in childbirth, people killed by drowning or lighting, and suicides, are often the object of special rites. Their bodies inspire the most intense horror and are got rid of precipitately. . . . Their unquiet and spiteful souls roam the earth for ever . . . It seems . . . that the transitory period extends indefinitely for these victims of a special malediction and that their death has no end."[8]

The charnel ground invites imagination to the margins, where death and danger can be sloughed off, into the forest, to the "wild" areas already infested with crawling insects, slithering cobras, tangled vines, sedimented foliage; they are prowled, at least in imagination, by dangerous beasts like man-eating tigers. Whereas people who died ordinary deaths would get at least a several-day wake in the home and a cremation ceremony in the paa-chaa, often those who died sudden deaths were quickly disposed of in the charnel forest. Sudden death was unnatural. The dead bodies and spirits seemed dangerous and polluted by this ominous breach. Untimely death is a bad death. Surrounding both the strange circumstances and the corporeal result hangs an aura of ill and foreboding. Such corpses were not often brought to the home for a funeral wake, for fear that the diffuse ill would rub off, as it were. Such unquiet souls can in turn cause more death, striking out spitefully at the living. Sorcerers, spirit mediums, and people unwillingly possessed by spirits often communicate warnings about such dangers to the living or, in the case of mysterious deaths, often diagnose malevolent spirits as the contagious cause of sudden death. People say that there would be bizarre rituals sometimes held in the paa-chaa for deaths that were particularly disturbing. One of these, so the tales go, was for the corpses of pregnant women (reminiscent of Bangkok's city pillar, and its source), which were feared would become terrible ghosts. It was felt that the deaths of women dying in childbirth were the most threatening. The husband of such a woman would return hastily from burying her corpse in the paa-chaa but would not go home, for fear of drawing the spirit into the house. He would often go straight to the temple and be ordained as a monk, temporarily, to cut himself off from the spirit and make merit to wash away the diffuse sense of danger hanging around him.[9] Sometimes sorcerers would be brought into the charnel forest to cut out the fetus from the dead body with a sickle, so it could be buried with the dead mother.[10] People say they would drive a nail into the dead woman's forehead to keep her haunting spirit trapped inside.

Some charnel forests acquire particularly ominous reputations, through stories and through the communications of sorcerers, spirit mediums, and victims of spirit attacks, as being intensely infested with such disembodied souls. The worst of these spiteful souls are *phii baub* and *phii dib*—vicious, murderous, hungry ghosts that possess people and engorge themselves on their intestines. These spirits, hungry for blood and entrails, these unquiet souls that disembowel the living to feed their tragic hunger and attachment, could have been particularly evil and avaricious persons in life. Or they might have been traumatized victims of phii baub or phii dib. Or they could carry a condition passed on in the family. Mingling among these terrifying spirits prowl all the other haunted and disembodied souls who died dangerous and sudden deaths, whose souls could not pass peacefully because of some horrible violence or perversion in their death, such as suicide or murder.

Such haunting is no light matter. Spirit possessions occur in many areas throughout rural and urban Thailand, and people sometimes really do die in the painful throes and trauma of spirit attack (the pain and shock, at least, are very real), unless an exorcism is performed. And even then the attack can kill one.

It was precisely into such a space of death and danger that the newly ordained monk Luang Bu Sangwaan Khemiko immersed himself, venturing to dwell alone and practice Buddhist meditation on death in the haunted charnel forest, the notorious *paa-chaa phii dib* on the outskirts of Baan Teung village, in his native Suphanburi province of central Thailand. He, like everyone around him, had grown up with these tales since childhood. But in the practice of Buddhist meditation on death, the charnel ground takes on an altered meaning, a higher purpose. One embarks to live alone in the haunted charnel forest to face such coarse fears and confront death in the heart of its most ambiguous and dangerous domain. Above all, the young monk was there for the opportunity to be near corpses as objects of Buddhist meditation. To an ardent practitioner in search of a higher truth and power in death, the corpse can be more than an object of fear and dread, more than a source of uncontrolled powers. There are practices in the charnel ground that, at least in their intention, aim beyond fear of death, of corpses, of women, of sex and reproduction, of viscera and hunger, of life and its pain, randomness, and dangers.

MEDITATION IN THE HAUNTED CHARNEL FOREST

Luang Bu Sangwaan was born in 2459 of the Buddhist Era, in Sam Chook district of Suphanburi province, central Thailand. He was born to a prosperous and landed rice-farming family in the rural central plains. He never had a formal education, and grew up working the rice paddies. He married, but the couple never had any children. Then his health began to deteriorate. His legs often gave out on him. He and his wife would have to take turns tilling the field, as he was often laid up by fevers. Eventually he became crippled and completely bedridden by the pains in his legs. The misery of this condition was a great influence on his life, as he became directly aware of how fragile the human body is and how much pain it can cause. Soon afterward, a palm-reader diagnosed him as about to die.

Luang Bu lay stricken, incapacitated, at home. One day, a nun was passing through and heard about his condition. She came to see the ailing man and taught him a simple concentration exercise, which involved visualization of a crystal-clear Buddha at the "center of the body," about two inches above the belly button, in the middle of the torso. In those days, although a monk had started the movement that focused on this form of meditation, it was the nuns who practiced it who were beginning to become famous for the healing powers that resulted from its practice. Later, a male-dominated meditation movement called Dhammakaya (Dhamma-body) Temple splintered off from the original practitioners. It went on to become the massive organization it is today, a mass-marketed religion drawing hundreds of thousands of urban middle-class followers who are attracted to Dhammakaya's emphasis on cleanliness and order. The temple reaches epiphanies of purity with large, orchestrated rituals of group discipline and order, and with meditation on the crystal-clear image of the clean new self within. Also appealing is the theory that clear sight of the crystal Buddha within will attract wealth to the meditator (this can also be helped along by donating heavily to the temple organization).

But, as Luang Bu Sangwaan told me, with this crystal meditation one was always supposed to enter into the center of the crystal-clean image, penetrate one layer and then another in what seemed like an endless series leading nowhere. Nevertheless, by practicing the meditation on the crystal imagery he achieved such concentration that he was able to heal himself, and after two years of practice, eventually he came to walk again, though he never returned to 100 percent capability. His hair, which had gone prematurely gray, began to turn black again. For a time, he practiced further, believing that this idealization of the "Dhamma-body" within would lead to a solution to his suffering.

Visualization meditation involves focusing the mind on the inner realm of images that most of us are capable of calling to mind. This inner realm of images is not fundamentally different from the realm in which one is producing images as one reads this text at this moment. As will be further explained below, what meditation does is train one to focus incessantly, practicing the ability to visualize to a point where it becomes far more vivid than ordinary inner picturing. And then it is continued beyond that, to the point where all else is excluded from consciousness.

In Thai Buddhism, the most common method by which the powers of mind are exercised to such a point that a realm of charnel visions is entered is by training with *ānāpānasati*, literally, "mindful of the in-breath and the out-breath." One begins by sitting still and noticing the active sensations of breaths as they are occurring in the present moment. To aid in this noticing, one chooses a single point of contact, usually the impact of breath passing in the nostril area, which is one of the most pronounced areas of sensation. One develops concentration by paying attention to the sense-contact at one point. The common simile has it that the breath is like a saw, which moves back and forth on a piece of wood, but though it is always moving back and forth, it makes contact continuously on the same, unmoving spot. One quietly tries to receive the sensations, watching at that point alone.

The purpose is to be awake, to awaken. The word for this in Pali, which is commonly recited in Thai mediation practices, is *buddho*, "knowing, awake, the mind of Buddha." Following the in-breath, one says silently, inwardly "buddh–," which is to call for a reminder: "I am awake now, I know the breath is going in now." Watching the breath as it goes out, one notes "–dho," which means: "I am awake now, I know that the breath is going out now." On the in-breath, one knows that one is breathing in, in repetitive reminder that it is happening, and notes, "buddh–." When breathing out, one is aware that *that* is in fact what is happening, and notes, "–dho."

Unfortunately, our minds are not ours to control and do with just as we will. We cannot always think what we want to think, any more than we can always dream at night what we want to dream (because thinking, like dreaming, occurs in a state of relative sleep). Thanks to a bit of relative wakefulness, we have some choice about what, or if, we think—about what we pay attention to, if anything. But ultimately waking thoughts slip like dreams because they are not ours to control, as becomes abundantly clear to anyone who tries meditation a few times (unwanted thoughts come on their own invitation, for instance). So concentrating on one point helps temporarily to alleviate this problem, and produces a relative power of focus called *samādhi*.[11] Samādhi is concentration that makes the mind temporarily strong and firm and ready for application to investigate what one wills. But even more, when the focus on one point becomes more and more intense, steady, and calm, this one-pointedness leads the mind into such an even and steady consistency that the mind, concentrating singularly on a single object, may begin to impinge upon the object, as I will explain further below, and be absorbed into that object of attention. Some forms of Buddhist meditation, like that practiced at Toong Samakhi Dhamm Temple, aim at developing such intense absorption, while others are more open-ended and work at a lower threshold of concentration.

The most intense level of samādhi concentration, so absorbing that it shatters the barriers between the mind and a single object of its attention, is jhāna. In jhāna the mind impinges upon its own object of attention and fascination. Sometimes when the mind approaches such intense concentration the breath becomes so refined, and the mind and its object so mutually absorbed, that the breath becomes indistinguishable—it appears as though one is not breathing at all. If this is misunderstood, it startles the mind out of jhāna for fear of suffocation. But, in fact, oxygenation is still happening. Only very refined material phenomena can appear to the mind in the realm of jhāna. Though there can be a sense of form to the body, it is not a coarse material form, and such relatively harsh material things as a breeze blowing over the skin or hot sun on one's back cannot even be felt, because "the body" in that coarse sense has been temporarily dropped out of the equation.

The kind of absorption one realizes, say, when one is concentrating on a task—when you get "really into it," perhaps writing, reading, playing a sport or an instrument, when the past and future drop away, extraneous thoughts drop away, various sights or background noises are excluded from attention—that kind of absorption, which everyone is familiar with, is a relatively small degree of absorption when compared to jhāna, though it is akin to it in some ways. Jhāna can thus be understood as an extreme form of an ordinary power of concentration we all use. We do not normally think of developing concentration on purpose, systematically, for its own sake. We only accumulate it as a by-product of our regular mental activities. Most people do not devote their whole lives, and overcome many hardships, exclusively for the sake of systematically developing concentration itself. Jhāna is an ordinary result of such an extraordinarily systematic application, based on techniques that have been worked out for thousands of years. It is not hard to imagine that such absorption leads to experiences very different from the kind of everyday absorption experiences that are not systematically trained. Jhāna comes with intense, full-time effort, which sometimes takes an entire lifetime, a discipline that isolates this absorbing tendency and works systematically toward enhancing it exclusively.

One of the things that this conditioned state, or we could say *cultured* state, of jhāna affords is a kind of "seeing" that is very far from the ordinary visual perception people are familiar with. Nevertheless, jhānic vision has been part of the conditioned sensory makeup of human beings for thousands of years. No one knows for how long some human beings have used this faculty of apprehension, which always exists as a potential mode of seeing, so long as the right conditions are present and the wrong conditions are absent. It is certainly not "Buddhist" per se. It existed long before Buddhism and will exist long after it. This seeing faculty is an extremely powerful inner visuality. It is not essentially unlike ordinary inner vision (the imaginary picturing that almost all people are able to call up to their "inner eye"), but it is very different in the sense of how vivid, clear, and sharp it is, how steady and focused the mind is when it uses the faculty and, especially, in the sense of what it is possible to see with it.

For Luang Bu Sangwaan, at that point in his practice of visualization, the concentration on an idealized body image was so absorbing that he had actually helped his physical body get better. Jhāna, absorption into the image, can give rise to a bodiless feeling that is quite pleasant. But Luang Bu did not feel that he was getting any nearer to a solution for the ultimate problem of his body's course of deterioration. His body was bound to deteriorate eventually; Luang Bu's real problem was to find out whether he was doomed to suffer along with it, or whether he could be free. The crystal meditation, even in absorption, did not in itself constitute a solution. It did not call up the other side of things, the harsh side that he ultimately needed to face if he was to realize his goal. In time, Luang Bu went on to have influential experiences that would lead him in the right direction.

One day, while walking past a full-length mirror, he turned to glance at his reflection.

A skeleton.

He had an *asubha-nimitta,* an "image" or "sign" of "the repulsiveness of the body." Nimitta are the stark mental images that arise in meditation. Asubha-nimitta are images of death and decay that reveal a visceral and fragile existence. He saw the danger in being a heap of being. In technical terms, he had a glimpse of what they call the *khanda*s, the aggregates. He saw himself as a composite, amalgamated collection of phenomena, rather than as a being that consists of a singular, homogenous, whole entity. He had an immediate and startling vision of himself simply as a heap of bones.

The experience is not simply visual but simultaneously includes a feeling of actually, physically *being* that pile of bones, feeling as though one were truly a walking skeleton. That is what makes it lead to what they call a *paññā* experience, a "wisdom-insight": it makes one able more truly to appreciate, because of its total and overwhelming nature, what is meant

179

when it is said that beings are a composite of aggregates—of body or form, sensation, habits of recognition and memory, thinking and concocting, and sense of presence or consciousness (that is, the five khandas: *rūpa, vedanā, saññā, sankāra, viññāna*). These five transitory heaps make up a being, which always tends to fall apart again (these five concepts are, of course, a culturally particular way of dividing things up that is motivated by their practical usefulness in meditation). Luang Bu was finally convinced in an intimate manner of the fact that it was in his body's nature to decay and die. Paññā like this is profoundly disturbing, and tends to cause the mind to want to do something about it, quite unlike a mere chain of association based on an outward observation that leads weakly back to oneself. It produces an extreme sense of urgency.

The point of asubha-nimitta is to see other sides to life, and other aspects of the body: beauty and pleasure to be sure, but also pain, sometimes, and death for everyone. Just focusing on what is pleasant creates a distorted picture. Staring down the negative creates a balance, and from this balance it may then become possible to stand outside of both sides and just take it the way it is. But it is easy to say all this and another thing to be able to do it. In the visceral reproduction of asubha kammatthāna, one tries to hold an awareness of the heterogenous, amassed, jalopylike conglomeration of the body foremost in one's experience, and to hold it all day long and with whatever degree of vividness possible. Normally one does not do this, let alone retire to full-time contemplation on the amalgamated nature of the body. A more flattering aspect is perhaps preferable, but Buddhist meditators in this school of training feel that the tendency to flattery does not need to be helped along, because the mind is already so inclined and society systematically valorizes it.

With the vision and experience of himself as a skeleton, Luang Bu developed needs different from those of the people around him. He grew bored with the homebody's life, which follows the same predictable patterns of work, marriage, children, old age, sickness, and death. It all seemed to lead nowhere, so he decided to be ordained as a bhikkhu again, this time for good, until he realized the end of Buddha's training or died trying. He and his wife came to an agreement, and together even settled on a new marriage partner for her, a kind and responsible man in the same village. Many years later, the second husband died, and she went on to be ordained as a nun in Luang Bu's temple, there practicing the Dhamma until her own death (after which "she" became a skeleton hanging in the meditation hall). Luang Bu was ordained at the age of thirty-five, at a temple on the edge of a haunted charnel forest, and set off into the paa-chaa to practice Buddhist meditation on death.

To have a sense of the power of the charnel ground meditation that set all of this in motion, it is important at least to imagine what life must be like in the haunted paa-chaa. Leaving family, friends, and to some degree society behind, one dwells alone in the forest on the bare edge of survival. Without any amenities, one is existentially very close to and conscious of how dependent the body is on certain conditions to keep it going, such as breath, food, water. One is highly conscious of the delicate balance, the fragility of life. One has no companions to lean on emotionally. One is living among corpses, constant reminders of one's fate. But if that is not enough, in this already contingent state one intentionally and systematically impresses upon oneself visions of death. It becomes humanly possible to perform an autopsy on oneself, without being dead and without being self or other.

This is an important move, one that transports our attention toward what might be said to be another kind of charnel ground, which is not a geographical place.

THE CHARNEL GROUND WITHIN

In death meditation, it is the subject matter of nimitta, mental imagery, that is of the greatest importance. The primary reason for dwelling in a charnel ground (or for dwelling in a temple that is replete with reminders of death) is that deliberate construction of nimitta images of death becomes easier for one's imagination in a charnel environment, and spontaneously occurring nimitta will, more likely than not, automatically be images on the themes of death, corpses, and the repulsiveness of body parts. The living environment has a great role to play in the content of the images that appear to the mind's eye (not completely unlike how in sleep we dream of things that are on our minds in waking life).

Though they often occur spontaneously, nimitta visions of the body are also deliberately constructed. In asubha kammatthāna, once the mind is settled and concentrated to an adequate degree through *ānāpānasati* (mindfulness of breath), one is then instructed to turn to alternately visualizing five outer parts of the body, which have traditionally been suggested for beginners: head hair, body hair, nails, teeth, and skin; these are sites with which one is visually most familiar, and which also are made up of dead matter. One takes each object in turn and simultaneously places mindfulness at that part. For instance, one directs mindfulness to the hair stalks growing out of and hanging from one's scalp, meaning that one is instructed to feel aware of the presence of hair. At the same time, one should picture the hair in one's inner eye. Sometimes it is hard to picture, in which case Luang Bu Sangwaan directs people to "just know" that the hair is there. If one can picture it, then one should concentrate on the visual awareness, which will become clearer and clearer with increasing samādhi.

As a further aid to building samādhi on the internal image, one might inwardly recite "hair, hair, hair," in order to isolate the phenomenon of hair for concentration. This practice aims at building awareness, rather like asking oneself continuously, "Where is the hair? What is it like?" until the "question" drops away and one is automatically aware of the presence of hair. In the case of beginning meditation on body parts, the standard practice is usually to move from part to part, traversing the body, rather than to stay on one part, in order to find those parts of the body that one finds easiest to work with. After a short while concentrating on one part, one turns to the next object: "body hair, body hair," then "nails, nails, teeth, teeth," covering all five, down to "skin, skin, skin," visualizing the skin and being aware of how it covers and enwraps the whole body, and then starting over—head hair, body hair, nails, teeth, skin, and so on, over and over.

From these basic five parts, one moves on to working with all conceivable parts of the body. Thai meditators will move throughout their bodies, singling out body parts along the way. Thirty-two parts of the body—skin, bones, heart, liver, and so on—are identified in ancient classifications for the purposes of this mediation (though there is no reason the body parts cannot be broken down according to modern anatomy). Thai meditators systematically contemplate various parts from head to toe, inside and out, simultaneously visualizing them and cultivating an intimate awareness of the reality of these parts located in one's actual body, until nimitta images arise, and capture all sense. In meditative apperception, when enough samādhi has built up to support it, body parts will pop up with a strange and stark clarity, or as the meditators put it, they "stick to the mind." In asubha kammatthāna the mind rubs itself into this feeling of repulsiveness inside the body. The intent of the practice, as least at first, is precisely that of enabling such intimate contact, ranging over the whole body. One tries to hold an awareness of the heterogenous, amassed, jalopylike conglomeration of the body foremost in one's experience, and tries to hold it to the fore continuously and with whatever degree of vividness ensues. A journey into the image realm of the charnel ground within demands, above all, the ability to be aware and detached while dangerous evocations press upon one, intimately and forcefully. And the challenges of the charnel ground within can be all the more compounded by a life in a charnel ground without, such as that which Luang Bu Sangwaan embarked upon. To live within a charnel ground, whether within the body or within a forest, is to confront necromantic power straight on; it is to use the power of abject images, to deliberately inhabit the space of impermanence and ruin. But with practice, or so some Buddhists claim, it is possible that one's heart does not have to follow likewise into ruin.

When Luang Bu Sangwaan went into the paa-chaa, he did not come out for six years straight. He got by on alms, and found an old discarded boat in the charnel forest to use as a crude shelter. He remained there alone, living on the edge, without a break for six years. At night he would drape a mosquito net over a hanging umbrella, in a fashion of wandering forest monks. The night air was so thick with blood-sucking insects that he could not venture out of the meter-wide perimeter of the umbrella-net. In the last hours of the long night, as he sat cross-legged and alone in the gloom of the forest, the wind would rip through the air, large branches would crack and snap throughout the whole forest. Surrounded by thunderous sounds in the dark, he did not abandon his meditation. He gave himself over to it even more, concentrating on the Buddha and his refuge, chanting aloud, "Buddho . . . Buddho . . . Buddho . . . ," until his throat was dry and parched.

And in the end, nothing too harmful ever befell him in that haunted charnel forest, although mischievous ghosts would sometimes come and flip open his mosquito net.

Luang Bu Sangwaan applied himself to the practice diligently for six years, alone and living in the old wooden boat in the paa-chaa phii dib. Planted firmly at the root of a tree, right in the midst of the space of death, and while the necromatic terror swirls, one sits cross-legged with spine straight, and establishes mindfulness in front of oneself. For six years of life on the edge, Luang Bu dwelled in the haunted forest with his mind focused on death.

"After one year, I didn't die. After two years, I didn't die. After three years, I didn't die. After four years, Dhamma had risen."

He stayed two more years in the paa-chaa phii dib. By this time, several villagers had come to respect and understand him. In that period of time, one lay woman and two lay men wound up becoming accomplished students, and eventually a temple organization grew up around Luang Bu Sangwaan. Nowadays, upward of a hundred nuns and thirty monks live in Toong Samakhi Dhamm temple, and thousands of lay people come for *kathin* (robes-giving) ceremony once a year. In turn, a monk-disciple of Luang Bu Sangwaan started a large temple organization, based on the outskirts of Bangkok, with thousands of dedicated urban lay adherents and many centers around the country.

But despite the relatively controlled atmosphere of routine temple life as compared to charnel-ground dwelling, there is no way to eliminate the dangers inherent to the work with abject imagery (as is indeed the case in the public sphere, as well). There is a great danger involved in traversing the charnel ground. This is not just an imaginary danger. Or if it is, then we might say that it is the imaginary which is dangerous. Given the forces of attraction and repulsion at work in the charnel ground, just as in the aesthetic politics of the public sphere, one cannot be heedlessly subject to every impulse, desire, or aversion that arises in the contest that death images present to the senses. In charnel-ground meditation, just as with the politics of public images, the stakes are high: there is much to gain, but also much to lose.

In this discipline of Buddhist ascesis, Luang Bu Sangwaan's teachers, all from the central plains, did not give him much technical information. Two simple statements were the core of his practice. One statement was, "Cultivate samādhi and you will see the truth." Dwelling in the ultimate charnel ground of the haunted paa-chaa, all he needed was enough samā-dhi, and, given the atmospheric situation, the death images would pro-duce themselves. The other instruction, more profound and even more simple, was, *ruu chaai, ruu chaai*, "just know, just know": bare aware-ness, uninvolved, still equanimity. The means and ends of the whole asce-sis is really just "ruu chaai, ruu chaai"—to develop the ability to know things clearly without distorting and disabling forces of attraction or aver-sion, which pull the mind out of balance.

Many accomplished nuns at Toong Temple, if their minds are inclined toward jhāna vision, have had widely disparate and challenging visions. But the challenges they face in the realm of jhāna visions require a con-stant attention to a sense of balance and perspective in which one does not become subject to the forces unleashed, whether they be pleasant or unpleasant.

"Your viscera are light," says the nun, Mae-Chi Liem, of the feeling when entering deep concentration. "There is no feeling of having to pee or excrete. It's like you are dead—just for a while." Even as one dwells in death-images, the mind and body can be light and at ease. Pleasant sensations and pleasant visions are as much a part of this ascesis as are their antitheses. In the unpleasant case, the mind is challenged with re-spect to aversion, hatred, anger, fear. In the pleasant case, one is chal-lenged with respect to greed and desire. One must find the mind that can discern without involvement, the nonreactionary mind, the mind that does not pile consequences upon consequences, reactions upon reactions, or what Thai Buddhists would call pile-up of kamma upon kamma.

While she was walking, the portly nun Mae-Chi Liem told me, some-times she would suddenly become light, "like you are floating on the tips of your toes. Golden trays would appear, there on the ground, to receive your feet each step. And every step, your feet are only bones, just feet of bones each step." On the other hand, she has seen her body engulfed in flames while contemplating the element of heat in her body.

Another nun, Mae-Chi Sa-ad, told me she once got up to stand after a restless meditation, and suddenly saw her corpse, bloated and rotting, and her heart was instantly stilled. Someone, whom she did not recognize, appeared before her, wearing magnificent clothes and with a hanging pendant of pure, priceless emerald. She watched the *naang*, "angel," and contemplated how beautiful she was. She came back to look down on her own person, now no longer a corpse, and saw that she too was decked out in such fine clothes, "like in a Chinese opera (*likee*)."

At this point in the conversation, another nun chimed in: "When I was sitting in the meditation hall I had a visions of corpses, some with clothes, some without. . . . I was sitting in great pain, and so I stood up to lean against a pillar. Suddenly, I saw three *devatā* [angels] dressed in glistening white. They touched my legs and told me to sit down again. I said it hurts, but I sat down and the pain disappeared. . . . I saw myself floating. The image of myself was floating closer and closer, shining with celestial light, and I wondered, why do I look so beautiful, when in fact I am not someone who is beautiful at all?"

Once, while Mae-Chi Liem was in walking meditation, a vision "split open" to reveal a space of rows and rows of funeral urns, "wide, spacious rows of funeral urns, all in good order." She could see yellow bone fragments inside them. Another time, during an assembly of the temple nuns and monks led in meditation by Luang Bu, in the main hall, she opened her eyes and saw radiant, celestial lights shining, and hundreds of sparkling devatā all kneeling around the meditators in so many dazzling rows and rows. Mae-Chi Liem also often has pleasant visions of Buddha images. Other times, there are unpleasant visions, such as one of a "great big mountain . . . very scary! . . . with someone throwing severed heads over a ledge . . . with strong winds blowing so that you can't climb up it."

Once, when she almost died from an illness, she had a long experience in a realm of near death. She saw herself rowing a boat in a stream that ran through a forest charnel ground, and a woman ghost came out of the trees, wearing a frilly blouse the color of a lotus flower, and laughing. It made her laugh too. She knew, somehow, that this ghost was the ghost of a woman who had died in childbirth. The spirit of Mae-Chi Liem's dead father, who had been born as a ghost, was also there, and he was very upset, almost out of his mind, that his daughter was dying. In this realm, she had an old house and an old boat, and she was being sent back and forth from bank to bank of the canal, on errands. Later, the ghost of her father brought monks to assemble around her, all holding candles. Someone put medicine into her mouth, while someone cut her hair. The monks chanted, and she fell asleep.[12] Later, she awoke out of the spell.

The horrible and pleasant journey into the charnel ground reaches heights of intensity that challenge, in every respect, the meditator to develop the discernment and detachment that can overthrow the magic of the self, the "I" and "mine" upon which all reactions of attraction and aversion depend for their force. One must be able to discern the valuable from the worthless, the vital from the extraneous, and cut to what is at stake in the personal matter of personal matter. Meditators who do not understand this will often not be able to develop the tranquility necessary for concentrated states of samādhi, nor will they be able to cull anything of value from the corpse. And even if they do achieve enough concentration to develop jhāna vision, by force of will or innate inclination, they will not be able to deal with what they find.

One day, I was meditating in the hall with a group that meets every afternoon for a two-hour sitting. Most people had left to go back to their huts, but five or six of the more dedicated aspiring nuns and I would stay on into evening. As we sat in silence among the skeletons, a loud raucous noise came toward us. It sounded like young people hooting and hollering, and I was quite annoyed with them. At the same time, I was quite ardently attempting to *ruu chaai, ruu chaai,* just know, just know, the disturbing sounds, as I am sure all the others were doing. But suddenly it was upon us. The doors burst open, and in rushed a group of monks, and they were carrying one monk who was screaming and writhing in their arms. He was yelling "I'm scared! I'm scared!" Over and over he screamed, his eyes wild, his arms lashing out, his legs thrashing, afraid of everything including the other monks who were trying to keep him under control. He screamed out at them, and then mumbled and whimpered that they were going to kill him. When they got him in the meditation hall, they let him loose and tried to reason with him, but he quickly jumped out a window and went running wild through the temple again. Eventually they caught him and brought him back.

It was several hours before they could control him, mostly by pinning him down on the floor. Luang Bu Sangwaan entered the meditation hall, and was by force of will able to command the hysterical monk to sit down, though just as soon as he would sit down, he would leap up again in a frenzy, screaming, "Luang Bu, I'm scared, scared, scared!"

He was one of the six monks who at that time were in intensive silent, solitary meditation. On the morning's alms round I had noticed, a few days before, that he had an unusually serious face, which I mistook for ardent effort. Also, shortly before this incident, word had somehow gone around that he was seeing terrible things in meditation, that he "had never seen anything so scary in his whole life." I do not know the actual content of his nimitta images. But I did get the unfortunate monk's story from another monk who knew him and who had, himself, been in intensive solitude before, who had "passed that test," as he put it.

The frenzied monk had gone into solitude only a few weeks previously. He had always been temperamental, the kind of person who got excited and happy about good things, and sad or angry about bad things. He had a reputation for exploding in anger. Before becoming a monk, he had apprenticed in black magic, and left that mostly because he was fascinated by the stories he had heard about visions and supernormal powers that were possible for accomplished Dhamma practitioners (and of which my own text is unfortunately one more exacerbation).

When he received permission to start silent solitude, he was, characteristically, overjoyed. "He was always happy when good things happened, and not happy when bad things happened." He merrily went to consult with this other monk who had been through intensive solitary meditation before, and asked him for advice in the practice. The more accomplished monk tried to impress upon him that the heart of the practice was not to get lost in happiness and sadness, but instead to cultivate *chid waang* (emptiness)—not to get excited about nice things and distressed about not-nice things; to watch over and guard the mind, so that, for instance, one is not pleased as punch when one gets a morsel of one's favorite food, or get uncomfortable because, say, it is too hot or too cold outside. In every aspect of life, the practice is founded upon cultivating that kind of detachment as a whole way of life, without exception.

Without chid waang, or emptiness, every kind of phenomena, whether mental or of bodily form, seems to approach one in a relation between "I" and "mine," a powerful relation forged in desire and aversion. Everything on some level seems to be happening to "me." Against this grain, in Buddhist ascesis every bond of attraction or repulsion must be exchanged for one of equanimity. Short of the development of equanimity in any and every aspect of life, there are soft spots, where one is still vulnerable to the powers of attraction, aversion, and delusion.

In this theory of meditation, oddly enough, personal identification is ultimately the nemesis of insightful contemplation of the abject body. Though it begins by taking abject visions right into one's own body, this "identification" ultimately must traverse the dangers of "taking things personally," even skirting the dangers of personally identifying with the suffering and misfortune of others. In short, it works toward an entirely different process of "identification" from that formed in humanist ideologies of sympathy and empathy, not to mention most forms of political appeal to the affects of death imagery. Beginning meditators, for instance, are admonished never to contemplate the possible death of anyone with whom the meditator already has a personal connection, or to meditate upon the corpse of anyone for whom one has sentimental attachments.

These emotions, certainly human and noble feelings in some sense, are in this particular practice ultimately inimical to insight. What kind of ethics could this be?

When the experienced monk finished telling the aspiring monk the facts about equanimity, he saw the monk's face "light up with happiness. He was really pleased and happy to be hearing all that good advice!"

Shaking his head, he went on, "Now, no one can say if he will ever recover. Not anytime soon, that's for sure. Sometimes they never get better. Their sanity is shattered forever."

In the ancient classic meditation manual, *Visuddhimagga*, Buddhaghosa wrote of the meditation on corpses, "For among the thirty-eight meditation subjects expounded in the texts there is no object so frightening as this one."[13] A month after the incident, the monk was still whimpering and fearful, and had to be watched over day and night lest he try to do himself in, though he did stop running wild.

It is not only ignorance of the right path, pertaining intimately to all aspects of one's mind and body, that unleashes the dangerous and powerful forces inherent in images of death, which can slip beyond control. For this economy of ascesis is never far from the cultural-economic systems that circulate around it, and to which this book must return, merging this charnel ground with that of the public sphere.

Even an entire secluded temple of renouncers, like Wat Toong Samakhi Dhamm, can be subject to the uncontrollable power of a sensational, international economy of images run wild.

Recently, a British tabloid newspaper got wind of the charnel smell, as it were, and they came to Toong Temple, and they photographed. The mechanical reproductions—of nuns taking the donated corpse of one of their friends apart in order to use it as a kammatthāna meditation tool—were published overseas with the caption, "THAI BUDDHIST NUNS EAT HUMAN FLESH!" When the outrageous news ricocheted back into the local market, a raging storm of national controversy exploded in the Thai newspapers.

It was bad for the public image of Thai Buddhism. It was destroying the national image. There was an investigation. The temple had to promise the ecclesiastic authorities that they would not use real corpses anymore.

Toong Samakhi Dhamm temple was ordained into the new world order.

THE TELEGRAPHIC ABJECT

With the aspect of repulsiveness, the image realm of the charnel ground of the body opens up, disrupts, and offends the presence and magic of being. Contemplation of the revolting attempts to cut through the aura of body and being that appears before the regard of beholding, to do it through means of an alternative aesthetics of repulsion, for the sake of a sight no less intimate than the touch.

But my employment of "intimacy" is obviously very different than that intended by the word as it is normally used in English. One might, quite clumsily and rather incorrectly, call the Buddhist work with abject imagery a "desensitized sensitivity" where it is successful, and a chaotic "hypersensitized sensationalism" where its power exceeds the capabilities of the minds that must negotiate its dangers. There is little room within its practice for personalizing sentiments, and it ultimately works against the grain of anything that could reasonably be called intimate contact between persons. Its dangerous potential to shatter all sensibility is extreme, and its intended result is perhaps even more extreme and alien to common sense. And yet it is not so alien as to not display a certain parallel resonance with the same problems that besiege abject imagery in the politics of the public sphere. Were we to assume that an ethical relation to the horrible misfortunes of others must be founded on an empathetic identification of common humanity, this repetitive practice of asubha kammatthāna could be said to produce hardened, jaded, and numbed subjects who have lost the ability to feel the human emotions that keep this world from falling to pieces.

The same approbrium, of course, is commonly hurled at the technological apparatus of media representation, and not without some merit. In the passing of the market of abject media in Black May, as in so many other instances, the sensational moment of breaking news can seem barely to leave a visible trace as history is processed at exponentially increasing speeds. Sustained political contemplation of events is perpetually deferred through the continual replacement of events, all within a broader representational environment in which the bar for the truly startling is raised higher and higher.

Perhaps the speed at which this processing of history proceeds would not be possible without the desensitization afforded by serial repetition of sensational death in commodity form. And perhaps there is something about the technological nature of mechanical reproduction that greases the wheels for forgetting. Perhaps the taking of profit and power in shock through mass media may lead to a need for more and more shocks, as mutated strains of death somehow lift like membranes off the surface of images and enter the ones who view them, also infecting the voyeurs with a deadening numbness.

But must this technology make us numb to images of death and violence? Though this question could hardly be settled even by the most extensive public polling techniques, it is of grave concern to theorists of modern visual media. It has become almost common sense that something momentous has happened in the proliferation of mechanical reproduction

and electronic simulation, transforming our sensory faculties to dangerous and largely disempowering effect. Some of the most radically histori-
cizing media theory written in recent years concerns the alteration of our
senses by discourses of vision or technologies of mass-mediated visuality.[14]
Such theory often turns on arguments about violent ruptures in modernity
between the body qua body and the body as represented visually, especially where it concerns the depiction of the abject, such as in graphic
violence and death. An overkill of body imagery circulates in what may
seem like a postmodern "hyperspace" without corporeal bearings, as
Jameson puts it.[15] It flows in "global mediascapes" without much regard
to the limitations of time and space, as Appadurai pictures it, in flattened
simulacra divested of multidimensional sensory embodiment, and in an
apparatus that enforces the privilege of the realm of vision over all other
sensory channels, as others have written.[16] Two-dimensional reproductions swirl over the surface of the planet, carrying impressions of the body
in violence and in death, graphic images that repeat themselves with such
serial regularity that we are possibly becoming inured to them, and ever
further distanced from the suffering they represent. Where our capacity
for empathy, outrage, and compassion disappears, there also goes our
ability to initiate sane reactions to insane actions.

In a world where the genocide of hundreds of thousands of Rwandans
can pass unhindered and even be shuffled from attention in the U.S. mass
media by the arrest of a celebrity athlete for murder, this critical position
stands on tenable ground. The culturally and historically particular effects
that contemporary visual media work upon our senses may help empower
everything from the racist policies of military intervention and humanitarian aid (compare Kosovar refugee camps and Rwandan camps), to the
conduct of seemingly blood-free war overseas (compare the living room
during the Vietnam War and the Gulf War), and arguably even to the
lack of inhibitions in spontaneous mass killings carried out in U.S. public
spaces.

It would be natural, when thinking critically, to pose against this violent
reworking of visual perception of the body a more organic sense of corporeality. The idea of a whole being, apprehended by a multisensory awareness of bodily existence, is often set off against the idea of a flattened body
and anesthetized senses, though often only implicitly. A lost, organic sense
of corporeal being might implicitly serve as the affronted ground to the
figure of what Jonathan Crary, for one, has called "the relentless abstrac-
tion of the visual," a "regime of vision" where "if images can be said
to refer to anything it is to millions of bits of electronic mathematical
data."[17]

The political meaning of shock effects is a complex subject, and where
it concerns the depiction of graphic death and violence—in a word,

gore—moral indignation rises in various, often contradictory ways. There is generally a great sense of urgency that violent acts, committed in so many places near and far, be brought to light and attention. Perhaps nothing has suited this purpose more powerfully than the ability of photography, film, and video to communicate the extremes of political violence and suffering, injecting abject evidence into otherwise politically sanitized environments. As John Taylor explores in an argument against the "compassion fatigue" thesis, and against strict propriety and fear of glut in news portrayals of "body horror," photojournalism often exerts powerful ethical pressure in political situations despite direct and indirect codes of censorship.[18] It seems, from Taylor's analysis of British discourse, that public discussion in England is focused on propriety: at what level is the graphic too offensive for public sensibility? By contrast, in the United States, discourse concerning violence in the media centers around the possible power of violent images to cause real violence. There is widespread condemnation in public discourse of attempts to exploit, profit from, or otherwise use graphic imagery in ways that might produce a voyeuristic thrill, or even pleasure, leading to desensitization and possibly even to violent acts.[19] In sum, there are in public debates over sensationalism ambivalent feelings that graphic detail can arouse true indignation and ethical sentiment, yet at the same time fears that too much will turn people's eyes away, offend them, or finally even bore them.

Theoretical writing has shared these common concerns. Susan Sontag's seminal *On Photography* is, of course, a classic expression of such suspicions about photographic representation. The photographic image, for Sontag, represents a loss—of contact, of intimacy, of reality—set up by false relations of proximity in photography between subjects distant from the viewer in time and space, which ultimately leads to increasing comfort in looking upon the horrible.[20]

Such a false contact with and pseudo witnessing of the horrible might be considerably enabled by a technology that serves vision from its spatial and material ties to place, and can circulate surrogate visions of the bodily form in pain far beyond connections to corporeal matter. Indeed, in step with this critique of photography, one might identify in technologies of image reproduction the general formation of a violent, "modern sensorium," as Susan Buck-Morss has called it.[21] She explains, for instance, that cinema spectators learn a peculiar form of phenomenological reduction whereby they cut off their normal relation to objects in the world. In this trained cinematic perception, the image of a speeding locomotive, for instance, no longer frightens the audience, as some say it once did in the early days of film, because the audience has learned a cognitive operation by which they are severed from both their own corporal existence and its relation to the bodiless images on the screen: "The surface of the cinema screen functions as an artificial organ," a "prosthetic" which does not "merely duplicate human cognitive perception, but changes its nature." This prosthesis represents a radical reordering of the perceptual status of reality: "On the screen moving images have a present meaning despite the absence of corporeal bodies, which thereby becomes a matter of indifference. What counts is the simulacrum, not the corporeal object behind it."[22]

Buck-Morss argues that this modern sensorium imposes a phenomenological-like reduction by severing film images from connection and identity with the material objects from which they derive. For instance, when film is projected on a screen there is no actor physically present. But even more, in the ideal-typical consumer experience, there is not really a corporeally present viewer either. Viewers are only sporadically aware of themselves as existing bodily presences during the absorbing moments of cinema experience that commercial filmmakers often strive for. They are transported from their bodies and into the cinematic world. In reaction to this cinema effect, Antonin Artaud, for instance, imagined a "Theater of Cruelty" that would rescue real pain by transmitting physically present vibrating emotions from the actor to the audience—from gut to gut—whereas the eviscerated cinematic experience of cruelty absorbs the audience in a state of distraction. Buck-Morss asserts that the bodily reaction of the audience is more or less cut off: no one rises out of their seat to rescue the victim. One sits still, as Siegfried Kracauer wrote, "spellbound" and "hypnotized."[23] Unable to move, unable to do anything, one is hypnotically pacified in the midst of the most extreme violence and agitation.

This is the ur-form of "simulacrum," Buck-Morss contends, for the cognitive operations by which the reality of the images is rendered irrelevant make the screen level the sole realm of reference: signification and reference collapse into each other.[24] There are only two-dimensional "bodies" ever up on the screen—nonmaterial, noncorporeal, nonreal except to the degree in which they have meaning and reference within the cinematic world of the screen itself.

I imagine that "hyperreality," to borrow Jean Baudrillard's loose term loosely, would be the ultimate dystopian culmination of these effects, where reference to the real carries exaggerated gravity, but only insofar as media representations themselves become the only valid index of what is real.[25] Moreover, it seems that within this realm the taking of profit and power in shock may lead to a need for more and more shocks. The technological and cultural operations of objectification performed on death may remake it into an exchangeable object of consumption, highly valued, highly profitable, and much consumed, but at that same time depleting, with every objectification, every exchange, every consumption, the very sensitivity and sensorial faculty to perceive death and know it has meaning. And yet, miraculously, at the same time the realm of reproduction is still somehow invigorated by this process, becoming in itself the authoritative venue for the staging of the real.

The quick turnover of history would probably not be possible without a process that Allen Feldman identifies as "cultural anesthesia," which is his "gloss on Adorno's insight that in a post-Holocaust and late capitalist modernity the quantitative and qualitative increase of objectification increases the social capacity to inflict pain on the Other"—and, Feldman adds, "render the Other's pain inadmissible to public discourse and culture." The media apparatus, as Feldman puts it, "jettisons the indigestible depth experience of sensory alterities." This is an observation easily verified by anyone's thoughtful reflection upon the representation of death in our time; it is also a crucial observation in all media criticism aligned more or less with Adorno. This holds that the operations that mechanical reproduction works upon perception flatten reality in such a way that images of violence, which should otherwise move us deeply, cease to signify the very real and embodied matters of pain and suffering they represent. It is as though, inherently, the reproduced images cannot transmit the multidimensional reality of pain, in part because they are two-dimensional, in part because they are produced and driven by reified profit-value. With respect to such anesthetizing effects of objectification, Feldman speculates that it is only a "re-perception," and "sensory alterity," that can provide an alternative.[26]

This is only one side to the story, however, and as such potentially recapitulates the singular dimension of a forward-moving story that modernity tells about itself. As in the present day, the turn of the last century was, as Ben Singer has argued, a particularly fruitful time to proliferate discourses on the "deadened nerves" that result from the "hyperstimulation" of modernity.[27] As Lynne Kirby has pointed out, at every recent stage of development in image reproduction—from painting to photography, photography to film, film to video, and video to digital imaging—a cry of alarm is sounded over the loss of authenticity in images of death.[28]

As Feldman suggests, there may indeed exist possibilities and conditions for opening alternative communications of perception and memory. Where could one find that kind of sensory alterity, or even the language to talk about it, were one to make contact with it? And was not the market of massacre on the charnel ground of Ratchadamnern Avenue capable, at least for a time, of transmitting several forms of insightful objectification, all of which carried more than a trace of the suffering they represented, making good—even through the "evils" of capitalism—on the significance of what transpired? What relation might these possibilities have to mechanical reproduction in general, to the economics of exchange, to death, and even to the spirits of the dead? In what does, or could, the positive value of sensory alterity in abject images of death, gore, violent death, and even the spirits of the dead consist?

Julia Kristeva's daunting *Powers of Horror* explores a conception of the abject that is unabashedly universalist in its assertions. For Kristeva, the abject—intentionally and repetitively overdefined in the book in order to perform its resistant excess—is simultaneously primal to, generative of, and reproductive of culture, language, and subjectivity. The abject is the necessary condition of these "things," or rather, of these primal refusals: I, language, culture. The abject is also their always-lurking, always-already-implied, undoing and defeat: "A weight of meaninglessness, about which there is nothing insignificant, and which crushes me. On the edge of non-existence and hallucination, of a reality that, if I acknowledge it, annihilates me." It is with analysis from a deliberate universal subjectivity that Kristeva contemplates "the utmost of abjection" in the corpse: "A wound with blood and pus, or the sickly, acrid smell of sweat, of decay, does not *signify* death. In the presence of signified death—a flat encephalograph, for instance—I would understand, react, or accept. No, as in true theater, without makeup or masks, refuse and corpses *show me* what I permanently thrust aside in order to live. These body fluids, this defilement, this shit are what life withstands, hardly and with difficulty, on the part of death."[29]

This distinction between signified death, itself signified through a sign of the modern, on the one hand, and the true theater inhering in the presence of death's substances which show their truth to you, on the other, may appear to be too simple. But that would be a predictable, orthodox response that fits the current templates of interpretation and the lockstep of what counts as knowledge in these constructivist days. What of that meaninglessness? The human sciences with their contemporary penchant for construction, context, and order rarely issue the license to generalize far enough to appreciate an insipidness that might conflict with, or even threaten, the sense-making of proper social thought. For Kristeva, literature's willingness and aptitude for taking on this task is what makes it the ultimate arbiter of the abject. By contrast, the refusal to acknowledge death as more significant for challenging systems that confer meaning than for being a product of them is perhaps part of that massive denial of the "nurturing horror" that Kristeva claims civilizations "attend to pushing aside by purifying, systematizing, and thinking: the horror that they seize on in order to build themselves up and function."[30]

And yet—seeming to prove the obvious criticism right—in valorizing this face-off with the abject, Kristeva constructs a hierarchy that is all too specifiable to her cultural and historical space. That mythology evoked by the sign of encephalographic signing, that is, the mythology of modernity, haunts the analysis at almost every turn. As Anna Tsing points out, "*Pow-*

ers of Horror follows an insulting evolutionary track from Africans and Indians to Judaism, Christianity, and, at last, to French poets."[31] For Kristeva, the deep psychosymbolic economy of the abject can be uncovered through analysis both in breadth—by assembling comparative ethnological difference for its demonstration of common denominators—and length—through abjection's teleological development from primary process, children, primitives, and madmen, toward modernity and its most cultured products. That is, Kristeva celebrates and anticipates the historical replacement of religion by transgressive art—specifically by literature, the highest cultural form ever to face and embrace the power of horror and reach "the sublime point at which the abject collapses in a burst of beauty that overwhelms us—and 'that cancels our existence' (Celine)."[32]

As a stepping stone to the bigger and better accomplishments of French transgressive literature, ethnological variation serves its purpose. This service is, as Anna Tsing has commented, to "an epistemological dichotomy between European 'theory' and global 'empirical' variation in which, by definition, the Third World can never be a source of theoretical insight."[33] The way to disrupt this boundary and subvert this equation is, however, not obvious.

The traditional method for identifying and valorizing sensory otherness through concepts of culture, unfortunately, is no less embedded in a narrative of modernity, and often warmly enlists the discipline of cultural anthropology in the performance of difference. Emblematic of this approach is Claudia Classen's *Worlds of Sense*, which retells the familiar story of "the rise of sight and science," and how the Enlightenment enthroned vision over the other senses, to their detriment.[34] *Worlds* necessarily includes the frequent subplot about those other cultures who do not think about perception or knowledge with predominantly visual metaphors, who privilege other sense channels or do not distinguish sense channels, and who upon contact with modernity are on the verge of losing their senses. *Worlds* is certainly a corrective to essentialist accounts such as Ackerman's *A Natural History of the Senses*, and part of the author's larger and richer history of European multisensory perception.[35] It depends, however, on an absolute otherness that virtually ensures that this otherness will have very little to say that is not rather vague: "For the Desana, existence in this world is a dream, a mere reflection of the reality which exists in the other dimension." The use of the visual metaphor "reflection" notwithstanding, these other worlds must be approached "within the context of a particular culture and not through generalized external sensory paradigms." But if these worlds are only valid within a particular culture, and cannot be generalized, then the initial promises of a liberating difference—or, short of that, a better insight into something valid more generally—can never be realized, since the audience of the work is presumably not a part of the other's sensory world and so there-fore excluded from the only context in which the cultural content has any validity. There is little possibility of translation—and certainly none for dialogue—when one party is a learned scholar and the other lives in a dream dimension. And yet somehow "these cosmologies are so powerful in their differing sensory symbolism that they shatter conventional west-ern perceptual models and open us up to completely new sensory uni-verses."[36] However alluring this sentiment may be, with sensory alterity confined at such an exoticized distance the likelihood is certainly low that even subtle shifts in attitude might result—let alone the shattering of our sensory universe consequent upon reading a book. It may be the case that the romantic wings of anthropology—which otherwise seriously consider the possibility that there is something to be learned from other people as well as about them—have done more to shuffle people off into irrelevance than to promote an engaged contest of thought.

The theory of comprehension only from "within" an exclusive alterity, confined to ethnographic context, precludes dialogue because only the analyst's ideas, theories, and categories are allowed to travel, to penetrate or at least to frame the others' world, whereas the others' theories, we are told, can only be understood in context and as culture. This may deliver, vaguely, a sense of difference situated in a distant, dying, or dead realm beyond modernity, while quite articulately it does more to perform the reality-effects of modernity discourse than to unsettle them.

Lurking behind this suspicion of the effects of modernity on our senses (but not of the sense of the modern itself), is the association of sight and science with literacy, and orality with the premodern and traditional, fol-lowing Walter Ong.[37] One wonders if the plot devices in the story of how literacy brought the death of orality are not also re-performed in the cri-tique of visual representations more generally. Indeed, there is a quite recognizable "metaphysics of presence" residing within many critiques of media imagery. It is not unlike what Jacques Derrida deconstructs from within the Western tradition of writing against writing.[38] According to this philosophical tradition, which Derrida argues is virtually ubiquitous in Western thought, the real purported "presence" and face-to-face inter-actions between real beings are replaced by the inferior and even "danger-ous supplement" of written discourse. The long history of writers writing against writing, in writing—beginning perhaps with Plato (also an ima-gophobic)—was Derrida's favorite scene for deconstruction of the meta-physics of presence, and for his dissemination of iterations about "arche-writing," an already-writing even before writers define what is not writing (in writing). These antiwriting rhetorics accumulate authority by referring truth to an extratextual something that they, by definition, have already named unrepresentable and so not presentable in the text. And yet the entirety is advocated through writing itself. In loose analogy with Derrida's critique of antiwriting rhetorics, we might consider many critiques of media representation as textual arguments that turn on a moral authority referred, similarly, to an extratextual "real presence." Critiques of death and violence in media images are, more often than not, pinned on arguments against the violent exclusion of presence—of real bodies, senses, and feelings—from two-dimensional reproductions. The authority of such arguments is nevertheless delivered in text, however, in precisely a medium that supposedly excludes those presences.

It is good to be cautious of falling too readily into a metaphysics of presence when contemplating both textual and imageric representations of "embodied existence" and "the senses." It is too easy to prey upon what I would call a "nostalgia for the body" that is common among contemporary intelligentsia who have dedicated themselves to a life of the intellect. For instance, it is typical to complain that there is "a tendency in contemporary anthropology to privilege the linguistic, discursive, and the cognized over the visceral and the tacit. We have lost an understanding of the body as an experiencing, soulful being," as Robert Desjarlais relates in an otherwise astute piece of fieldwork, *Body and Emotion*. To remedy such modern loss, the new ethnography of the senses will have a new way of writing that can actually afford bodily exchange between the author and the reader: "a way of writing ethnography that includes the reader's body as much as the author's in the conversation at hand."[39] Analytic frameworks surrounding the return of phenomenology to social theory, and signaled in current anthropological discourse in such terms as "embodied knowledge" and even "sensuous scholarship," as insightful and creative as they are, may be even more interesting when informed by an interrogation of yearnings for a metaphysical transcendence of the text.[40]

In contrast to these approaches, a counterintuitive criticism of mass-mediated imagery, even if only partly faithful to deconstruction of the metaphysics of presence, might open up unexpected avenues for the formation of critical practice. Where do we stop, and representations begin? How could the media be divested of "real life," when the media is, to some extent, our life? And we might also ask, practically speaking, what is the point of single-minded critique of the flatness of media representation when there is no force on this earth that could ever rid us of it?

What would it mean for media criticism, for instance, to assert that photographs do not destroy the bodily nature they represent, but that bodily "nature" is itself already akin to photography even before the dawn of its technology?

Sometimes the situation calls for—no, cries out for—the classic critique of representation and its humanist message and call for presence. Why should it not, in some sense? Is there no difference between suffering and

197

its representation? Is there no difference between suffering the wrath of an authoritarian crackdown, or being shot, or being tortured, and the mere representation of these experiences, after the fact? Only the most self-absorbed philosophe would deny the significance of such distinctions.

Refracting the technology of mechanical reproduction through Buddhist visions of the corpse may dishevel the arrangement of contradictions at work here. This encounter will depend on dislodging ethnographic content from a prison house of ethnographic context that might otherwise obscure the potential of alternative visual practice as a source of theoretical insight rather than as a source of empirical global variation. Attention to Buddhist visualization may help redeem mechanical reproduction from a metaphysics of presence that can cloak the powerful and radical potential of image-copying technologies. This powerful potential in media reproducibility—and this is my central argument—far from excluding the "real presence" of bodies and feelings, may heighten awareness of them.

CORPORE OBSCURO

Objects, reflecting light, press outward from themselves, leaving their imprints on photographic negatives like footprints in the sand. Or, as André Bazin said of the ontology of the photographic image, like the face of a corpse on a death mask.[41] And so is it with Buddhist meditation on death among the nuns and monks in the central Thai monastery of Toong Samakhi Dhamm Temple (Wat Toong). In fact, corpses are of the greatest worth for impressing upon the mind an eidetic reminder of mortality, almost as though one's mind were light-sensitive paper. To make that impression, nuns and monks retire to intensive, sometimes lifelong meditation on the corpse. Although seemingly morbid, this attention to the body in death is integral to the Buddhist soteriological path, as the nuns and monks of Wat Toong understand it. The body must fall apart and die, as universal law, but that one must also fall apart emotionally along with it is not written in stone, as it were. The organizing trope in Thai Buddhism of dukkha, "suffering," necessarily demands an intimate confrontation with the painful and disappointing tendency of the body to fall apart and die. It is the practitioners' belief that only by coming to terms with this truth can one ever escape from being emotionally subject to it. And yet, it seems as if they have as much difficulty as anyone else in trying to realize the significance of the one thing humans seem most adept at avoiding—but that is necessary, as they explain, for marking a relatively systematic route toward an awareness of death. They take aim, as it were, by means of vision and imagination.

Techniques for harnessing vision for this purpose are ancient, as far as texts can tell us, and yet are also fairly well represented in contemporary Thailand in temples such as Wat Toong. To enter into an atmosphere infused with death, nuns and monks avoid the diversions of everyday life; they sometimes live in cremation and burial grounds, sometimes alone in the forest, sometimes in a reclusive monastery, and all the while dedicate their life to training mental attention systematically, eventually cultivating a pronounced ability to visualize. Most important in this cultivation of vision is the instruction to spend as much time as possible around a cadaver. There the meditators should clearly inspect every detail of it, and use the detail to commit it to eidetic memory. The corpse should be stared at over and over, with particular attention to its most gruesome details. Buddhaghosa, in the *Visuddhimagga*, lists ten such details or aspects worth impressing on the mind: the bloated, the livid, the festering, the cut up, the gnawed, the scattered, the hacked and scattered, the bleeding, the worm-infested, the skeleton. The text goes on to describe further each aspect of decomposition in the most lurid and prurient detail; it almost seems deliberately in bad taste. The livid, for instance, is "reddish-colored where flesh is prominent, whitish-colored in places where pus has collected, but mostly blue-black." The festering "is trickling with pus in broken places." The gnawed "has been chewed here and there in various ways by dogs, jackals, etc." The scattered "is strewed here and there in this way: 'Here a hand, there a foot, there the head.'" The hacked and scattered is "scattered . . . after it has been hacked with a knife in a crows-foot pattern on every limb." The bleeding "sprinkles, scatters, blood and it trickles here and there . . . smeared with trickling blood." The worm-infested is "full of maggots."[42]

Here the corpse in its gory, abject, and repulsive state is the most desirable aesthetic. Once thoroughly immersed in this aesthetic of gore, meditators perform the crucial next step of imagining themselves as such a corpse, applying the visualization to their own body as if it were in a state of exposed internal organs and repulsive detail. The sensationally hideous aspect of such images can affect a meditator deeply, and suddenly. But it is not only physical corpses that are used as sources of the abject detail. Given that fiasco of British tabloid journalists depicting "cannibalism" at the temple, the meditators now generally avoid using real corpses, in accordance with their promise to Thai authorities not to appear too dark in the eyes of the world. This is the way to best serve the national image. Instead they use, as in many other Buddhist temples in Thailand, photographs of corpses for their meditation; these are usually culled from hospital autopsy procedures.

How great a loss is this? Would the "real presence" of a corpse be essential to impressing upon the mind the details of corporeal mortality?

Is the physical presence of the cadaver different in nature from the two-dimensional "mere reproduction" of the body in death?

In fact, not only is photography employed by Buddhist nuns and monks to produce visions of death, but so too is a variety of material tools and visual aids drawn from biomedical anatomy instruction. These are precisely the artifacts of Western science that are said to divest our being of its holistic nature and narrowly hypostatize it in the objectified, medicalized form of "the body." In fact, Michel Foucault has argued that the techniques of seeing formed in autopsy are the source not only of clinical knowledge but of the entire disciplinary matrix upon which modern power rests. "Medicine becomes modern with the corpse," he wrote in *The Birth of the Clinic.* "It will no doubt remain a decisive fact about our culture that its first scientific discourse concerning the individual had to pass through this stage of death."[43]

Thai Buddhist meditators acquire for their purposes both autopsy photographs and the Western medical anatomy representations that are used by Thai doctors. *Gray's Anatomy* cutouts and plastic statues are common Buddhist paraphernalia, even at temples that do not practice corpse meditation. The practice of medical autopsy, and especially the clinical photographic record of it, are images and frames that have been taken over by Buddhists and used in new ways. Monks and nuns regularly visit hospital autopsy rooms, and many temples have autopsy photographs on display for the public, sometimes with captions under, say, a mutilated face, that read "I was once like you. You will one day be like me!" And meditators use autopsy photographs and biomedical anatomy representations in the formal practice of asubha kammatthāna, to enter into their modes for the intimate observance of mortality.

Such photography of abject bodily dismemberment can be directly incorporated into the practice of meditation, and in Wat Toong is often pivotal to its effectiveness. The first step in the process, however, involves cultivating the basic ability to concentrate on an object of mental attention, regardless of its content. Samādhi, concentration, is usually built up through the technique of mindfulness of the breath. This may require hours, days, or weeks of sitting with the mind focused on the sensation of the breath at one point, most commonly where it passes the nostrils. One focuses on that point alone, constantly returning to it when distracted, until one builds up enough momentum in concentration to hold to the one point easily. With the ability to focus the mind to near one-pointedness based on attention to tactile sensation, meditators then transfer concentration to vision of a physical meditation object: the photograph of a corpse. Meditators impress the physical sight of the autopsy photograph on their minds by concentrating first on the outer sight, with special attention to the graphic details. They then attempt to reconstruct the image within "inner seeing" (*hen pai nai*) or "inner looking" (*maung pai nai*). In Thai Buddhism, what is referred to in English as the "mind's eye" would fall within the rubric of the mind as the sixth differentiated sense organ, in addition to the Euro-American five. In this conception, the mind as a sense organ has as its objects the appearance of any phenomena that do not have material contact as a condition of their immediate possibility: in other words, inner picturing, monologue, intentions, thoughts. The advantage in Thai meditation of this six-sense perceptual model is that it does not privilege the mind as a separate receptor of the five senses, but treats it as a sense like any other, which, as will become clear later, is central to the theoretical orientation of meditation.

This meditation is hard practical work, and different from simply making theoretical declarations that there is no inner or outer, that dualism is false, or that there are people who do not distinguish body and mind. The hard work consists in taking the abject object inward, since the abject at first may indeed appear to be what Kristeva describes as having only one quality of an object, "that of being opposed to *I*."[44] One begins with roving back and forth between the physical image and the mental image, each time staring, concentrating, trying to be more and more accurate in the inner visualization, and then comparing it with the outer, physical sight of the object, developing a closer and closer match. If one is a cultural other who does not distinguish between inner mind and outer world (*lok pai nai / lok pai naug*), then of course this cannot be practiced. But in Thailand this technique, which is also called "touring the cemetery within" (*bai teio ba cha pai nai*), is possible both to conceive of and to perform. The exercise itself can bring the mind to a fairly concentrated degree of samādhi, so that a clear and detailed image of a body part or an entire corpse is impressed on the mind's eye.

The practitioners can then work on that image alone, in the absence of the physical object, and focus on it just as one would focus on the breath as a meditation object. The point is to be able to cull from the material world a reproduction in the realm of inner vision, which one can work in formal sitting meditation without need of any physical sign. One calls the mental image to mind over and over, hour after hour, day after day, week after week.

There are three patterns of experience in samādhi that meditators report one might pass through, with enough continuous effort. The first is called "momentary concentration" (*kannika samādhi*), when concentration becomes focused but only in temporary spurts. In the initial momentary concentration, one gets what could be characterized as merely an unusually clear version of ordinary inner picturing. The second is "threshold concentration" (*upajhāna samādhi*), which is on the verge of absorption. Threshold concentration is deeper and lasts longer than momentary concentration, and it is in threshold concentration that the mind may start to see clear and whole inner mental images. At threshold samādhi, the inner visualization is of another order. It has its own momentum and appears seemingly without volition, popping up more or less clear, detailed, and complete so that it can be taken as an object of meditation, which is to say, as something already "there" that one can focus on. The third kind of samādhi is called "attainment concentration" (*āpāna samādhi*). In this case, absorption has occurred and the image has become absolutely stark and clear; it becomes the only thing present, so that there is no longer any reference point outside this absorption from which the image can be said to be "out" or "in," or even "there" in the usual sense of the terms. Through continuous practice, one's samādhi builds up toward absorption in the image, until the immaterial image-object itself is taken in so deeply that it is not much like an object anymore, and it snatches one into a spiraling descent, heading straight into its repulsiveness, until one is dwelling right in the heart of an image of death. In all this, it is the graphic and gory aspect, the foul and repulsive detail that carries the greatest eidetic-mnemonic power.

The bodily details "stick to the heart," *did chai*, as the nuns of Wat Toong say. Mae-Chi Liem has regular experiences of seeing into her body: "It cracks open, divides, and separates. This body opens up for you to see. You see bodily ooze, clear ooze like in the brain; thick, filmy ooze and clear ooze. The body splits open into intestines, intestines the size of your wrist, *na*. Liver, kidneys, intestines, the stomach, you can see it all."

She got her first look at herself in the form of a corpse when, after a teacher admonished her for being proficient at falling asleep while sitting, she stood up and leaned against a pillar, and saw that her body was a carcass, "rotten, disintegrating." She followed the instructions to use this image as a meditation object, to focus and sustain it, to guard it and return to it over and over, then and in the future. She has since often been cultivating visions of her corpse: "I see my body bloated and rotting. I see clear greasy pus and thick, filmy pus. I see the head and brains, and from there see all the way down to the neck. . . . I see the bones in my skeleton, all yellow, yellow. . . . This body of ours, there is nothing to it. There is only the four elements—earth, air, fire, water—and the parts of the body. It is all dukkha—birth dukkha, old-age dukkha, pain dukkha, death dukkha, dukkha-sensations, pain and stiffness."

Just like her best friend Mae-Chi Liem, Mae-Chi Sangiam began practicing meditation with the five basic asubha kammatthāna objects in order to familiarize herself with death and dukkha: head hair, body hair, nails, teeth, and skin. She got her first kammatthāna, or meditation tool, after about one month of intensive solitary practice. She saw her form, *rūpa*, and saw her skin close up: "I saw the greasy skin hairs all separately, far,

far apart! And it looked disgusting, and *scary.* I saw the flesh along the holes of skin pores, each hole far, far apart! The holes of the skin pores were huge. I saw how crude, crude flesh is."

She was shocked at how "filthy" (*sogkaprog*) it all was. After seeing the filth, her *chid salod,* her mind had a great letdown. The word *salod* is precise here, and often used in this context; one might use it to describe the feeling when one is really elated, and then something happens to suddenly bring you down, a deflation. She says it was a terrible "letdown," to see for the first time what we are really covered in. As she describes her amazement at the time: "We people don't have anything good at all. We have only filth, filth. People in this world are all the same. There is nothing truly clean; we have only the filth. My mind was let down so much, so much."

It may seem counterintuitive that this experience is so valued and desired. As Stephen Collins writes of asubha meditation in Sri Lankan Theravāda Buddhism, the contemplation of the negative and averse characteristics of the body is often balanced by practice ideals of positive and cheerful comportment.[45] Over the course of studying in Wat Toong, I came to know several practitioners for whom such a balance of emotional forces was obviously necessary, but more for whom this was not necessary and who expressed suspicion of such emotional needs. Rather, as Collins also discerns, the demonstration of positive external signs of contentment may be both a necessary social exchange in presenting the value of Buddhism to the rest of society, and perhaps also an actual effect of the beneficial practices of this form of meditation.[46] Mentioning the "positive side" of Buddhism can also assuage the concerns of academic readers who might receive undesired impressions about Buddhists because they do not share the same values. On the other hand, there can be no doubt that this meditation on seemingly morbid subjects can become, in fact, morbid. An early Buddhist text in the disciplinary rules for nuns and monks tells of the occasion when Buddha came up with the rule forbidding suicide, after a group of monks became so despondent after contemplating corpses that they took their own lives, or had others kill them, en masse.[47] As I have explained in the incident of the crazed monk, I have witnessed people go into nervous breakdowns, for lack of better words, during the practice of Buddhist corpse meditation, including what clinicians might identify as psychotic hallucinations and fantasies. At the temple there is a short but significant history of the meditators whose "minds cracked" (*sati taeg*), as they term it, at the sight of meditation imagery; most of them never recovered.

A particularly telling analysis of the difficulties in appraising the values woven into Buddhist meditation on death and repulsiveness is explored in Gananath Obeyesekere's reflections on the cross-cultural salience of the clinical psychological category "depression." The interrogation of the category was sparked by a Western doctor's pronouncement that the author's associate, a Sri Lankan lay practitioner of Buddhist meditation on death, had "a classic case of depression."[48] Rather than interpret the man's preoccupations through the Buddhist notions of dukkha or "suffering," the doctor deduced a clinical disorder. Similarly, Obeyesekere argues, "semen loss" disorder, a common diagnosis in South Asia deduced through signs such as weight loss, sexual fantasies, night emissions, and urine discoloration, could in the same manner as "depression" be easily "proven" to be a universal disease if the classic constellation of symptoms in semen loss are present everywhere, which happens to be the case.[49]

If Obeyesekere's critique is applied to the example of the modern media disorder called "desensitization," or perhaps to the diagnosis of "body loss" in sick forms of media, a complicated picture results. What is the constellation of symptoms in "desensitization?" In Thailand it is not unusual to find oneself in a room with the corpse of a deceased loved one where family members are crying, and not one arm's length away a monk and others are cracking jokes and laughing. No one present finds this a violation, or assumes that mental states, like colored cloths, must be modulated to avoid clashing. This would be unthinkable behavior for, say, a doctor in the United States. And yet the corpse-naming, organ fights, and other antics that go on after hours routinely in U.S. medical school anatomy classes no doubt are intimately bound up in another specialized relation to the visceral that is shaped by institutions and that may be necessary for analytical acts such as surgery.

These practices and artifacts do not in themselves contain any particular meaning by virtue of a technological nature inhering in the medium. Imputing an essential effect of the technologies of medical science on consciousness is no different from imputing it to a work of art: is there really a style of painting or way of writing a novel that serves the revolution, and another style that is inherently decadent? Is the biomedical conception of the body necessarily more violent and available to power than that conceived in acupuncture meridians? Is there a style of media violence that we can identify as dangerous simply by describing its technological form? Or more to the point here, is "body-loss" mandated by the nature of photography as a medium?

The use of actual corpses in Buddhist meditation in not necessarily more effective than the use of photography. To help further characterize the possibility of exchange in eidetic power between photography and corpse meditation, and at the risk of adding a "dangerous supplement" to the words of Thai aspirants in this practice, I might include a few of my own.[50] An experience of the interplay between corpses, photography, and intense eidetic memory in the special sense that is of interest here came upon me after viewing the corpse of Luang Bu Sangwaan's teacher, Luang Bu Maha Tong, the senior monk who had taught Luang Bu back in the 1950s when he ventured into the haunted charnel forest. For some time after his death, Luang Bu Maha Tong's corpse was kept in a closed coffin. I slept beside and lived with the corpse, because it happened to be stored in the same room that I was housed in, when I wasn't staying in Luang Bu Sangwaan's room. Later they took out the corpse, which had been injected with formaldehyde, and put it on display under a glass case on board the large meditation hall, which had been built in the shape of a ship. It is the tradition among meditation temples in central Thailand that the corpse of a respected teacher, instead of being cremated, is kept on display in an altar, as a relic and meditation object. I spent considerable time contemplating his corpse, the first sight of which was very startling: shrunken, black, all skin and bones, dried out and hollow, wisps of disintegrating hair falling over the shriveled skin of his cavernous face; long spindly fingers and long gray fingernails.

Although I frequently spent time viewing his wrinkled cadaver, I did not intentionally pursue reconstruction of the image mentally. One day, while doing walking meditation and taking my footsteps as the object of mindfulness (walking meditation is a good complement both physically and mentally to sitting meditation), I was having a particularly difficult time with wandering thoughts and distractions, mostly because of too-intense effort, and finally I became frustrated and sat down in defeat. As soon as I gave up, and my body sank to sitting down, the whole body was suddenly just such a corpse as I had been viewing. My arms and legs and hands and face and skin—everything—was all dried out, black, and shriveled. In an intense total-body awareness, I was all fragile, hollow, brittle. I both felt this almost as a sensation and saw it vividly in my mind's eye. I was dead, a shriveled corpse, through and through.

And yet even more than physical corpses it was the physical objects of charnel photographs—mechanical reproductions arrayed in the meditation hall full of death-reminder *kammatthāna* (meditation tools)—that I found catalytic to the practice of cultivating nimitta (see figure 8). An experience early on is telling in this respect. After a period of practicing intensive awareness of the body at Wat Toong, one day, before the afternoon two-hour sitting, I knelt near the altar and spent a good deal of time inspecting photographs placed there. These were photographs of a nun (Luang Bu's former wife, it so happens), who had died and given her corpse over to the temple residents for use as a kammatthāna. The photographs captured the various things done to hone that tool: first the nuns and monks got together and placed the corpse outside on a bamboo table, to watch it decompose for awhile, though not for too long because red ants would eat it all up. Then they boiled the cadaver in a big pot. They

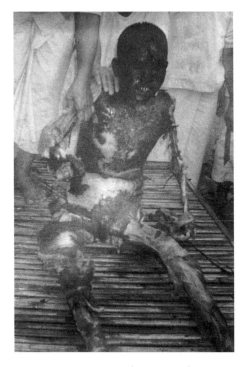

Figure 8. Meditation tool

took out the cooked body with black, charred pieces of flesh hanging from it, and put it back on the bamboo table for more viewing. After that, the nuns took a meat cleaver to it, and scraped the burnt skin and grizzled fat and muscle from her bones, and with bare hands pulled out all her intestines and internal organs. Finally they boiled and cleaned the bones again, strung them together, and hung them just to the right of the altar in the meditation hall, where they remained, hanging over my shoulder while I viewed the photographs.

I was particularly affected by one picture of the nun's corpse sitting up on the bamboo table after being boiled. Her seared face was grinning. The cooked flesh had been scraped off of one arm, so that I could see, poking out from her stewed torso, the thin bones in her arm with flecks of wet meat sticking to them.

Beginning the two-hour sitting, I had a bit more sincerity to my practice that day. It was as though there was a corpse waiting to happen. It was easy to gather my awareness together into a tight bundle, as it were. I could easily follow the reminder of the breath as it was going in, as it was going out, breathing in, breathing out, noting *Buddho, Buddho, Bud-*

dho. . . . There was a feeling of being on top of everything, gathered together: the low-grade, general sensation of the body; the more acute aches or rumblings; the thoughts; and the "shape" and "consistency" of concentration. It was all rounded up into one singular awareness. With the mind gathered in such a fashion, it is easy to focus on a single meditation theme, in my case the breath in the nostrils, and that focus only gathers the mind into more singularity.

Less than a half an hour into the afternoon meditation, a choice was available to me, a direction of movement was open to my mind, and I just knew what to do, strangely, as if I had always known and as if it was the most natural thing in the world. From a more coarse, gathered presence, focusing toward a single-minded point, the concentration went from that pinpoint to opening up into a more refined, rarefied presence. There was a diving into a totally different realm. The physical body ceased to exist as a coarse object (which is merely to say that such an awareness of it was temporarily excluded), and at the very same instant there was a seeing of my own skeleton suddenly leaping out into view. I saw bones in vivid shape, texture, and color as they were piled upon each other. The bones were strikingly clearer than seeing an object with the physical eyes. They seemed exactly anatomically accurate (I checked the hanging skeletons afterward). And they were quite startling—too startling, in fact, for a fledgling meditator like me to handle for very long. Yet after I leapt out of the experience in this realm, which lasted only a short time, there was nevertheless a lingering awareness of the bones, and of the entire skeleton inside the body. This lingering skeleton persisted for a few days, wherever I went and whatever I was doing, so long as I was trying to be mindful of the body: an awareness of both the simple presence of the skeleton in my body, and simultaneously of its visual image, seen, as it were, in a corner of my inner eye (as opposed to the very tangible and direct visual presence in the initial experience of it), whether with eyes closed or open. The continuous, lingering presence was such that whenever other temple residents glanced my way, I would feel suddenly embarrassed and naked, with my bones exposed like that, before I reminded myself that they couldn't see what I was seeing. One feels as though one were actually a skeleton walking around. Kind of eerie. But also peaceful because it is supported by lingering momentum from a high degree of concentration, which is generally calming and pleasant.

This consciousness of the body is to be carefully maintained, cultivated, and guarded with mindfulness and equanimity (which I was subsequently unable to do). The initial breakthrough is what meditators call, in Thai, *dai kammatharn*, to "get a meditation tool." The meditation tool can be cared for by mindful attendance to the point that it is vividly present in everyday life, and so also easily reentered into during formal sitting, returning the meditator to the intimate clarity of jhāna. Once this abject imagery has "stuck to the heart" (*did chai*), meditators at Wat Toong go around in their day-to-day life intensely aware of, say, their skeleton, their skin hairs, or their heart, actually seeing it inwardly all the time, and they build this awareness over long periods of time until it induces and provokes them to touch the charnel ground within, and brush against an insight into their existence. We all know, of course, that there are bones in our bodies, that the body is a delicate and impermanent construction, that it will definitely wear out, get sick, be painful, and finally die. But this kind of knowing or consciousness is usually an objectified form of knowledge. We know the body as an *object* that will fall apart. It is possible to make the intellectual association that this falling apart pertains to "me." But the immediate consciousness of the truth of the body is much more rare and precious, and glimmers of it usually come only under extremely unfortunate circumstances, circumstances that can sometimes be too overwhelming and upsetting to support the instruction of inspection, such as with serious pain and illness, childbirth, fatal diagnosis, or as we die. To know the body not as an object linked in a string of thoughts to a hypothetical "me," but as, say, a heap of bones, an intricate jalopy of a skeleton clunking along, is to glimpse a very powerful form for contemplating death and impermanence.

Living an ascetic life in Wat Toong, resident ascetics are engaged in a wide array of everyday practices that make it difficult to avoid familiarity with the more unfortunate aspects of such an existence. But the crucial catalyst to acquiring the internal kammatthāna has, for many practitioners at the temple whom I know well and probably many more, consisted precisely of viewing these same photographs of the charred corpse of the nun, with burnt flesh dangling from her lips and nose; with brittle, crumbling hairs and white teeth, still smiling; with stringy, cooked tendons poking out of the blistered skin.

For their soteriological purposes, the nuns and monks of Wat Toong seek out the salod chai, letdown, of repulsiveness. But the "truth" of these images is ultimately not located in the image. It is the graphic, gory detail that "sticks to the heart" (*did chai*), and toward which this Buddhist pedagogy of visual images, and often also this Buddhist use of photography, leads (figure 9); ultimately, however, the image realm of charnel ground may not be the realm of the physical eye, an organ that contacts things in an outer visual field. And yet asubha kammatthāna can have a connection to mechanically reproduced visual objects, which do operate that way. In the most absorbing photographic, video, and cinematic perception, of course, outer physical sight is the primary mode of contact, and in that sense the material body of the viewers themselves are not ordinarily the object of attention. But this is not a truth inherent to the "nature" of such

Figure 9. Buddhist fruit

visual media. Photographic images of death, corpses, and the repulsiveness of the body can be exchanged in a constant relation to eidetic visions of the body. And though they do not consist of matter, nevertheless these asubha images lead to an intimate awareness, a seeing of the body in the body, a reproduction in which, ultimately, a copy of a body can be retransformed and restored into an original—into a body once again.

"I look deeply into the parts of the being," Mae-Chi Sa-ad says. "What do I see? I see from the scalp to the skull, all the way down. And then I contemplate, *na*. I contemplate the mind, let the mind stay put with the mind, let the mind *phicarana-aaa* [contemplate] *lo-ooong* [sink down, down] to the feet. Go down and up, up and down . . . see my body, watch to see what this body really is for sure. . . . In my tummy," she laughs, "what kinds of things are in there? I look throughout my parts. If the mind is calm or the mind is distracted, I simply make note of it, that's all. If the mind is quiet, the mind is buoyant. No pain or stiffness. When sitting, it's like . . . it's not as though our body is a body of ours."

Then, after a pause, she says (with a tone something like awe, or reverence), "Cetanā khau yuu nai tua kaung man." The meaning of that statement is strange, almost ungrammatical in Thai, and phrased enigmatically: the intentions of "her" are located in the body belonging to it, or, "The will of her resides within its body."

209

Nuns like Mae-Chi Sa-ad are held in high regard at Wat Toong because they are believed to have realized something about the intensely personal matter of personal matter—that is, that it isn't (ours). But they claim it is possible to face this fact squarely rather than be engulfed by it when the time of its most pressing manifestation comes, as it does for us all. According to this theory, although we may "know" these things about the body as not ours—as not under our control, ultimately unstable, and with a "will" of its own—that does not mean we realize it completely. It is for this reason that the nuns at Wat Toong dedicate themselves to acquiring this faculty of seeing born in intense states of concentration. Spending continuous moments, minutes, hours, days, weeks in meditation on repetitive and sensational images of the abject body, they access an image realm with profound impact on what they understand as a realization of *anicca*, "impermanence," and *anatta*, "no-self": in the body there never was anything present that could permanently keep it together, and nothing there that can ever be held to as "Self."

In contrast to dominant strains of media criticism, this exchange of images operates on very different assumptions about the nature of what is real about "presence," because this transformed reproduction, passing through photography and into the body, is taken by the practitioners quite literally as an insight into the characteristic emptiness of bodily existence, rather than as a simulacrum. Or, more precisely, we might say that a two-dimensional reproduction, which may divest the body of its physical aura, is reenvisioned into a materiality, and yet that vision shows that there never was a stable, essential, physical presence to begin with.

On those rare occasions when a corpse is available for dismemberment, some of the nuns and monks do avail themselves of the multiple sensory attributes of a dismembered body. That this is useful is not in doubt. But that bodily presence and multisensory embodiment is essential to the work of asubha kammatthāna should be placed in great doubt, not only because of its empirical contradiction in the practice of the nuns and monks at Wat Toong but also because of its theoretical supposition that the source of the abject is ultimately located in the external matter of bodies, if not also for its metaphysical belief that there is anything at all that can ever be fully or finally present.

ARCHE-PHOTOGRAPHY

The practice of asubha kammatthāna is nothing if not repetitive. Yet meditators take images of death and make them more and more vivid, and powerfully transformative, as they attend to them. It is a common observation, by contrast, that in the realm of mechanical reproduction precisely

210

the opposite is often the case—the most extreme and obvious example being the cheapest sensationalism, plugged straight into the reified directives of the profit drive. In a mechanically reproduced memory it may become easier and easier to behold images of greater and greater atrocity. It seems that the more gory and sensational the images become, the more gory and sensational they need to be. The chasms that seem to have opened up between the sensorial suffering of victims, on one hand, and the bodiless viewers and acorporeal bodies on the mechanical screen, on the other, are more a departure from a significant and meaningful contact than a potential for liberation through imagery, such as Walter Benjamin, for instance, hoped for.[51]

And yet the problem of the divestment of "the aura of the object" was not a problem for Benjamin. Quite the opposite. In contrast to the line of argument outlined above, which is premised on a metaphysics of presence, Benjamin found something wondrous in the divestment of the aura: "For the first time—and this is the effect of the film—man has to operate with his whole living person, yet forgoing its aura. For aura is tied to his presence; there can be no replica of it."[52] It may seem easy to cry devil in the face of modern mechanical reproductions, and perhaps in some cases also correct to do so. As Martin Jay demonstrates, that would contribute to the stream of a long tradition of the "denigration" of sight that began when philosophers first woke up from naive assumptions about "the noble sense" and continued in the more recent critique of Western "ocularcentrism"; contributors to this stream include intellectuals as diverse as Bergson, Foucault, Sartre, Irigary, Lacan, and Barthes, even to some degree Bataille and Derrida, and the criticism even reaches an extreme form among, of all things, film theorists such as Metz and his generation of *Cahiers du Cinéma* writers.[53] But after all, if we only deride the dominance of visual imagery in our world, see it only as illusion to be unmasked, or essentialize it as a Western, modern, regime of ocularcentrism, perhaps that is an exercise in futility. The proliferation of mass-mediated visual culture has been accomplished. It is now counterintuitive, and therefore intriguing, to note that at the dawn of the ascendance of this image sphere Benjamin harbored no metaphysics of presence for the image and rather saw something potentially liberating in the seeming negation of presence that mechanical reproduction represented for our senses. Is there, then, another dimension to two-sided mechanical reproductions, another side that, however compelling and true to life the critique of mass media may be, nevertheless defies it and connects with that utopian hope Benjamin had concerning a radical altering of the relation between people and their world?

It is easy to drift from the aspiration for such a pedagogy of images into a hazy ontology of cinema consumption. There are some theorists who would seize upon filmic dimensions of "experience" as though they represented a way to transcend "modernity" and alienation, and restore a more natural relation to life. Take, for instance, the philosophy outlined in Maurice Merleau-Ponty's "Film and the New Psychology."[54] Merleau-Ponty's position on vision in his essay on film, even though an affirmation of film, still shares many of the assumptions implicit in the critique of the hegemony of vision. As such, it serves to outline certain structures of feeling about "presence" that are chronic and widespread. Though Martin Jay explains, almost convincingly, that Merleau-Ponty was not seeking a mystical union with the natural senses, he acknowledges the persistence of appeals in Merleau-Ponty's body of work to a "primordial sensorium prior to the differentiation of the senses."[55] These are also common longings, at least implicitly, in much of contemporary social theory. In his book on vision and modernity, *Techniques of the Observer*, Jonathan Crary states that the most crucial questions facing the critique of "an ongoing mutation in the nature of visuality" include "What forms are being left behind?" and "How is the body, including the observing body, becoming a component of new machines, economies, apparatuses . . . ?"[56] To that add Fredric Jameson's long, bewildered, yet incredibly articulate cry of vertigo over "hyperspace" in his book *Postmodernism*.[57] It is not much of a leap from these still historical yet credulously linear wonderings about loss and an implied affront to the human dignity of a previously less alienated self to the more generalized desires, still loitering in the more romantic wings of cultural anthropology, for an undifferentiated mode of being in which all the violent, "modern," and "Western" distinctions, conceptions, notions, dualisms, and dichotomies dissolve in a great mushy whole.

Merleau-Ponty, like many before and after him, attributes these "violent" differentiations to the intellectual disturbance caused by the dualism of Descartes. To this Cartesian differentiation of the senses he counters that "perception of the whole is more natural and more primary than the perception of isolated elements," and "should be considered our spontaneous way of seeing," as opposed to "the scientist who observes or the philosopher who reflects." "My perception is not a sum of visual, tactile, audible givens: I perceive in a total way with my whole being; I grasp a unique structure of the thing, a unique way of being, which speaks to all my senses at once." For Merleau-Ponty, "being-in-the-world" is always holistic, a matter of gestalts, "a being thrown into the world and attached to it by a natural bond." It is only by analytic error that we divide experience, segment ourselves, separate ourselves from the objects around us. And that is why for Merleau-Ponty, film, of all things, undoes this modern and unnatural division. Film blends the senses, and re-presents us with the truth about perception. It is film that "directly presents to us that special way of being in the world." In film, just as in life, the world is preconstructed, preexistent, and causes its own perception.[58]

When Merleau-Ponty reflects upon "experience"—always after the fact (which he himself attributes to science, philosophical analysis, and Cartesian philosophy)—it appears as though existence is situated in an undifferentiated whole and continuum of being. That is how it appears to anyone who is merely thinking and remembering (as they are writing philosophy on how wrong philosophy is) about how it really feels to "be in the world," perhaps because it is one of the mind's many capabilities to reconstruct life in wholes and continua. It may even be more pleasant that way; I know I would rather be a continuous being-in-the-world than a sequence of fragments. But is experience given to us all in this form? For instance, does the approach to its observation change it in any way, or is "experience" completely separate from the act of observation?

Ironically, Buddhist meditation disciplines are often and wrongly considered to be similar to phenomenology because of what seems to be their valuation of attention to experience "just as it appears." But in practice Buddhist meditators display attitudes toward "experience" that are very different from those of popular phenomenology. According to the Thai nuns of Wat Toong, if one were to pay extremely intense attention to every moment (backed up of course by particular techniques, traditions, and disciplinary tactics to sustain such observation from moment to moment, such as informants report about meditation on the body), one might find that being-in-the-world is not so homogeneous after all. It may seem to be seamless when we inattentively reflect on our *memory* of "experience" in life as it is lived, with relatively low awareness. But when one pays careful attention, under appropriate circumstances such as reclusive meditation, practitioners report that it is not too difficult to see, for instance, that phenomena change from seeing, hearing, touching, and thinking, back and forth in a most fragmentary and startling way. One's attention must be quick enough to pick up this alternation. Consider this analogy: the four blades of an electric fan (read: multiple senses), run at high speed, appear to be one continuous, whole, circle of matter, but when you slow them down, it may no longer look like one continuous entity.

According to Buddhist meditation theory, the magic of being operates by the fast succession of sensory occurrences, making it possible for one to cling to a singular self-identity, in this case as a "knower" of phenomena, when in fact all that has happened is that phenomena *were there*. The "being there" is what Buddha labeled *viññāna*, usually translated as "consciousness" but better translated as something more like "presence." Perception occurs when "there is" a sense object, a sense organ, and their contact ("there is" being viññāna). Viññāna depends upon this. When visual contact happens, for instance, there is eye viññāna (sight-presence).

When auditory contact happens, viññāna is the there-ness of sound. When tactile contact happens, viññāna is the presence of a touch. When thinking happens (involving likewise a mind organ, mind object, and viññāna), viññāna is the presence of a mental event. Without viññāna, there can be no occurrence of phenomena, *that is, they are not there*, such as when an unconscious person is kicked. In that case there is the sense object (a boot), the sense organ (the nerve receptors in the body), but no viññāna (no "consciousness," no actual there-is-ness).[59] Similarly—and here's the rub—there can be no consciousness, viññāna, without the other two elements. "Consciousness is always consciousness of something," as Sartre wrote.[60]

As conscious experience happens very rapidly from one contact to the next, it appears as though there is one person, or one viññāna, before which these various phenomena are appearing. But this is a magic trick. They are all different viññāna: eye-seeing-thereness, ear-hearing-thereness, mind-knowing-thereness, and so on, occurring in rapid succession, too fast for an untrained attention to follow. There is no viññāna without something as its object. Yet it appears as though viññāna exists independently of its objects. It seems as though presence, "consciousness," or "the knower," has its own independent existence before which these phenomena make their appearance.

Viññāna is the ultimate magic trick, according to Buddhist meditation theory, because what merely appears as "presence" or "there-ness" is instead taken to be "I-am-ness," taken to be self, thus feeding the fundamental conceit of the presence of the self, "I am." Somehow the simple "thereness" that may occur in conjunction with things and sense organs by a sleight of hand is experienced as a presence of oneself, "I am," such as in the problematic "*I* experience the world."

Thai Buddhists call the belief in this magic of the self *sakkāyaditthi,* the view (*ditthi*) of personality (*sakkāya*). Sakkāyaditthi is not simply a mistaken conception or belief about oneself, which one can simply choose to exchange for a better one, but a more fundamental conceit that is extremely difficult to uproot. It needs the discipline of an arduous ascesis that aims to wear down the conceit and eventually overturn the belief in the personality view, thus beginning to undercut the fundamental unawareness that underlies it, *avijjā*, ignorance.

Merleau-Ponty's critique of "Cartesian rationalism," specifically, may not be completely off the mark. But just as the differentiation of bodily organs through anatomy charts or viewing autopsy procedures does not, in itself, dictate that a practice that uses them, like corpse meditation, must arrive at a biomedical consciousness of "the body," so too differentiating the senses does not necessarily lead to a Cartesian epistemology. There is always a romantic longing for being that urges critics to argue that any and all differentiation of the senses is a fabrication of modernity or of Western civilization. For Merleau-Ponty, along with the idea of "ge-stalts," the phenomenon of "synesthesia" was particularly interesting as a language game to construct this version of life.[61] Synesthesia (the blend-ing of senses, such as smells having color, or the seeing of sounds), is often cited as evidence that the differentiated senses are merely a modern aberration, alienation, sinister power operation, and so on.[62] But Buddhist meditators claim that even synesthesia can, if mindfulness is quick enough, be observed as it actually happens. They report that so-called synesthesia (and some practitioners are what has come to be called "synes-thetes") is always a translation or reencoding from one sense faculty into another, which happens so fast that it usually experienced as a blending of two senses, that is, as synesthesia. The translation follows the original sense contact faster than a lightning bolt.

But this is not a complete refutation of Merleau-Ponty's philosophy, for now we are entering an entirely different language game. Merleau-Ponty's world is like that of the deaf percussionist who uses vision and tactility to make music (I am thinking of an actual master classical perfor-mer here). The music is still music, even to the deaf percussionist, whether or not the ear provides any sensation. It is not based on sensations of *sound*, but in the perception of *music*, which is greater than the sum of its sensual parts. By contrast, the investigation of bare attention to the senses in meditation, were Merleau-Ponty aware of it, would be neither here nor there according to the manner in which he interprets the phenom-enological reduction of Husserl, and upon which his philosophy is predi-cated. Quite reasonably for Merleau-Ponty, alternations between the sen-sory happenings, if not consciously perceived, are therefore not as real or as important as the holistic, gestalt experience of existence in sensory experience that he claims is consciously perceived: a singular, holistic being-in-the-world. Through phenomenological reduction, the apparent phenomenon of a continuous being-in-the-world becomes the ground of the philosophical real, whereas any nonconsciously perceived "natural world" processes, like the differentiated senses (or, as the meditators see it, discontinuous fragments of "things that occur," as it were), are brack-eted out of consideration, leaving only experience, supposedly just as it appears to one. Although this does make some sense logically—and here is the fundamental flaw—in fact in this case it is not "experience" just as it is, but a memory, reflection, and intellectual speculation that occurs after the fact, which is taken to be an object of experience (ironically, precisely what Merleau-Ponty claimed to be overcoming). Paying atten-tion to experience "just as it is"—if that is truly what one wants—presum-ably would require that one pay sustained attention, closely from moment to moment, and that would not be something easy or perhaps even possible to accomplish. But were one to marshal the discipline to try, the nature of "experience" might well turn out to be different from what it is when just remembering it. "It" may necessarily change the closer one gets to it, may appear differently with the speed and quality of the mindfulness that follows it. Experience "just as it is" does not really exist, or, if it can be said to exist in some sense, it does not until one can follow "experience" in close tandem with its occurrence, and then, necessarily, it may not display the same characteristics you once thought you saw in it. And that might be something of a salod chai, a letdown.

This is a critical emphasis necessary to understanding the difference between Buddhist meditation and popular phenomenology. If it sounds like a simple metaphysics of presence or, to be more precise, an out-presence-ing of Merleau-Ponty's metaphysics of presence, the one thing to remember is that in the Thai meditation's attention to and mindfulness of the present, there is no essential presence in presence. And this is not a pleasant thing to discover. Merleau-Ponty is absolutely right in saying film is like life because, like "life," it depends for its appearances upon blurred attention. The mind perceives a series of still film-frames, fluttering by too rapidly for anyone to be mindful of their change from one to another, and so the mind experiences a lifelike movement and seamless reality in film. In fact it is lifelike above all because we already are cinema, because in life we also let sensory contacts pass by too rapidly to observe how they arise, linger, and pass away, and rather misperceive to a great degree just as Merleau-Ponty would have it.

And yet . . . there is nothing outside the film frame. Cinema depends on erasing the gaps, the starts and stops, of the technological apparatus of projection; just so the holistic version of being-in-the-world depends on a degree of inattention that makes the gaps between sensory phenomena invisible and unnoticed. Film may take the fundamental principle and illusion of life as a "being" and raise it to a new level of technological accomplishment. But perhaps that is precisely why it was in montage, juxtaposition, collision, and conflict that Benjamin formulated his hopes for a utopian power unleashed in the dialectical image. In that case, the strange confluences and divergences between filmic apprehension and the image-realm of jhāna are not necessarily, or essentially, a matter of their different technological nature but rather very much a matter of the relation to, and the presentation of, the image. What can be so potentially startling, liberating, revolutionary about mechanical reproduction is that not only can it take the illusion of the life continuum and raise it to an extreme and ideal state but also that then, as cinema, it can just as quickly dash itself against itself again, creating moments of shock effect and fragmentary consciousness that in turn play back not only against the grain of film projection but against a fundamental illusion of life itself, which cinema mimics. It is this more fundamental rendering of life—that cinema copies by the very act of projecting its copies—that makes film also potentially subversive on the most basic of levels, training the mind's eye either to generate or to disperse the homogenous magic of being-in-the-world.

DIALECTIC OF ENLIGHTENMENT

How one actually arrives at the point where sakkāyadhitti—the magic of the self—is overthrown and the training in asubha kammatthāna brought to fulfill its purpose is not something most people who know for themselves are willing to talk about with others, because it gives rise to all sorts of misconceptions and preconceptions. I would not even bother to ask my teacher, Luang Bu Sangwaan, about such matters. The nuns at Wat Toong also avoid too much direct reference to these things, though they are not bound by strict rules, as are the monks, against talking about experience. In a rare and articulate disclosure, however, one of the key disciples of Acharn Mun, founder of a meditation school of Thai Buddhism cognate to that of Wat Toong, has allowed his words on this subject be recorded and transcribed.[63]

Phra Acharn Maha Boowa, whom I will refer to as Luang Ta, "venerable grandfather," as is popular in Thailand, is probably the most highly respected living Arahant in Thailand today, which is to say he is considered to have practiced the Dhamma to its very result: the complete release from subjugation to the *kilesa* (defilements) that cause suffering: greed, anger, and delusion. Unfortunately, because he is a heterosexual male (at least in Euro-American categories), it is easy to interpret the following account of sexual desire, liberation, and meditation on death as simply misogyny. That is certainly, I suppose, one valid interpretation, especially if you ignore the fact that a parallel and identical process also occurs among nuns. But the fact is that everything he might say about his struggle over desire for the female form has its analogy in the practice of nuns, who practice it in relation to the male form. Also, it should be noted that it is implicitly recognized among advanced practitioners that homosexual attraction is inherent in all people (celibate ascetics practicing mindfulness of the body could hardly miss this fact!), and so fixating on male-female bonds is a distortion of the reality of the situation. Following Thai manners, however, this aspect of the practice is rarely spoken of in public forums (the brief reference Luang Ta makes below about attraction to male form is therefore unusual in that respect).

Through Luang Ta Maha Boowa's words we can get a sense of the later stages of practice, which concern minute attention to matters that people like you and I (I am assuming) are far from concerned with. His account of the final stages of practice describes aspirations that few readers would hold out for themselves, or think were in any way valuable, good, or desirable: release from desire. It is not that desire is "evil" in the Dhamma, but that at the highest levels and in the extremely ideal telos of Dhamma practice, desire, or *rāga* (passion) and *tanhā* (clinging), are no longer worthy of being seen as the most important of all values in life. It is possible to misunderstand this through associations with Victorian moralism or, say, Catholic priests, who are often seen in U.S. culture as being some sort of deviants for not having sex. In a dark, cavernous cathedral, a Catholic monk waits to whip you with leather straps. Dried up old nuns tragically endure a gray existence, deprived of the thing they need. . . .

With the practice of awakening in Buddhism, it might be better to understand the practical meaning of disengagement with desire in a less anxious and more matter-of-fact way: desire is a conditioned phenomenon, a part of convention, and clarity of discernment will not have the necessary power while one is in a state of reaction to it. So, if the ideal of clear discernment is your goal, then glorifying and pursuing desirous passions would not be beneficial. If clear discernment is not your goal, however, then it does not matter. Rāga, for instance, has its place in everyday life for Thai lay Buddhists. Lay people are encouraged to have sex in kind and loyal ways, while nuns and monks practice celibacy, a few to the point where desire is not an issue for them anymore—they do not give it a second thought. They have a sense different from, say, that of a D. H. Lawrence, of what is urgent and important in their life, as Ñanavira Thera has put it.[64]

Luang Ta Maha Boowa was attempting to realize freedom from reaction to conditions of body and mind, and that included realizing freedom from reaction to the conditioning of desire. After years of meditation in which he periodically held all-night vigils in a sitting position, keeping still and racked with incredible pain, he had developed a quiet strength of mind that he said was so nearly perfect that he got stuck on his daily practice of concentration for almost five years before he had the sense to break out of it. He was stalled in the pleasant, steady-minded effect of concentration, which is only a temporary and conditioned phenomenon, dependent as it is on the application of oneself to certain specific disciplines like mindful breathing, described above. The Thai expression for this is *hin thab yaa,* a rock upon grass, which is to say concentration is like a rock that prevents grass from growing under it, but if you remove the rock the grass sprouts up again. Samādhi, in the relative sense of the word signifying concentration, is only a temporary, conditioned phenom-enon, and in itself produces no lasting transformation. However, samādhi does help empower the mind to do what really is the point of Dhamma, which is to observe calmly, and then to discern, to have insight and wis-dom into the general characteristics of existence: suffering, imperma-nence, and not-self. As far as the simple, raw power of samādhi was con-cerned, Luang Bu was adept at the concentration on the repulsiveness of the body parts, so that he could see inside of his own body and gaze into the bodies of others. He was confident:

> When I contemplated repulsiveness, it was remarkable, you know. Really remarkable. The mind, when it contemplated, was adroit and audacious. I could see right through whatever I looked at—man, woman, no matter how young. To tell you frankly . . . (and here I have to ask the forgiveness of both the men and women involved if it's wrong to speak too frankly), it wouldn't have to be a question of old women you know. If the gathering was full of young women, I could march right in without any sign of lust appearing at all. . . .
>
> Looking at a person, there would be just the bones wrapped up in skin, nothing but flesh all glaring and red. So where could I see any beauty? The power of the repulsiveness was really strong. No matter whose body I saw, that's how I would perceive it. So where would there be any beauty to make me feel desire?
>
> As soon as I saw another person's body, I would see right through it. There would be nothing but flesh and bones in that body . . . the power of my contemplation of repulsiveness was so strong that I'd perceive everyone as a pile of bones.[65]

But the vision of asubha, repulsiveness, is not in itself the ultimate truth of the matter. It is like a rock atop grass, not true discernment and free-dom. It is still mere construction in the realm of form. He had no certainty that "lust or passion for the male or female body had disappeared at this or that point in time and place." Although he could, through condition-ing, prevent sexual desire from arising noticeably at any given time, he had never had the experience of a certain knowledge of sexual desire pass-ing away, once and for all. In fact, while the attention to asubha had its value for a time, it was just a temporary tool: "But this daring wasn't right, in terms of the point at which the mind really had its fill of lust, which is why I criticized myself afterwards, after the mind had passed this point. This daring was a kind of madness, but while I was following the path, it was right, because that was how I had to follow it through. This is like critizing food after you've eaten your fill."[66]

Luang Ta changed strategies, to a dialectical method. He reversed the momentum of his mind from repulsion to attraction, and consciously willed himself to cover all these walking skeletons with skin. Although it went against the grain of his previous practice, he forced his mind to cover the bones with skin, and he visualized a beautiful body contiguous with his:

> I'd do walking meditation visualizing the beauty of that body clinging to mine, clinging right to mine as I walked back and forth. . . . I practiced this way for four full days without any physical attraction or desire appearing at all. . . . The image kept trying to change into a pile of bones wrapped in skin, but I forced the mind to stay just at the skin level. . . . I kept on contemplating every facet to find which facet would make the mind feel desire, to see at which moment the desire would arise, so that I could then take whatever might appear and focus on it as the object to be contemplated and uprooted. . . .
>
> [T]he night of the fourth day, there was a flickering, as if the mind was going to feel lust for that beautiful body which had been clinging to me constantly during that period. It was a peculiar kind of flickering. As soon as the flickering appeared, I kept encouraging it. . . . I focused in on it. That flickering was simply a condition of the mind which appeared only slightly. It had no effect on the body at all. It was inside the mind. When I encouraged it, it would flicker again, which proved that it wasn't all gone. So now that it wasn't all gone, what was I supposed to do?[67]

He switched tactics again. Now he alternated between the poles of beauty and repulsiveness. He would let his contemplation take apart the body down to its bones and then build it back up again, back and forth. One day, while visualizing an image of repulsiveness, he willed the image to remain unchanged. He describes the development of beginning stages of discernment, of letting go, of extricating himself from his necessary madness:

> If it was an image of bones wrapped in skin or a pile of bones with the skin removed, I had it stay right there in front of me. The mind stared right at it, with mindfulness focused, waiting to learn the truth from that image of repulsiveness, to see what it would do, how this pile of repulsiveness would move or change. . . .
>
> As I kept focusing in, the image of unattractiveness standing there before me was gradually sucked into the mind, absorbed into the mind, so that I finally realized that repulsiveness was a matter of the mind itself. The state of mind which had fixed on the idea of unattractiveness sucked it in—which meant that attractiveness and unattractiveness were simply a matter of the mind deceiving itself. Then the mind let go in a flash. It let go of unattractiveness. It understood now, because it had made the break. "This is how it's supposed to be. It's been simply a matter of the mind painting pictures to

deceive itself, getting excited over its shadows. Those external things aren't passion, aversion, delusion. The mind is what has passion, aversion, delusion." As soon as the mind knew this clearly, it extricated itself from external affairs and came inwards. As soon as the mind would "blip" outwards, it knew that these external affairs were displaying themselves. So now the image of unattractiveness appeared exclusively within the mind.[68]

Despite frequent admonitions in Theravāda Buddhism to view corpses in order to see the unsavory truth about your body, in fact in later stages, the practice of asubha kammatthāna deconstructs this discourse of truth. Even so general an attribution as "realism" to the interest in death imagery in Thai Buddhism becomes complicated upon deeper inspection. The point in asubha kammatthāna, for advanced practice, is not to tear off the mask of beauty as illusion and see the stark reality, as though the ultimate truth inhered in abject detail and constructedness inhered in beauty; least of all is it to balance the positive and negative so as not to be "too dark." Instead the purpose is to see the constructedness of both the attractive and the repulsive themselves, proving to the heart (*chai*) that there is no essential truth that inheres in objective form, whether that of abjection "in the body" or that of beauty. In this practice, abjection is necessary and effective, but is neither fixed in nor originates from external forms. Luang Ta describes the practice of seeing attraction and repulsion in external forms as "a kind of madness, but while I was following the path, it was right, because that was how I had to follow it through." But even to understand *this* necessary madness as illusion would be "like criticizing food after you've eaten your fill."[69]

Even within the highly directed practice of asubha kammatthāna there is no stable nature to the medium. In this case, the work with what may seem at first sight to be a negotiation with a "natural emotion," aversion to the abject, is not accomplished through "deadened nerves" or through any other metaphor that posits a short-circuit interruption—by faulty media conduits—of the connection between an objective truth of the body and a perceiver on the other, damaged, end. What remains instead is a more subtle observance of a reactivity to imagery, at least when the mind understands. Luang Ta, at that point, could now deal with the very matter of reactivity in the only place it is truly possible to work with it, within the mind. But even this "within the mind" was susceptible to a Buddhist deconstruction of presence. Luang Ta found that as soon as he would conjure any image up, it would dissipate in the next instant. Within the mind, all imagery was clearly subject to anicca, passing away:

[I]t was just like a lightning flash: as soon as I focused on making an image, it would vanish immediately, so there was no time to elaborate on its being attractive or unattractive or anything at all, because of the speed of the arising and disappearing. The instant it would appear—blip!—it would vanish. . . . As for external unattractiveness, that problem had already been taken care of. I had understood it from the moment it had been sucked in towards the mind, and the mind had immediately let go of external unattractiveness. It let go of sights, sounds, smells, tastes, everything external—because the mind was what had been the deceiver. Once I understood this point clearly, those other things were no longer any problem. . . .

After the internal images had all disappeared, the mind was empty. Completely empty. Whatever I focused on was completely empty. I'd look at trees, mountains, buildings, and see them simply as shades, as shadows. . . . Even when I'd look at my own body, I'd see it simply as a shadow. . . . Even though it was that empty, I would form mental pictures as a way of exercising it. Whatever image I would form would be a means of exercising the mind to make it even more adept at emptiness, to the point where after a single blip it'd be empty—a single blip, and it'd be empty. The moment anything was formed—blip!—it'd be empty right then.[70]

Objects of attraction or repulsion can display no essential nature in a world of disintegrating shadows. But that was not the end of the line, for what remained extremely problematic was the position of presence in the "knower." Out of the emptiness this arresting and convincing sense of insight arose: *"If there is a point or center of the knower anywhere, that is the essence of . . . being."* He saw it as a bewildering sensibility that had dawned on the mind and held him in its sway for some time. He searched for that "point of the knower" within this awareness he had cultivated. Eventually that point arose like a wonderful radiance, filling the empty world with a marvel of bright and pure awareness. He paid no more heed to the five khandas, but exercised his mindfulness and discernment on this awareness, searching it throughout, but finally concluded: "the 'point' . . . was still a conventional reality. No matter how magnificent it might be, it was still magnificence in the realm of convention. No matter how radiant or splendid it might be, *it was still radiance and splendor in the realm of convention, because there was still ignorance (avijja) within it."*[71]

The closer he focused on this core of ignorance within the point of the knower, the more he was able to discern that it, too, was subject to variability, that it alternated from states of ease to disease—impermanent and suffering—although only in the most extremely subtle manner. He practiced continuous awareness of the general characteristics of this marvelous radiance—moment by moment, minute by minute, day by day—until the second half of the epiphany dawned on him. *"Defilement (kilesa), radiance, ease, and suffering: these are all conventional realities. They are all annatta—not-self.*"[72] And he says that it was at this moment of realization that the mind was able to completely let go of this point of the knower, this seeming essence of being, the magic of the self,

> that state of mind immersed in ignorance was a conventional reality which should simply be let go. It shouldn't be held to. A moment after this realiza-tion arose to warn mindfulness and discernment, which were acting as senti-nels at that moment, it was as if the mind, mindfulness, and discernment each became impartial and impassive, not stirring themselves to perform any duty at all. At that moment the mind was neutral, not focused on anything, not alluding absent-mindedly to anything anywhere. Discernment didn't do any work. Mindfulness was alert in its normal way, without being focused on anything.
>
> *That moment—when the mind, mindfulness, and discernment were each impassive and impartial—was the moment when the cosmos in the mind over which unawareness held sway trembled and quaked.* Unawareness was thrown down from its throne on the heart. In its place, the pure mind ap-peared at the same moment that unawareness was toppled, smashed, and eradicated through the power of triumphant mindfulness and discernment—the moment that the sky came crashing down and the cosmos (within) trem-bled and quaked, showing its final marvel on the border between convention and release.[73]

PROFANE ILLUMINATION

Walter Benjamin's enigmatic hope was for a secular, materialist gnosis of a nature and power analogous to religious revelation: a "profane illumi-nation," which was, as Michael Taussig put it, "the single most important shock, the single most effective step, in opening up the 'long-sought image sphere' to the bodily impact of the 'dialectical image.'"[74] In his famous analogy, Benjamin likened film to a surgical operation. The camera, dis-cerned Benjamin, slices through reality as the surgeon penetrates into the patient's body: "his hand moves among the organs. . . ." And thus an optical unconscious would be flushed out of hiding: an image-realm that the photograph can resuscitate from sleep, "meaningful yet covert enough to find a hiding place in waking dreams."[75]

Benjamin placed the fulcrum of the lever that would crack open the unawareness haunting the material scene of modernity in the power of mechanical reproduction to divest material objects of their "aura." With respect to the work of art, this meant that the elite cult of art objects and of artists would give way under the pressure of a technology that could reproduce objects ad infinitum. As Eduardo Cadava has pointed out, "technical reproducibility" (what has in a mishap been translated as "mechanical reproduction") was for Benjamin a quality of all art objects, of any era, each of which represents a series of technological procedures performed on matter that is, theoretically, reproducible.[76] "Mechanical reproduction" through film and photography (as well as through video and digital imaging, for that matter) represents not the eruption of a completely new phenomenon but the articulation and enhancement of what art already was. It is a rapid, dizzying expansion of reproducibility at such a pace and on such a scale that it appears to be a flash of the entirely new.

A technical reproducibility that can proliferate at such great speed and across great distances has the potential to undermine the bourgeois aesthetic of art consumption, an aesthetic that sees value in the physical presence of an object or original, rather than locating its value within the inherent reproducibility of the object, which was always a technical potential in the making of it. Widespread and rapid technical reproduction highlights rather than obscures what artistry always was: the intervention of human action in the making of the world. Where elite art consumption requires the acquisition of high taste and a distanced, solitary contemplation of the art object by which spectators immerse themselves singularly and behold the work and its aura, submitting to the object, technical reproducibility makes art accessible, collective, plebeian, a mass phenomenon where the secret of human agency is raised to the level of the explicit and conscious. This is presumably a discovery the ruling order, for obvious reasons, would not benefit from if it were popularized.

With respect to the work of film, Benjamin placed great faith in the distracting, repellent, and ballistic shock effects to empower this new politics of the aesthetic. But in this he unfurled a too-neat distinction between his idea and the fascist politics arising all around him. Fascism is a betrayal, he wrote, that gives satisfaction to an experience of violent destruction, "the situation of politics which Fascism is rendering aesthetic," and to this we must respond "by politicizing art."[77]

In actual practice, these two tendencies have almost always arisen together, and are almost always muddled and indistinguishable. Aesthetic satisfaction in violent consumption, as well as in the way political realities come to be imbued by the aesthetic properties of the public image realm that "represents" them, is persistently powerful in this realm of mechanical reproduction because it represents a violence linked to what may have become a de facto historical nature. Where some may see new utopian hope in the surgical operations of the camera's expansions and contractions—its cuttings, tiltings, trackings—the operations in their actual history of practice have resonated more with the brutality that these tactics suggest than with the liberation they may have seemed to promise. And yet, we are already living in a dissected world of shock effects—situated in it, oriented toward it, and constituted by it in such a way that, under these conditions of altered sensoria, we may no longer be able to refuse the necessity of working in and with this strange realm of forms.

Given this situation, our fate hangs on a peculiar meathook, on the pointed contradiction between the absolute necessity that mechanical reproduction unleash the liberating power of images and the seeming impossibility that this image-realm will ever do so. The market of images absorbs into itself the nature of economic systems, and reality starts to conform to representations as though it were trying to portray them accurately. That was the great danger in the aestheticization of politics—a force of aesthetic satisfaction in violence and taking pleasure in destruction, a spirit of fascism which, if so characterized, certainly has not been kicked out of our world but has, rather, seeped into it with the anonymous quiet of capillary proliferation. At the same time, more loudly and clearly in the realm of mechanical reproduction than anywhere else, that violent destruction has taken on tremendous economic value. It is perhaps the potential of mechanical reproduction violently to rework perception that may cut death loose and allow it to circulate freely and harmoniously with the values of high liberal economics.

Yet the practice of Thai Buddhist meditation on graphic imagery—even on photographs—shows us that in principle this violence on perception is not foreordained in the technological nature of the medium, that image reproductions do not necessarily have to have the effect of hyperreality, but can have an effect precisely opposite to everything that has been attributed to them.

When they are incorporated into particular practices, image reproductions afford particularly powerful effects, the range of which may be opaque to those with too radical a skepticism about vision or who shiver at the thought of photography. If these effects of meditation on corpse photography are possible, why not others? In Thailand, for instance, and in Asia generally, photography of the corpses of historic massacres are central to explicitly political rituals. These demonstrations of graphic photography in political memorials negotiate memory of the past with protest in the present. Photographic shock effects are used to seize control of vision and transfer the witnessing of past atrocity onto a seeing of the present condition. In any case, it is only this text's presentation of corpse meditation in the still rather traditional anthropological form of alterity that may distract from the fact that there are multiple cultural arenas—ranging from the cinema of political memory to the increasingly democratic camera surveillance of previously "quiet" police brutality—in which the witnessing of suffering is delivered through abject imagery to deliberately ethical and political effect. Like Buddhist meditation on gory photographs, traces of the body in this imagery wander into our own form, and are scratched, however lightly or deeply, on our eyes. It is true that with an argument pinned strongly on a metaphysics of presence one might be convinced that there is no genuine witnessing, that in the distanced voyeurism of visual media "you were not really there." But one has only to look carefully: if one was not there, then why are there flecks of the uncountable political murders one has witnessed still "sticking to the heart?" Just look.

In this, not even the most straightforward argument about the flatness of representation and the objectification of body imagery can be held stable, and the "apparatus" is potentially subject to the human hand. In some sense, then, Benjamin must have been absolutely right about the liberating powers of the image realm, though no one fully knows how to work them. And what thoughtful person could deny the importance that he be right, if there is to be any hope?

The problematic statement by Benjamin—the distinction between the aestheticization of politics and the politicizing of art—makes all the difference in the world here. As Buck-Morss interprets that enigmatic, late addition to the Artwork essay, it was an argument not for art as communist propaganda but a demand from art of "a task far more difficult—that is, to undo the alienation of the corporeal sensorium, to *restore the instinctual power of the human bodily senses for the sake of humanity's self-preservation*, and to do this, not by avoiding the new technologies, but by *passing through* them."[78] Though I would suggest it is not entirely clear that the restoration of a lost, instinctual bodily experience is necessary to this movement, the critical idea Buck-Morss articulates here is this sense of "passing through" technologies of vision, a passage I would assert is entirely possible, because we never were not photographs. Although this is far from participating in a knee-jerk reaction against new technologies for the production of aesthetic objects, one should still be aware that political life itself can be rendered into such an object, a political "consummation of art for art's sake" such that humanity can, as Benjamin put it, "experience its own destruction as an aesthetic pleasure of the first order."[79]

Beholding the object of politics as art, as it unfolds and demands service in the pursuit of its form, is a surrender not so different from observing, dizzied, the transformations of technologies as though they contain within themselves an autonomous identity, subjecthood, or historical moral. I would argue that a decidedly different shift in attitude toward the proliferation of image reproductions—with the will if not confidence that these technologies are at least as malleable as we are—is essential to a vigorous social critique, not to mention powerful visual practice. Certainly, the violence of media perception can and often does follow an aesthetic logic specific to its own historical force. And in some sense, or in all of our senses, we certainly may all be historical constructs, down to the bone. But "cultural construction" can obscure our power and potential for . . . well, cultural construction. However true to life the critique of what flat and repetitive representation of deadly violence is doing to us, when its authority is too steeped in a metaphysics of presence this critique itself becomes a narrative of loss and nostalgia. Referring to an imaginary elsewhere of embodiment that once was but is now lost, or deferring to an "outside to the text," or eliciting desires for a reversal of an historical process that is not, practically speaking, reversible, can have the unintended conservative effect of encouraging an exit from the game, a withdrawal from engagement in the important task of making history through vision. This leaves that task to the political bad taste of the active "aesthetes," in exchange for what may amount to little more than fleeting feelings of poignancy.

The problem with making history through vision—what reminds us to remain in the relentless presence of the negative—is precisely the nature of the system that carries death away and converts its value. Buddhist meditation on corpses lasts, thousands of years, but it does not accomplish social liberation just the way we want it. Black markets of massacre images may accomplish what we want, but not for long.

With respect to visions in general and mechanical reproduction in particular, it is certainly not technological nature in itself that makes the critical difference between a liberating power and a destructive violence. There must be a more fundamental problem: practices of relation to the images, which are ultimately inseparable from the form of social and political relations between ourselves. Concentration upon the image-realm arrives at this, the critical point, and highlights the fact that the effect of a cultural practice with images can theoretically go either way, and yet seems to go mostly one way. The infinitely mutable practices for viewing corporeal images are narrowed by the condition of social relations in which they occur; but other image practices can likewise mutate those social conditions, which is why Benjamin saw technical reproducibility as more than a highly efficient propaganda content-delivery system and rather as a form for social refabrication.

The current proclivity for using graphic image media in political protest, especially in Asia, is more than simply a question of convenient historical availability. Technical reproducibility is more than an aid to remembrance. The destabilizing potential of abject image reproduction can powerfully abrade the illusions of individual subjectivity. In that destabilization fixed identities are repetitively deferred, and so also the personalization and individual possession of responsibility are destabilized. Personal possession of responsibility can divert the formation of collective

227

conscience, or even preclude, as Thomas Keenan has argued, ethics and politics themselves in the metaphysics of the responsible subject.[80]

The assault on the self that graphically violent imagery affords cannot be separated from the fact that this destabilization of personhood is, at least in Thailand, linked to collective projects not only of memory but of the aspiration to reconstitute the social in form, where death is shared even in and among the living. The misfortune of death is the disturbing occasion in which the living are called upon to re-form themselves not as "subjects of," or as "subject to," or as "subjected by" something so portentous as modernity but as something quite oblique to "subjectivity" itself, even violently opposed to it, and which they already "are" in their essenceless essence. The focus of so much scholarship on establishing how cultural histories constitute and construct "subjectivity" and the faith that subjectivity itself exists or at least is fixed through historical-processual orders with an agency all their own are rather askant of a project of social refabrication enabled by the violence that it is only possible to inflict through culture. This is not a violence on our organic senses, nor an undoing of a previously integral individual or cultural system, but a violence to destroy that which conditions. It is a deconstruction and deconditioning that the products of violence—particularly the body of the violently killed—transmit in a way that cannot be made to stop at the intentions of the original act, or limit itself to the body or victim proper, but can be made to transmit its work subversively back upon the ontological principles of violent orders themselves. That the "origin" of such acts is unfortunate is not to be denied. But this is not a question of origins or of simple condemnation of what has happened, but of projecting insight into the inherent instability of the social order through which radical democracy reaches for both its exercise and its aims. This projection is only possible because we never were not violated, because the social order never was not fragmentary, never was not brutal, and was only peaceful and reasonable to the degree by which it was able to obscure its genealogy in violence and so render massacre and other atrocity as exceptional and aberrant.

And that is why humanitarianism, human rights, and humanist calls for sympathetic identification, as long as they are premised on apolitical interventions into the violation upon the universal ground of being—that which Giorgio Agamben has called "bare life" and "homo sacer"—often create an "out" for the founding violences that exist before spectacular brutality. This foundational violence may have been a condition for sensational events, that is at work, and very close, long before any viewing subject encounters a distant violation.[81] The humanitarian impulse to "make it go away" is, on a practical level, certainly noble and necessary, but in a political philosophy dangerous in the extreme. Humanitarian action is, even in its own explicit practical program, always stop-gap ac-

tion. Stopping the gap is in fact a political program with far greater implications and ambitions: offering as substitute for politics the moralistic
observance of "bare" and "sacred" life, a deep tradition in which moral
action is purported to derive from personal encounter and identification
with the suffering of others, affording a mystical leap between what are
taken to be irreducibly separate beings. The "untranslatability of pain,"
taken as the unsignifiable ground of the real aloneness of subjectivity that
is such a staple of violence studies only furthers an I-thou metaphysics
that misses the point of the excess that is generated in the expenditure of
life. This excess is quite capable of sending its intrusive work into the
heart of social existence itself, to the benefit of collective reformation,
because the "units" already were in a state of shared culpability and responsibility.[82] Abjection alone is not up to this task of bringing the culpable to realization—which is to say, understanding what is already the
case—when reduced to the inadequate techniques of sympathy and empathy based on identification of "oneself" with "another." Such identification assumes that this difference, this separation of individual entities, was
real—as though this separation of individual entities or the separation of
the dead from the living was not the aim of murder in the first place.
Instead, the abject can be made to transmit indeterminancy into the very
ontological conditions of possibility and reality of this difference. It thus
offers a deconditioning of that which prevents realization of a social form
that is not, and never ultimately can be, fixed in relations of autonomous
individuality or in a consensus without contradiction, conflict, or exclusion without remainder. The graphic depiction of violence is a technique
for mnemonics, but at the same time it can wander into our forms, offend
the magic of being, depersonalize the referent of existence, and potentiate
social reformation in ways that might make of memory something that
could eventually matter.

Thai Buddhists have a wealth of philosophical conceptions and practical techniques through which to work through conditioned barriers to
their communitarian aspirations, and to assault and unsettle the sense of
self; this is a great fortune and advantage for them, which is my unrelativ-
istic reason for availing myself of it here, placing it in the unorthodox
position of ethnography as theory, a practice I will continue in the chapter
to follow. Their usages of photographic images of death can lead to a
perception of the charnel ground within, as in asubha kammatthāna, and
they can bring down an army, as in Black May.

And yet at the same time, in the realm of public culture the memory of
the dead is as unstable as the self, and can therefore lose its exchange value
very rapidly with the turnover of history's shelf stock—not to mention all
the other dangers inherent in necromantic power. The settled constitution
of embedded social practice is critical to sustaining the unsettling political

work of the abject, and this is inseparable from the practice of exchange. The aspiring dominant social formations of new-era historical exchange, such as they are, cannot make death meaningful enough to stick in people's minds, despite the potentially awesome sticking power of gory death. The dead are cast out and forgotten so easily, as history picks up speed in its journey into the future. And they who have lent the angel of history its source of propulsion are left behind, as though they had no role to play in the economics of this movement. What would it take to acknowledge our debt to the dead and to death, even to be able to see what it consists of? What refabrication of the social does not depend on body presence for its constitution of powerful social relations, and yet can call to account the expansive deficits accrued between people, times, and eras?

Like the body as arche-photography, it was already there in the fabric of these events all along. The troublesome venture is, and always was, to recognize it.

The Funeral Casino

A MINDFUL ECONOMY

Origins of knowledge.—Over immense periods of time the
intellect produced nothing but errors. A few of these proved to
be useful and helped to preserve our species: those who hit
upon or inherited these had better luck in their struggle for
themselves and their progeny. Such erroneous articles of faith,
which were continually inherited, until they became almost
a part of the basic endowment of the species, include the
following: that there are enduring things; that there are equal
things; that there are things, substances, bodies; that a thing
is what it appears to be; that our will is free; that what is
good for me is also good in itself.

FRIEDRICH NIETZSCHE[1]

THE EXCHANGE RATE

For change to come, it seems, someone must die. Only catastrophe can
work the magic of necromancy on history. This is something any number
of "third hands" in the Black May situation implicitly knew. There must
be death, it seems, in the gift economy of historical agency—a life-and-
death exchange between the living and the dead.

And yet the long-term effects in the exchange of acts and their return
show that the revolting history of sacrifice never works out the way people
intend it. It is almost as though it would have been better if no one had
died at all, and General Suchinda had been allowed to reign on, and the
student and activist opposition forced to muster itself for a long and protracted struggle.

Would it have been better that way? The students had always thought
so. In their conversations with me at the time, that is precisely what the
student leaders said that they had wanted all along, though it was the
politicians and not they who ultimately gained control of the movement.
As the students explained, with the military in power there is a clear
enemy, a clear moral transgression, and the opportunity for a protracted
campaign in which to engage in a prodemocracy pedagogy. But with sud-

den victory, with the trade of corpses for power, where does that leave them? Where do you apply pressure once a dominant mode of movement through history settles in with its subtle diffusion? No, the students, unlike the politicians, already knew it would be better if no one died. They already knew what I am saying, and in fact I learned it from them, because they remain in contact with this revolting history and know, because it is their own painful history, the lessons that it has to teach.

But it is different now, once the deed is done and the sacrifice made, when it cannot be revoked. And this is all the more problematic when its force has been usurped by a system that cannot recognize that there are inevitable consequences for leaving its obligations behind. But is this a law of symbolic exchange with the dead that is real, obligatory, and inevitable? Or is the circulation of goods in a market of scarcity and demand the true reality of economy and so, consequently, of history as well? In other words, is it possible to hold to a different sense of economy, in an expansive sense that includes principles of exchange that go beyond the narrow range of an economy that refuses to acknowledge its debt on the gifts it has received?

For a few days in May 1992, the Black May dead were objects of intense value, traded over the surface of the earth and right on the killing ground. The evocative power of their images displaced the military and ushered in a democratic government, and they gave to the public sphere a powerful argument for the need of media freedoms, not to mention generating in their death great profits all around. But after only three years, the dead are of little interest or value, and those who profited the most from their death can now say of those who lost the most that they are avaricious and improper in their desire to benefit from the deaths. "Don't use corpses for your own gain."

This is the strange neoliberal economy of history by which the value of the dead is inverted, an unquiet photographic negative of what it should be. The new world order has no obligation or connection to the old one, and the U.S. president disapproves of the violent use of M-16s.

But you may remember a different moment in this story, when the exchange between the living and the dead was very immediate. The air was filled with the smell of rotting flesh, with the oily smoke of burnt-out vehicles, and with the incense and candles of grateful, horrified, and generous people aware and present with the unquiet dead. From that charnel ground of exchange there did erupt a market of commodified death images, but in a way that coexisted, at least for a time, with this other sense of exchange, the commerce serving only to transmit the shock effects of violent death more loudly and widely.

But it seems that with the quick movement of the public image-realm, death can only dream its way back in through a bizarre misdirection of the memory of its own forms of disappearance. Those who strive to recognize the value of exchange with the dead, even their relatives, are as in a photographic negative themselves turned inside out, transfigured, made to appear as though it is they who are the capitalizing profiteers, and then are discarded as politically obsolescent. That is precisely why it may be necessary one day to disinter the mass grave of neoliberal economy.

There are many moments in this story in which a kind of exchange is enacted that seems to open to quite a different sense of the real, and of the value of death and of the dead, from what a new, improved neoliberal economy could possibly acknowledge. The funeral market of massacre on Ratchadamnern, and the smaller commemorations returning to that same space, with a cyclical sense of time, bring with them a spirited commerce of gifts, candles, incense, good intentions, and good wishes for the dead, which in turn are all circulated focus points for reciprocity, memory, gratitude, and even a kind of political power. Perhaps all this exchange is simply a quaint, fanciful expression. Perhaps it is all a way to imbue with "kulchural" meaning something that in its essence is meaningless, and see spiritual consequences where there are in fact none.[2] But what would "economy" mean if it were possible to recognize these connections with the dead and the spirit of their gift, a mindful economy of real consequence?

THE ANGER OF THE GIFT

The second to last conversation I ever had with Boonyern, my father-in-law, was about the massacre. It was an argument, actually, and that was a bit strange because our relationship was not one in which you would want to let your anger show. But at that moment in May 1992, I was still a bit piqued. For instance, after the first night of killing, I went to buy some cigarettes in the morning because I had sucked down a lot, between episodes of lying flat in the streets. I got a pack of Winstons from a guesthouse for tourists. The military-installed government had recently made foreign cigarettes legal, and it had become my habit when among friends for entertainment purposes to thank the "National Peace Keeping Council" before lighting up. But as I lit up this particular Winston cigarette, expecting the familiar, soothing feeling to fit my lungs like a glove, I was dismayed to discover that instead of consuming a relaxing moment of relief after a long tense night, I had been sold a throat-tickling pack of *fake* Winstons, and charged extra to boot. I stormed back to the guesthouse and demanded my money back from the proprietor (who was familiar with me as an occasional patron). When she refused, I threw the fake pack against the wall violently, and roared the worst insults I knew in Thai and English. A young man, maybe her son, picked up a curved knife

233

and came at me, but Patcharee, my partner in investigating these incidents, stepped in and pointed her finger right in his face, and said in a cool, vile tongue, "Don't even try it." He was frozen stiff right there in his tracks, and after we walked away I suppose all those involved were scratching their heads. I could not believe how I could have blown up like that, in a fury so far out of proportion to the event. Patcharee could not believe she had the force of mind to throw up a psychic brick wall in the tracks of the enraged man. And certainly for the guesthouse proprietors, kept up all night by the sound of machine guns on the next block, it was a bad way to start off the first day of what was certain to be a slump period for their business in the tourist trade.

The young man with the knife had spent the night in his bed, I suppose, and the force of his mind, pampered by pillowed sleep, couldn't match the pathos of a woman who had lived and slept in the streets on and off over the course of a month of demonstrations, and had just seen much worse than he would ever have imagined he might do with a mere knife. It was as though for that moment, even though each party had spent the night only a few hundred meters apart, we were from one world and he was from another. There was no comparison, no way to know how to react to the glaring eyes of a woman with bloody murder flashing in them.

Or was it that he was filled with the same repercussions, though perhaps weaker, of anger? Perhaps he never would have reacted with a knife if he hadn't heard those machine guns all night in the first place, knowing perfectly well the history of such sounds, especially when they come from the area around the nearby Democracy Monument. Was he caught up all night between waking and dream, staring at the dark ceiling, projecting all manner of probable and improbable visions of murder into the black (as I know others in the area were)? At the very least, he was reacting to the gunfire that had passed though me and into him. I was not the army's target, and he was not mine. Could it be that we were, all three of us, filled with physical vibrations of rage, like empty vessels and against our wills, performing a pathetic exchange of the angry sights and sounds and imaginations we were subjected to?

This fouled tobacco exchange on the streets of Bangkok could only have occurred in precisely the way it did after the Black May massacre of 1992. It could only occur in the context of what was then called the new world order, a time of neoliberal market openings when a military dictatorship in Thailand could only squeak by if it traded its potential violence against the desire for commodities that bought them their time in office. Lowered tariffs on imported cars and legalization of foreign cigarettes were among the new regime's first pronouncements. Myself, I was a Winston man. Now, at the "End of History," this could be true regardless of where I was, spatially speaking, in the world. But more: at that very time the U.S. undersecretary for trade was visiting Bangkok, pressuring the government to put a stop to all the Thai counterfeiting of U.S. trade goods. The Vietnam War, the string of U.S.-backed military dictatorships in Thailand, the whole Cold War itself, which was not so "cold" at these lower latitudes—it was no longer the time for such scenes of conflict, but for other scenes. While unarmed civilian Thais faced off against M-16s in the streets, he and I, the undersecretary for trade and I, struggled with our Thai counterparts over the very spiritual principle of trade, over the very identity of the substances that pass to and fro.

The undersecretary was probably advised to stay indoors until the trouble in the streets abated. Could he still hear the gunshots as distant memories struggling with and yet vaguely connected to the whole new world of peaceful trade and reason?

Though of course rhetorical, this question is in effect the fundamental question of this book—a question about time and the spirit of the gift, "the gift" being a fundamental anthropological distinction which affirms that items of exchange embody the persistence of social relationships in time. It seems, then, that it is in the spirit of the gift that anthropology has something to give against new worlds that want to forget where they came from.

There is something about anger that is akin to this gift exchange. Once anger is given to you, it is passed along as quickly as possible. But either returning it straight back to the original donor or keeping it to yourself is problematic. There in the street, as the army fired over our heads, but also at us, the first impulse was to return the gift of death straight back to the original donor, with no lapse of time. But, in that case, you would be killed. So you pass it along, and it just leaps out, somewhere else and at another time.

There were a lot of people who could not help but perpetually keep it to themselves and were therefore bent out of shape by the shooting— not necessarily the shooting at defenseless people but just the incessant shooting into the air, the angry sound of exploding discharges, day and night. There were a lot of people who returned to their everyday life unable to control their anger, and exploded into senseless rage at the slightest trifles for months afterward. And then there were those who were shattered and broken, and a year later—the last time I checked—were wards of a concerned Buddhist temple, where they were cared for while they marched around, day in day out, in angry circles within the temple walls, wild-eyed and shouting the same old protest slogans, "Lizard Suchinda, get out," as if it was still yesterday, always yesterday—haunted people out of time, or perhaps terribly stuck in it, the living dead unable to return the gift.

They are not unlike those meditators in asubha kammatthāna who cannot abstain from piling kamma upon kamma, who cannot manage their sentiments and who subject themselves to an economy of attraction and aversion, whose "mindfulness cracks" (sati taeg) at the sight of frightening images. It is said that those minds which tend toward anger will in meditation tend to encounter fearsome images in return.

Haunted victims madly stuck in the past, and insane monks victimized by the visual return of their anger . . . this can be treacherous talk, this talking to the anger of the gift. As Marcel Mauss, and even his critic Derrida, knew—instantly it seems—language is at its limits just as soon as the gift "seems to give itself to be thought here," as Derrida put it.[3] It is just as Nietzsche says of the origins of knowledge in the error of things, substances, bodies. Just as soon as one thinks of a gift, of an exchange, of objects or substances passing to and fro, it is already too late; for although anger passes through paths of exchange, like a substance or some thing, it is also not so at all, and it is only at your peril that you understand it so. You can give your anger, but you cannot give it away. You can pass it on to someone, but that does not expend its force in you. In the pressure-cooker theory of anger, one is encouraged to let it out as though anger were a discrete substance like steam which if not released will result in an explosion. Anger is not such matter, and it is not energy either. There is no conservation of energy here, for every angry discharge produces anger in others and reproduces anger in oneself, over time. Angry people never become less angry by being more angry. So the "discharge," the expenditure of anger, is also a production of anger, never consuming it but rather all-consuming, if anything. And that is not the way of things and substances, which can be consumed, expended, which can go up in a puff of smoke.

It is difficult to resist the temptation of smoke, of tobacco, of that sumptuary pleasure that serves no purpose but to go up in a puff of smoke. In an anthropological figuring of potlatch, tobacco is wasted by throwing heaps of it, in seeming defiance of economizing, on the fire. That is how its meaning appears in writing on *The Gift*, as Derrida discerns, where it similarly functions to symbolize that other way of evaluating value, where value seems to have a purpose: expenditure itself. Here tobacco comes to symbolize the symbolic itself, as Derrida has said in his writing on the gift. Tobacco comes to symbolize the Other of rational economizing exchange: it is sumptuary expenditure, consuming pleasure, going up in smoke and leaving nothing but traces, ashes.[4]

In my tantrum, what was I really striking back at, then—the sin of violating the social contract of the free marketplace? Was I recapitulating the mission of the U.S. undersecretary for trade, pressuring the Thai government to enforce the protection of our intellectual property rights? Or was it that this connecting value and symbol of expenditure had suddenly turned counterfeit when I needed it most? That morning, when I hurled insults at counterfeiters, probably marked the peak of my anger over the killing, anger that was to stay with me a long time, and that still lingers in me as I write, though sometimes I don't notice it. After that bloody morning, confused as to what to do next, we went north to Lampang province for a couple of nights, to get away from it all, and that's where I became entangled in the second-to-last conversation I ever had with my father-in-law, that disagreement about the massacre.

It was not a heated argument, but that there could be any disagreement at all was unusual; one gets used to showing no reaction to what your elders say and think; what they say is no reflection on you, after all, and it never seems worthwhile to disturb anyone's peacefulness over it. He had only been watching government- and army-controlled TV, had never picked up a newspaper, and he was not believing what we were telling him about the protest. But still—how could he side with those who had tried to kill his daughter? I am sure he never thought of it that way, and I never had the gall to put the issue to him like that. And yet it seems that where talk is cheap only such rhetorical shock tactics ever have the power to turn people around to see another, negative side to things.

Our last conversation was a couple of months later. He had just finished building a two-story cement and teak house he had been dreaming of for years. Our last conversation was about cigarettes and gruesome death; he, wishing his wife Kamnoi would quit smoking, and I, having just quit myself, were in amicable and self-righteous agreement as to the ill effects of smoking on the health. It was as though the male bonding through sharing tobacco had passed between us, simply by speaking of smoke in this inside-out, ascetic-potlatch exchange. Meanwhile, just like smokers in the United States, his wife had to sit there and submit to the self-satis-fied and zealous health talk of renunciation circling around and about her. That was precisely what he and I were cheerily voicing the last time I saw him alive.

A few weeks later he died of lung cancer. He had been a technician in the local electric power plant, which provides a large part of Thailand's domestically produced electricity, and which was fueled by an on-site, coal-dusty lignite strip mine.

The fact that so many people seem to die of lung cancer in that area is something most people are not willing to talk about. I was told that any-one who was foolish enough to try and compile statistics from the local hospitals would be putting themselves in considerable danger. And there is no local popular movement that would fall in behind them. Most people with any participation in the economy of the power plant unplug them-selves when the subject of the health effects comes up. They are a privileged class, after all, for if it was not for the plant they would simply be farmers struggling against falling market prices and the rising cost of chemical fertilizers and insecticides, which are no less carcinogenic—an expensive way to purchase your death. And in fact it turns out that it is only the health of these farmers that ever breaks the surface of inattention, when an occasional cloud of sulphur-intense exhaust from the power plant's smoke stacks gets caught in high air pressure and descends over their domiciles, burning the leaves off of their trees, the hair off the hides of their water buffalos, and giving them severe rashes, respiratory failures, and hospital bills they cannot afford. That gets into the national press, and it can even appear—during periods of civilian government—on TV. In that case, the Electricity Generating Authority of Thailand marches its own selection of locals before the camera. They go on the air talking about how long they have worked in the plant and never had any health problems, and how good it is for the economy and how well their family is doing because of it. Patcharee recognizes them by name when they go on the air with their big thrilled grins: "That's Mr. Aart. He can't stop gambling. Sometimes he loses ten thousand in a night," and so on.

Patcharee's older brother Deng doesn't want to have anything to do with that sort of critical talk, either. He is a technician at the plant just like his father. It's a good job. If you press him he will fault the high-pressure systems, not the plant. Who could blame him? His wife is having their first baby. Their vision of their life depends on everything proceeding as always; the alternative would be worse, much worse, than simply not having the things that working for power brings. Questioning the power station, which may or may not have shortened his father's life and may one day extinguish his own, disrupts the picture. Damn those high-pressure systems. It's nature, something you can't change.

But it is not as if Patcharee's elder brother Deng has tuned out all manner of critical thought. For instance, when the power station sent him to Bangkok in May 1992 for extra technical training, he stayed at our place, and since we were spending the nights outdoors on Ratchadamnern Avenue in the heart of the old city, he joined us and surprised us both with his verve for participation in the protests being staged there against General Suchinda Kraprayoon's usurpation of the prime minister's seat, the public gatherings that were reaching new heights of attendance in that first half of May 1992. This might have had something to do with the junta's outlawing his union of workers for the Electricity Generating Authority of Thailand. Deng had surprising ascetic powers at his disposal. He stayed up all night listening to the speeches that expounded the value of democracy and the nonviolent measures that must be taken to achieve it, and then spent all day studying power.

THE THING GIVEN

I move this book forward over the corpse of a man. Since he is someone I knew very well, what is at stake is hauntingly real for me. I am using him and his death. And what do I have to exchange with the dead? For others, he may have little value in the capital sense of the word; he was neither a central figure nor was he marginal enough to make marginality vivid. He was neither rich nor poor, and though an ordinary man, he was not as ordinary as many of the people around him; even the circumstances of his death, shrouded in uncertainty, allow no one to make any clear political statement, of one sort or another, out of his demise. For my part, I know what I owe him, but you do not owe him anything. Unless . . . unless it is possibly the case that in general everyone owes something to the dead whether they realize it or not, which is to say, whether or not they are mindful that there is "economy" in a possible, true sense of the term between the living and the dead. A life-and-death obligation, you might say.

I at least owe it to him not to misuse his death, just as I owe the same to all the other corpses spirited into these pages, and to death itself. But what one might shudder at is not spirits but the "spirit of the gift." It is not the phantasm of corpses disinterred from these pages that stalks me but rather a concern that I return the gift they have given me. It can be drawn in the same words that Tamati Ranaipiri used to invoke a spiritual principle of reciprocity in the gift, the famous Maori words that Marcel Mauss used to disseminate an anthropology of "the spirit of the thing given":

> I will speak to you about the *hau*. . . . The *hau* is not the wind that blows—not at all. Let us suppose that you possess a certain article (*taonga*) and that you give me this article. You give it me without setting a price on it. We strike no bargain about it. Now, I give this article to a third person who, after a certain lapse of time, decides to give me something as payment in return (*utu*). He makes a present to me of something (*taonga*). Now, this *taonga* that he gives me is the spirit (*hau*) of the *taonga* that I had received from you and that I had given to *him*. The *taonga* that I received for these *taonga* (which came from you) must be returned to you. It would not be fair (*tika*) on my part to keep these *taonga* for myself, whether they were desirable (*rawe*) or undesirable (*kino*). I must give them to you because they are a *hau* of the *taonga* that you gave me. If I kept this *taonga* for myself, serious harm might befall me, even death. This is the nature of *hau*, the *hau* of personal property, the *hau* of the *taonga*, the *hau* of the forest. *Kati ena* (but enough on this subject).[5]

"The *hau* follows after anyone possessing the thing," Mauss echoes.[6] Unlike the free-market transaction, purely conceived, where each party comes together for a moment, exchanges, and then completely relinquishes possession of values that circulate willy-nilly with no relation to the previous owners, in gift exchange a "spiritual power" compels and propels exchange from person to person and back again, because "I must return to you what is in reality the effect of the *hau* of your *taonga*."[7] The giver has a hold over the receiver because the thing given away always contains within it a bit of the giver, the "spirit of the gift," a connection between people established in exchange and threaded through its paths by the personal implications that continue beyond the range of the sensible, beyond the physical instant of the exchange, where the effects echo afterward in further exchanges beyond one's own hand, before returning back again once more to the giver: I must return to you what is in reality the effect of the spirit of your gift.

My concern with what is owed to the dead is no different. "If I kept this *taonga* for myself, serious harm might befall me, even death." This is all about the insensible connections between people. I might make my living by stepping over the dead bodies of people who are not from the same country that I am from, and whose deaths, some of them, are directly connected to the foreign policies of my nation, and the violent gifts that it has given. And all the value I receive from this exchange, and that is generated by it, I try to pass on through writing from me to you, in return for which I get a degree, publication, and also a career, salary, health insurance. Given the return I get, it is spiritual poison not find some way, some path, some connection through which to return it to where it belongs, with the dead. This is one way we have of speaking about the spirit of the gift.

Another way of talking about the spirit of the gift comes to me from a language I learned attending funerals in a northern Thai village, as well as in moments of commemoration and protest on the streets of Bangkok, and even in a charnel ground, as far as it is experienced in practicing Buddhist meditation on death and the body as a corpse. I suspect that mindfulness of death can go a long way toward undoing the ontological assumptions that conspire against our acknowledging the debts we have incurred, toward dissolving the vision of a phantasmagoria of discrete individuals exchanging valuable matter. And yet, using Buddhist awakening as a language game is ultimately elusive. For all the sense of sensory alterity that reclusive meditation can suggest to us, it is also necessary to take hold of those insights through a lay language, a practical language. In rural Lampang, that language would express a law of economics not much more exotic than the idea that you reap what you sow. I am speaking, of course, of kamma, and kamma talk in Thailand has this ring of

240

the obvious; any strictly wordy definition of it always seems to fall terribly short of the excessive meaning that even the word *kamma* itself can close off from your mind. As a result, exegesis abounds, and I will get to that in time; but there is also a truth expressed in the fact that if you press most Thais for an explanation of why kamma works, the best answer is usually because it does.

For every action there is a return reaction (even for thinking this thought). The return on the original is far from random and unrelated to it. The return effect always carries something of the spirit of the cause—it is a descendant of it, just as a fruit is descended from a seed, and if the return is not forthcoming then it hangs over you, hauntingly, until the right conditions are present for it to reach fruition, to come back to the original giver.

It is hardly accidental, or original, to associate the spirit of the gift with kamma. This is because, first, the spirit of the gift that comes down to us from Mauss is really a collaboration between himself and at least two others (though all the authority seemed to go to him). First among these "collaborators" was, of course, Tamati Ranaipiri and his people, who authored the critical passage quoted above. And second, there is a more diffuse and nagging sense of reciprocity, of return, of spiritual likeness between an act of giving and its return that seems foreordained to be mixed up with the idea of kamma and its tendency to return. Mauss had immersed himself in Vedic texts from the Indian subcontinent and worked through their ideas of karma, and the *dāna*-giving oriented by it, for years before writing the *Essay on the Gift*. As both Mary Douglas and Jonathan Parry argue separately, in addition to the influence of these ideas on the thinker before the writing of the seminal essay, the ideas also play a pivotal role in argument of the essay itself, as go-betweens for archaic exchange and our modern contracts.[8]

It is as though we have at least three very different ancestors, one European, one Melanesian, the other South Asian. Parry urged a strict disentangling of this weave, and advocated drawing a fast distinction between the economic world of Melanesians, on the one hand, and that of "world religions" ubiquitous for the Asian Indians, French, and all capitalists, on the other.[9] By contrast, Mauss did not want to cut people out of the exchange. He wanted to mix the fast distinctions that depleted the wealth of economy, in the more general sense he was aiming at.

For our purposes this would mean including an obligation to the dead such that the spirit of their gift is imbricated in the narrative of economy itself. For what must be made accountable in this last funereal story I have to give is simply that there really is, or can be, deficit accrued by the passage to new eras. The story is about the kamma of the gift, about the death of a worker in the business of producing electricity, and about

241

the currents of sentiment that pass between people in the same way that value does, that is, both self-interestedly and generously. For Mauss's part, he wanted to "jumble up together, color and define differently the principle notions that we have used." He wanted to short out the terminals of self-interest and pure generosity—of, on the one hand, "useless" expenditure like potlatch, and on the other hand, utilitarian savings with interest: "it would be good to put them into the melting pot once more."[10] This line of mixed thinking does not describe a reality so much as it mimics it, exchanging thoughts and imitating gift economy in a way that is indebted to it, which is to say, is in exchange with it. "Everything passes to and fro as if there was a constant exchange of spiritual matter, including things and men, between clans and individuals, distributed between social ranks, the sexes, and the generations."[11]

To this list of "everything" we might include theories, epistemologies, vocabularies, and grammars. And to this sense of the delight in exchange we might also add how unnerving it is as well, how shadowy and similar to this circulating "spiritual matter" is the justly feared equivalence of numerals and people in scaled systems of commodity value. Yet the critical difference might lie precisely in such spiritual matters as possess me now, the matter of finding a way, if there is one, for someone imbricated in market forces nevertheless to return the gift. The obligation does not cease, even if the market I am in does not recognize the economic realism of an obligation to return what was given to me by the death in these pages, deaths that are probably not unconnected, in a series of exchanged histories, to the privileged place of the reader.

Such thinking is not very different from how Georges Bataille imagined a science of "general economy," an economy of ends in themselves. His was an attempt to imagine an alternative to political economy, choosing to predicate a vision of economy on the problem of *surplus*, rather counterintuitively for a culture of utilitarian assumptions. Every economy is shaped not by how it meets its needs according to the principle of scarcity, but how it deals with the problem of its excess, its "accursed share." While retaining a certain functionalist trope, the focus of his imagination was not efficiency but expenditure—*dépense*: to use up, to consume, to spend, expend, to exchange value in an economy of the broadest, widest, most expansive, expensive, and wasteful wealth of the term.[12]

The place of death in this narrative ethnography aims at opening to this very different sense of economy. Considering this idea in relation to tales of the dead and of violent death, Michael Taussig's Bataillian considerations of his excessive stories about pacts with the devil can paint the image much more clearly: "The stories' relation in time to the events they depict is reminiscent of Bataille's pointedly anti-utilitarian interpretation of the paintings of animals and hunting in the Lascaux caves not as images the magical power of which shall ensure the success of the hunt and the satisfaction of need, but as images demanded by the opening to the sacred consequent to the violence of violating the prohibition against killing."[13]

Taussig is feeding here on the light in that Bataillian phrase that jumbles up wealth, energy, excess, and the gift—"the sun gives without receiving"—illuminating the wealth in poetry and tales that give excessively, connected to a scriptural economy very unlike that pinched into utilitarian valuations. "This leaves the status of the image, no less than . . . stories," Taussig continues, "in a strange vacuum of testimony, sanctity, and obligation—not unlike the gift itself."[14] Narrative ethnography exceeds predatory analytics. And although a story, or an ethnography, can be reduced to an economical phrasing or two, the functionalism of which is to tell us what it was that the story was supposed to tell us, what that does not tell us is why, then, one should bother to tell the story in the first place. Unless . . . unless there is an obligation, and unless there is something in tales and poetry that can give like a gift, and return like a gift.

It is excessive, melting language that can imitate death and violence, ugly words that can look like corpses, and it is only stories about the connections between people that can exchange the connections between yourself and other people.

DUKKHA

This story, about the circulation of energy on the surface of the earth, begins under its skin, with a mortal wound, actually, with skincrust peeled back to expose the ancient, long-decomposed corpses of life forms that have become coal, lignite, ghostly fossil fuels disinterred from their grave, returning to us from another time, and carrying, into our linear time, their power. Lines of power, power lines, an electrical connection is wired from this single point in the universe, in a northern Thai valley, and radiates out on strings that transmit energy to the beyond in a radial sundial of cables metallically suspended over the land of the living. They impart life into the economy and kingdom, connect it to the life of other lands, and communicate beyond that out into the atmospheric currents of histories that zap across this world, almost instantly plugging right back into the wires of the same northern Thai valley. There rocks, spit up with stripmine dynamite, leave a toothless grin in the hills, and towering stacks cough smoke up at heaven; there a turbine generator, which by seeming to return eternally in circles, propels the organism forward in a straight line to the future.

When Patcharee called me saying that this time it looked really bad for her father, I immediately hopped on an all-night tour bus from Bangkok to Lampang. By chance her father's brother was on the same bus, and together we went to the hospital in the morning, only to be told at the counter that it was *riab raoy laew*, which means, literally, already proper and tidy and everything neatly in its place. He winced, and then we went to the new house for which the dead father had been saving all his life. There were a lot of people sitting there in the common room, on the shiny new shellacked floorboards.

Stepping into that house was like stepping into another world, like stepping out of a physical world, where the hot sun beats down on your head, where red dirt billows dust in your face and aggravates the mild discomfort you already feel inhabiting a physical body, like stepping out of all of that, and into a *room*, a human space not so much occupied with physical objects and sensations as it is inhabited by the minds of people—grieving minds, confused, weeping minds, disbelieving and believing minds. As I stepped through the door, a thick cloud of mourning brushed me instantly. I saw from the corners of my eyes the faces of close family, flashing out from all the rest with their heightened state of sadness. I looked across the crowded floor of gathered mourners, and exchanged glances first with my mother-in-law, Kamnoi, who was crying, and then my two sisters-in-law, who were also in tears. Boonyern was only fifty-seven years old.

They were a close family, all best friends, very casual and open with each other, as befits a family that had begun with an impulsive and far from proper elopement. The young Kamnoi had escaped out of a window on what was supposed to be her wedding day, just when she could hear the sounds of the unwanted wedding party coming closer, marching from their village to her house, beating drums and cymbals and singing on the way with the chosen groom. She ran away with this other man to Chiang Mai town to the north, even though the groom's family had given the bride's family a brand new bicycle and this other man had no economic substance whatever, and because of that was anything but liked by her family.

When things cooled down, they came back. Boonyern took up a menial labor job at the sugar mill, until the state entered the softly rolling hills outside Lampang town, all set to open them and release the power buried under their lignite mounds. First they would need to cull, from the local peasantry, technicians who could help them harness the energy unleashed from the earth. As fate would have it, despite his humble origins Boonyern was literate, having learned books as a boy while ordained as a Buddhist novice at a temple—the poor man's long-cut to social mobility (there is no equivalent for women). So he was among those trained for the power plant. Eventually he put in over thirty years there. He was renowned among the workforce for the whole barbecued steers he could roast over an open fire to such delectable effect at the annual Electricity Generating

Authority of Thailand's New Year's party, an extravagant show of the state company's love for its workers, complete with a stage, a light show, a cavalcade of live bands and musical performers, freely flowing whiskey, and over five hundred table-and-chair sets put out for a sea of party-goers to sit and drink at while they await the free gifts of food.

No one had realized what a popular guy he was. Scores of friends came to visit him in the hospital, and hundreds paid their respects at the funeral wake, a continuous event for seven days and nights, staged in the home.

For two years he had been secretly visiting a hospital to the north in Chiang Mai because he had been sick with something and they were giving him medicine. He did not tell anyone about it until the treatment was over and was told he could go back to sipping whiskey with his friends again. That lasted a few weeks, before he became suddenly racked with back pains, which became chest pains; they brought him to the hospital the first time for tests, and the next week to die.

He was to experience torture for only three days, and it would have been less if they had not kept him going with artificial respiration. At first, without that accordion hose in his mouth, he was able to call out "Deng, Deng" for his son whom he especially loved, and beckon his son closer to him, and beg his son to go home and get a gun, to please get a gun and kill him.

With the best intentions, the doctors had prolonged his torture by filling his mouth with a vacuum-pumping breathing machine. That would be the recurrent image that would surface again and again with startling clarity, and still does come to his daughter—the image of her father's death that first inspired her to apply herself to Buddhist meditation and that the meditation itself would stir up again and again, crystallizing it into an unusually clear image, a memory arising in the stark visions of deep concentration.

My father is lying there with that hose in his mouth, and we are looking at each other. He is looking in my eyes and I am looking in his eyes. He is crying as he looks at me. He is in such pain, and knows he is about to die, and he doesn't want to leave me. He wants to talk with me, say something to me, but he can't say anything with that hose in his mouth. He can't even say good-bye to me. Only look into my eyes, with his eyes full of tears, painful and so sad. That is how we parted, that is how he died, silenced, the last time I see my father, the last time we see each other.

Whenever the mind approached the one-pointed strength of firm concentration—there—it would suddenly appear, her father dying and unable to speak with the respirator pumping him. The mind would react to that image and then itself erupt out of its balance. At the time, the mind had little experience and could hardly do anything about this. It was basically helpless and had to follow the power of the image. Looking at disturbing images of death, with neither blinding furor nor dulling insensitivity to the truth that they convey, is an art form of mindfulness that is not easy to master.

Now the technological breathing apparatus of biomedicine, which tries to master his death through its power over life, covers his mouth and he cannot talk back to us. It has invaded and occupied her mind as it had his dying body. More thoroughly, in fact, for it was the biomedical technology that made the moment of death itself more painful to her and so in a strange way had the power to reach back out from beyond death and keep the image painfully alive, unnaturally respirating in the starkest regions of her memory. And he had no say in it.

THE SPIRIT OF THE GIFT

There is something about both death and giving that draws each to haunt the other, something that silences us with the seeming impossibility of speaking about these matters. Perhaps it is the losing, that is, the giving up and the release and, ultimately, the parting. What wants to live and exist is killed by the same conditions that give it its existence. A person, a being, and the feeling of being a personality, are given their life by the same organic conditions that give them their death. And so it is with the gift, it seems. The idea of a pure gift between people seems as impossible to conceive as it is to know what happens in time after death. In the way that Jacques Derrida writes of the impossible language of giving, once the recognition of the gift event occurs, the gift is annulled, most of all by its noble identification.[15] Once a gift has been identified as such it cannot help but enter the circle of debt in which it ceases to truly be a gift, freely given. As Parry suggests in a partly compatible argument, the whole idea that there should be a pure gift or pure giving is itself a product of characteristically Western notions whose propriety demands that there be an opposite to self-interest, and as such has little to do with the idea of the gift that Mauss lifted from Tamati Ranaipiri.[16] Derrida attempts another track, using a deconstructive method that does not depend on radical othering, as Parry does. Rather, he attempts to subvert the discourse of the gift with itself. He interrogates Mauss's appeal to a logos beyond the materiality of the gift, that is, the "spirit of the gift," and subverts the romantic-humanist morality that Mauss's essay on the gift intended to pose against materialism and narrow self-interest. For Derrida the discourse of pure giving is itself bound up in a tautological circle and worldly wheel that we could identify variously with obligation, superiority and inferiority, or at the very least, with the immediate gift-canceling return of self-satisfaction in "giving."[17] And yet this seems to bear the echoes of the postulate Parry was trying to unsettle, lingering assumptions that pure giving is what the gift *should* mean, though there is no assumption, for Derrida, that this is what it *can* mean. The gift dies at the same time it is born, for Derrida, or—and this is the same thing as the gift and death for him—as soon as it tries to speak:

> In order for there to be gift, gift event, some "one" has to give some "thing" to someone other, without which "giving" would be meaningless. In other words, if giving indeed means what, in speaking about it among ourselves, we think it means, then it is necessary, in a certain situation, that some "one" give some "thing" to some "one other.". . .
>
> For this is the impossible that seems to give itself to be thought here: These conditions of possibility of the gift (that some "one" gives some "thing" to some "one other") designate simultaneously the conditions of the impossibility of the gift. And already we could translate this into other terms: these conditions of possibility define or produce the annulment, annihilation, the destruction of the gift.[18]

At least as far as Derrida understands it ("if giving indeed means what, in speaking about it among ourselves, we think it means"), we must part with "the gift" even before the giving, just as soon as the intention to give arises, so long as the intention to give involves a subject of giving, an object, and a subject of receiving, as though, like the death of our selves, the gift passes entirely out of our control precisely because of the same conditions that bring it within our grasp.

The Funeral Casino

After the medical separation of death, the corpse of Boonyern was not parted from the family for long, and just as quickly as possible the family brought the corpse home. And they quickly brought others to him for a funeral wake, as many as possible, so that he would not be lonely. In the mornings of the seven days and nights, many people would pass in and out of the home to bow to the corpse, to give funeral wreaths and light candles for it, to bring gifts of money in honor of the dead man, and to give alms to monks who were invited for a meal and chanting every day before noon. After gifts were given to the monks, an eight-piece band of musicians would start up and unfurl into the air their tense requiem dirge of crying clarinets, sighing wind pipes, fist-pounding drums, and showering scales of xylophonic tears, weeping on and off like that all day and into the night. Funeral dirges in northern Thailand are composed and played to sound like crying.

247

As afternoon passed into dusk and darkness, mourners would keep gravitating in on the funeral. But it was also for the gambling that they would pour forth in great numbers.

Some people came with big stacks of bright purple 500-baht bills. Dealers came and set up roulette wheels. Or they came with a bowl of dice and a big betting rug, each one good for a crowd of ten or twenty gamblers to sit around and cast their lots. The house family let loose, on the crowds, quart-sized bottles of Mekong brand rice rum to navigate through the spaces between bodies, with mixer bottles of Coke, Pepsi, Singha soda water, and tin buckets of ice in hot pursuit. Packs of slicing and dicing cousins and aunts were spinning out plates of fried meats, raw pork, and saucy vegetables from their encampment in the kitchen. Family members were sent forth onto the casino floor, to extract from time to time a cut of the dealers' profits. And the dealers were raking it in all over the place, starting from gambling operations set up right next to and under the coffin of the dead father, fanning out over the whole living room floor space, out onto the porch, and beyond that, spilling into the open air of the yard in front. Over this space, billions of words and tens of thousands of baht were exchanged in rapid-fire succession. Eruptions of laughter among the many drowned out the sighs of the few. And they kept coming—mourners, gamblers, and dealers. Whatever tables and chairs there were, whatever mats, plates, glasses, pitchers were at hand, all were set out to accommodate them. The pros brought along their own equipment. They had their own mats, their own cookie tins for cash registers—ready to break a 500 or a 50, it's up to you.

Of course, no one would sit down to play without first bowing to the corpse—could you imagine that, placing your precious money at risk with a big coffin standing over you, to which you haven't paid respects? But that being done, people would get off their knees, get down on their butts, and—rubbing their hands or blowing on the dice in just the way that had worked before—let it all hang out, let themselves loose on the waves of spinning wheels and tumbling cubes stirred briskly around in swirls of fateful passing from person to person, in fractures of laughter, breaths held in suspense and released in great expenditures of happiness and disappointment. Some people were there playing along just to rub elbows, others were just watching, and yet others were basking in the attention and wonder, in the tremendous drama they were willing to put on, to risk, and to offer up to everyone, so that their fate would be spectacularly put on line, there for everyone to see and feel, for they know or can just imagine what it must be like to have 2,000 baht riding on a single turn of the wheel, or what it must be like to be sunk in a desperate situation, your back against the wall, where you have lost almost everything, made a wreck of almost everything, maybe your whole life, and the life of your loved ones and children too, and only a godly twist of fate can save you from this dark pit of doom, or what it must be like to have one's head reeling and drunk with excitement as the money keeps coming at you like you are an invincible magnet, to feel the very ecstatic heart of fortune beating in you, and that dreamy feeling that it will never end.

Perhaps the endless, eternal value of capital culture takes root from the seed and phantasmagoric truth that capital can reproduce itself, or as Benjamin Franklin advised the young tradesmen, "Money can beget money, and its offspring can beget more."[19] But this is something that is spelled out just as clearly in the circulation of wealth over a funeral casino as it is in the fiscal flows of value signaled in binary code across a worldwide web of cable and satellites. Wagering a stake is like an investment that returns in kind, though the founding fathers of the spirit of capitalism would hardly approve. And there, precisely, is the difference so clearly expressed in the fact that it is precisely the casino economy that can become black, underground, illegal, and even funereal when high capitalism tries to settle all accounts. Gambling does not pretend to asceticism. The spirit of capital as a jail-cell asceticism is a truth of capitalist discipline so obviously flaunted in nearly every consuming moment of its own existence, an existence driven by desirous ends in themselves as much as by the pretension of mean necessity. Wherever it is outlawed, gambling nevertheless implicitly flaunts the contradiction between the ascetic, disciplinarian, and austere practices of penny pinching and life lived through an account book, on the one hand, and the extravagant excesses of consumer society, on the other. Depending on the analyst, one or the other of these gestalt alternatives is made to seem like the necessary condition for the reproduction of capital. To outlaw gambling is to state a utilitarian signpost, a prohibition on black economy, on expenditure and destruction of value for its own sake, of consumption for consumption's sake, a taboo on the kind of uneconomical economic intercourse that exposes, in a carnivalesque manner, something inherent to high-capitalist finance: the way in which money eats money, the carnivorous way wealth destroys itself and through that, miraculously, reproduces itself as well. It is truly mystifying—how can value reproduce itself, how can money beget money? But in a funeral casino the birth of investment capital in a space of death is no secret, of the fetishism of commodities or otherwise. That is one of the problems with funeral casinos. There money is set free to expend itself openly, to fritter away in an explosion of gains and losses, seesawing before the eyes of those who are so intensively active in surrendering themselves to the helpless passivity of the gamble, but perhaps other exchanges as well. It is as Artaud wrote of the Theater of Cruelty, "The breath of events will travel in material waves over the spectacle, fixing here and there certain lines of force, and on these waves the dwindling, rebellious, or despairing consciousness of individuals will float like straws."[20] The wagering minds float on waves lolling back and forth, back and forth, between fate and randomness—like the sea, but also like death, striking surely but unsurely, giving no warning, no sign, no certainty, yet in a sense more certain than anything.

Small-time gambling in the midst of an entrepreneurial economy provides visions of both liberation and fear, which are not desirable apprehensions in a populus that is to relinquish freedom for the sake of a "free" market dominated by centralized capital, and that is not to fear to do so, at the same time.

In the moment, it seems that nothing could be so sensational, electrifying, and lurid as this bubbling exchange. Everyone laughed their heads off when Gai Chohkdee ran out of cash and had to take off his wristwatch. Half the mouths stopped moving and half the cards stopped sliding across the floor and half the roulette balls stopped dancing when Gai put down the keys to his brand-new motorbike on lucky number nine. And when he started rambling on about the choice teak furniture he had at home, half the spectators cried out, "You just go back there and don't come back," and even the dealer wearing his wristwatch was in agreement that enough was enough, as she certainly could not complain about her profits and everyone else had relished the debacle. And so, driven off by the roaring shoos and embarrassing giggles of the crowd, Gai Chohkdee exited the funeral casino as though through a humiliating gauntlet, and started off alone on his long walk home.

And yet even he was lucky, if you consider the fate of another guy, whose name nobody seemed to know, who had come to the funeral not to gamble at all but only to drink deeply of the free-flowing Mekong rum, which in the late hours of the night splattered and spilled between people as much as it was poured from person to person, and finally having had his fill, started off on his own lonely walk to wherever was home. He did not get more than a hundred meters from the last dice game before he lost real big and was hit by some vehicle speeding off to the power station. He left behind a big stain in the road and one rubber sandal.

❖

Gambling is strictly illegal in Thailand. Not only that, although people may do it they also generally consider it slightly profligate and indecent. Husbands don't approve of their wives doing it, and wives certainly don't approve of their husbands doing it, especially northern wives, who often control the family purse strings. Nevertheless, on occasions such as funeral casinos, as in most spheres related to religious observance, women have a majority representation, and they make up the majority of both dealers and gamblers. Ultimately, regular folks are quite a bit more easy-going than is the Thai state, which for all the notorious and illegal nasti-nesses that it allows for some reason has a pretty firm fist when it comes to public gambling (unless it's organized crime)—at least when it involves defenseless villagers doing it up with dice and roulette wheels in some-one's front yard, which is precisely what often happens at funeral wakes in the Lampang countryside.

As time goes on, the state has been trying, with mild success, to consoli-date and routinize its power more and more efficiently on the local level, and funeral casinos are becoming more unstable and difficult to attend. Women table runners are becoming increasingly dependent on securing protection with both bribes to police and payoffs to criminal rackets. Both organizations are controlled almost exclusively by males. Nevertheless, and for reasons owing to anything but luck, a funeral remains the sole "legitimate" space for casino gambling, according to a wobbly rural con-sensus. It has been explained to me in a utilitarian fashion, in so many words, that given an irrepressible desire to gamble, supply meets demand in funereal space/time because it is a sacred space/time into which the profane state is the least comfortable penetrating. Not that it is impenetra-ble—no one would argue that—but that it offers, at least, a bit of resis-tance in the form of social discomfort, impropriety, and an accentuated sense of violation that agents of public security are bound to feel in any crackdown on a family's mourning rites. So, since supply must meet de-mand somewhere, the space of death is the best, or least bad, spot for such a meeting.

This is all very true, but there is another "utilitarian" reason, which is much more enlightening if you loved the person who has died, and that involves not so much the work of supply meeting demand, or the fulfill-ment of illicit desires, as it does the work of a desire for more desire itself—not producing supply (gambling), but producing a demand, at-tracting the desire to gamble because that desire will materialize what is ultimately the desired product and supply: people themselves. The econ-omy of the funeral casino's telos is not simply an excuse to supply a prod-uct to satisfy a community's urges. It has far more to do with the needs of the dead. The dead are lonely. The telos of the funeral casino is, as they say of the gift economy, to establish relationships between people—to produce a community, in this case a community of gamblers for the sake of the dead. The funeral economy is centered around and surrounds the corpse, on purpose. Indeed, the entire funeral casino is a gift to the dead, the gift of camaraderie, a gift of a relationship between people, and that means between the living and the dead. Society is the gift. What the family wants above all, and what the funeral gamblers feel morally comfortable in providing, is company for the deceased spirit. No one wants the poor departed person to have to spend the night alone. The purpose of the funeral casino is to *ben peuen sope,* "to be the friend of the corpse," to keep it company.

The corpse needs friends because, soon after death, the spirit is the only one present who is dead, and in that lonely state is in a sense separated from family and community. Every relationship ends in separation. It is absolutely certain that you will be separated from every single person that you love. No relationship can ever end in any other way. And just as people do not often consider that this is where their relationships with each other are heading, so too, for a time, is the dead person ignorant of this truth, even though it has in fact already come true. In the first few days after death, the dead do not normally even know that they are dead. They may think they are in a dream, or in a nightmare, but even that degree of lucidity—enough to have any reflection at all on their condition—would itself be a remarkable example of powers of mindfulness. Many are in a dazed, confused, or even terrified state. Instinctively, in their confusion, they hang around near their former body, near the corpse, and are also drawn emotionally to the hurt, emptiness, and lacking of the living, which of course also hovers near the corpse and which, just as it feels to you like a bottomless pit in your heart when you miss a dead person whom you love, seems like a pit of gravity to the dead, who cannot resist it. It is not easy to stay up all night, and it is not easy to get a lot of people to stay up all night. But if you have got an all-night casino running right under the coffin, you can be sure they'll come, one and all, and keep a happy, convivial and vibrantly social atmosphere circulating around the dead, running through the long, lonely hours of the unbearable night and until the break of day—an economy of the most fluid, rapid, and energetic sociality possible, where money meets money and begets more money, passing from person to person in the most animated way, a funeral economy where value is more of a self-reproductive principle than even the value of investment capital circulating under the sign of utilitarian economics, and yet at the same time given a celebratory chance to expend itself, uselessly. The entire economy, the entire funeral casino, itself is a gift, and a most compassionate gift spent, expended, for the departed.

Self-interest in profit making and taking obviously runs through the funeral economy in the individual wagers placed by the individual gamblers, the individual table owners, and even the economic interests of the bereaved house, which takes a cut. As soon as the news broke that Patcharee's father had died, word spread like wildfire to the gambling table runners, who seem to have psychic powers to detect such momentous events in human affairs, and at great distances. There are numerous full-time and part-time roulette wheel or dice game proprietors who make a whole or part of their living traveling from funeral to funeral, wherever they can get up a game. There are also a few habitual gamblers who follow the funerals with similar regularity. When he was alive, Boonyern never lost out to that kind of excessive expense because his spouse saw to it that he didn't. Indeed, Patcharee has vivid memories that as a child she had to go foraging in the forest for edible leaves with her father every day for a few weeks, because he had lost the family savings while gambling at a funeral; that was the last time for him, since he wanted eventually to be let back in the house to sleep, as this was the choice he was offered.

Perhaps by the law of kamma, whatever value he had uselessly expended in the past was coming back to him now, in what was an exceptionally large funeral casino with upward of a hundred participants at a time. This is another way of going to show that such expense is never completely useless, or rather never *finally* so, because all losses one expends at a funeral casino are a gift to the dead. Not only is your personal presence itself a gift to the dead, and the more zestfully you give it over to the casino economy the more is given (lost), but the proprietors of every dice and wheel game will themselves regularly present a cash gift to the family of the deceased, a cut of their profits, which after all are originally coming from the gamblers. The wager at a funeral casino is at one and the same time a mundane gamble for personal profit and a donation of spiritual value for a good cause. It is expensive to feed and entertain so many guests, excessively expensive to present this gift of society to the dead, and anything one can do to help the family is for an extremely good cause, especially, as was the case with Boonyern's death, when the breadwinner of the family is the one who is gone. One reason wives and husbands allow each other or themselves to gamble at a funeral, and one of the little devilish inner voices that intervenes when someone is thinking that maybe they have already lost enough, is that every wager is connected to this spiritual economy of death. The gift of the wager in a funeral casino is, in part, also a donation in the spirit of generosity, good kamma, and merit making.

Now the corpse was reaping what he once sowed. But not, of course, just from that wonderful night during which he lost his head at the roulette wheel. More important, there was the friendship and love he had sown while alive. All manner of exchanges that ranged from gift presentations as tiny and common as a friendly smile to ones as exceptionally neighborly as the forgiving of debts helped make him very popular and so bring in all those high-rolling mourners. Also present were not a few of his friends who owed him money, sometimes from more than ten years earlier. They were among the first to show up at the wake, nervously crashing the scene, with money if they could get it or, if not that, then whatever object of value they could lay their hands on, like a lamp or an engraved headboard—whatever they could do to settle accounts with the dead man before he could come knocking.

But of all the reasons for the sizable attendance at the funeral casino, there was one more, curious thing: one of the most unusual sacrifices and gift presentations I have ever heard of in the Lampang countryside. A long story, which I will make short, ultimately leads, by a chain of kammic cause and effect, to one other reason why there were so many people there—people who felt particularly safe gambling at this funeral. This particular funeral was widely reputed to enjoy special protection from a crackdown by the state because, as everyone could see when they arrived at the front gate, there was conspicuously present a four-man squad of khaki-uniformed military police, with white helmets, arm patches, and pistol holsters, sitting out front eating fried meats and drinking whiskey courtesy of the house, occasionally helping to sort out parked trucks, cars, and motorbikes, but also standing guard lest the police attempt a raid.

A Sacrifice, and a Bit of State Power

This story is one of the most important ones in the dead father's life, and I must tell it from a point of view sympathetic to his position in the conflict. It begins a long while before his funeral casino. Around the time that Boonyern first got the job producing power for the state (which may or may not have killed him), he and his young wife had made a very strange personal sacrifice. They gave away their firstborn son.

Kamnoi entered a local hospital in labor one morning, while Boonyern was away selling his labor at the power plant. She gave birth to a healthy baby boy. Her older sister (Patcharee's aunt), who took after their mother in having a powerful and dominant personality, but who had none of the matriarch's well-known generosity to both neighbors and the Buddhist temple, was a childless woman. It was in fact the younger, timid sister who had inherited the generous nature, as though the matriarch's qualities had been split into two equal shares. Although generous, she was anything but a forceful personality. The elder sister had been in a childless marriage for years, and besides being renowned as a stingy groceries merchant and a stickler for the minutest details of debt, throughout the pregnancy she had inwardly harbored a secret desire for the baby in her younger sister's womb. When the baby boy was born, she had her husband go to the hospital and impersonate the father, Boonyern, sign for the baby at the desk, and take it away, leaving the mother behind. Only when the biological father got off his shift at the power plant did he discover that the baby had been stolen. It did not take long after that to figure out who was behind it. Boonyern stormed into their village, brandishing a machete,

254

only to find that the childless couple had disappeared. In those days, there were not many ways to hide out from the net of gossip, but the baby-takers managed to stay out of reach just long enough for the impulse to commit murder to pass. It was also just long enough for Patcharee's mother to get pregnant again.

What followed was a series of arguments, fights, and negotiations, the rationale and ultimate result of which none of the concerned parties can completely explain today. As far as Patcharee and I can make out, it came down to a relationship between sisters, and the force of one sister's wants prevailing on another's generosity. At first the older sister returned the baby, and Kamnoi nursed it. But her older sister did not stop coming around. Neither did all her allies and some relatives. They incessantly beseeched Kamnoi for the baby. They kept pointing out to the young couple how poor they were: they were never supposed to be married in the first place, not with the father such a pauper. Now it was in the baby's interest that he grow up with some means and substance, that he have a bright future and get a good education. They told them to have *mettā*, compassion, for the boy, and mettā for the unfortunate barren sister as well. They said it was the boy's kamma, his fate, that he should be raised in a household of opportunity. Eventually, the older sister convinced her younger sister to let her have the son that she wanted so desperately. The younger sister was going to have another baby soon, anyway. And, in what was also an apparently powerful argument, she reasoned that such generosity and self-sacrifice for the sake of her elder sister would be an act of great merit, which now seemed proven true, as the second baby turned out to be a son who, after his father died, was moving into the new house and was set to take care of his mother for the rest of her life.

Anyway, and somehow, Kamnoi had in the end relented. She went on to give birth to the second son, Deng, then Patcharee two years later, then another daughter, Yah, the following year, and by mistake, four years after that, a third daughter, Noi. The four children were told about their eldest brother, but no one talked openly with him about this until he was almost eighteen. Patcharee's aunt and uncle lived in a neighboring village and were meticulous in keeping him from playing with his brother and sisters.

What Patcharee's aunt did not figure in when doing the merit account-ing for her younger sister was that just as it appeared that a great amount of merit or good kamma might be made by the sacrifice and generosity of such an intimate gift between sisters, so might there be certain demerit or bad kamma to be earned by the acquisition. For although the younger sister's second son turned out to be a good egg, and was at the time of the funeral all set to take care of the generous woman in her old age, the older sister's adopted son turned out to be—in what is an uncanny turn of correspondences, given where we are situated in the narrative—a burdensome and irredeemable gambler.

He was an extremely bright young boy, and well taught at a good school, so that at eighteen he had managed to pass the state entrance examinations for nothing short of the Chulajomklao Military Academy, with little or no bribery as far as we know, and not so much as a distant uncle thrice removed to serve as an alumnus "noodle" (*sen*), which is Thai for what we call "connection" or "string." The Chulajomklao Military Academy is the only institution that produces the country's line of military dictators and elite military-businessmen. By the time the young man entered his cadet class, it had already adopted a curriculum and class structure modeled on the West Point Academy, as indeed the Thai military had thrown in its lot with the Yanks' military-industrial complex, eagerly accepting martial aid and air-base investment in the billions of dollars. Now in accordance with this aid, the West Point class system was a sticking point for U.S. international security experts, because it encouraged intense loyalties among the young officers to their age-group class. The United States wanted precisely such a rock-solid military elite to guarantee their air bases and their ideological goals, and sure enough the Thai cadets merged as desired into tightly knit class groups, which sometimes turned into factions, but nevertheless provided enough of a coherent ethos of loyalty, code of silence, and worship of the soldier's honor to ice the cake of the young men's already pronounced proclivity for "Big Man" (*phu yai*) patronage loyalties. This West Point class structure is widely seen by political analysts as a major cause for recurrent coups in Thailand.

So the given son entered the military elite's class system, which they call a "generation" (*roon*) system. In the academy he developed his voracious appetite for gambling, often getting involved with gamblers in possession of far greater resources than he, since he mixed with gambling cadets from the elite social classes; gambling sometimes has in its rapid circulating exchange nature the tendency to blur distinctions. His adoptive father and mother had some measure of surplus wealth at their disposal, and he often called on them for continuing support of his gambling habit. One time, they made him a gift of a brand new automobile. A car was a gift of value almost out of this world at that time and place, not so long ago, given the relative weakness of the Thai economy and the massive import taxes on cars that used to be levied in commercial self-defense by the state. He converted that car into cash and lost it all while gambling. After he graduated and was commissioned an officer in the army, they gave him a second car, and he lost that, too. He served in a supply and reconnaissance division of the army, where he supervised requisitions. On several occasions he used army requisition money to gamble with, and on several occasions lost it all. Every time he lost the money, he called on his adoptive parents for the cash, and on and on, until, by the time of his birth father's funeral casino, not only were the adoptive parents so far in debt, mortgages, and remortgages of their house and property that they were on the verge of losing it all, but he was also in big trouble with the army, which because of class loyalties had never considered prosecuting him but was now, after all these years, giving him an ultimatum of either paying up or shipping out.

So before the time came for the funeral casino for Patcharee's father, her aunt and uncle were almost destitute and faced the unbearably shameful prospect of homelessness. This is what the given son had brought on them. When Patcharee and I would visit the aunt around this time—and she could never come to visit us because so long as he was still alive she was not welcome in Patcharee's father's house—she had already come to regret everything, from taking the boy to the stingy way she had related to all her nieces and nephews, not even allowing them little pieces of candy from her store. She had learned the hard way, and we would find her in a terrible funk of relentless, obsessive suffering. One time, while recounting to us her financial woes in a spiraling emotional ascension, she collapsed into a heap on the ground, nearly unconscious.

Her son, on the other hand, was welcome at the house and, when the time came, more than welcome at his first father's funeral. His relationship with his birth father and mother had always been difficult and uncomfortable. One day, it all came to an epiphany, during a special moment in life between a son and his parents. After graduation from the military academy the time came for him, like most young males, to be ordained temporarily as a Buddhist monk. It was the most difficult moment for both him and his natural parents. A good son takes the yellow robe in order to make merit for his parents. It is a great occasion for them, which calls for a party on almost the same scale as a funeral wake (without the casino). The merit of good kamma made at such ordinations, and during the subsequent tenure as a monk, is thought to go to the parents. In the ordination ceremony itself, at one point, the merit is consciously *phrae*, spread or dedicated, to the parents in the "spilling water" ritual act, where one pours water from one container, over one's finger, and into another container, while monks chant blessings.[21] Parents generally look forward, avidly, to this return gift of spiritual value from child to mother and father.

✧

A television commercial breaks into the program.

A man's head and naked shoulders are bowed forward in submission. Military snare drums rattle in the distance. A tense hand comes and violently digs its fingers into the man's hair, and clutches a clump of it. A razor appears, glinting white steel in the harsh light. Whoosh, whack. The razor cuts through his hair. The snare drums are flaring nervously as the blade lands like an ax, over and over. Then it glides smoothly, scalping. Cool water pours over the shaven head, and the bare-backed man, kneeling, holds his arms out submissively, palms pressed together, to receive on his outstretched forearms a folded pair of blue jeans.

"There comes a time, once each man's life, when he gets his first pair of Wranglers."

✤

When the given son was ordained as a bhikkhu, it was Patcharee's mother who had sponsored the rites, which involve a big party for the celebrants and cash gifts to the temple and presiding monks. As she had always regretted giving her baby away, she was more than eager to pay for the rite. And even though it was normally the parents who were responsible for incurring that expense, her elder sister, being the way she was about money, was not going to complain. For the young man's biological mother and father, however, it was hardly a satisfying arrangement. Before the ordination ceremony, there was the usual drunken procession of relatives and villagers carrying the young man to the temple on their shoulders, accompanied by the drums, cymbals, and whining clarinets of a ten-piece band playing atop a creeping cattle truck. People sang and danced all the way, carrying gifts of flowers, fruit, food, and cash for the monks in the temple. At the head of the procession, the initiate was held aloft. He is considered to be in an intermediary state, having a shaven head and having donned white garments the night before in preparation for the ordainment proper. After him followed the adoptive parents, who carried the one gift that carries the greatest merit: the actual yellow robes that he will wear as a monk. Even though she didn't sponsor the rites, Patcharee's aunt insisted that *she* be the one to give the robes. Boonyern and Kamnoi had to walk behind them, with fruit.

And so under these circumstances, which were without precedent in anyone's memory, they could hardly be expected to feel as festive as the others, who were happy to share in the merit of the occasion in the typical manner. After carrying the young initiate up all the way to the door of the "chapel," or *bood,* where the monks wait for him, those carrying him raised him up so he could touch the door's threshold, a gesture of sharing merit that carries you to the heavens. Everyone crowds in, the closest family touching the initiate at that moment and so partaking of the merit, while whoever can't touch the initiate tries to touch the ones who can, and those who can't physically do that try to establish physical connection with someone who can touch one who can touch the initiate, and so forth, until everyone is touching everyone, and all are connected in some way to the currents of merit surging from the merit-making initiate who touches the threshold to heaven, before they all release him and give the gift of the young man over to the Sangha (order) of monks, waiting inside.

The night before, at the big party, Patcharee's aunt insisted, when it came time to shave the young man's head, that she be the one to cut the first lock, which was no surprise to anyone. So she cut off his first lock of hair, and after that her husband cut off the second lock of hair. Next came Patcharee's parents, then various elders and relatives. And then someone who had skill with a razor shaved the remaining hair, clean off. After that, the white-clad initiate was blessed by his elders, while a ritual singer sang an ode to the boy's life. He sang in his high-pitched, nasally shrills a standard song about the son's moment of conception, of his gestation, of the weight of his body in his mother's womb, of the pain and effort of childbirth—and here the band comes in with a dramatic, staccato refrain—of the mother's strains in childbirth, of her giving of life-nourishing suckling milk to the infant, of her care for the infant, her bathing of the infant, the love she gave him and so on.

While this song was being sung, the elders tied white strings around the young man's wrist, which is a way to give blessing, the good wishes serving to protect the one who receives them. Patcharee's aunt wanted to be first to tie a string, of course, then her husband, then Patcharee's parents. When the original parents approached the young man, who had been and should have been their son all along, and tied the blessing on his wrist, when they looked each other in the eyes, the given son broke down crying, and his birth father and mother broke down, too, following him into sobs; then almost everyone else in the room, who all knew the sad story and this strange situation, fell like dominoes into the same tears and sniffles.

It is this moment of connection, in the tying of strings within the imbricated bodies in tactile contiguity, in the meeting look of the eye, in the shared implicit historical knowledge of this radical break in the family, that characterizes the potential force in such moments of kammic ritual. Rather than bridge or stop the gap that has opened up consequent to a tear in the social fabric, these moments of connectivity actually reopen the wound, and it is here, especially in communalized binding, that the rupture is most forcefully rendered present. Quite different from the ordinary assumption of unity and wholeness as the purpose of collective rites, these communitarian forms can bring forth an enhancement of the coarse splintering that was already insidious to that connectivity. And this lack of closure, precisely in moments that formally resemble closure, is the discharge that lends them their force.

259

There is no necessary zero-sum game between collectivity and fracture, and this is perhaps even more the case within northern Thai funeral rites, which are communitarian gatherings premised upon separation itself. Precisely at the epiphany of communalism is the aporia—the impassable gap—of social relations rendered most present, and that is the special power of the funeral idiom, here and—in funerary politics—elsewhere. Nor is there a necessary zero-sum game between individual interest and communal exchange in these rites, as the ostensive zero-sum gaming of gambling itself is simultaneously enveloped in a broader communitarian system for the generation of value. Here, as in politics elsewhere, the strict heuristic divisions between gift and commodity are inappropriate, as for instance the market of massacre imagery makes abundantly clear: the more the entrepreneurial vendors prosper, so also does the communitarian project of the funereal space. The obvious amenability of gambling to harsh critique, according to a rather puritan strain in the critique of capital (something it shares not randomly with the puritan praise of capital), is of course undeniable. Gambling has even become a unifying cipher for everything that is wrong, unreal, and "fetishistic" in global economy. But at the same time, such a critique employs something of a heuristic codebook which assumes that gambling has an essential nature and that social relations embodied in gambling are necessarily the epitome of what is dark in the heart of capitalism, and that the "fetishism" of value reproducing itself is inherently inimical to rendering social relations present to consciousness—when precisely the opposite can be the case.

That may be why, at least in Southeast Asia, village gambling was often a target of colonial-entrepreneurial regimes. Village gambling did not contribute to a production of individuality that might be folded into a new economic order. The values it generated, specifically a "commerce" in community itself, were in this regime simply a frittering away of what counted as potential time for productivity. Gambling even threatened, as Mary Steedly has argued, to create an alternative sponge of monetary circulation that might absorb the liquidity necessary for the broader markets, perhaps becoming a relatively autonomous economic formation.[22]

CALCULATING GIFTS

It was the given-away army officer's connection to networks of military patronage that afforded the possibility that this especially populous community of the funeral casino could form. Although his military career was stunted by the professional improprieties resulting from his passion for gambling, he eventually managed to rise to *pan drie,* or major, in the Thai army's extremely top-heavy officer rankings—it has, so I have heard, the most generals per hundred noncommissioned soldiers of any standing army in the world. Although he was stationed on a base in the south, it was no problem for him to rustle up some "noodles" in Lampang province and get a contingent of military police to keep guard at the gate of the funeral wake. He also happened to be in the same "generation" as an officer who was in control of the local police situation, and explained to the classmate that his father was having his funeral, that there might be some gambling going down, and to please keep the police grunts off their backs. So the first day of the wake saw scores of gamblers show up for the funeral casino, and by the second and third day, word was out that this was a choice funeral, complete with army guards—the really good stuff. The sacrificed son was now affording a sizable gift of society to his dead first father. Given the uncanny scent of the state wafting over the countryside, given the instability of outlaw gambling, and given the spreading word of special protection for an eruptive funeral casino, the crowds came out from all around and in droves to expend whatever cash they could spare (or really could not spare, whatever the case) in the exuberance of the moment.

Not only does one have to stay up all night to keep the corpse company, but one has to keep an eye on the gambling tables, as well. Sometimes a not-so-grateful roulette wheel owner will underestimate his or her takings; it depends on individual disposition for greed and relationship to the grieving family. The operators could be almost perfect strangers, and sharp professionals, so you have to keep an eye out and see who is raking what in. Periodically, you also go around and take the house cut. Patcharee's elder brother, Deng, and the eldest brother were mostly in charge of this monitoring and collecting. Sometimes, despite the military guard, low-ranking and underpaid police officers would show up, surreptitiously and casually dressed, looking for a cut of the funeral economy's profits, but the given son would shoo them away from the gambling as soon as he discovered their snooping.

The casino is not the only conduit of fiscal liquidity in the funeral economy, however. A staple form of value flow in a funeral economy are cash gifts, which follow what is to anthropologists a classic pattern. One classic idea of gift exchange is that a gift is not an instant transaction like a sale of merchandise, or a wager, but an object of value that is handed over without immediate strings attached, and yet with an obligation to return it at some time in the future. In the Lampang countryside, where money is essential to survival, mortuary cash gift exchange looks a bit like social security. In fact, one of the rhetorical points of Mauss's *Essay on the Gift* was to argue that the state must increasingly take on the role of such giftlike and, as he saw it, humane forms of exchange. Almost all visitors to a funeral will bring money for the grieving family. If they have a lot of cash to spare, they will certainly consider the economic situation of the family when deciding how much to give. If a breadwinner dies, as was the case here, then people will feel especially sorry for the family. The funeral wake then serves to help them out during a bad time.

Naturally, in Lampang, the social exuberance of the funeral gathering is more often than not far more powerful than any cash calculations, and the expenses incurred for the food, music, and drinks turn out to be far greater than the incoming gifts, even including, when there is a casino, the house cut of gambling losses. And all that is not even counting the expenses of actual mortuary rites: gifts of food, requisites, and cash to monks during every day of the wake, and then at the cremation the cost of sponsoring the cremation rites, buying the coffin, buying a fancy multi-colored cremation spire, and more gifts to monks after that.

Every night of the wake, while the elder brothers were on the funeral casino floor, Patcharee, her sisters, and I would do the books. Every cash gift is given in an envelope, and every night we would open the envelopes, read off the names, count up the money, and someone would write it all down in a ledger: who gave what and how much, just as the gifts that this family had made at the funerals of others in the past had been recorded in their household ledgers, records that were consulted before they came to our house, and before they decided how much we would be able to record under their name in our ledger. The gift-exchange ideal is that you ought to give the same amount you once got, or a bit more.

This family had lost its breadwinner, so the counting of the money at the end of the night had a bit of excitement to it, given the fiscal uncertainty of the future. We did it privately and quietly in an upstairs room, where no one could overhear us making jokes and wisecracks about those gifts that were smaller than they should have been, or those gifts that were practically insignificant. Those insignificant gifts, like ten baht, which "even a little tyke wouldn't be happy with for lunch money," were in another sense meaningful, because they were such a glaring sign of the times. In one sense, the circulation of cash in mortuary exchange is timeless and selfless: the money value has been circulating between families since before anyone can remember. There is no true, rock-bottom owner of the value in the gift because it is always a return of the gift from the past. But now a different historical narrative had intervened, for it was not selfishness that was behind the ten-baht gift, but the fact that the giver was in a different league from the receiver. To those who were connected to the Thai developing machine, a time machine plugged into the electric currents of the world historical economic order as much as it is plugged into the electric currents of the surging power station whose astringent smokestacks lay just over the next hill—to such people in step with the time line, ten baht is nothing, a penny. Although the joke was not accurate—actually our niece who lived in that house is quite happy with ten baht for lunch money—it also has its own expressive accuracy. Some peoples' mortuary ledgers have been jump-started into another stratosphere of value, leaving the long, bottomless history of the gift far behind. And that's not the half of it. After all, those left behind on earth have little choice but to enter into an exchange relationship with that same stratospheric value. They are obligated to survive as best they can, just as they have no choice but to present their gift, just as it is and just as it can be, when they come to a funeral. Given their situation, that ten-baht gift becomes a greater sacrifice to them than it should be, while to the receiver it is less than it should be. That disjuncture in the value of the gift is an historical story that even the World Bank can tell; even they know it and worry about it—what might be the return on the developmental "gift" that they have given, the story of a massive, growing, left-out underclass, which can only spell I-N-S-T-A-B-I-L-I-T-Y.

If one were to calculate only in terms of the nominal value of money, this sort of visitor consumes far more money value, just counting the cost of the food eaten, than is given. If one looks at it that way, then by coming to the house they have not brought a gift at all. It's a good thing there are jokes to dissipate that thought when it arises. And it does arise. Everyone must make a living. So it must arise, and one should not miscalculate its power.

Still, it is not the point. Nowadays, Kamnoi, who as a widow given to a little loneliness now and then, depends very much on funerals for company. Also because she is a widow, she has accumulated the obligation to visit many wakes because so many people came to her husband's. She attends at least three or four wakes every month, whether for just one night or for several or all of the nights of the wake. And she always gives generous gifts. Her sons and daughters try to rein her in, but she always wants to give a lot. Often she gives much more than was given to her. She explains how badly she feels for the families. After all, she knows how it can be, losing someone and then throwing a big wake. And for many people, like the ten-baht people, it's much worse. When someone dies, they're in big trouble. She considers that giving a lot is good kamma, making merit.

She puts on her most expensive jewelry before going out to the wake, and always brings what her children feel is much too much cash with her. Although she has no source of income of her own, between the severance pay from the power station and gifts from her children, particularly from her daughter Yah whose husband is a rich contractor operating out of Bangkok, Kamnoi has acquired a handsome stash of gold jewelry: a thick chain bracelet, a chunky necklace chain, rings, earrings, and so on. She has a silver belt, but whenever she gets the chance she will borrow her sister-in-law's gold belt. It is the next thing on her list, a gold belt, costing about 30,000 baht (US $1,200). This jewelry is worn on special occasions, and most often at funeral wakes, where everyone wants to show off what they have if they've got it.

Conspicuous consumption is no less "traditional" than the mortuary gift exchange, however. What is more, the construction of "public image" is also no less traditional (which may partially account for both the success of Thailand in the international market of images and the success of the international market of images in Thailand). Class status marking has been in vogue for as long as there are historical memories of the presentation of self. There have long been sumptuary displays of wealth to mark one off: the aristocracy from the commoner, the commoner from the poor, the poor from the slave. And yet, although this public identification and participation between persons and their things certainly does not depend solely on what we might think of as modern commodity consumption, it is tremendously helped along by it. At the time of the funeral, the most prestigious such items were passenger cars and cellphones (which were soon to become commonplace).

Many of the people who showed up at the wake with a cell phone and an expensive car are people who have sold their land. It fetches a high price in a good spot these days. In fact, the piece of land inhabited by a transitory casino, and upon which was built the new two-story cement and teak house, could be purchased only ten years ago for 1,500 baht per *rai* (the local measure), while now it would go for 30,000 baht per rai, and that's for land that does not even have a clear and free title to it. Indeed, the dead man had in fact acquired it at the going rate ten years earlier, from very poor peasants who were so out of their element in trading earth for cash that they requested not to be paid all at once, for fear they would spend it all, but rather asked that they could drop by, from time to time, to collect the money when they needed it, bit by bit, as though it were the return on a gift. This was actually very intelligent of them, because a lot of other people do not understand what it is that they do not understand. A lot of the people with these cars and mobile phones had, ultimately, bartered their land for these things, the land which was the only thing that they knew how to work so that it would yield them a living. So although they had acquired the signifying implements for constructing a public image for themselves, they did not know how to work that image as they do a rice paddy. They did not know how to work an image and make it produce value. It is an endemic problem in the northern countryside—people who sell off their land at a dazzling price, thinking they have it made, only to find that they had not counted on everything.

But others, like that half of Patcharee's relatives who are plugged into the power plant economy, are more prudent and really do become entrepreneurs. Her uncle Sert owns a new townhouse with a shopfront where he sells groceries, while continuing to live in an old teak shack where he raises and slaughters pigs when not at work in the transport division of the power station. His wife sells the pork in the village market. He has been negotiating the sale of a titled piece of land. When that deal is settled he is going to get a Mercedes-Benz to go with his mobile phone. He is a loudly generous man, and a thunderous talker and joker. He wears the loudest gold jewelry. His wife has a gold belt. He picks up the tab at dinner. He has to drink only foreign whiskey. He throws the most gigantic parties, once sending out one hundred thousand invitations to his son's Buddhist ordainment party, which was a miniature version of the state electricity company's New Year's party with pop-rock bands, stage, dance floor, and light show. And he is accumulating bottles of Chivas Regal, over a hundred bottles now, for his daughter's wedding. He is going to give away the taste of the finest whiskey to fellow bourgeoisie and ten-baht peasant alike, indiscriminately, and he will be talking about it for years to come after that. In fact, he has already been talking about it for years.

Ultimately, the funeral economy is a similar statement of loud generosity. As it turned out, the funeral wake did not turn a profit, even with the exceptional casino going on downstairs. There were huge food and drink expenses, gifts to monks, and mortuary paraphernalia to pay for. Moreover, even though he was the one responsible for creating such an exuberant casino, the eldest, given brother wound up subverting its profit aspect, for no sooner would he collect the house cut from the dealers than he would himself get carried away by his personal demon and lose it all again, and through the wager return the gift almost instantly to the giver, almost as though he were refusing it.

He had that annoying knack. After sinking his adoptive parents, he had often come to members of his lost family to ask for loans for his habit, and he got more than a few. Then one day his birth father said enough was enough, he wasn't going to let him pull the whole family down. Even during the funeral wake he asked us for loans. Sometimes it would devolve into an extremely awkward situation, and he would almost start crying, saying his family didn't give a damn about him. One could only shake one's head in disbelief.

Just so, he would also shake *his* head in disbelief, alienated while listening in the corner of the room while we told our stories about the killings in the streets. Dragging on a cigarette, with his arms folded across his chest, he would shake his head, exhaling a sputtering laugh, when Patcharee, Deng, and I would tell the others about what had happened. He was a major in the army after all, and spent the whole episode on base, where he was treated to stories of communist insurgents manipulating gullible people, of roving motorcycle gangs, of paracriminal youths bankrolled by supposedly antimonarchist politicians, and of religious fanatics out to replace Buddhism with the cult of a treacherous antiprophet.

Much later, after people in his wife's family sold their land and gave him a big loan to rescue his parents and himself from debt, after he got back on his feet, and got a little shop going on the side while staying on in the army, after he quit smoking and gambling and turned his life around, and after the mass media won a virtual victory for itself in the wake of the 1992 Black May massacre in Bangkok, he came around to accepting that it was not self-defense, as the military said at first, nor was it an accident, as they said afterward, that so many defenseless, unarmed people were gunned down. But still he insisted that the prime minister at the time, General Suchinda Kraprayoon, was not such a bad guy. He had met him at a few officers' parties.

THE CRACKDOWN

The sound of panic. Patcharee and I would be dead tired at the end of each day, and drop off to sleep before the end of the night. One night we were woken up by a great, roaring sound beneath us. We both knew that sound well. The sound of a stampede. But not just a sound, an overwhelming wave of emotion, *panic*, that gets inside you and carries you along with it. Hundreds of feet multiplied to thousands and thousands, like an earthquake sent rocking down deep into the earth and rebounding off of its core and shaking everything to the foundations. People running, hiding, scattering, moaning.

The black sound of fear vibrating through you. Anyone who has been through it knows exactly what I am referring to. It was just like being back there again.

We ran out onto the balcony, to see that the casino below was in a complete disarray. There were cards and dice and roulette wheels and betting cloths spilled everywhere like blood at the scene of a crime. Tables and chairs were overturned and broken up, there were discarded rubber or leather sandals and shoes flung everywhere, their owners missing—a haunting, scattering absence right in what had been the center of a droning, hobnobbing space that had hummed us to sleep just moments before. Everyone had stampeded around the house and disappeared into the banana fields in back, where you could still hear men and women shouting in the dark, "Run! Run!" Meanwhile, out front there was an indistinguishable chaos of shouting voices, a confusion of uniformed bodies with their chests thrust out, all bunched up near the front gate.

266

The much-renowned guard of military police had been enjoying themselves, and their free whiskey and snacks, with such carefree abandon that they had failed to notice the police pickup truck, chock full of officers, creeping up on the funeral casino with its headlights off. It was much too late by the time they hoisted up their potbellies, emerged from their collapsible chairs, and started fruitlessly blowing on their whistles as the police truck whisked past them through the front gate and into the yard, where it discharged a squadron of police officers onto the startled crowds, who, while climbing over each other, picked up the money and ran.

For all the advantage of the element of surprise that the police had gained in their raid, in the panicked stampede the officers managed to capture only one dealer, a middle-aged woman from a nearby village. They took her ID card and wrote down her name. They put her in the cab of the pickup. The MPs and the police were all in a huddle talking things over. The given son, being a major in the army, sought out the police squadron leader. They had a long, private discussion, during which the crowds started trickling back in from the dark banana fields. The villagers would ogle poor Jarunai in the front seat, pointing and chuckling, while she sat there sad-faced and silent. People were complaining to the dealers that they had been losing all night, and now, just when the damn roulette ball fell in the right slot, their wager had disappeared. Dealers were complaining that all the bets had spilled on the ground, or that someone had stolen them. People were making accusations at each other, at the police. They were looking for their shoes, or helping to put the tables and chairs back upright, or holding up a broken piece of furniture for inspection as if it was a dead duck they had found in the road.

The negotiations were going well. The two officers were smiling and laughing. They were establishing which cadet class they had come from, establishing through which patronage connections they were connected to each other. They had it all sorted out. Poor Jarunai was released from the pickup truck and given back her craps-betting rug, which she hugged to herself like a blanky. Everyone cheered, and laughed. Whooping and hollering, they set out the gambling mats and went back at it with a replenished sense of élan and adventure.

Spiritual Value: The Kamma of the Gift

It could hardly be coincidental that a space of death should be the site of a rapid-fire economy of exchange; that the corpse should be the sign under which such a resilient society should be encompassed; that the cadaver, both as an object and as the grave emotional aura that it casts, should exert such gravitational pull that almost without forethought people come running to each other, bringing along all manner of gifts, money, commodities, wagers, donations, and histories of exchange; that without even being called all manner of dealers and high rollers nevertheless materialize on the funereal spot; or that such an exchange-based society can spontaneously be generated, and even if dispersed by a whack of state security force can just as quickly recharge its flow of animation and recompile its public mass. They are hardly coincidental, death and economy.

It is no different with political commemorations. The same confluence of death and economy alighted on the funereal space of Ratchadamnern Avenue in Black May—the space of the political dead whose corpses, though in a material sense absent, were nevertheless incorporated into the very fabric of the wagering blanket. A market of massacre images assembled around the candles and incense and remembrances of the unquiet dead. These were not two contradictory forces, the market and the gifts. The gains and losses of entrepreneurial funeral activities only appear to be tense and awkward composites of the individual and collective, of private and public interest, when one is convinced that individuals are in fact the reference points for deciding where the gaining or losing occurs, or convinced that it is simply the matter which is exchanged between them that is in its meaning exchangeable, or coterminous, with the meaning of value itself.

The funeral wake was a chance for Patcharee's family to create a material spectacle to show their father how much they loved him—a chance to give him something really big, really special. It was also all show. Just as everyone has a greater or lesser zest for adorning their social skin, showing off their wealth and status, their ability to consume, and their ability to give away by throwing large, lavish parties for large numbers of people (or making hefty, conspicuous donations to Buddhist temples), so is the funeral wake a spectacular continuation of that life project, only in this case the person, being dead, is not personally able to make any showy prestations to everyone anymore. The funeral wake was Boonyern's last big gift to everyone, but he needed the living to help him give it: they must give it *for* him. A funeral is given for the dead both in the sense of being given *over to* the dead but also in this sense of being given to others *on behalf of* the dead. The continuation of exchange beyond death is one in which, by proxy as it were, the dead man loudly gave a gathering to the community of the living, and the community gave the gathering to the dead man at the same time. The gathering is the gift, but who is the giver and who is the receiver cannot really be determined by words because, at any one time, the gift is being given both ways. Those "directions" are not really spatialized and that "movement" is not really temporalized because in a sense the gift itself, the gathering, is its own destination and it has already arrived; that is, the gift is also the giver and the receiver, which calls back to mind that what is really uncanny in

268

exchange with the dead is the status of giving itself. It makes one wonder what it is, really—"giving"—especially the kind of giving in which the material object of giving does not observe the reality principle of *things,* any one of which is not supposed to be able to be in two places at once.

Just this tiny degree of visibility interred in an image of the funeral economy already goes a long way toward sowing the seeds of doubt about what we know for sure when we put the gift into words, including a seed of doubt over the deconstruction of the gift so long as it is premised on the assumption that "giving indeed means what, in speaking about it among ourselves, we think it means," and the assumption that the words used to identify the gift are, in all times, all places, and forever, those of the "one" who gives, the "thing" given, and some "one other" who receives, as Derrida does in his deliberately and profoundly literal manner.[23] But this form of reduction to linguistic definition hoards the authority to define the point and purpose of giving in a way that is profoundly ungenerous. The aporia of the gift, that it must be a "gift without exchange" and the simultaneous impossibility that it could ever be so, is premised on the surety that it is not so and yet also on the assumption that somehow it *should* be so, to be properly termed a gift—that universally the problem of the gift lies in the fact that pure generosity is impossible because all forms of giving are already inscribed in orders of exchange. What if "the gift without exchange" already was the state of affairs? What if the practice of exchange were seen through different moral eyes, ones not so full of an unfulfilled desire for the absence of interest, hierarchy, asymmetry, or—and this is forceful—not haunted by the deep cosmological tradition of the "evil" of money? In almost every instance money is the unspoken thought that lines the secret pockets of such impossible gift theory. What if there is no "thing" given, no "one" and no "one other" in the first and last place? What if in giving practices it were possible to mimic, which is to say inconsistently figure, the "pure" giving that is already the state of affairs, that giving between selves and others that is already happening constantly without recognition, that is always perfectly transmitted and requires neither acceptance, rejection, forgetting, nor nonrecognition to remain "pure," because there is nothing that can destroy it, stop it, or alter it, and in fact there is nothing anyone can do about it all, as there is nothing the least bit self or other, not the least bit human, good, or evil about it?

MINDFUL ECONOMY

After cremation, it was believed, the spirit of Boonyern would become aware that he was dead. Realizing that he would have to leave the company of the living, he would come back one last time to the home, "to pick up all the footsteps and fingerprints he had left behind there," before going off to his destiny.

The actions we do, with our feet and hands as well as with our mouths and meanings, indeed, even with our thoughts and intentions, leave traces on the spirit, leave their imprints in the heart, and echo long after in the mind. Most people have some awareness of this causative relationship. They are aware, say, that certain lines of thought and courses of action, because they have taken them before, tend to lead to bad feelings or despair, whereas other sorts lead to better feelings and happiness. They may even be aware that repeated courses of thought, speech, and action actually change the person who does them. To use an example a monk once related to me, there are people who can kick a dog for no good reason and feel nothing, while others, should they kick a dog, would feel really bad about it, would have a refined sense of the consequences, as the consequences come back as bad feelings in the perpetrator's mind. Some people even know that, were they to continue kicking the dog, over time the consequences of that too would cause them to become more and more insensitive to its suffering, less and less likely to feel unpleasantness, and so less likely to see what that action is doing to their minds, until their awareness of the consequences are so coarse and blunted that they are themselves changed, and now far more likely, because of unawareness, to commit more and more such acts, more and more easily, which would, in turn, make them even coarser, and so more likely to act in such a manner, and so on and so on.

Just as unawareness leads into a self-perpetuating spiral, the awareness of this process guides most people, keeping them out of deep trouble and leading them toward wisdom and insight into life as they grow older, even if they have never thought of it this way or formulated it so. And no one could survive very long without some ability to detach from cycles of kamma. They would just follow their first impulse and, who knows—splat—be hit by a car because they saw an ice cream stand across the road. Almost everyone has a practical awareness of cause and effect in this sense, and can often skillfully manage some measure of disengagement from its cycles when necessary.

But "cause and effect," as we more often use the terms, as a law of material science, is according to Thai Buddhism but a ghost of kamma, a pale reflection of the law of cause and effect that rules every being that is not free. In the Buddhist reckoning of kamma, thoughts piled one atop the other eventually spill over and become intentions. Intentions piled up become actions. Actions accumulated become habits; habits amassed become character, and a character sustained becomes a destiny. In this model, generosity is skillful: it gives you beneficial thoughts, beneficial intentions, and leads to beneficial actions, habits, to a beneficial character and, eventually, to a destiny. That is the sentiment in an idea of giving where it is terribly unclear whether the giver is actually ever giving anything away or whether the giver is constantly raking it in. It is actually selfish to be generous—so seems the paradox, aporia, impossibility of the "gift without exchange" to Derrida. But this contradiction is ultimately counterfeit, minted by a presence that does not understand its own false relation to itself. I will try now to raise a possible explanation of this, and of why the always already "pure" operation of the gifting of kamma subverts this false relationship of oneself with oneself, through generosity.

It is possible, more or less, to understand the idea of kamma intellectually. But it is different when considering the actual process by which effects come back. The fruit, or "result," of kamma is something the Buddha warned was *acindeyya*, not accessible by normal thought processes. He argued, or so I have heard, that you could spend an eternity trying to grasp the fruit of kamma, but you will never get to the bottom of it, and you may even drive yourself crazy in the process.[24] That is the warning Buddha gave about the things that are acindeyya. The gift is its own return, and ultimately there is no referent we can point to outside this law of exchange, the law of kamma, of cause and effect, reciprocity: for every gift there is a return gift.

This is usually intended as a teaching about heightening consciousness of the consequences of one's thoughts, speech, and actions, as these circulate through others and back to you, and as they take shape over time. But its point of reference is ultimately not the moral being but the thoughts, speech, and actions themselves, the origin of which in themselves is beyond good and evil, inhuman, and acindeyya or unknowable. Unfortunately, often the warnings against claims to final knowledge of the acindeyya go unheeded, and sometimes the idea of a return on kamma is read backward from the result to an imputed cause, such as when explaining "unfortunate events" or unjust divisions in society as justified because they are a just return on kamma. Such speculation is not only an objectification of what is unfathomable but harmful in its assignation of states of moral being and in the ignorant way it moves backward from result to cause. In fact, kamma is not the same thing as "poetic justice." It is not even justice. It is a blind, unjudging, impersonal, and sometimes (seemingly) vicious law of cause and effect, and nothing to be happy or rest assured about. Rather, it is something that must be addressed. No one deserves their suffering, which ultimately is always innocent in that it occurs because of material and/or mental conditions that prevent realization of how to address it. And whatever the inheritance from past lives, or past moments, it is some other life or moment that impersonally bequeathed that inheritance into this one, along a chain of ignorant clinging to self that causes the impersonal continuity of the personal to occur, and which no one has chosen for his or herself. It is not the same person from life to life, any more than it is from year to year or hour to hour. No one deserves to suffer for the inconsideration of some past person who was not really yourself. The idea of deserved suffering, of crime and punishment and law, is the province of ideology, and of the necessary practical interpersonal workings of law and order in the social world. It is something decidedly other than the impersonal force of kamma, though sometimes it is layered over kamma in Buddhist ideologies, which can, like all human cocktails, have sinister side effects.

Generosity brings a return for someone else, a stranger, some other person in the future (even in the next moment), to whom you might habitually refer as "yourself." One is being generous in giving a good inheritance over to *that* person, and inconsiderate by leaving a bad inheritance, whether we are referring to "this life" or "between lives" (there is no essential difference). But this "good" and "bad" only makes sense from a relative perspective, for the personal recipients of these qualities cannot, strictly speaking, actually be there to receive them. And yet what is a "person" supposed to signify if not an enduring entity in time? In that sense one cannot even rightly say that the gift is for someone else, either. What one is ultimately left with is the acts themselves, and this is something of profound significance for the formation of certain forms of Buddhist ethics, which are, at least among some, strangely devoid of personhood. Although this ethics of observance of kamma ostensively entails being generous to all who must suffer the effects of thoughts, words, and actions, whoever they might be, self or other (there is no essential difference), that "they" is ultimately only other thoughts, words, and actions.

To raise observance of kamma is to be mindful to create the best possible inheritance, or gift. It requires very careful and refined attention to the only place that can matter in the matter of kamma, careful attentiveness in the only place that can ultimately make a difference—*cetenā*—intention, the moment of arising of thought, speech, and action. This is the only place where one amalgamation of acts can influence the situation of another amalgamation of acts. And yet this not fully or finally so, but only in the relative sense of setting up conditions for the refinement of intentions in the future. There is no way to determine or control now what some other "self," as it tends to be called, will do later. At the same time, any sensitivity to cetenā (intention) now is not, strictly speaking, "intentional" (in the English sense), because it has already been conditioned to occur. In short, this ethics could be said to be less about "doing good," or "being good," and more about "causing skillfulness" in dealing with these chains of impersonality, for which, delusions aside, there is no choice. If there can be any basis here for "moral action," and I am not sure that such a phrase makes sense in this Dhamma, it certainly cannot lie in confusion over the existence of a moral being, who endures and chooses. Instead, wherever such observance of, and respect for, the unfathomably intricate strands of the already culpable and conditioned act occurs—in the "unknowable" (*acindeyya*) arising of "intention" (*cetenā*)—that is where the gift is already being given, to no one in particular or, alternately, where it can be said, in a relative sense, that it is given to all others, of which the "self" is one. Thus, to be generous in the biggest way, at least according to this conception, one ought to support careful awareness of and investigation into acts and the aporia of intention wherever it is occurring, in self or other, with conducive material and/or mental conditions and acts.

To many Thais such mindfulness would be represented, and embodied, by the Buddha, Dhamma, and Sangha. But this is not the only place such attention is happening. These symbols are called upon repeatedly in funerary rites of exchange, whether those of the village or the nation, rites in which participants are called upon to observe the force of relations of kamma that must be respected, even if they cannot be understood or finally known. The reminder, the memory, the mindfulness is nothing other than "realization"—which is to say a realization that something is so, has always been so, though one did not realize it before. In meditation this amounts to cultivating mindful observance of existence, but in funerary rites this "mindfulness" works upon history, and its most powerful manifestation need consist in nothing more than arresting a realization that what has happened cannot be denied and cannot be made to go away, however much some may try. This must be respected and observed. There is no choice here, and that is what must be realized.

But this is a technical and philosophical manner of speaking that only some nuns, monks, and lay people share. Its vernacular idiom is far more articulate.

Every morning right before noon, while the funeral casino was shut down, monks would come to receive gifts of food, necessities, and cash from the family. This gift is called *tam bun*, making/doing merit. After the gift prestations, the monks chant blessings, which are mentally and orally verbalized good wishes, wishing for all the lay people there health, prosperity, good luck, long life, a rebirth in heaven, and ultimately, nibbāna just as soon as possible; nibbāna is to be finally free of the reactivity of kamma, of submission to the forces of birth, death, rebirth, and the inevitable effect of being subject to kamma, suffering, or dukkha, or so those who have not finished the Buddha's training to the end *believe*. Buddha, or so I have heard, suggested that there was a way, but he also stressed that nobody can take his word for it, nor should they. You can only know by finding out for yourself that it is so. Short of that you can only have a conditional belief. So people believe that the Buddhist training leads to a realization, to knowing what the Buddha knew.

The Buddhist discipline of ascesis, if it is to remain available and accessible to believers who aspire to more than just belief, requires material support. Buddha is reported even to have made some strict rules for the order of monks and nuns, to enhance the exchange relation of that economy with the everyday economy of laypeople. The aspirants should be completely dependent on gifts. For instance, they were not to cook food for themselves, nor were they to store food overnight. In order to eat, for every single day of their lives they would need a gift. Even the robes on their backs must be gifts. Thus, ideally, the political economy of the Buddhist Dhamma would be in a continuous exchange relation with the society at large. By the time Patcharee's father died, gifts to monks had been for a long time both a routine and a very special way to give gifts.

As one can see in the funeral wake and even in the funeral casino, all kinds of gifts can carry spiritual value. They are in whole or in part beneficial causes, in whole or in part skillful actions, and so lead to beneficial results in the mind and make merit for the giver; this is true even without awareness of the operations of kamma. Economy is always operating in both senses at once, in material exchange and in what we might call spiritual exchange. It is a two-way relation, two-way causation, and every participant is subject to the spiritual consequences of this economy whether it is recognized or not. There is no other kind of economy than gift economy. There is always a return on any transaction, whether visible or not. There is nothing outside the gift. And yet although exchange is always the rule, there is nothing that is not at the same time a "pure gift," in that it is impossible ever finally or fully to know what has been given and what returns. In short, there is never a final gift-canceling recognition of "the thing given" because there is nothing that does not escape the power of language and thought to recognize it.

In the particular case of this Thai context, the culturally particular connection that makes it possible to gain an inkling of that which is beyond good and evil—though imperfectly and never fully or finally knowable (*acindeyya*)—and that organizes the material exchange imbricated in spiritual economy is the idea that the apex of value in giving is the gift that leads precisely to such a beyond, to what the Buddha knew. In their reasoning, if you are not wholeheartedly pursuing that gift yourself (which is the same as doing it for "one other"), for the sake of all others who must cross paths with you in this life or another life (which is the same as oneself), then the next best thing is to help give that gift to others who are pursuing it, that is, to support materially others who in their act of trying to know what Buddha knew are the representation of that which is beyond good and evil. A gift to the Sangha, the order of nuns and monks, may help to keep the Buddhist Dhamma available for such pursuit. So by giving such a gift of spiritual value, you make merit for "yourself." If you give it without regret, with as much sincerity and good intention as you are capable of, so much the better for this gift connected to an economy of already high aspirations. It is said that the practice of *dāna*, charitable giving, can in all these ways lead to skillful results that ennoble the mind. But this valance is simultaneously defied in the practices of sharing merit in connections that do not recognize personal possession of this value, or even recognize merit as a thing subject to the singular placement of mass or to the laws of conservation of energy.

In its ostensive terms it is, after all, both a spiritual and a material economy of gift exchange, and so Patcharee's father was not able to participate in its material aspect directly, since he was dead. That is why the monks were invited to the funeral every day of the wake, so that the family could give the gifts on his behalf. While the monks chanted blessings over the givers, the merit makers themselves concentrated on spilling the merit made over to the dead man's spirit. Just as the funeral economy is in a total sense itself both a gift given by others to the dead and one given on behalf of the dead to others, so is the exchange of spiritual value between the merit makers and Buddhist Sangha in its entirety itself the gift, given both over to the dead and on their behalf. That circulation of spiritual value is even more socially rapid, interconnected, and instantaneous than the most fast-paced and reeling casino economy, which is, after all, not entirely plugged into the spiritual economy of the funeral wake alone. The gift givers in spreading merit have much higher aspirations, wanting to give away even the merit that is personally earned in the act of their giving to the Sangha. As the monks chanted blessings, the lay donors poured water from a glass, over their finger, and into a bowl, manipulating these material, ritual tools to help them concentrate on being a conduit through which spiritual value merely passes through on its way to the dead. But even that spirit of giving, where you wish your own merit for another, is itself such a noble intention that it is, in turn, productive of more merit for yourself. Self-interest is a tenuous thing to define in this practice. One can see how if you are really adept at generosity, there is no limit—just as with anger—to the merit that can be made, shared, produced, and returned to you in greater proportions the more you give it away.

When the monks would chant in the living room, lined up beside the coffin of Patcharee's father, the room would be packed with his friends and family all there to make and spread merit. The material economy of the exchange of spiritual value was limited by scarcity: there were only so many sets of glasses, water, and bowls, and only so many gifts given to the monks. But no matter; even if you did not give anything you still shared in the merit so long as you adopted the giving state of mind, and those who did not have a set of merit-sharing bowls and water would just place their hands on the shoulder or back or leg of someone who did have a set and was spilling water to spread merit. If you are touching them then you are sharing in the merit that is being collected and dispersed at the same time. And if you cannot reach them, then you touch someone who can touch someone who was spreading the merit, thereby sharing in the merit being made and sharing in the sharing off of that merit, and so on, so that everyone was in tactile imbrication and connected to everyone, both making merit and spreading merit, raking it in the more they try to give it away, so that it is terribly difficult to say who among the monks, the laity, and the dead are the givers and who are the receivers. Indeed, it is hard to say what it is that is being given or received, because even calling it *bun*, merit, or spiritual value is obviously a reification of this gift, grammatically making it into something that it cannot possibly be, since it seems to know neither limits nor boundaries between people, or between givers and receivers, or between production and consumption; the act of expenditure can be at one and the same time an act of production, which is not the way of things, which once they are expended are gone and must be reproduced.

"Spiritual value" is only a clumsy signifier for this kammic effect of generosity so unlike the utilization of things, in the sense that the mode of its production is also its mode of expenditure, and spending is its accumulation.

The spiritual economy of the funeral wake is a two-way exchange with the dead. The family of the dead man, and his friends, make a big show of their generosity, and although sometimes such merit making is notorious even among its most avid participants for being only that—just showing off—the spectacle of the giving can at the same time, in whole or in part, be sincerely intended as given away, mind to mind, spirit to spirit, love for love, in exchange with the dead.

THE STATE GHOSTS

One hundred days after Boonyern died, it was time for another big merit-making venture, on his behalf and given to him. In the family's reckoning, by one hundred days Boonyern would have been completely on his way to his next destination, his next birth—that is, unless he was a "hungry ghost," someone whose heart was ruled by greed and consequently after death is obsessed, and like a broken record repeats itself over and over, haunting the same spaces with only a modicum of consciousness.

On the day of his cremation, Boonyern did not look as if he would be a ghost. He looked quite well, peaceful and content. Everyone thought so. Just before they burned the body they opened the coffin and everyone who wanted could take a last look at the grayish skin, the whiskers and long fingernails of the cadaver hollowed of life, and yet also strangely animated in expression. Children were held aloft so that they could take in that uncanny sense.

Just before they cremated the body, everyone assembled to give robes to monks in the "charnel ground" cremation area in the forest behind the temple. A few of the dead man's nephews were ordained as novices for the day, to make merit for their uncle. Together they recited a dedication of merit for the dead man, wishing him a heavenly rebirth and, eventually, nibbānna as soon as possible. On the one hundredth day after his death, a final burst of generosity was sent off to him. Since then, the family has been going merit making on his behalf on every anniversary of the death.

If memory serves us right there is another spirit hovering over this scene, however, always present but only occasionally making contact. Throughout the funeral wake, I never heard a single soul speak about any possible connection between the state electricity generator, the strip mining, the lignite dust, and the man's death. It seemed as if I alone had been trained in that kind of anger, so that my mind instantly seizes upon any possible blame of power. Members of the national parliament who represented the district sent funeral wreaths to the wake, of course with their names and party affiliation printed boldly upon them. When I scoffed at these, I was reminded to keep quiet because the designate who brought them might still be present, and that would be impolite of me. Such politicians have extensive, capillary patronage networks that seep through the countryside, and the same political apparatus that distributes money to each constituent, buying votes at election time, is ready to hand out funeral wreaths whenever anyone dies.

This is the other side to the gift economy, the relations of reciprocity that organize the gift economy of democracy and the state in Thailand. They haunt the state relentlessly, so that even secular Thai political analysts have in the past been convinced that a cyclical, eternally returning pattern infects the historical line of progress like a ghost in the time machine: a cycle of political corruption leading to military coups, which over time eventually leads to a return of democracy but then also more corruption, and so more coups, and so on.[25] They say the problem is vote buying: greedy people who invest politically so that they can extract their payback once in control of the state. But the word "buying" is used by them only to convey the sense of banality and desecration of the pure representation of public interest which it is desired that democracy express rationally. In fact it is not simply "buying" but the chasm between that and a fatal reciprocity of giving that is at work here. The politicians are investing capital on expectations of a proportional return, but to some of the villagers it is a gift, and they feel obligated, when alone at the ballot box, to return the present. And when, as always happens after election day, numerous vote canvassers turn up dead with bullets in the backs of their heads, it is clear that the political machinery also considers it a gift, carrying the full force of reciprocity with death. "If I kept this *taonga* for myself, serious harm might befall me, even death," suggested Tamati Ranaipiri, though surely he was not speaking of a such an inverted economy of things in which material weapons can stand for a spiritual economy of consequences, and hungry ghosts can walk the earth alive.[26]

After the giving of robes in the charnel ground cremation site, and right before they take the coffin and the cremation spire, painted in dazzling fluorescent colors, to the cremation pyre, the master of ceremony, a layman who specializes in leading cremation ceremonies, speaks into the microphone an impersonation, or reimpersonation, of the dead man's voice. The man is not considered possessed by a spirit, but he talks as if he were the dead man, saying good-bye to his family. He mentions them all by name, and says how he does not want to leave them, how much he loves them; then his voice starts to waver and it becomes a crying wail as he says, "good-bye, good-bye everyone. . . ."

To them this is not maudlin, because to feel maudlin you have to recoil out of the sorrow and reflect on the technique that is inciting it. To them, to hear the man on the microphone crying in a high-pitched voice is almost as if it really was their father crying to them as he goes off to be burned, off to the beyond, and they all let out great wails in response. His wife cries, his sons and daughters cry, his relatives and friends cry, and the cry of the departing man is all mixed up in that, and so many in the audience can feel the sorrow building on sorrow, the sound building on sound, into one big sob, so that they, in turn, fall into the play of tears.

DISTRACTION AND SOCIAL CONCENTRATION

In thin rain, the students, the families of the Black May martyrs, some rural farmers, and some interested Bangkok citizens line up, as is customary in all political activities, behind the portraits of king and queen, and the national flag. Tonight is a memorial night, the third anniversary of the 1992 Black May massacre. The commemoration assembles at Thammasaat University, to move down Ratchadamnern Avenue and toward the Democracy Monument, the sites of the three major massacres of unarmed civilians in the last two decades. The short march in the dark drizzle leaves Thammasaat's front gate behind, where police and right-wing terror groups desecrated student corpses in 1976, and covers one-quarter of the oval loop of road surrounding the grassy field of Sanam Luang, site of the old marketplace where students and urban citizens first joined up in 1973. On the horizon and lit up with spotlights are the golden spires and majestic colored roofs of the ceremonial royal palace and royal temple compound. People were murdered here on Sanam Luang every time, 1973, 1976, 1992. The march continues down Ratchadamnern Avenue, where most of the killing was done in 1992, proceeds about half a kilometer, and then reaches the looming wing-towers of the Democracy Monument, a focal site for both the amassing and dispersing of bodies in 1973 and 1992.

Surrounded by the cement brick fringes of a city of seven million people, between two and three hundred commemorators form a thread that curls down the scenes of crime, snakes through the city streets pulsating with the electric verve of progress. The long cloth signs that the procession carries on their streetside flank are barely legible, held as they are in darkness, below neon signs that flash clearly on buildings mostly three to six stories high. Tall air-conditioned city buses also tower over the commemorators. So does a sequence of fifty-foot-tall royal portraits suspended on steel rigging from the divider island in the center of the avenue. One is a profile of the king holding a large camera. The profile of a coronated technology of image reproduction coincidentally faces the protesters' side of the street, so that it looks precisely as though the king was taking pictures of them, from above the car engines that gun sound and smoke screens on ground level.

It is a murky, moonless, starless night. The procession is made just visible by the tall streetlights and the headlights of traffic, which are heavy because of the drizzle. The sidewalks are much wider than the column of marchers, and Ratchadamnern itself is a wide, modernist avenue, with four lanes in each direction. Where they had once flooded the avenue with oceans of people, dwarfing the cityscape, now they are puny specks meandering, unnoticed, in a giant's world of cement, metal, electric, and smoking mass.

Bustling harried bodies, in the midst of urban transport, not only make of the scene an engulfing wave of material density spilling over and around and dwarfing the protesters in its tidal proportions but also evoke an abstract and immaterial sense of a single giant mind milling in restless preoccupation. Perched up in the backlit windows of an air-conditioned bus, by happenstance some passengers find themselves backed up in traffic alongside their fellow countrywomen and -men in the street. The bus passengers are in a state of distraction. A bored, resigned face is drawn to the miniature spectacle below just as easily as it turns away when the fare collector snaps her aluminum change purse, and the head and hands turn to her. The head turns back again just as distractedly, and anonymously peruses the curiosity, from a perch screened of rain and noise and smoke by the droning hum of the air-conditioned window-sealed environment.

The commemorators file past a rock'n'roll club with big blue neon tubes forming musical notes, and a billboard behind glass with photographs of the girl singers who will appear nightly in frilled and sequined dresses. Passing under the lighted caption "The Tourist Walk," the demonstrators file by the open front of a tourist bar with bamboo paneling and hardly anyone in it. Inside, a couple of middle-aged foreign men turn away from beer and satellite TV and watch for a spell. In ten minutes the column has passed and disappeared into the distance.

Behind the national flag and monarchical portraits follows a pickup truck, rolling slowly along curbside and up to the Democracy Monument. Aboard, one student leader addresses the column from a soapbox and megaphone, while two others hold each of his legs so he does not fall off. They park the pickup and set up a stage on the top steps of the monument, which gradually ascends from the street with increasingly smaller concentric circles of platform levels, leading up to a tomblike, domed structure rimmed by four monumental wings raised in the four cardinal directions in an austere style reminiscent of 1930s fascist architecture, which is the period in which it was built. On top of the domed tomb is the likeness of a gold-colored tray, the kind on which one places donations to senior monks or gifts to royalty. On the tray is a gold-colored folded object, which looks like monk's robes being presented for donation but which actually represents the constitution on a golden tray, the way a constitution is presented to a king for signing and the way it is then presented when it is given back by the king to the people. Although it was constructed as a monument to democracy, it has come to be known as a tomb of democracy, for the killing that has taken place there and that has sanctified it as site of power.

There are just enough people present to fill up one-half of the monument's area, though people mill around from one side to the other. On one side a stage is set up, where student leaders introduce the father of a young man once killed here. He makes speeches on behalf of the dead and their relatives. On the other side a temporary shrine is set up. There, against the side of the tomb, they lean a soldier's khaki helmet and a black baton of superdense plastic, and around that, cardboard signs with photographs of bloody corpses pasted on them. On the top step they arrange more images of the dead.

The pictures are lit up with candles, which keep getting blown out by a finicky wind and have to be relit constantly by attendants. People file past, and take a good look at the photos. Many haven't seen the images for some time, but they are the same photos that were sold on the streets after it happened, the same ones sold in newspapers and gore magazines, that were posted up in a kilometer-long sidewalk exhibit after the violence. The color photographs are of the street-sale variety, which were printed up with such great haste that the coloring is of poor quality. Though vivid, the colors are blotchy, crude, and seem to run into each other. A few of the corpses are swaddled in the national flag. They were demonstration corpses that could be toted around in a big bloodstained flag for everyone to see, or plopped down on the ground for whoever had a camera ready. Now, as the corpses are laid out once again for viewing, the faces of most of those who pass by the photographic display once again reel in mild revulsion and a deeper distress. Many stand there a long time, while others sit at their feet, staring at the images, impressing them into their minds.

The colors are sopping wet. Traffic circles around the monument. Bodies collapse within the mush of the photographic frame and then topple out of it. Vehicles weave and cut each other off. In one of the photos, a skull-cracked head is scalped by machine-gun fire; pieces of brain float in a black pool. Traffic lights change from red to green. Dead eyeballs, partly dislodged, are vacant of everything but an ogling last moment. Motorcycles rip and roar their engines, peal their tires. Furious exhaust spumes out from the motorcycles that race to get ahead of the cars and beat the next red light. A motionless heap of corpses is unstirred by life but at the same time viciously animated by the hideous, photogenic propulsion of violence.

The cars and buses and motorcycles and trucks, which enter the center of the city via Ratchadamnern Avenue, have no choice but to go around the Democracy Monument, a traffic circle that spins voyagers off north, south, east, and west. Beside the preserved monuments to ancient kingly rule, it circulates the urban populace through its heart and around its monumental architecture of power.

The demonstrators, surrounded by both the broader darkness and the circling of headlights, solemnly hold candles alight against the wind, as they too circle the monument in the same clockwise direction as the car beams. Three times around the tomb, like the candlelit circling at a Buddhist temple on a holy day. When the candlelit procession is completed, the mourners assemble in a vigil together. The families of the Black May dead hold candles in the background, while singers lead the mourners in songs of lament for the martyrs of democracy. At the end of the song, they shout "victory" in the name of the dead, "Chaiyo!" three times.

In silence, and ensconced in the lurching noise of traffic, all approach the foot of the tomb, where they go to their knees and bring their palms together, raising the candles up and over their heads, bowing in reverence and offering to the dead. The candles are set down on melted wax, surrounding the tomb in fire lights. Many candles are amassed near the photographic menagerie of death. The mourners kneel, some recollecting the dead, and generously spread *mettā*, compassion, to the unquiet spirits. Others just look. The most solemn mourners make determinations in their minds and hearts that the dead be at peace, dwell in happiness, and one day achieve nibbānna, the final liberation from dukkha, circulating the good wishes among one another, each other, and then giving them over to the other side.

Or is it the case that what really circulates here is only the mobile vehicles of the world casino's smoky, combustible development?

After the wind blows out many of the candles, and the mourners gather them up, the Bangkok Metropolitan Authority (which is controlled by a sympathetic political party), brings in trucks with water cannons to hose down the monument and restore it to a state of cleanliness no other antagonistic parties would want to blame on the students. The city is as it was before.

Although Bangkok did not see what had just happened, recollecting the dead does not, essentially, require the eye of beholding. The memorial quiet may have been drowned out by car horns, but the memory of the virachon was kept alive—perhaps just barely. But barely might be enough, so that one day, should conditions and events be such as again to warrant the assembly of people in defiance of tyrants, they may flock to the occasion, drawn to the fount and focus point of necromantic power as though the day of remembrance for the dead had always been foremost in their hearts, each and every one of them, all these years. The day of recollecting the dead is a forceful day for only a very few today, but those are the few who help keep the day ready and waiting, to be resurrected, possibly, once again. Or at least it has worked that way in the past. And, at least, that is the hope for the future of contacts and contracts with the spirits of the dead. It remains to be seen whether there will always be eyes to perceive that this exchange with the dead matters, and whether this spiritual economics and this awareness of the repulsiveness of the body politic can be harnessed in defiance of a tyranny without tyrants, an economy built out of and contiguous with the old style of U.S. imperialism, Thai military rule, and shared massacre, but not obviously culpable in these matters.

TIME AND THE GIFT

Consider it this way: How long, for instance, can the police occupy Tiananmen Square, suppressing commemorations and memory? The question should really be, if they want to remain in totalitarian power: How long *must* they? Forever. Forever is how long they must control the space, because memorial comes every year, without respect for linear time. You can control physical space, and through it you can seem to control the eternal return of anniversary time, but for how long? Tiananmen began with a funeral for a sympathetic Communist Party official, and it will probably end in the power of funerary memoriam, because forever is too long. No one can control forever. That is both the hope and danger—the return that death brings.

But then again, it is not as though linear time is not real, or does not matter here. It is certainly possible that oppositional sentiments could, over time and under hegemony, lose touch with the dead. There are countervailing forces, however. One reason that forgetting the dead may be an unlikely cultural scenario in Asia is the implicit social knowledge of spiritual economy, of symbolic exchange with the dead, that is ensconced there (and yet, who can estimate the power of the neoliberal economy of history?). The second reason the spiritual debt may not pass out of awareness has to do with the material economy of expanding technologies of eidetic memory. The power of mechanical reproduction to capture artifacts of memory surely increases the longevity of those images of danger that can call our obligations to mind, though of course not without all the dangers of necromancy. In terms of the mummification effects attributed to this realm of image reproduction, there is certainly a difference between historical events that are captured on film and those that are not. Precisely because of the divestment of the aura of the object, precisely because it is not necessary to have been materially present, say, at napalmed Vietnamese villages, Tiananmen Square, or Ratchadamnern Avenue, nor necessary to return for commemoration to the physical sites of charnel ground (though such returns are certainly of political value)—precisely because presence is not of the essence when deaths live on in material representations that defy physical controls on matters of time and space—it is unlikely that awareness of the debt will be completely erased even under the material, violent control of physical spaces of memory, or under the hegemony of an economy of history in which international leaders can clink glasses over economic cooperation as though nothing had ever happened.

These dangers and others are perpetually at work. In return for placement in the neoliberal economy of history, Thailand has been forced to accommodate a massive downsizing of the value of its economy to the same global investors who almost balked and walked after the events of Black May. The economic policies of the successors to military rule turned out to be as open to free-flowing finance as were the initiatives of the government set in place by General Suchinda's coup, and almost as hostile to labor. This was one key factor in enabling, first, the overextension of credit in the country and, second, the legal ease of capital flight that enhanced the trauma of the economic crisis of 1997. The country has subsequently been focused on rationalizing all forms of economic and cultural life. One ironic though not least amusing twist in this development has been the simultaneous proliferation of organized illegal casinos in the country (though they are nothing new) and the even more pervasive consciousness of this proliferation, created by a mass media focused on exposing the irrational and corrupt. This focus on illegal gambling has especially been the case with a new television network, iTV (independent Television), which was granted a license to form a private corporation in response to censorship in the events of Black May. A large portion of iTV stock was acquired by the telecom company of the media tycoon Thaksin Shinawatra, who set up his own political party and won a landslide victory, becoming prime minister and forming a government in 2001. Right after the election twenty-three workers in iTV's news department were fired for, as the journalists claimed, attempting to unionize and for refusing to avoid mention of damaging news about Thaksin in the days before the election. That a telecom giant would eventually rule the country could almost have been predicted in the first moments after Black May. The relatives of Black May did not let this firing of journalists go without public comment of course, raising the memory that the network itself could have existed with the deaths of their kin.

Strangely, the new iTV news department—brought in to replace the more troublesome one—immediately kicked off its tenure by conducting secret camera investigations of illegal gambling in several provinces, which created quite a stir and forced immediate transfers of police officers by the highest police authorities. So far, iTV has not shown up in Lampang. The last funeral casino I witnessed was crashed, however, not by a police raid but by a caller on cell phone, into the funeral, claiming that iTV was coming to film them, which resulted in an immediate panic as well as orders by the local police (who faced transfer if caught by iTV) to halt all funeral casinos for the time being. At the time of writing, funeral casinos remain in a state of complete suspension. Meanwhile, an organized illegal casino in the area—less public, more focused on money alone, and with more of a tendency to wreak havoc on the lives of its customers than a funeral casino—has benefited greatly from the "iTV ban." It is the opinion of almost everyone in the area that the caller was connected to this casino.

In any case, the secret eyes of the mass media are everywhere, and gambling is therefore driven into the more secretive and even truly dangerous arms of organized crime. But perhaps it is not appropriate to bemoan this loss of public illegality at the hands of progressive rationalization of economic and cultural life—for in the face of the even more severe winds of international finance, the neoliberal world order and disorder, the stakes of gambling have been raised exponentially higher on the local level. This is true of both the amounts of money wagered in the hopes of winning big, and the consequences of devastating loss and destruction through gambling that are wrought on all forms of social relations. The frequency of truly dysfunctional betting behavior has become far greater than it was only a few years previously, at least in Lampang, and this has not been helped by the separation of gambling from public social life and from the economy of funeral giving. The "funeral casino"—at least as a figurative entity—will have to migrate elsewhere, and find new forms and sites for the application of its "black" market models and heightened consciousness of social obligation.

Things must always be done differently. The funeral casino has disappeared, at least in a literal sense, at least temporarily. But, by contrast, in recent years the relatives of the Black May dead have adapted and become far more adept at capturing attention, and their leader, Adul Kiewboriboon, has become an articulate voice in all matters of concern to the ongoing project of democracy in Thailand. Meanwhile, the monk Luang Ta Maha Boowa, cited earlier for his insights on reclusive meditation on corpses, and disciple of the "world renouncing" tradition of Acharn Mun, has now come out of the forest and become an activist raising money—especially gold and U.S. dollars—for the national reserves, while his followers have attached all kinds of strings to the money donated to the government, thus creating a new form of public voice in macroeconomic policy.

It may be unlikely that awareness of the debt, and the gift of death, will disappear, particularly in a field so scorched by financial liberalization. But it is certainly possible, at least, that it might fade. For the society that adopts a cultural economic form which exiles the dead, however, there are dire consequences in store: a quiet, capillary proliferation of surrogate death-effects, as well as the surprise, come-from-behind return of catastrophic violence that breeds on the delusional ground of progress in trade and reason.

It is not, then, such a great leap to see that opposition movements of funeral commemoration are fighting not only for the dead but also for the living, for us. In these struggles of eidetic memory are connected the fates of both the living and the dead. Either way there is a return. One way or another, Tiananmen will come back. There is always a return.

And remember that even if this idea I am suggesting of actions and their return is framed in recognition that is intentionally heretical to contemporary theory for what I hope are clear reasons, the ultimate point here about what is owed to the dead, as northern Thai funeral casinos show, is that society is the gift. The obligation to continually reform society, as return on the gift of death, is a debt we all share.

The spiritual economy of a funeral wake, however, settles nothing once and for all. It is not as though an economy of remembrance can be exchanged, finally, for an economy of forgetting. The cycle of gift exchange is without beginning and without end, and the kamma of world relations hangs relentlessly over the body politic.

There is nothing that can release the living from that, nothing save an all-out ascesis with images of death, the work of the corpse taken all the way to its terminus. The funeral casino, by contrast, may release the play of tears, but it does not—cannot—expend it. It could hardly be otherwise. For there is a difference between meditation on the charnel ground and such funeral scenes as these, the likes of which first shocked Buddha, so I have heard, into finding a different way. There is a difference between the ascetic work with corpse images and the love of life and love of each other which—whether in the aspirations to bring memory to the state or to the village—gives to death a meaning that is unexpendable, that repeats itself, and that hurts forever.

The nature of connection to that suffering is what is really the issue here: whether we are to understand such connections as a contiguity of mechanical causes and effects, or in some other sense of actions and their return. This question itself is not a question of which view is "true," which view describes the reality of history, which one semiotically adheres to the way things are in the natural world. It is a question, rather, of which view can draw people into an observance of and respect for connection and responsibility to these matters the most forcefully, and which view can sow seeds of sufficient doubt about precisely that economy of history that has been of concern throughout this text, an historical progression that does not recognize its obligations to the death that gives it its life.

In this respect one could say, in Thai at least but perhaps in other languages too, that kamma is the unbreakable principle of connection between the dead and the economy of history circulating over the surface of the globe. In this, the practice of meditation on death has its say, both as a real act performed by real people but also as a fertility principle of critical significations, as it appears in this text. Just as it is with the economics of everyday life, the intent practice of Buddha-Dhamma is dependent upon a conducive situation. So the lay adepts, monks, and nuns need their different but not separate peace by which they depend for their existence not only upon the same conditions that support the others' lives but also upon coming to know what some of those conditions are really like, even if it is an unpleasant sight. In this they depend upon the shocking sight of what happens to people when life goes wrong and they die and that good life passes, as it always will, world without end. This relatively infinitesimal population lives to call attention to the negative, and through sharing wisdom, helps assuage its relentless pressure, while in their different spiritual economy they take on the image of eternally returning death, straight up, and exchange it—some of them—for release. And that is shared, too. That too, spilling over at least in some measure, is excessive:

never to have to cry again, never to have to die again, never to be placed upon the funeral pyre again, never to be born again, never to exist, and never not exist.

And yet throughout this text I have been compelled to return, not content with a story of how the Thai people threw off the yoke of tyrants, which—speaking in certain relative terms—they did do, but to seek out the unhappiness and unfinished business that unravels the closure. This is what the listening function of ethnography can transmit into political philosophy, but only accurately so when incompletely, raggedly so. The moments of closure that funeral memoria ostensibly seek are never finally possible, and that is why the funeral idiom has such force for political mobilization. I have focused on collective recognitions that one would be tempted to call "good," but of course this is merely a bias, as the call to answer for the dead is as often as not the call to further violence and war. Where the communitarian rite of answer to the dead closes its ranks is where it gets scary. Where the eyes meet and join in seamless union, rather than in recognition of an always already present rupture and open wound, is where an "organic" solidarity loses touch with reality.

By contrast, a radical democratic project can never achieve final society, can never present a final gift of society that answers the call of the dead, because radical democracy is, must be, an incomplete and impossible project. The consummation of a society without irreconcilable conflict and in peaceful consensus without disintegration would, were it possible, be founded upon a final and impassable exclusion of those who cannot meet its terms. And that is precisely the defeat of radical democracy, which itself depends for both its opportunities and its aims upon what Ernesto Laclau has identified as "the impossibility of society."[27] The moments of political protest commemoration that embody a national stand of justice and unity call attention precisely to their impossibility and to the actual condition of affairs as they stand, which is the opposite of justice and unity. In any case, the violence can never be undone, and the return to the state of the whole—whether that be of the social or individual organism—the whole before the lesion, can never happen because such integral states themselves never were there to begin with.

The alternative temptation, in response to the impossibility of society and the impossibility of a final social gift to the dead that settles accounts once and for all, is of course an ethics of personal responsibility. But this ethics of personal identification with others, an ethics of sympathy and empathy and of I-thou horizons, however strategic as fiction, straddles, ignorantly, the aporia of the self-self relation, which is the truly impossible that has given itself to be thought here. Neither self nor society, neither private nor public, the funerary idiom works best when communitarian aspirations to unity bring the always already ruptured polis into vivid presence precisely at the most consummate moment—in the very act of gathering, realizing the impossibility of society; in the very collection of individuals, realizing the impossibility of individuals; voicing the call and attempt for justice, as Derrida discerns, in the impossibility of justice.[28] The prevention of final suture of perpetually open wounds forestalls the profoundly apolitical closure whereby violence and trauma appear as aberrant exceptions to the rule of previously intact individuals inhabiting a previously unviolated and unviolating order.[29] Here, the fiction of individual autonomy in responsibility is as dangerous to democracy as the fiction of the social whole, or even more so because of its clandestine location within the heart of democratic ideologies. This is the special danger of solely empathetic and sympathetic identification in humanist calls within this new world order, calls that increasingly provide moral cover for political action to pass as apolitical—something all sides, and including this text, cannot help but be complicit in. The surreptitious use of the abject in awakening conscience can further, as Giorgio Agamben has called it, the schema of "bare" or "sacred" life in the formulation of a moral program that seems to be beyond politics and so is all the more acutely political in effect.[30] But the abject carries another force, one that is violently subversive of personal and humane identifications, that cannot promise to bind what was has come undone, what always was and will be undone. Kneeling at the tomb of democracy, under candlelight, some Thais stare into a hideous body, rent apart. They do not know the person pictured there. What is there is barely even recognizable as a person or a human, and in any case there is none anyway. This is something else, open, clung, and beset. The world is formless and screaming.

The "End"

There can be no end point to this thought, and even in imagination it certainly cannot be muzzled with either literary closure in the figure of the Buddhist Arahant or with the story of a family's wake and their chance to cheat fate and say goodbye to their father, and hear his final hail back to them, despite a power over life that had stepped in and cheated them of that. Even for them death is no perfect closure, but a dissolution. It is no note to end on, or string to tie up a bundle with, but an unraveling. And so, to eschew any suggestion that death is a final end (which is the last thing it is), I am obligated to return to those who did not get to say goodbye, who did not get their closure, and who—most of them—were even cheated of their corpses.

The kamma has been made. It chains us to each other. And that fact will not just go away.

When the 1995 virachon commemoration lets out in the morning following the remembrance in the night, we soon become aware of the presence of military intelligence workers in our midst. As though collecting the husk of the bodies was not really what they wanted, now the military is still drawn to them, wanting more, seeking information about the state of their mind and soul. They claim to be "news reporters." The telltale questions they ask include their perennial favorite, "How much did they pay you to come here?" One mother of the dead tells me they suggested some figures to her, "Was it ten thousand? Seven thousand, six thousand?" Even now, they still cannot believe that anyone has genuine sentiments, not even the loved ones of the military's murder victims. There are always interested elements out there, hiring the people to come out against them. After all, that is what they themselves have always done—pay people and give them cardboard signs to hold up.

The two casually dressed men try to sidle up to us, probably trying to see what Patcharee and I are doing there with a video camera, which we proceed to point at them. We sit with some virachon relatives on a bench at Thammasaat University, on the field where the students were massacred October 6, 1976. Uniformed students are playing soccer on the field, occasionally raising, over our voices, loud shrieks of alarm or distress, or cheers. Both of the casually dressed men walk up to us with their arms folded in front of their chests, as though they were more comfortable that way. One even manages to hold a cigarette like that, his elbow stuck close to his ribs. They try to make small talk for a few seconds, then Patcharee asks them how they feel, as soldiers, about these poor families, but before she can finish, the one with the cigarette blurts out, "We're not! We're not [soldiers]!" Now he is really hugging himself tight.

"Okay, then just as people—nothing to do with your line of work—just personally how do you feel, yourself, about their situation?"

"Well, I guess I feel sorry for them," the nonsmoker says.

"They ought to get more," the other one adds.

"It's normal that we should feel that way. It was their flesh and blood."

"It's natural that we would feel for them, right?"

"Yes, it's natural," Patcharee reassures them. And now the hook is set. Sitting with us are three mothers of dead sons, and one young wife of a dead husband. I watch as they reverse, for a short, fleeting time, the reversal that had been worked upon their sacrifice.

Like two bad but polite boys who want to be liked again, the soldiers answer their questions respectfully. The air does not seem to be tense. It does not seem to be personal. Everyone is smiling. The soldiers admit that they would rather not be soldiers. One says he wishes he could be in the United States. Then the "reporters" give a robotic line about following orders, "Collecting information has to be done completely straight. We can't leave anything out. If you curse the military, then we can't write down that you praised them."

One of the mothers tells him, "If you really want some information then go see how we live, and tell your bosses, the ones that did this to us, to give us some help."

The "reporters" want to change the subject to something other than what they are doing here, so they ask Patcharee and me what we are doing here, and we say that we are collecting information.

"Write that down!" someone suggests to them.

"Good. Go ahead," another mother says. "Doing whatever you want—that's true Thainess. There is no lack of freedom anywhere."

Trying to make them feel more at home (sort of!), one of the mothers says, "Thailand is the greatest country! Thai people are a people of good heart and mind. We are people with *mettā* (compassion and generosity). People who are warm and—"

"Kind," another mother interjects.

"Ungrudging!"

"—and forgiving!" With big nods to her helpers, she continues to inform the soldiers, "If you shoot us to death, if you kill us we just SMILE, SMILE, and say, 'Don't worry about it! We'll be born again!'"

"Thai people forget easily," one of the soldiers says, showing them that he can be serious about it.

"Right. Right. They forget easily. But Thai people are not afraid of bullets, *na*!" She points her finger, moving it in chopping motions up and down as she tells it to them, "Thai people are afraid of rain. Rain falls and they all run away. But they shoot bullets at us and we don't run."

Trying to squirm out of this, the reporters change the subject to the fact that there are some Korean dissidents, a lawyer and his wife, milling around. "Their problems are not our problems," one of the soldiers says with finality.

"Oh yes they are. Same problem. Bullets stick in them just like us."

"And Koreans have mettā," once more from the mother who likes this point, "They are generous just like us. When they have extra bullets they give them away to the people in the countryside. They lend them some in the arms, some in the legs, some in their bellies."

"Hey, where are you going?"

"Now don't you miss the benefit concert tomorrow!"

"Hey, don't go yet! There's been no incident yet! Stay a while and wait for something good to happen!"

But the two casually dressed men skulk off, sort of sideways, half turning their faces toward the women, though not so far as would cause the men to face their smiles.

❖ Notes ❖

CHAPTER ONE
INTRODUCTION

1. Marcel Mauss, *The Gift*.

2. Susan Buck-Morss, *The Dialectics of Seeing*, 77, 55.

3. See Rosalind Morris, *In the Place of Origins*, for an alternative method of ethnographic practice using unorthodox combinations of spatial and temporal locations within Thailand. Morris goes farther than the present work toward breaking up the ideological nexus of Thai nation-statehood in her attention to the complexities of regional identity. One of many emblematic moments of this difference is her account of Black May 1992 politics through northern Thai participation at a distance from the Bangkok main stage. Such a treatment runs against the grain of national narratives. The concentration on Bangkok in the present book is, in this sense, an unsurprising choice of location. For a study of the literal use of mapping in bringing national identity into being, see Thongchai Winichakul, *Siam Mapped*.

4. Arjun Appadurai, *Modernity at Large*.

5. For insightful writing on the mutually bound helix of the ethical and the political, and the profound relinquishment of responsibility consequent upon either the complete separation of ethics and politics or the collapse of one into the other, see Thomas Keenan, *Fables of Responsibility*.

6. For an alternative to my approach, see Jean Comaroff and John L. Comaroff, "Millennial Capitalism: First Thoughts on a Second Coming."

7. Marshal Sahlins, *Stone Age Economics*, 171–83.

8. Benedict Anderson, *Imagined Communities*.

9. Jacques Derrida, "Force of Law."

10. Comaroff and Comaroff, "Millennial Capitalism." On the "impossibility of society," see Ernesto Laclau, *New Reflections on the Revolution of Our Times*.

11. Keenan, *Fables of Responsibility*.

12. Jacques Derrida, *Spectres of Marx*, 11.

13. Even within their own social context, these Buddhist principles offer no final resolution, or any way to avoid the exclusion upon which consensus and community are based. For instance, not everyone in Thailand is Buddhist (up to 10 percent are not), or Thai in citizenship, though almost everyone killed in the democracy movements and almost every killer was a Thai Buddhist. As the economic disaster of 1997 distributes its effects from finance to rest finally with the marginalized and poor, for instance the hill-dwelling minorities and their urban representatives, how then will politics and ethics be expressed, when the majority of those who are most directly sacrificed are no longer Buddhists or even Thai citizens?

14. I thank Sanjib Baruah for naming the practice of "contextualizing the exotic."

15. Thongchai, *Siam Mapped*, 6–9, 12.

16. Morris, *In the Place of Origins*, 5.

17. Thongchai, *Siam Mapped*, 10–11.

18. Robert H. Sharf, "Zen and the Art of Japanese Nationalism."

19. Richard Gombrich and Gananath Obeyesekere, *Buddhism Transformed*.

20. See Anne Blackburn, *Buddhist Learning and Textual Practice in Eighteenth-Century Lankan Monastic Culture*, for an account of religious change in Sri Lanka that deliberately emphasizes pre-Theosophical currents.

21. Charles Taylor, "Toward an Unforced Consensus on Human Rights."

22. Ibid., 76.

23. Again, Gombrich and Obeyesekere, *Buddhism Transformed* (also cited by Taylor) would be a good place to start on the mutually constitutive relations between Buddhist modernism and the West.

24. Taylor, "Toward an Unforced Consensus on Human Rights," 83.

25. Ibid., 86. In the characterization of the "gamut of western philosophical emotions" Taylor may have allowed deconstruction to slip his mind.

26. See Charles F. Keyes, "Buddhist Politics and Their Revolutionary Origins in Thailand," and Peter A. Jackson, *Buddhism, Legitimation, and Conflict*. In fact, much of the scholarship of the eighties was prophetic in the common apprehension that eventually something in Thai politics had to give. Black May 1992 was it. It is the task of the scholar to anticipate and theorize such fissures, and Keyes and Jackson wrote some of the most insightful material at the time. Perhaps a firm belief in the solidity of the structure of the Buddhist nation-state, mirroring nationalist ideology (in the way Thongchai criticizes), may lead to the belief that changes in Buddhism would transmit their force along the pillars of that structure. Stanley Tambiah, *Buddhist Saints of the Forest and the Cult of the Amulets*, makes a similar, slightly auto-critical, prophesy that forest monks might lead a violent insurrection in the countryside; his was not as reasonable an analysis as that offered by either Keyes or Jackson.

27. See Anderson, *Imagined Communities*.

28. See Rita Gross, *Buddhism after Patriarchy* for a trenchant critique of the politics of riding roughshod over Buddhist women with critiques that leave them no place in the tradition. Gross argues instead for rewriting the tradition. Chatsumarn Kabilsingh, *Women in Thai Buddhism*, conducts a study that demonstrates how diverse and changing the roles of women in Thai Buddhism are, without deferring, as Gross does, to the idea of the Western woman as the necessary agent of such change.

29. In fact, the practice of Buddhism among women in Thailand thrives in many ways, sometimes amid adverse conditions, most of which are not understood by the participants in the same way as they are understood by a critical scholar from the academy. None of the women meditators I have studied with see gender as sociologically relevant to their practice (which is not to say that it is not relevant, or cannot be examined that way). For this reason, the practitioners who enter into this text are not presented particularly marked as women, for that is not how they understand their practice. To themselves they are practitioners of the Buddhist Dhamma plain and simple. There is a purpose to their practice that, at least in their minds, is of greater importance than any other way of achieving or speaking about power and freedom. If their voices are to be used, and all ethnography uses voice in some way, one of those ways includes them as unmarked spokespersons authorized to speak generally about Buddhism and not only "as

women." Although this approach is inadequate and does not settle any questions about women and Buddhism in Thailand, I believe it must be a key ingredient in any further investigation that aspires to value the choices and achievements made by women in Thai Buddhism.

30. Antonio Gramsci, *Prison Notebooks*. I thank John D. Kelly for this point, though he is not responsible for my use of it.

31. Thanks to Kaushik Ghosh for pointing out the ironies of such questions and in sharing mutual perplexity with me over it, within a graduate structure that was so accommodating and supportive of eccentricity and irregular attitude.

32. I thank Jennifer McLuhan for first raising this issue.

CHAPTER TWO
THE NEW WORLD

1. Walter Benjamin, "Paris, Capital of the Nineteenth Century," in *Reflections*, 162.
2. *Bangkok Post*, 1 October 1991.
3. *Thai Rath*, 1 October 1991.
4. Ibid.
5. Paul Handley, "Tarting Up for Company," 32.
6. *Bangkok Post*, 7 October 1991.
7. *Bangkok Post*, 10 October 1991.
8. Handley, "Tarting Up for Company," 32.
9. Ibid.
10. *Bangkok Post*, 6 October 1991.
11. Handley, "Tarting up for Company," 32.
12. Paul Bowring, "Traveller's Tales," 32.
13. *Bangkok Post*, 2 October 1991.
14. Ibid.
15. P. Shenon, "Where Beauty Queens Preen, No Eyesores, Please."
16. Ibid.
17. *Bangkok Post*, 2 October 1991.
18. *Bangkok Post*, 8 October 1991.
19. *Bangkok Post*, 15 October 1991.
20. *Bangkok Post*, 11 October 1991.
21. Michel Foucault, *Discipline and Punish*, 151–56.
22. Bowring, "Traveller's Tales," 32.
23. *Bangkok Post*, 18 October 1991.
24. Bowring, "Traveller's Tales," 32.
25. Foucault, *Discipline and Punish*, 195–228.

CHAPTER THREE
REVOLTING HISTORY

1. Georges Bataille, *Visions of Excess: Selected Writings 1927–1939*.
2. Paul Bowring, "Traveller's Tales," 32.
3. The Tiananmen Square movement, for instance, began as memorial and will, as in Bangkok, probably return as one.

4. It has been said by sources inside the army that Thanong, who had a heart condition, was deprived of his medication after being captured by Suchinda, and died of heart failure under interrogation. Others suspect murder.

5. This is the other side to "terror as usual" as explained in Michael Taussig, *The Nervous System*.

6. Somporn Sangchai and Lim Joo-Jock, eds., *Trends in Thailand*, 84, 85.

7. The infamous "class system" was instituted on the model of West Point Academy, and was intended to foster class camaraderie and mutual identification. That it did, enhancing a culture already dominated by patronage systems. By 1973 several of the classes were out, with two in particular, Class Five, at the major-general rank, and the "Young Turk" colonels of Class Seven, having coalesced into tight ranks that would vie for power in the years to come, and to this day. On factional army politics, see Chai-anan Samudavanija, *The Thai Young Turks*.

8. Ross Prizzia, *Thailand in Transition*, 50–52.

9. Ibid., 63, 16.

10. Thak Chaloemtiarana, *Thailand: The Politics of Despotic Paternalism*.

11. The elite politics of behind-the-scenes maneuvers are of course still a main-stay of Thai politics, but this space was once a sovereign space.

12. Benedict Anderson, "Murder and Progress in Modern Siam," 178.

13. Frank Reynolds, "Legitimation and Rebellion: Thailand's Civil Religion and the Student Uprising of October, 1973," 140–41.

14. Jidbhand Kambhu, "Thailand, Death of a Regime," 16.

15. Reynolds, "Legitimation and Rebellion," 141–42.

16. Prizzia, *Thailand in Transition*, 66. The division of bodily and mental labor in the protest reflected a class consciousness that would become far more powerful than this contingent organization: two years later the students would be bitterly and disastrously divided along these same class lines. On this see Benedict Anderson, "Withdrawal Symptoms: Social and Cultural Aspects of the October 6 Coup."

17. Reynolds, "Legitimation and Rebellion," 141.

18. Prizzia, *Thailand in Transition*, 66.

19. Joseph Wright, *The Balancing Act*, 205.

20. Jidbhand, "Thailand, Death of a Regime," 16.

21. Prizzia, *Thailand in Transition*, 67.

22. Ibid., 67–68; Wright, *The Balancing Act*, 206–7.

23. Prizzia, 68.

24. Ibid.

25. Ibid.; Jidbhand, "Thailand, Death of a Regime," 16.

26. Prizzia, *Thailand in Transition*, 69.

27. Reynolds, "Legitimation and Rebellion," 146n.7.

28. Wright, *The Balancing Act*, 208.

29. Reynolds, "Legitimation and Rebellion," 142–43.

30. Prizzia, *Thailand in Transition*, 69. As with all public massacres, the battle over the precise body count continues forever, as the horror is reified and quantified into so many votes of death, for and against. Frank Reynolds reports that rumor had it at the time that thousands were killed. This sort of rumor is deliberately spread as part of the tactics of waging war in the public sphere.

31. Jidbhand Khambu, "Panic, Death, and Lies," 19.

32. Prizzia, *Thailand in Transition*, 70.

33. Reynolds, "Legitimation and Rebellion," 142; Wright, *The Balancing Act*, 208.

34. Jidbhand,"Panic, Death, and Lies," 19.

35. Prizzia, *Thailand in Transition*, 70.

36. Ibid.

37. Ibid., 70–71; Wright, *The Balancing Act*, 210.

38. Prizzia, *Thailand in Transition*, 71.

39. Jidbhand, "Thailand: Death of a Regime," 17.

40. Jidbhand, "Panic, Death, and Lies," 19.

41. Prizzia, *Thailand in Transition*, 71. In truth, Thanom left Bangkok separately two days later, and it was never clear whether this was due to a rift between him and the others.

42. Jidhbhand, "Panic, Death, and Lies," 19.

43. Prizzia, *Thailand in Transition*, 71.

44. Harold Stockwin, "The Unholy Gross," 45.

45. Ibid., 10.

46. Benedict Anderson, "Withdrawal Symptoms," 19, 20. Anderson notes how these rewards mirror those that the upwardly mobile and democratically minded students could expect from their career futures. Although in 1973 both classes of students, from vocational schools and from the universities, united against the military regime (though the division of bodily and mental labor was reproduced when the vocational students took the "front-line" duties because they were considered more rough-and-tumble types), by 1975 counterinsurgency operations easily exploited chronic class conflicts to their purposes.

47. Puey Ungpakorn, "Violence and the Military Coup in Thailand," 10.

48. Wright, *The Balancing Act*, 244.

49. Puey, "Violence and the Military Coup in Thailand," 11.

50. Marion Mallet, "Causes and Consequences of the October '76 Coup," 84.

51. Puey, "Violence and the Military Coup in Thailand," 11; for more on the role of the infamous monk Khittivuttho in these events, see Charles Keyes, "Political Crisis and Militant Buddhism in Contemporary Thailand."

52. Anderson, "Withdrawal Symptoms," 20.

53. Katherine Bowie, *Rituals of National Loyalty: An Anthropology of the State and the Village Scout Movement in Thailand*.

54. Puey, "Violence and the Military Coup in Thailand," 11; Anderson, "Withdrawal Symptoms," 20.

55. Anderson, "Withdrawal Symptoms," 10.

56. Wright, *The Balancing Act*, 243; Mallet, "Causes and Consequences," 87.

57. Mallet, "Causes and Consequences," 85.

58. Wright, *The Balancing Act*, 244.

59. Mallet, "Causes and Consequences," 88.

60. After escaping Bangkok, the students reemerged with the communist insurgency in the countryside. After the events of October 6, 1976, many other students joined them for the peak years of the Communist Party of Thailand's ranks, until

amnesty was granted to communists after the authorities discovered that state terrorism was actually creating the problem.

61. Mallet, "Causes and Consequences," 86. Mallet reports that U.S. aid was cut from $39 million in 1973 to $17 million in 1975. Japanese investment fell in a single year from $749.6 million in 1974 to $423.6 million in 1975.

62. Puey, "Violence and the Military Coup in Thailand," 4.

63. Mallet, "Causes and Consequences," 89.

64. Anderson, "Withdrawal Symptoms," 24.

65. Ibid.

66. I take my facts about this heavily censored time from foreign news reports and from an amalgamation of anonymously submitted Thai journalist accounts that were put together by Dr. Puey Ungpakorn, then rector of Thammasaat University. He was, as the historian Thongchai Winichakul has pointed out to me, a partisan for democracy, a consciousness raiser who hoped to intervene in the public memory and alter the course of subsequent political campaigns. In short, his account (as well as that of foreign correspondents, in their own fashion), was created to shock and send a message. What follows, then, is a politics of writing that is not very different in its use of the graphic from what Dr. Puey was doing, and what the Thai students in fact were doing at the time—for that is the point: what do we do with the evocative power of the public cadaver, once its necromantic power has been tapped? I not only write about this question but also participate in it, in the morally dubious but perhaps also necessary practice of manipulating images, as the students of October 1976 were to do.

67. Richard Nations, "All Aboard the Seni-Go-Round."

68. Puey, "Violence and the Military Coup in Thailand," 5.

69. Anderson, "Withdrawal Symptoms," 24.

70. Puey, "Violence and the Military Coup in Thailand," 5.

71. Ibid., 6. It should be noted that Dr. Puey Ungpakorn's account is interspersed with direct reports that the *Bulletin of Concerned Asian Scholars* wove into the same article, eyewitness accounts by anonymous reporters for Thailand Information Center's news and features services, which will nevertheless be cited as if by Puey Ungpakorn.

72. Ibid., 5–6.

73. Ibid, 6.

74. Ibid., 6–7.

75. Ibid., 7.

76. Ibid.

77. Ibid.

78. Richard Nations, "October Revolution—Part II," 11.

79. Puey, "Violence and the Military Coup in Thailand," 8.

80. Ibid.

81. Nations, "October Revolution—Part II," 11.

82. The new regime put the official figure at forty-one, whereas those at the Chinese Benevolent Foundation, which handled the cremation of many of the dead, claimed handling "over a hundred corpses" (Puey, "Violence and the Military Coup in Thailand," 8). That several hundred were killed is a reasonable supposition.

83. Ibid.

84. Ibid.

85. Michael Taussig, *Shamanism, Colonialism, and the Wildman*, 370.

86. Ibid., 442.

87. Student Federation of Thailand, *Samut phap du"an Tula: pramuan phap hetkan 14 Tulakhom 2516 læœ Tulakhom 2519*.

88. Thongchai Winichakul, "Jodmai Chaebob Thi Neung."

89. Taussig, *The Nervous System*.

90. Nelson Peagam, "Judge Picks up the Reins," 9.

91. Keyes, "Political Crisis and Militant Buddhism in Contemporary Thailand."

92. Peagam, "Judge Picks up the Reins," 9.

93. Mallet, "Causes and Consequences," 91.

94. Nelson Peagam, "Challenges for the New Order," 8. Kriangsak led a successful overthrow of Thanin less than a year later. Thanin's was perhaps the most bizarre regime ever to control Thailand, and the military soon tired of it.

95. *Bangkok Post*, 11 October 1976.

CHAPTER FOUR
BLOODLESS POWER

1. *The Nation*, 9 April 1992.

2. Ibid., 10 April 1992.

3. Ibid., 16 April 1992.

4. Ibid.

5. Ibid., 8 May 1992.

6. Ibid.

7. Ibid., 2 May 1992.

8. *Matichon*, 2 May 1992.

9. See *The Nation*, 5 May 1992.

10. Ibid., 7 May 1992.

11. Ibid., 18 May 1992.

12. Ibid.

13. Ibid.

14. Ibid., 12 May 1992.

15. This is my liberal translation of the idiomatic message, in which I substitute the terms of exchange with "gold" and "dust," which are meaningful for the reader in English. The message is reprinted in Chamlong Sri-Muang, *Ruam Gan Su*, 105.

16. Some late modernist theorists, following Benjamin, have returned to the assertion that photography and film are the only mediums that can bring the masses into perception as a collective agent, but this event proves that a little clever innovation can produce the same effect, or better. On the sense of collective agent as existing only in film, see Susan Buck-Morss, "The Cinema Screen as a Prosthesis of Perception: A Historical Account."

17. *The Nation*, 13 May 1992.

18. Ibid.

19. Ibid.
20. Ibid., 7 May 1992.
21. E. P. Thompson, "The Moral Economy of the English Crowd in the Eighteenth Century."
22. *The Nation*, 14 May 1992.
23. Ibid., 12 May 1992, 16 May 1992.
24. Ibid., 13 May 1992.
25. I thank Rosalind Morris for first alerting me to the scale of the profits.

CHAPTER FIVE
REPULSIVENESS OF THE BODY POLITIC

1. Antonin Artaud, *Oeuvres Complètes*, vol. 13, 118; cf. Stephen Barber, "Cruel Journey," 75.
2. *The Nation*, 2 June 1992.
3. Ibid., 25 May 1992.
4. *Bangkok Post*, 22 May 1992.
5. *The Nation*, 25 May 1992.
6. *Bangkok Post*, 19 May 1992, 22, 23.
7. Ibid.
8. Ibid., 26 May 1992.
9. *The Nation*, 22 May 1992.
10. *Bangkok Post,* 20 May 1992.
11. Ibid., 21 May 1992.
12. Ibid., 23 May 1992.
13. *The Nation*, 21 May 1992, 23 May 1992.
14. Ibid., 23 May 1992.
15. Ibid., 28 May 1992.
16. David Harvey, *The Condition of Postmodernity*.
17. Anthony Giddens, *The Consequences of Modernity*.
18. Scott Lash and John Urry, *The End of Organized Capitalism*; Arjun Appadaurai, *Modernity at Large: Cultural Dimensions of Globalization*, 4.
19. Appadurai, *Modernity at Large*, 40.
20. Ibid., 10.
21. Jean Comaroff and John L. Comaroff, "Millennial Capitalism: First Thoughts on a Second Coming," 313.
22. Appadurai, *Modernity at Large*.
23. Comaroff and Comaroff, "Millennial Capitalism," 313.
24. *The Nation*, 22 May 1992.
25. Ibid., 23 May 1992.
26. Ibid., 22 May 1992.
27. *Bangkok Post*, 24 May 1992.
28. *The Nation*, 22 May 1992.
29. Ibid., 5 June 1992.
30. Ibid., 4 June 1992.
31. *Bangkok Post*, 4 June 1992.
32. *The Nation*, 4 June 1992.

33. Ibid., 5 June 1992.

34. Ibid., 31 May 1992.

35. *Bangkok Post*, 19 May 1992.

36. *The Nation*, 29 May 1992.

37. Ibid., 30 May 1992.

38. Ibid.

39. Ibid., 5 June 1992.

40. *Bangkok Post*, 1 June 1992.

41. Annette Hamilton, "Video Crackdown, or the Sacrificial Pirate."

42. *The Nation*, 23 May 1992; *Bangkok Post*, 25 May 1992.

43. *Bangkok Post,* 23 May 1992.

44. Ibid.

45. *The Nation*, 24 May 1992.

46. *The Nation*, 19 May 1992; *Bangkok Post*, 19 May 1992.

47. *Bangkok Post*, 19 May 1992.

48. Ibid., 22 May 1992.

49. *The Nation*, 25 May 1992.

50. Ibid.

51. Ibid.

52. *Bangkok Post*, 23 May 1992.

53. *The Nation*, 22 May 1992; *Bangkok Post*, 25 May 1992.

54. Christine E. Gray, "Thailand: The Soteriological State in the 1970s."

55. *The Nation*, 26 May 1992.

56. Ibid.

57. Ibid., 24 May 1992.

58. *Bangkok Post,* 29 May 1992.

59. Hamilton, "Video Crackdown."

60. *The Nation*, 26 May 1992.

61. Ibid.

62. Ibid.

63. Ibid.

64. Ibid.

65. Ibid.

66. Ibid.

67. Ibid., 24 May 1992.

68. Ibid., 20 May 1992.

69. *Bangkok Post*, 23 May 1992.

70. Ibid.

71. For more on this, see Stanley Tambiah, *World Conqueror and World Renouncer: A Study of Buddhism and Polity against an Historical Background.*

72. Appadurai, *Modernity at Large.*

73. Alan Klima, "Exchange and the Unquiet of Photographic Memory."

74. Hamilton, "Video Crackdown," and Rosalind Morris, "Surviving Pleasure at the Periphery."

75. Eventually, in 1997, a new constitution was ratified, but at the pleasure of the political parties and with only token deference to prodemocracy action groups.

CHAPTER SIX
THE CHARNEL GROUND

1. Walter Benjamin, *Trauerspeil* (I, 343), cited by Susan Buck-Morss, *The Dialectics of Seeing*, 161.

2. Thongchai Winichakul, "Remembering/Silencing the Traumatic Past: The Ambivalence Narratives of the October 6, 1976, Massacre in Bangkok"; see also his *Ramleuk Hok Tula: Thammai lae Yangrai*. 13–22.

3. Thongchai, "Remembering/Silencing the Traumatic Past."

4. The possible exception to low attendance at 1976 commemorations may be the well-organized twenty-year anniversary of Bloody October in 1996. I was not able to attend that commemoration.

5. Katherine Verdery, *The Political Lives of Dead Bodies: Reburial and Postsocialist Change*, 28, 137n.16, 32.

6. Ibid., 33.

7. The truth of this historical attribution has been called into question by Stanley K. Abe, "Inside the Wonder House: Buddhist Art and the West." Abe demonstrates that the idea of the Greek source for Buddha imagery may reflect a projection of a European fantasy of influence in the construction of tradition. The analysis seems sound in principle, yet there is no evidence to suggest that in fact the diffusion did not occur this way, as even the author acknowledges.

8. Robert Hertz, *Death and the Right Hand*, 85.

9. For more vivid descriptions of these ideas, see Phra Khru Anusaranasanakiarti and Charles F. Keyes, "Funerary Rites and the Buddhist Meaning of Death: An Interpretive Text from Northern Thailand," 15.

10. There is much more to be understood in these fears, in a general and comparative sense. One might want to note the guilt and responsibility men often feel for causing a women's death by impregnating her, not to mention the common fear and dread of woman's reproductive organs and functions and, last but not least, the fear of women in general and of women's power in particular. I can only note here that with both the lag muang and the paa-chaa, it is women and their reproductive power that carry the greatest charge. There is much more going on here that is worthy of further concern and that would go far beyond my understanding in both breadth and depth.

11. Although other forms of Buddhism might use the word *samādhi* to refer only to something "off the charts" as far as any experience of body and mind are concerned, in Thailand the word is used sometimes absolutely in that sense, but also relatively to signify stages of concentration.

12. I can't help noticing how amenable this dream is to a psychoanalytic interpretation, but I would suggest that such interpretations are violent assertions of ethnographic authority where they are not accompanied by a detailed case study of personal history such as those of Gananath Obeyesekere, *Medusa's Hair*, for instance. Often, especially in Lacanian approaches in anthropology, ethnographic subjects have their minds interpretively plumbed in facile and offhand statements.

13. Buddhaghosa, *The Path of Purification (Visuddhimagga)*, 193.

14. Jonathan Crary, *Techniques of the Observer: On Vision and Modernity in the Nineteenth Century;* Susan Buck-Morss, "The Cinema Screen as a Prosthesis

of Perception: A Historical Account," and Buck-Morss, "Aesthetics and Anaesthetics: Walter Benjamin's Artwork Essay Reconsidered"; Allen Feldman, "From Desert Storm to Rodney King via ex-Yugoslavia: On Cultural Anaesthesia"; David M. Levin, ed., *Modernity and the Hegemony of Vision*.

15. Frederic Jameson, *Postmodernism, or, The Cultural Logic of Late Capitalism*.

16. Arjun Appadurai, *Modernity at Large: Cultural Dimensions of Globalization*; Buck-Morss, "The Cinema Screen as Prosthesis of Perception," and "Aesthetics and Anaesthetics"; Feldman, "From Desert Storm to Rodney King"; Crary, *Techniques of the Observer*; Levin, *Modernity and the Hegemony of Vision*.

17. Crary, *Techniques of the Observer*, 10–11.

18. John Taylor, *Body Horror: Photojournalism, Catastrophe, and War*.

19. Sissela Bok, *Mayhem: Violence as Public Entertainment*; Susan D. Moeller, *Compassion Fatigue*.

20. Susan Sontag, *On Photography*, 21, 16, 41.

21. Buck-Morss, "The Cinema Screen as Prosthesis of Perception," and "Aesthetics and Anaesthetics."

22. Buck-Morss, "The Cinema Screen as Prosthesis of Perception," 48–50.

23. Antonin Artaud, *The Theater and Its Double*; Buck-Morss, "The Cinema Screen as Prosthesis of Perception," 56–57; Siegfried Kracauer, *Theory of Film*, 160.

24. Buck-Morss, "The Cinema Screen as Prosthesis of Perception," 50–53.

25. Jean Baudrillard, *Simulations*.

26. Feldman, "From Desert Storm to Rodney King," and 87–97, especially pp. 90, 91.

27. Ben Singer, "Modernity, Hyperstimulus, and the Rise of Popular Sensationalism."

28. Lynne Kirby, "Death and the Photographic Body."

29. Julia Kristeva, *Powers of Horror: An Essay on Abjection*, 2, 3, 4.

30. Ibid., 210.

31. Anna L. Tsing, *In the Realm of the Diamond Queen*, 180.

32. Kristeva, *Powers of Horror*, 210.

33. Tsing, *In the Realm of the Diamond Queen*, 180–81.

34. Constance Classen, *Worlds of Sense*, 7.

35. Diane Ackerman, *A Natural History of the Senses*; Constance Classen, *Aroma: The Cultural History of Smell*; and Classen, *The Color of Angels*.

36. Classen, *Worlds of Sense*, 11, 135.

37. Walter J. Ong, *Orality and Literacy*.

38. Jacques Derrida, *Of Grammatology*.

39. Robert R. Desjarlais, *Body and Emotion*, 29, 20.

40. Michael Jackson, ed., *Things as They Are: New Directions in Phenomenological Anthropology*; Jackson, *Paths toward a Clearing: Radical Empiricism and Ethnographic Inquiry*; Thomas Csordas, *Embodiment and Experience: The Existential Ground of Culture and Self*; Paul Stoller, *The Taste of Ethnographic Things: The Senses in Anthropology*. See also David Howes, ed., *The Varieties of Sensory Experience: A Sourcebook in the Anthropology of the Senses*; George Steiner, *Real Presences*; Paul Stoller, *Sensuous Scholarship*.

41. André Bazin, *What Is Cinema?*, 12.

42. Buddhaghosa, *The Path of Purification* (*Visuddhimagga*), 185–86.

43. Michel Foucault, *The Birth of the Clinic*, 197, cited in Jean Baudrillard, "Political Economy and Death," in *Symbolic Exchange and Death*, 183.

44. Kristeva, *Powers of Horror*, 1.

45. Stephen Collins, "The Body in Theravāda Buddhist Monasticism," 195–196.

46. Ibid., 201–2.

47. Ibid., 195.

48. Gananath Obeyesekere, "Depression, Buddhism, and the Work of Culture in Sri Lanka," 139–40.

49. Ibid., 136–37.

50. I can translate to the audience of this text my own senses of this practice better than I can those of my informants, who in speaking on the subject were always addressing a fellow practitioner who spoke their language and shared their interests. Whether my investigation of these techniques is the "same" as those of Thai practitioners cannot be settled, perhaps, by the fact that they themselves assert that these investigations are indeed the same. According to their conception of what they are doing, the deliberate training of the mind through standardized forms in meditation creates standardized results, the more so the more repetitive and standardized the work that is applied. This makes sense to them because they operate according to an epistemology that recognizes only cause and effect: similar causes, repeated deliberately, therefore lead to increasingly similar effects. By deliberately patterning the mind, recognizable patterns result—this much should be obvious—though only those who embark on any given patterning of conditions can recognize its result, by definition. For a critique of such arguments and a scathing rebuttal of Buddhist claims to knowledge of their own practices, see Robert H. Sharf, "Buddhist Modernism and the Rhetoric of Meditative Experience."

51. Walter Benjamin, "The Work of Art in the Age of Mechanical Reproduction" in his *Illuminations*, 217–42.

52. Ibid., 229.

53. Martin Jay, *Downcast Eyes: The Denigration of Vision in Twentieth-Century French Thought*.

54. Maurice Merleau-Ponty, *Sense and Non-Sense*.

55. Jay, *Downcast Eyes*, 309.

56. Crary, *Techniques of the Observer*, 3.

57. Jameson, *Postmodernism, or, The Cultural Logic of Late Capitalism*.

58. Maurice Merleau-Ponty, "Film and the New Psychology," in *Sense and Non-Sense*, 49, 50, 53, 58.

59. Ñanavira Thera, *Clearing the Path*, 103–6.

60. Jean-Paul Sartre, *Being and Nothingness*, xi; cf. Ñanavira, *Clearing the Path*, 458.

61. Merleau-Ponty, "Film and the New Psychology," 49–50.

62. See Buck-Morss, "Cinema as a Prosthesis of Perception"; Feldman, From Desert Storm to Rodney King."

63. Acariya Maha Boowa Nanasampanno, *Straight from the Heart*.

64. Ñanavira, *Clearing the Path*, 227.

65. Maha Boowa Nanasampano, *Straight form the Heart*, 118–19.

66. Ibid., 119.

67. Ibid., 119–20.

68. Ibid., 120.

69. Ibid.

70. Ibid., 121.

71. Ibid., 122. Emphasis in original.

72. Ibid., 123. Emphasis in original.

73. Ibid. Emphasis in original.

74. Michael Taussig, "The Physiognomic Aspects of Visual Worlds," 207–8.

75. Benjamin, "The Work of Art in the Age of Mechanical Reproduction," 233.

76. Eduardo Cadava, "Words of Light: Theses on the Photography of History."

77. Benjamin, "The Work of Art in the Age of Mechanical Reproduction," 242.

78. Buck-Morss, "Aesthetics and Anaesthetics," 377. Emphasis in original.

79. Benjamin, "The Work of Art in the Age of Mechanical Reproduction," 242.

80. Thomas Keenan, *Fables of Responsibility: Aberrations and Predicaments in Ethics and Politics*.

81. Giorgio Agamben, "Biopolitics and the Rights of Man."

82. The canonical text in this literature is Elaine Scarry, *The Body in Pain: The Making and Unmaking of the World*. For a treatment that works, at times, partly against the grain of this canon, see E. Valentine Daniels, *Charred Lullabies*.

CHAPTER SEVEN
THE FUNERAL CASINO

1. Friedrich Nietzsche, *The Gay Science* 169.

2. I believe I have lifted this word "kulchural" from somewhere in Allen Ginsberg's writing.

3. Marcel Mauss, *The Gift*; Jacques Derrida, *Given Time: I. Counterfeit Money*, 12.

4. Derrida, *Given Time*, 107, 112.

5. Marcel Mauss, *The Gift*, 11.

6. Ibid., 12.

7. Ibid., 11.

8. Mary Douglas, "Forward: No Free Gifts," vii–xviii; Jonathan Parry, "*The Gift*, the Indian Gift, and the 'Indian Gift.' "

9. "*The Gift*, the Indian Gift, and the 'Indian Gift,' " 468–69.

10. Mauss, *The Gift*, 72–73.

11. Ibid., 14.

12. Georges Bataille, *The Accursed Share*, vol. I.

13. Michael Taussig, "The Sun Gives without Receiving: An Old Story," 397.

14. Ibid.

15. Derrida, *Given Time*, 87, 142, 147.

16. Parry, "*The Gift*, the Indian Gift, and the 'Indian Gift.' "

17. Derrida, *Given Time.*

18. Ibid., 11.

19. From Benjamin Franklin, "Advice to a Young Tradesman," cited in Max Weber, *The Protestant Ethic and the Spirit of Capitalism,* 49; cf. Taussig, "The Sun Gives without Receiving," 394.

20. Antonin Artaud, *The Theater and Its Double,* 128.

21. Some commentators translate *phrae* overmechanistically as "merit transference," objectifying the merit into a physical-like thing which is then, as they say, "transferred," a word that does not correspond, in the sense of literal translation, with any of the words that the participants use to describe the act, and in a figurative sense does not correspond with the sentiments involved, as the case I discuss here exemplifies. Here, obviously, something more than an abstract value is being "transferred," as though wiring money between bank accounts. On the other hand, the translation is not exactly wrong either, for such ideas do express the conceptions of some Thais. Merit making can be made entirely compatible with a such reified idea of exchange if people choose to look at it and work with it in a singularly objectifying way. It can even be compatible with the commodity form, and indeed it is made so in many cases when contributors are promised material reward as a result of their gifts, a kind of merit-account-book-in-the-sky approach. However, as this chapter shows, merit making nevertheless can often in practice encompass a scope far broader than that.

22. See, for instance, the analysis in Mary Margaret Steedly, *Hanging without a Rope: Narrative Experience in Colonial and Postcolonial Karoland,* 110–11; and see also pp. 84, 92, 214–17.

23. The same terms of doubt concern Derrida, *Given Time,* 11.

24. Bhikkhu P. A. Payutto, *Good, Evil, and Beyond,* 47–48.

25. The political scientist Chai-anand Samudavanija has formulated this perception, which seems to be proven by the historical facts of frequently recurrent coups. For a specific and detailed examination of this process, and the most insightful work existing on the factional struggles within the Thai army, see Chai-anand Samudavanija, *The Thai Young Turks.*

26. Marcel Mauss, *The Gift,* 11.

27. Ernesto Laclau, *New Reflections on the Revolution of Our Times.*

28. Jacques Derrida, "Force of Law."

29. I thank Yates McKee for conversations on the matter of articulating irreconcilable memories in an idiom of "open wounds."

30. Giorgio Agamben, *Homo Sacer.*

❖ *Bibliography* ❖

Abe, Stanley. "Inside the Wonder House: Buddhist Art and the West." In Donald Lopez, ed., *Curators of the Buddha*. Chicago: University of Chicago Press, 1995, 63–106.

Ackerman, Diane. *A Natural History of the Senses*. New York: Random House, 1991.

Adorno, Theodore. *The Culture Industry: Selected Essays on Mass Culture*. New York: Routledge, 1991.

Agamben, Giorgio. "Biopolitics and the Rights of Man." In Agamben, *Homo Sacer*. Stanford: Stanford University Press, 1988.

Anderson, Benedict. *Imagined Communities: Reflections on the Origin and Spread of Nationalism*. 2nd ed. London: Verso, 1991.

———. "Murder and Progress in Modern Siam." *New Left Review* 181 (1990): 33–48.

———. "Withdrawal Symptoms: Social and Cultural Aspects of the October 6 Coup." *Bulletin of Concerned Asian Scholars* 9, no. 3 (1977): 13–20.

Anusaranasanakiarti, Phra Khru, and Charles F. Keyes. "Funerary Rites and the Buddhist Meaning of Death: An Interpretive Text from Northern Thailand." *Journal of the Siam Society* 68, no.1 (1980).

Appadurai, Arjun. *Modernity at Large: Cultural Dimensions of Globalization*. Minneapolis: University of Minnesota Press, 1996.

Artaud, Antonin. *Oeuvres Complètes*. Vol. 13. Paris: Gallimard, 1974.

———. *The Theater and Its Double*. New York: Grove Press, 1958.

Barber, Stephen. "Cruel Journey." *Art in America*, February 1995: 71–75.

Bataille, Georges. *The Accursed Share*. Vol. 1. Translated by Robert Hurley. New York: Zone Books, 1991.

———. *Visions of Excess: Selected Writings 1927–1939*. Edited by Allan Stoekle. Minneapolis: University of Minnesota Press, 1994.

Baudrillard, Jean. *Simulations*. New York: Autonomedia, 1997.

———. *Symbolic Exchange and Death*. Translated by Iain Hamilton Grant. Thousand Oaks, Calif.: Sage Publications, 1993.

Bazin, André. *What Is Cinema?* Vol. 1. Berkeley and Los Angeles: University of California Press, 1968.

Benjamin, Walter. *Illuminations*. Edited by Hannah Arendt, translated by Harry Zohn. New York: Schocken Books, 1968.

———. *One-Way Street and Other Writings*. Translated by Edward Jephcott and K. Shorter. London: New Left Books, 1979.

———. *Reflections*. Edited by Peter Demetz, translated by Edmund Jephcott. New York: Schoken Books, 1978.

Blackburn, Anne. *Buddhist Learning and Textual Practice in Eighteenth-Century Lankan Monastic Culture*. Princeton: Princeton University Press, forthcoming.

Bok, Sissela. *Mayhem: Violence as Public Entertainment*. Reading, Mass.: Perseus Books, 1998.

Bowie, Katherine. *Rituals of National Loyalty: An Anthropology of the State and the Village Scout Movement in Thailand*. New York: Columbia University Press, 1997.

Bowring, Paul. "Traveller's Tales." *Far Eastern Economic Review*, 31 October 1991: 32.

Buck-Morss, Susan. "Aesthetics and Anaesthetics: Walter Benjamin's Artwork Essay Reconsidered." In *October: The Second Decade*, edited by Rosalind Krauss et al. Cambridge: MIT Press, 1997, 375–413.

———. "The Cinema Screen as a Prosthesis of Perception: A Historical Account." In *The Senses Still*, edited by C. N. Seremetakis. Boulder, Colo.: Westview, 1994, 45–62.

———. *The Dialectics of Seeing*. Cambridge: MIT Press, 1989.

Buddhaghosa Bhadantācariya. *The Path of Purification (Visuddhimagga)*. Translated by Bhikkhu Nyanamoli. Columbo, Sri Lanka: A. Semage, 1964.

Cadava, Eduardo. "Words of Light: Theses on the Photography of History." In *Fugitive Images*, edited by Patrice Petro. Bloomington: Indiana University Press, 1995, 221–234.

Chai-anand Samudavanija. *The Thai Young Turks*. Singapore: Institute of South East Asian Studies, 1982.

Chamlong Sri-Muang. *Ruam Gan Su* [Our Struggle]. Bangkok: Tiragon Publishing, 1992.

Chatsumarn Kabilsingh. *Women in Thai Buddhism*. Berkeley: Parallax, 1991.

Classen, Constance. *Aroma: The Cultural History of Smell*. New York: Routledge, 1994.

———. *The Color of Angels*. New York: Routledge, 1998.

———. *Worlds of Sense*. New York: Routledge, 1993.

Collins, Stephen. "The Body in Theravāda Buddhist Monasticism." In *Religion and the Body*, edited by S. Coakley. Cambridge: Cambridge University Press, 1996, 185–204.

Comaroff, Jean, and John L. Comaroff. "Millennial Capitalism: First Thoughts on a Second Coming." *Public Culture* 12 (2000): 291–343.

Cornell, Drucilla, Michel Rosenfeld, and David G. Carlson, eds. *Deconstruction and the Possibility of Justice*. New York: Routledge, 1992.

Crary, Jonathan. *Techniques of the Observer: On Vision and Modernity in the Nineteenth Century*. Cambridge: MIT Press, 1990.

Csordas, Thomas. *Embodiment and Experience: The Existential Ground of Culture and Self*. Cambridge: Cambridge University Press, 1994.

Daniels, E. Valentine. *Charred Lullabies*. Princeton: Princeton University Press, 1996.

Derrida, Jacques. "Force of Law." In *Deconstruction and the Possibility of Justice*, edited by D. Cornell, M. Rosenfeld, and D. Carlson. New York: Routledge, 1992.

———. *Given Time: I. Counterfeit Money*. Translated by Peggy Kamul. Chicago: University of Chicago Press, 1992.

———. *Of Grammatology*. Translated by Gayatri Spivak. 1967; Baltimore: Johns Hopkins University Press, 1998.

———. *Spectres of Marx: The State of the Debt, the Work of Mourning, and the New International*. Translated by Peggy Kamuf. New York: Routledge, 1994.

Desjarlais, Robert R. *Body and Emotion*. Philadelphia: University of Pennsylvania Press, 1992.

Douglas, Mary. "Forward: No Free Gifts." In Marcel Mauss, *The Gift*. New York: W. W. Norton, 1990, vii–xviii.

Eisenstein, Sergei. *Film Form*. New York: Meridian Books, 1957.

Feldman, Allen. "From Desert Storm to Rodney King via ex-Yugoslavia: On Cultural Anaesthesia." In *The Senses Still*, edited by C. N. Seremetakis. Boulder, Colo.: Westview, 1994, 63–107.

Foucault, Michel. *The Birth of the Clinic: An Archeology of Medical Perception*. Translated by A.M.S. Smith. London: Tavistock, 1973.

———. *Discipline and Punish*. Translated by Alan Sheridan. New York: Vintage Books, 1979.

Giddens, Anthony. *The Consequences of Modernity*. Stanford: Stanford University Press, 1990.

Gombrich, Richard, and Gananath Obeyesekere. *Buddhism Transformed: Religious Change in Sri Lanka*. Princeton: Princeton University Press, 1988.

Gramsci, Antonio. *Prison Notebooks*. Translated by Joseph A. Buttigieg and Antonio Callari. New York: Columbia University Press, 1992.

Gray, Christine E. "Thailand: The Soteriological State in the 1970's." Ph.D. dissertation, University of Chicago, 1986.

Gross, Rita. *Buddhism after Patriarchy*. Albany: State University of New York Press, 1993.

Hamilton, Annette. "Video Crackdown, or the Sacrificial Pirate." *Public Culture* 5 (1993): 515–31.

Handley, Paul. "Tarting up for Company." *Far Eastern Economic Review*, 26 September 1991, 32.

Harvey, David. *The Condition of Postmodernity*. New York: Blackwell, 1988.

Hertz, Robert. *Death and the Right Hand*. Aberdeen: Cohen and West, 1960.

Howes, David, ed. *The Varieties of Sensory Experience: A Sourcebook in the Anthropology of the Senses*. Toronto: University of Toronto Press, 1991.

Jackson, Michael. *Paths toward a Clearing: Radical Empiricism and Ethnographic Inquiry*. Bloomington: Indiana University Press, 1994.

Jackson, Michael, ed. *Things as They Are: New Directions in Phenomenological Anthropology*. Bloomington: Indiana University Press, 1996.

Jackson, Peter A. *Buddhism, Legitimation, and Conflict.* Canberral Institute of Southeast Asian Studies, 1989.

Jameson, Fredric. *Postmodernism, or, The Cultural Logic of Late Capitalism.* Durham: Duke University Press, 1991.

Jay, Martin. *Downcast Eyes: The Denigration of Vision in Twentieth-Century French Thought.* Berkeley and Los Angeles: University of California Press, 1993.

Jibhand Kambhu. "Panic, Death, and Lies." *Far Eastern Economic Review,* 29 October 1973, 19.

———. "Thailand, Death of a Regime." *Far Eastern Economic Review,* 22 October 1973, 16.

Keenan, Thomas. *Fables of Responsibility: Aberrations and Predicaments in Ethics and Politics.* Stanford: Stanford University Press, 1997.

Keyes, Charles F. "Buddhist Politics and Their Revolutionary Origins in Thailand." *International Political Science Review* 10, no. 2 (1989): 121–22.

———. "Political Crisis and Militant Buddhism in Contemporary Thailand." In *Religion and the Legitimation of Power in Thailand, Laos, and Burma,* edited by Bardwell L. Smith. Chambersburg, Pa.: Anima Books, 1978.

Kirby, Lynne. "Death and the Photographic Body." In *Fugitive Images,* edited by Patrice Petro. Bloomington: Indiana University Press, 1995, 72–84.

Klima, Alan. "Exchange and the Unquiet of Photographic Memory." Manuscript.

Kracauer, Siegfried. *Theory of Film.* New York: Meridian Books, 1960.

Krauss, Rosalind, et al., eds. *October: The Second Decade.* Cambridge: MIT Press, 1997.

Kristeva, Julia. *Powers of Horror: An Essay on Abjection.* New York: Columbia University Press, 1982.

Laclau, Ernesto. *New Reflections on the Revolution of Our Times.* New York: W. W. Norton, 1991.

Lash, Scott, and John Urry. *The End of Organized Capitalism.* Madison: University of Wisconsin Press, 1987.

Levin, David M., ed. *Modernity and the Hegemony of Vision.* Berkeley and Los Angeles: University of California Press, 1993.

Likhit Dhiravegin. *Thai Politics.* Bangkok: Tri-Sciences Publishing House, 1985.

Lopez, Donald S., ed. *Curators of the Buddha: The Study of Buddhism under Colonialism.* Chicago: University of Chicago Press, 1995.

Maha Boowa Nanasampanno, Acariya, *Straight from the Heart.* Translated by Thanissaro Bhikkhu, n.p., 1987.

Mallet, Marion. "Causes and Consequences of the October '76 Coup." In *Thailand: Roots of Conflict,* edited by Andrew Turton et al. Nottingham: Russel Press, 1978.

Mauss, Marcel. *The Gift.* Translated by W. D. Halls. New York: W. W. Norton, 1990.

Merleau-Ponty, Maurice. *Sense and Non-Sense*. Evanston: Northwestern University Press, 1964.

Moeller, Susan D. *Compassion Fatigue*. New York: Routledge, 1999.

Morris, Rosalind. *In the Place of Origins: Modernity and Its Mediums in Northern Thailand*. Durham: Duke University Press, 2000.

———. "Surviving Pleasure at the Periphery." *Public Culture* 10 (1994): 341–70.

Ñanavira Thera. *Clearing the Path*. Colombo: Path Press, 1987.

Nations, Richard. "All Aboard the Seni-Go-Round." *Far Eastern Economic Review*, 8 October 1976, 9.

———. "October Revolution—Part II." *Far Eastern Economic Review*, 15 October 1976, 11.

Nietzsche, Friedrich. *The Gay Science*. Translated by Walter Kaufman. New York: Vintage Books, 1974.

Obeyesekere, Gananath. "Depression, Buddhism, and the Work of Culture in Sri Lanka." In *Culture and Depression*, edited by A. Klein and B. Good. Berkeley and Los Angeles: University of California Press, 1985, 134–52.

———. *Medusa's Hair*. Chicago: University of Chicago Press, 1976.

Ong, Walter J. *Orality and Literacy*. New York: Routledge, 1988.

Parry, Jonathan. "*The Gift*, the Indian Gift, and the 'Indian Gift.'" *Man* 21 (1986): 453–73.

Payutto, Bhikkhu P. A. *Good, Evil, and Beyond*. Translated by Bhikkhu Puriso. Bangkok: Buddhadhamma Foundation, 1993.

Peagam, Nelson. "Challenges for the New Order" and "Judge Picks up the Reigns." *Far Eastern Economic Review*, 5 November 1976, 8, 9.

Petro, Patrice, ed. *Fugitive Images*. Bloomington: Indiana University Press, 1995.

Prizzia, Ross. *Thailand in Transition*. Honolulu: University of Hawaii Press, 1985.

Puey Ungpakorn. "Violence and the Military Coup in Thailand." *Bulletin of Concerned Asian Scholars* 9, no. 3 (1977): 3–12.

Reynolds, Frank. "Legitimation and Rebellion: Thailand's Civic Religion and the Student Uprising of October, 1973." In *Religion and Legitimation of Power in Thailand, Laos, and Burma*, edited by Bardwell Smith. Chambersburg, Pa.: Anima Books, 1978, 134–52.

Sahlins, Marshal. *Stone Age Economics*. New York: Aldine de Gruyter, 1972.

Sartre, Jean-Paul. *Being and Nothingness*. Translated by Hazel E. Barnes. New York: Philosophical Library, 1957.

Scarry, Elaine. *The Body in Pain: The Making and Unmaking of the World*. Oxford: Oxford University Press, 1985.

Seremetakis, C. Nadia. *The Senses Still: Perception and Memory as Material Culture in Modernity*. Boulder, Colo.: Westview, 1994.

Sharf, Robert H. "Buddhist Modernism and the Rhetoric of Meditative Experience." *Numen* 42 (1995): 228–83.

Sharf, Robert H. "Zen and the Art of Japanese Nationalism." In *Curators of the Buddha: The Study of Buddhism under Colonialism*, edited by Donald S. Lopez. Chicago: University of Chicago Press, 1995, 107–60.

Shawcross, W. "Legacy of a Revolt." *Far Eastern Economic Review*, 19 November 1973, 29.

Shenon, P. "Where Beauty Queens Preen, No Eyesores, Please." *New York Times*, 21 August 1991, A4.

Singer, Ben. "Modernity, Hyperstimulus, and the Rise of Popular Sensationalism." In *Cinema and the Invention of Modern Life*, edited by Leo Charney and Vanessa R. Schwartz. Berkeley and Los Angeles: University of California Press, 1995, 72–99.

Smith, Bardwell, ed., *Religion and Legitimation of Power in Thailand, Laos and Burma*. Chambersburg, Pa.: Anima Books, 1978.

Somporn Songchai and Lim Joo-Jock, eds. *Trends in Thailand*. Singapore: Singapore University Press, 1976.

Sontag, Susan. *On Photography*. New York: Doubleday, 1978.

Steedly, Mary M. *Hanging without a Rope: Narrative Experience in Colonial and Postcolonial Karoland*. Princeton: Princeton University Press, 1993.

Steiner, George. *Real Presences*. Chicago: University of Chicago Press, 1989.

Stockwin, Harold. "The Unholy Gross." *Far Eastern Economic Review*, 5 November 1973, 45.

Stoller, Paul. *Sensuous Scholarship*. Philadelphia: University of Pennsylvania Press, 1997.

———. *The Taste of Ethnographic Things: The Senses in Anthropology*. Philadelphia: University of Pennsylvania Press, 1998.

Student Federation of Thailand. *Samut phap du"an Tula: pramuan phap hetkan 14 Tulakhom 2516 læœ Tulakhom 2519* (October Album: Collected Photos of the Events of 14 October 1973 and October 1976). 3rd ed. Bangkok: Samnakphim Thang Thai, Chatchamnai Saisong su"ksit Khlet Thai, 1989.

Tambiah, Stanley J. *Buddhist Saints of the Forest and the Cult of the Amulets*. Cambridge: Cambridge University Press, 1984.

———. *World Conqueror and World Renouncer: A Study of Buddhism and Polity against an Historical Background*. Cambridge: Cambridge University Press, 1976.

Taussig, Michael. *The Nervous System*. New York: Routledge, 1992.

———. "The Physiognomic Aspects of Visual Worlds." In *Visualizing Theory*, edited by Lucien Taylor. New York: Routledge, 1994.

———. *Shamanism, Colonialism, and the Wildman: A Study in Terror and Healing*. Chicago: University of Chicago Press, 1987.

———. "The Sun Gives without Receiving: An Old Story." *Comparative Studies of Society and History* 37, no. 2 (1995): 368–98.

Taylor, Charles. "Toward an Unforced Consensus on Human Rights." *Beogradski Krug* (Belgrade Circle), no. 3–4 [no. 1–2] (1995 [1996]): 76–94.

Taylor, John. *Body Horror: Photojournalism, Catastrophe, and War.* New York: New York University Press, 1998.

Thak Chaloemtiarana. *Thailand: The Politics of Despotic Paternalism.* Bangkok: Social Science Association of Thailand, 1979.

Thompson, Edward P. "The Moral Economy of the English Crowd in the Eighteenth Century." *Past and Present* 50 (1971): 76–136.

Thongchai Winichakul, "Jodmai Chaebob Thi Neung" (Letter Number One). In *Rao Mai Lyym Hok Tula* (We Don't Forget October 6). Bangkok: 20th Anniversary Memorial Publication, 1995, 184–86.

———. *Ramleuk Hok Tula: Thammai lae Yangrai* (Remembering October 6: Why and How). In *Rao Mai Lyym Hok Tula* (We Don't Forget October 6). Bangkok: 20th Anniversary Memorial Publication, 1995, 13–22.

———. "Remembering/Silencing the Traumatic Past: The Ambivalence Narratives of the October 6, 1976 Massacre in Bangkok." In *Proceedings of the 6th International Conference on Thai Studies, Theme II.* Chiang Mai, 1996, 473–93.

———. *Siam Mapped: A History of the Geo-Body of a Nation.* Honolulu: University of Hawaii Press, 1994.

Tsing, Anna L. *In the Realm of the Diamond Queen.* Princeton: Princeton University Press, 1993.

Turton, Andrew, et al., eds. *Thailand: Roots of Conflict.* Nottingham: Russell Press, 1978.

Verdery, Katherine. *The Political Lives of Dead Bodies: Reburial and Postsocialist Change.* New York: Columbia University Press, 1999.

Weber, Max. *The Protestant Ethic and the Spirit of Capitalism.* New York: Scribner's, 1958.

Wright, Joseph. *The Balancing Act.* Bangkok: Asia Books, 1991.

311

✢ *Index* ✢

315